Of all the questions students a

evil and suffering top the list. B

head-on. His helpful response is biblically accurate and intellectually stimulating.

John Book.
Campus Director, Campus Crusade for Christ

Although suffering and evil are common to all peoples in all cultures, satisfying explanations for evil elude us. The issues are especially acute for theists who believe in an all good, all powerful and all knowing God. Professor Brian Morley has provided us with a wise, comprehensive and thoughtful exploration of suffering and evil within a Christian worldview. Believers and skeptics alike will benefit from this sensitive and sensible discussion.

Harold Netland,
Professor of Philosophy of Religion and Intercultural Studies,
Trinity Evangelical Divinity School, Deerfield, Illinois

This work is thorough in its scope covering these immensely crucial topics from the theological, philosophical, psychological and personal perspectives. It is well reasoned and practical. As a teaching chaplain I will highly recommend *God in the Shadows* to pastors and hospital chaplains as a learning tool and resource that provides an up to date framework regarding the crucial issues of life.

Chaplain Phil Manly
USC Hospitals, Healthcare Chaplains Ministry Association,
Placentia, California

God in the Shadows

Evil in God's World

Brian Morley

CHRISTIAN FOCUS

To my father, who endured the childhood loss of his mother, the great depression, the bombing of London, jungle fighting in Burma, and then strove to raise a family in America. He is a model of taking evil seriously while never losing idealism. And to the memory of my mother, who always sought in this fallen world, to find the good, the true, and the beautiful.

10 9 8 7 6 5 4 3 2 1

ISBN 1-84550-175-6
ISBN 978-1-84550-175-4

Published in 2006
by
Christian Focus Publications, Ltd.,
Geanies House, Fearn, Ross-shire,
IV20 1TW, Scotland.

www.christianfocus.com

Cover design by Moose77.com

Printed and bound by J. H. Haynes & Co. Ltd., Sparkford

Contents

Acknowledgement

A number of people deserve thanks for their contributions to this project. Editor and writer Steve Miller saw potential in it from the beginning, and his expert opinion convinced me that it would be worth all the effort. Malcolm Maclean's immediate support at Christian Focus Publications is what made the book possible (and his patience through a number of setbacks on my end allowed me to finish it the way I had envisioned). Also, over the years I've been encouraged by the serious interest of students who were part of my class entitled, "The Problem of Evil."

I had the benefit of several readers to comment on the manuscript. Jennie Kay's candor and insights helped smooth some things. I was grateful and relieved to get a thumbs up from both Dennis Huchison, Th.M., Th.D., and Tom Halstead, M.Div., Ed.D., who incidently, was glad to read the manuscript in spite of his marathon summer of travels through India, Japan, and the United States. I was glad too, to get the thoughts Eric Thomas, pastor of Christ Community Church, a man of practical spirituality if ever there was one. A friend from my doctoral days, Peter Payne, Ph.D., is an evangelism and apologetics specialist with InterVarsity Christian Fellowship's Grad/Faculty Ministries. He gave me the benefit of his expansive intellect, in spite of the busyness of moving to Oxford. Another friend, Harold Netland, Ph.D., gave me some very helpful insights in spite of his already overloaded schedule. He is professor of philosophy of religion and intercultural studies at Trinity Evangelical Divinity School in Illinois.

Through the years I've benefitted from the kindness and depth of people across the theological spectrum. Just a few who stand out are Dallas Willard, Mark Hanna, Robert Saucy, Robert Thomas, Stephen Davis, Richard Swinburne, and John Hick. I shall always carry their investment in my life.

I've appreciated the example of Phil Manley, Los Angeles Area Director for Health Care Chaplains Ministry Association. As a chaplain for over thirty years, he has been able, day after day, to share in the lives of those who are experiencing the very worst life has to offer, and somehow he never becomes callous, jaded, or disillusioned.

I'd like to thank my wife and spiritual partner, Donna, a helpmate in so many ways, who offered her insights from the manuscript's beginning. Always an energetic wife and mother, she still finds time to minister to women by writing her own books. As for my son, Johnathan, watching him struggle gallantly on a daily basis with severe eczema motivated me to keep writing about why a loving God allows suffering. Watching my daughter experience, and bear with grace, some things only a parent would know, has provided similar motivation. She also helped by doing some fact checking and compiling the Scripture index.

Special recognition goes to my father, who taught me to be realistic about pain and evil while never surrendering idealism; and to my mother, who strove as hard to look beyond evil as my father did to meet it head on.

Of course, the deepest gratitude goes to God Himself, who enabled me to somehow write this book in spite of a very full teaching load, a five hundred mile weekly commute, raising and homeschooling our two (wonderful) children, and a myriad of other responsibilities. I hope that in some small way, this book will help His image emerge from the shadows.

INTRODUCTION

LORD, I DON'T THINK I WANT TO KNOW YOU

I sat on the edge of my bed one night, reflecting on the pain, evil, and misery in the world. It was overwhelming. There were the major sources of suffering, from the hopelessness and violence of ghettos, to crime, famine, disease, and warfare. Though the century still had three decades to go, it had already been one of the bloodiest in history.

The cold-war brought tensions all around. I had grown up with bomb drills in school during which we dropped under our desks. For a time the government maintained bomb shelters in case of a nuclear attack. There was civil unrest – race riots, several assassinations, and protests of everything that represented traditional values. Organized crime was quietly thriving, as was the drug trade. Serial killers made the news from time to time.

In addition to the spectacular evils, I contemplated a myriad of lesser hurts, the daily ones that never show up on the news but that tear at us nonetheless. These are the "little murders" caused by gossip, backstabbing, disloyalty, rejection, and ridicule. Then there are relationships that grow cold and die, not from deliberate cruelty, but from neglect, or wrong priorities, or misunderstandings.

Besides interpersonal pains there are natural ones – wretched diseases that kill millions, tornados, fires, earthquakes, floods, and on and on.

At that time, too, I was struggling to work through the normal stresses and strains of growing up.

Sitting in the dim light that night, as a non-Christian adolescent trying to understand God and His world, I boldly voiced my feelings to God Himself. "Lord," I said candidly, "if this is the world you have made – if this is your world – I don't think I want to know you."

I had been searching to understand God for some months. I had concluded that the world must be a fairly accurate portrait of its creator. It wasn't a pretty picture.

I thought my brief prayer would bring closure to my search for God. I had been a bit brazen and I knew that God had every right to be displeased. Given His power that was a bit scary. But I had been honest, which I supposed was better than saying something I didn't believe in order to get a favor. And anyway, if God is responsible for the miserable world then I didn't mind Him keeping me at arm's length from now on.

Just then, to my surprise, I felt flooded with God's love. With it came the clear sense that He Himself loathed evil, which I then realized comes from the things people do with the powers they have been given. I sensed too that God grieves over the world's tragedies far more than I ever could.

I was relieved and puzzled at the same time. How could the world not reflect the will of God if He is its creator, and so powerful?

I decided that I would trust God even though I did not understand it all.

It was my first real attempt to understand God's relationship to pain and evil. It would be a subject to which I would return many times over the years.

A few years later I came to believe that the cross of Christ was God's solution for a fallen world. In Christ God had accepted the punishment for our wrongdoing so that we could have an intimate relationship with Him. Justice was satisfied and swallowed up in love.

That answered some of the problem of evil, but it also invited deeper searching. Yet when I turned to other believers for answers I found that so many of them had little more than incomplete, cliche responses to the profound questions which remained.

I went on to major in philosophy at the University of Southern California. Working my way through school as an ambulance attendant and training in a busy emergency room, I had plenty of time to think about suffering. Some of the things I saw were shocking and horrible. I also dealt with psychiatric emergencies so I saw mental pain that was, if possible, more tragic than the physical pain – people shattered from struggles and tragedies, some real and some merely notional. Working twenty-four hour shifts I would sometimes lay awake at night between calls, trying to deal with – or forget – what I had seen that day.

But at the same time I came to realize that divine grace and providence were also at work. The healing process, for example, sometimes seemed miraculous. One young woman was brought to the emergency room after a bad traffic accident in which she was thrown through the windshield of her car. Her face and body were shredded and she was completely unaware of anything, yet she was mindlessly thrashing about in shards of glass. We were trying to restrain her, stitch her back together, and put blood and fluids into her veins. We frankly didn't think she would make it. Yet only a week later a co-worker and I visited her hospital room. The transformation was astonishing. The skillfully stitched cuts were healing beautifully; she was up joking around and eager to leave the hospital. She had no recollection of the accident nor how badly she had been injured. Neither had she any idea how close she had come to dying, so she even avoided mental scars. I saw it as another example of the healing power God had graciously built into the human body.

On a broader scale I could see how an orderly society limits evil and suffering. I constantly saw how ambulances and hospitals took care of the injured, fire fighters arrived to put out fires, police caught evil doers and prisons kept them from continually harming the public. It seemed as though a hidden hand of grace were behind it all, providentially caring through human compassion and order.

The picture of the world was coming into focus as a place of not only great tragedy but also of great grace.

Going on for graduate work in seminary and then for a doctorate gave me a lot of time to develop my thinking. At the Christian college where I am starting my seventeenth year of teaching biblical studies and philosophy, one of my courses is entitled, the "Problem of Evil." The topic has a way of showing up in my other courses, such as those on theology, world religions, philosophy, logic, ethics, and apologetics.

The subject still holds plenty of mysteries for me, but answers have become much more distinct. This book is my attempt to share that picture that has been getting clearer over the years. The clarity has not removed the shadows from the picture because, as I've discovered, life's shadows have a vital role. They give depth and shape, making the picture more vivid. As I'll explain later in the book, the picture which emerges, shadows and all, is a portrait.

The topic of this book is in many ways the central issue of the age. Suffering of every kind, the struggle between good and evil, and resolving diverse conflicts, are the themes of a thousand stories, epic poems, novels, and movies; as well as part of the subject of ethics, psychology, counseling, sociology, anthropology, and more. The struggle of a person against his or her inner self, of one person against another, and of people against nature – all at root aspects of the problem of pain and evil – fill our culture, our personal lives, and the daily news.

Some of the most successful modern authors have focused most poignantly on the theme of good and evil. Nowhere is this more evident than in two of the most popular writers of our time, C. S. Lewis and J. R. R. Tolkien. The focus is no less evident in works like George Orwell's *Nineteen Eighty-Four*, and *Animal Farm*, about the cold realities of utopian ideals gone awry; and William Golding's *Lord of the Flies*, which shows how even the most innocent among us are capable of the darkest deeds.

Other authors have revealed not only their thoughts on evil, but their deep struggle over it. Herman Melville heavily marked his Bible in the books of Job and Ecclesiastes. Raised in the Dutch Reformed Church, he had come to question orthodoxy. In *Moby-Dick*, captain Ahab abandons his Quaker roots in his quest to vanquish evil, personified for him in the great white whale. Ahab seems to challenge God Himself, asking, "Who's to doom, when the judge himself is dragged to the bar [of justice]?"[1] Author Nathaniel Hawthorne revealed the struggles of his friend Melville when he said of him, "He can neither believe, nor be comfortable in his unbelief..."[2] The writings of Nathaniel Hawthorne reveal his own inner turmoil, some of which arose from learning of his ancestor's role in the prosecution of supposed witches in the Salem trials.

Some lost the struggle to hold onto faith in the face of evil. It was said that Mark Twain became embittered against God after the death of his favorite daughter in 1896. W. Somerset Maugham recounted how he prayed earnestly as a boy that God would remove his stammer. The next morning he was sure it had been answered – until he had to speak. He was so profoundly disappointed that he never believed in God again.

Of course the problem of evil has had a deep affect on other opinion makers. A devoutly religious young man in Tennessee was a prayer group leader and planned to become a missionary. Then his sister died of leukemia, after which his father committed suicide. In the aftermath of these tragedies the young man lost his faith completely. Growing up to become an outspoken non-believer, Ted Turner went on to found the Cable News Network (CNN).[3]

A school teacher recently told me that when he began working at a middle school he immediately noticed that another teacher would scream continually at students on the playground. This went on day after day, for a decade. Then one day it stopped. He expected it to start up again, but after about a year of no screaming he asked his colleague what had changed. The colleague explained that many years ago his son had died, and the school children were a constant reminder of him. He had struggled with hostility toward God – even though, he also revealed, he had been a Christian for many years. He said he had finally resolved his feelings about a year ago. Unresolved grief affects many people more deeply than they let on.

The Bible sheds light on the ultimate resolution of the problem of evil, which has been so central to human experience.

Most believers are quick to appeal to mystery and the need for faith when it comes to serious questions about pain and evil. "We'll never know," it is often said; or, "we'll never know this side of heaven – we just have to trust God." Deuteronomy 29:29 is often quoted, "The secret things belong to the Lord our God...."* There is even a mentality that associates original sin with the desire for forbidden knowledge; then it associates forbidden knowledge with pushing too far for answers to the truly difficult questions of the faith.

This book emphasizes the second part of Deuteronomy 29:29, "...but the things revealed belong to us and to our sons forever...." We will explore what can be known, pushing toward the boundaries. We need not fear that we will discover something God wants kept hidden. If He wants it hidden there is no way we will find it out (as Prov. 25:2 says, "it is the glory of God to conceal a matter").

The Bible says that God is pleased when we strive to understand Him deeply. We are to "seek His face continually" (Ps. 105:4), to search for Him with all our heart (Jer. 29:13), and to "press on to know the Lord" (Hos. 6:3). Paul thought that knowing God in a deep way is so valuable that by comparison everything else looks like garbage (Phil. 3:8 σκύβαλον, "refuse," "dung"). We are not to glory in riches, strength, or even wisdom (Jer. 9:23). But we are to glory in knowing God. We are told, "'Let him who boasts boast of this, that he understands and knows Me, that I am the Lord who exercises lovingkindness, justice and righteousness on earth; for I delight in these things,' declares the Lord" (Jer. 9:24).[4]

This book explores how there can be a God who is loving, just, and righteous – in spite of the fact that the world is so full of pain and evil.

The "problem of evil" is a way of referring to the problem that the existence of God does not seem to fit with the existence of either pain (including mental suffering) or moral evil. It is called simply "the problem of evil" rather than "the problem of pain and evil" because pain is regarded as a type of evil. But when not used in the phrase "the problem of evil," evil still generally refers to moral evil only.

There are several parts to the problem. The first is the logical problem of evil. That is the argument that any amount of pain or evil is logically inconsistent with the existence of God. The issue was debated in the 1960s and 70s, but eventually nearly everyone, including atheists, have come to agree that this argument against the existence of God doesn't work. As was decisively shown by Christian philosopher Alvin Plantinga, that is because there is no way to rule out conditions that would allow for the existence of both God and some pain or evil. It may be impossible, for example, for humans to be given free will and for God to guarantee that no one ever does wrong.

So since the 1980s the focus has shifted to the evidential problem of evil. It argues that the amount or type of evil that exists means that God *probably* does not exist. It depends a lot on the idea that some suffering is pointless and that without such suffering there would be just about as much goodness. This book will explore a number of answers to this challenge. It will show that God has good reasons to allow a world like ours, and that furthermore, we are simply not in a position to know otherwise (more about our ignorance in chapter 13).

That still leaves what is sometimes called the pastoral problem of evil: how to practically deal with the pain and evil we face in life. This problem exists because sometimes we need more than intellectual answers (we will look at practical issues in part four of the book).

As we get started in section one, we will take a brief look in the first chapter at various views that are unacceptable to traditional believers in God (theists). These unacceptable views hold, for example, that evil does not really exist, or that God does not exist, or that He is not powerful enough to prevent evil, or that He is not purely good and thus does not want to eliminate evil. Rejecting such alternatives will leave us to defend the orthodox view that God is good and all powerful in spite of the existence of evil. Although nearly everyone will find it helpful to understand what is wrong with alternative answers to the problem of evil, readers who are not particularly interested can skip this chapter and will not be disadvantaged later. For that matter, each chapter was designed to stand alone as much as possible, so the reader can skip a chapter and perhaps come back to it later; as well, a single chapter can be shared with a friend.

In chapter two we will see just what it means for God to be good. We will see why some of our expectations of a good God are unfounded. We will see why, for example, a good God does not need to make the happiness of every creature His top priority, and why He need not be more gracious to any of His creatures than He has been.

Part two looks at major reasons for pain and evil. Within that section, chapter three shows that if we are to be physical beings who can make moral choices we must have a certain type of environment. It has to be consistent, for example. That means God cannot constantly intervene to prevent all harm. Then chapter four looks at the controversy over what it means to be free and how that impacts the problem of evil. In chapter five we see that this world is not a place where everyone is as happy as can be, but that it accomplishes a much more important goal. Chapter six shows why God is just to bring some pain on those who make evil choices. We will see why He is still good even if the punishment does not result in the betterment of the wrongdoer. That means that God does not have to be loving to be good; He can simply be just.

Part three deals with a lot of important special issues. Answers to the puzzling problem of animal suffering are explored in chapter seven, where we find out, for example, how easy it is to overestimate the problem. Chapter eight explores religious misconceptions about God and illnesses, and shows how illness can make important contributions to human life. Then in chapter nine we consider death as a consequence of human fallenness and how it leads to a blessing for some people. Chapter ten looks at the difficult problems of birth defects, the diverse origins of poverty, and the causes of war.

Chapter eleven shows how the future figures into the problem of evil, healing the hurts of some, yet tragically – though justly – leaving those who refuse divine grace to suffer. We will see how God is good even though hell exists, because justice is a type of goodness, and the highest good is not pleasure but something else. Whether God feels the sufferings of His creatures or instead cannot be affected by anything outside Himself is taken up in chapter twelve.

Part four, "Application," begins with chapter thirteen in which we answer skeptics. We will look at how we reason and hold worldviews, and why our mental capabilities fall far short of what we would need to conclude that a good and all-powerful God does not exist. We also look at a wide array of reasons to believe that God exists apart from the problem of evil. In chapter fourteen we glean valuable lessons from some of God's most distinguished followers, each of whom had an important insight into the problem of evil that we can apply to our lives. Finally, in chapter fifteen we emphasize our personal part in resolving the problem of evil. We need to go far beyond merely understanding why God allows pain and evil. We have to take the opportunity to help resolve the problem evil by, for example, showing kindness and meeting the needs of people around us. In so doing we act as God would act, thereby glorifying Him.

Having said something about the plan of this book I need to say something about its method. I will use a lot of the Bible but I hope by the end of the book I will have gone far beyond quoting and discussing individual verses (important as that is). I aim to use the nuts and bolts of individual passages to build the superstructure of a Christian view of pain and evil.

To put it another way, we will connect the dots of individual passages to form the big picture of God and evil. Drawing lines between dots requires a bit of reasoning. Generally, the farther apart the dots, the more skill is required to form the picture. Some of the biblical dots on the problem of evil are rather far apart, which is why Christian thinkers can disagree on where to draw the lines (as we'll see for example in chapter four, on what it means to be free).

To form a picture of anything – of what is ethically right and wrong, a Christian view of history, the nature of God – we have to go beyond the dots, beyond the nuts and bolts. We have to put the biblical specifics together to form Christian ideas.[5]

Some people are uncomfortable doing that because they think of it as usurping God's authority and supplanting revelation with reason. But I think God expects us to take what He has given us and form a cohesive view of things, such as who we are and who He is, what we ought to do and think – and why He allows pain and evil. To live as believers we have to build cognitive superstructures, we cannot live among piles of nuts and bolts. Building these big ideas is something we do whether we realize it or not. If you go beyond specifics to think about an entire subject, you are using the nuts and bolts to build a cognitive superstructure. To think about God's omnipotence, or what you should do about a situation, or to think about virtually anything, you must draw the lines between the dots.

In drawing the big picture, this book will do more than exhort the reader to do what is right. Though there will be some of that, we will invest a lot of time forming an answer to one of life's hardest questions. So we will invest a lot of time in what we should think and believe, because that is the foundation for what we feel and do. If the foundation isn't there, whatever is built up will not stand.

To help deepen our thoughts and personalize them, as well as to integrate them with our actions, I have added questions after each chapter. Some questions review the content, some invite the reader to draw out implications, and some lead to application. A glossary reviews concepts crucial to the book.[6]

In the end we will not remove mystery from this issue, nor the need for faith. But we will see that God has understandable and wonderful reasons for bringing about a world like ours. Nevertheless the good things that can come from it are mostly opportunities rather than guarantees. Cancer, for example, can cause us to have more faith, hope, patience, and sensitivity to those around us; or it can make us doubtful, bitter, angry, and full of self-pity.

Whether pain and evil benefit us has a lot to do with what we know and how we respond. So let us press on to a better understanding of God and how to make the most of our brief sojourn in this fallen world.

NOTES

[*]All Scriptural quotations are in the New American Standard (NASB) unless otherwise noted.

1. Herman Melville, *Moby-Dick* (New York, NY: Barnes and Noble, 1993), 453 (ch. 132). For pointing me to this reference, I am indebted to D. Bruce Lockerbie, *Dismissing God: Modern Writers' Struggle Against Religion* (Grand Rapids, MI: Baker, 1998), 87.

2. Eleanor Melville Metcalf, ed., *Herman Melville: Cycle and Epicycle* (Cambridge, MA: Harvard University Press, 1953), 83; quoted in Lockerbie, 89.

3. For the examples of Hawthorne, Twain, Maugham, and Turner, I am indebted to Lockerbie, 72-77, 232.

4. Of course God is not a sexual being and therefore has no gender in a literal sense, however I will use the traditional masculine pronoun ("He") since that is how God represents Himself in Scripture.

5. Going from what I have been calling the nuts and bolts of specific biblical passages (or the dots, if you like) to the superstructure can be described in much more detail. Subjects like linguistics, history, archeology, and the study of the original biblical languages (Greek and Hebrew) help to do exegesis. Exegesis gives us the straightforward meaning of the text. To do this we use principles of interpretation, or hermeneutics (the concepts undergirding the application of hermeneutics are sometimes called philosophical hermeneutics).

We can put these exegetical blocks together to construct "biblical" theology, which looks at the style, themes, and theology of specific biblical writers, thus giving us, for example, Pauline theology (i.e., the theology of the apostle Paul). (In this technical sense "biblical" theology does not mean biblically correct theology as opposed to biblically incorrect theology.) Bible exposition expounds the themes and issues that run through individual biblical books, biblical writers, or whole divisions of the Bible (such as the gospels, or the entire Old or New Testament). Theology puts all the pieces together to form the superstructure. It does not just deal with what a particular passage tells us, for example, about God's goodness and evil (exegesis); or what the apostle Paul said about the subject ("biblical" theology), or how the subject appears in the flow and thought of books and major sections of the Bible (Bible exposition). Rather, theology deals with what the entire Bible says about God's goodness and evil. Theologians sometimes also benefit from historical theology, which deals with past Christian thought on a subject. For instance, as we deal with God and evil in this book we will find the thoughts of Calvin and Augustine especially relevant.

I've simplified this description of how it works since in actual practice going from text to theology may not always be a straight line upward. Considerations from biblical theology, for example, may influence how we interpret a particular passage.

Finally, the content from exegesis, biblical theology, Bible exposition, and theology, are applied to life through activities such as preaching and counseling. It is obvious that it would be difficult to effectively apply the Bible to life without first building upward from exegesis, in other words, without "connecting the dots." We will go from text to application in this book, but we will spend a lot of time putting the big picture together.

6. In some of the illustrations I have changed one or more details to preserve the anonymity of people involved.

CHAPTER ONE

ANSWERS THAT DON'T ANSWER

During one of many sleepless, miserable nights, my son Johnathan, then five, looked up at me with tears in his eyes. In a burst of frustration he asked, "Why do I have these bumps?" "Why does God make me have them?" Nearly a quarter of his body was broken out with eczema, so irritating that he would scratch until he bled. It was his second summer with the condition. Because we had to keep him from anything that might aggravate it, he couldn't be in the sun for long periods, play on the grass, swim with his friends, or even enjoy the relief of a warm bath. In the winter he was limited as to what he could wear to keep warm, and even his pajamas had to be sent to us from a relative in Europe, because those sold in America irritated his skin. And, because the main medication for his condition had the side effect of possibly stopping his growth, we had to use it very sparingly.

I said, "Johnathan, do you sometimes wonder why God allows you to go through this if He loves you and can do anything, including heal you?" After pausing, he answered a firm, "Yes!", as if I had just helped him identify the worst part of it.

I told him that God can indeed do anything, including heal him, and that He certainly loves him very much; but sometimes He allows things to happen for a special reason – and we can know some of those reasons. I also told him that watching him struggle and knowing that others did too, had been a major reason I wanted to write a book exploring this whole difficult issue.

Everyone experiences pain and evil to some extent, and we are affected by others who experience it as well. The suffering is often made worse by our difficulty understanding it all. Stating it logically, as a syllogism, we could put it this way:

Premise One:	If God is good He would want to eliminate evil.
Premise Two:	If God is all powerful, He would be able to eliminate evil.
Premise Three:	But evil exists.
Therefore:	There does not exist a God who is both good and all powerful.

Virtually every religion and major philosophy attempts some answer to the problem of evil. Many of the answers are not acceptable to the traditional theist, who believes that God is both good and all powerful. This chapter will examine and critique those unacceptable answers (though it's helpful to know the problems with the alternative views, readers who want skip ahead to the next chapter will not find the gap a problem for their understanding of the orthodox solution to the problem of evil).

Of course the most fundamental question regarding the problem of evil, and one we need to answer before we answer anything else, is why we think God exists. It is to that we now turn.

There is No God – Atheism

Russell Baker, the *New York Times* journalist and humorist, became an atheist at age five, when his father suddenly died. He said, "If God could do things like this to people, then God was hateful and I had no more use for Him.... That day I decided that God was not entirely to be trusted."[1]

One option is to accept the conclusion of the syllogism above and to deny the existence of any supreme being. An atheist should have no intellectual problem with the existence of pain and evil since without God there is no reason to think that things should be better than they are. There can be no conflict between the world as he finds it and the world as he thinks it should be.

Though the atheist may have an easier time on an intellectual level (there being no conflict between how things are and how they should be), he may have a harder time on a practical level, trying to cope with experiences of pain and evil. The skeptical British playwright George Bernard Shaw once remarked that, "Alcohol is the anesthesia by which we endure the operation of life."[2]

By contrast, while the theist may experience some intellectual tension, he has the comfort of trusting that events are under the control of a loving God. He can trust that troubles have some greater purpose, and that someday things will be better, if only in a future life.

To some extent the theist can find confirmation for his faith in the world around him, for example, by seeing that it is an ordered place. Order is best explained by an orderer (a line of reasoning called the teleological argument).[3] For example, so many conditions have to be finely tuned for life to be possible. The earth has to have just the right amount of gravity, oxygen, carbon, heat (it has to be within a minute fraction of the total temperature range) – even the wind speed can't be too high. The basic forces of nature have to be just right, including the force that binds atoms together, gravity, and the electromagnetic force. Such details as the mass of the proton has to be within an extremely narrow range (more about this in the chapter about answering skeptics).[4]

It is clear, too, that things do not come into existence by themselves, uncaused, and that God is the only cause sufficient for the universe (called the cosmological argument).[5]

Moreover, common moral sensibilities tell us that right and wrong are more than a matter of mere personal whims or conventions of society, that evils like genocide are wrong even if whole societies like Nazi Germany approve them. If indeed morality is something that transcends humanity, it must be rooted in some higher moral authority. So morals, too, point to God (called the moral argument).

Paul seems to be alluding to arguments of these sorts in the book of Romans, showing that the nature of the world and our moral consciousness both point to God, leaving the rejecter without excuse for his failure to know God. Paul said, "For since the creation of the world His invisible attributes, His eternal power and divine nature, have been clearly seen, *being understood through what has been made*, so that they are without excuse" (Rom. 1:20; italics added). Thus the basics about God's existence and nature can be known through a simple and obvious conclusion drawn from the world. Though Paul is not specific, it seems that the sort of reasoning characterized as the teleological and cosmological arguments could describe how these inferences are made. Whatever he has in mind, he is clear that everyone can know that God exists.

Paul also says that people are aware that evil deserves God's punishment (Rom. 1:32). As well, the basics of right and wrong are known to people, having been "written in their hearts, their conscience bearing witness..." (Rom. 2:15). This knowledge of the moral dimension of life is further testimony to a creator (a type of the moral argument).

When talking to the Greeks at Lystra, Paul appealed to their knowledge of a creator, saying that God did not leave Himself "without a witness" (ἀμάρτυρος). There has always been the witness of providential care: "He did good and gave you rains from heaven and fruitful seasons, satisfying your hearts with food and gladness" (Acts 14:17). Not only is there order in the world, but the kind of order gives evidence of a loving creator (a type of the teleological argument)

The Psalmist, too, says that the universe testifies to the existence of God. "The heavens are telling of the glory of God; and their expanse is declaring the work of His hands" (Ps. 19:1). The proclamation is non-verbal ("there is no speech, nor are there words," 19:3), but continual ("telling" and "declaring" are participles), and known "through all the earth" (v. 4; cf. Job 36:25).

Denial of God's existence then, amounts to ignoring or suppressing the evidence that is inside us and all around us (Rom. 1:20), a source known in theology as general revelation.

What everyone can get from general revelation is knowledge of the generic God of theism, one who is powerful, knowledgeable, holy, creator, and the like. (However it does not follow that everyone has, through the knowledge of creation, access to the more specific knowledge of Christ, the plan of salvation, the Trinity, details of His will, how He has acted in history, and so on. For that a person needs special revelation, such as is found in the Bible. There is more about this in chapter thirteen, on answering skeptics.)

The evidence for God in general revelation is *not* as overwhelming as it could possibly be. Evidence from general revelation can be suppressed, although God could provide virtually unsuppressible experience of Himself, as we expect will be the case on judgement day. So while the case for God is not so weak as to be undecidable (as philosopher John Hick would insist[6]), neither is it as overwhelming as it could be.

British philosopher Bertrand Russell, author of *Why I Am Not a Christian*,[7] was one of the most famous atheists of the twentieth century. He said that if he ever had to face God and give account for his unbelief, he would say there had not been enough evidence.[8] Yet lack of belief in God left a large hole in his world view. He was a passionate social reformer, but realized that without God he had no basis for his ethics. He therefore found his own views "incredible." "I do not know the solution," he admitted.[9] He contemplated suicide many times. As theists would interpret it, he spent much of his life groping for God. In his terms, he sought the reason for a sense of awe at the universe, and why some truths (like those of mathematics) *have* to be true and do not just *happen* to be true.[10] He admitted to a mistress,

> The centre [sic] of me is always and eternally a terrible pain – a curious wild pain – a searching for something beyond what the world contains, something transfigured and infinite – the beatific vision – God – I do not find it, I do not think it is to be found – but the love of it is my life – it's like a passionate love for a ghost. At times it fills me with rage, at times with wild despair...[11]

While theists sometimes struggle to reconcile their belief in God with the harsh realities of the world, Russell shows how some atheists struggle to deal with life apart from God.

In essence, by claiming to know God does not exist, the atheist makes the bold claim that he has all the capabilities and information necessary to know if there is a God, and that he can presently decide that there is no such being. That is quite a claim. Further, he claims to know that no one else knows there is a God either. There is plenty of reason to think otherwise.

Even though this is a very sketchy outline of the case for theism, it is enough to suggest that atheism has serious trouble on a world view level.

On a practical level, atheism offers little or no help in dealing with pain and evil. As a religion that has no formal view of God, Buddhism is unusual, however. While it neither affirms nor denies God's existence,[12] its entire focus is on the elimination of pain. It teaches that life is suffering, but that suffering can be avoided by extinguishing desires that hold us to this life. Those desires can be extinguished through leading a moral life. If we live successfully, at death we will enter nirvana, which is a kind of non-existence in which there can be no pain. The solution it proposes is to stop craving the things of this life, which are too unstable to grasp anyway. Yet Buddha chose not to develop the deeper issues of a world view, such as the nature of ultimate reality and of the world; and he even said little about the nature of the soul (though some of his followers have speculated on things much more than he).

Christianity, by contrast, provides the framework for a highly developed world view, one in which the parts connect to other parts. For example, goodness is grounded in the nature of God, who is loving and just. Evil comes from beings choosing to act in a way contrary to God's character, a choice which causes harm to others. So the solution to humanity's problem is not merely a matter of getting right information or becoming enlightened, but one of reconciliation to a moral God by means of His forgiveness, and working out moral changes in our life.[13]

Any adequate strategy for coping with pain and evil must be built on a fully developed and fully connected world view. Anything less will leave us under equipped for the troubles of this life. This book attempts to ensure that the reader has that vital equipment with which to go through life successfully.

Everything is God – Pantheism

The opposite of regarding nothing as God is regarding everything as God. According to pantheism, everything is God and God is everything. This makes evil a part of the same reality as good, not something essentially different from it.

Various forms of pantheism appear in the New Age movement, Hinduism and eastern thought in general (including some forms of Zen Buddhism), as well as the teachings of some western philosophers, such as Spinoza (and Hegel comes close).

Critics accuse pantheism of being unintelligible and self-contradictory. The view typically claims that all things are one, which means that there can be no real distinctions between things. That erases not only the ultimate difference between right and wrong, but between anything. In pantheism, becoming enlightened is supposedly a matter of knowing not to make distinctions. According to the critic, what follows is that we have no reason for caring about anything. If, for example, good and bad are ultimately the same, why care what happens?

A more fundamental problem with pantheism is that claiming there is no difference between things is self-contradictory in that the very claim depends on making a distinction. Pantheism makes a distinction between the (supposedly correct) view that everything is one and the (supposedly incorrect) view that everything is not one. So pantheism's main claim is self-contradictory. It is like someone claiming in English, "I cannot speak a word of English." The statement refutes itself. This is known as being self-referentially incoherent; or to put it less technically, it is "shooting oneself in the foot."

Pantheists usually claim that objections like this show that a person is still locked into a lower level of thinking and is not yet enlightened. But it seems more accurate to say that the pantheist's claim amounts to nonsense. It would be a little like the claim that only enlightened persons can understand the sentence, "Infinite ships dream from without wise pink." It seems better to say that those ideas just don't fit together – not that they fit according to some higher, unexplainable reality.

The critic would also say that some circular reasoning lies at the heart of most forms of pantheism. Supposedly, the distinctions between things are mere illusions. That is why Vedic Hindu enlightenment consists of coming to see that we are part of the divine whole rather than the separate beings we appear to be. But then we have to ask, how did the illusion get there? The answer is, from ignorance. But where does the ignorance come from? The answer is, from the illusion.[14] This seems blatantly circular.

Whatever problems beset pantheism, the Bible makes it clear that the evidence which is around us and in us telling us that God exists also tells us that God is different from us and the rest of creation. Those distinctions are not illusory, they are real and permanent; and they mean that we will never become God, no matter how much we think it. In biblical terms, what is at the root of the problem of evil is not a failure to realize we are divine but a lack of holiness, which has separated us from a holy God. The way back is not trying to merge with God by convincing ourselves we are divine, but allowing Him to reconcile us by His love, manifested in the sacrifice of Christ on the cross.

Evil is Not Real – Christian Science

Pantheism's cousin is a strong form of idealism according to which reality is an all encompassing cosmic mind.[15] Christian Science is an example of such a view and claims that evil is less than real. Founder Mary Baker Eddy claimed, "Evil has no reality. It is neither person, place, nor thing, but is simply a belief, an illusion of material sense."[16] She reasons from its illusory status to the solution: "If God, or good, is real, then evil, the unlikeness of God, is unreal. And evil can only seem to be real by giving reality to the unreal."[17] Supposedly evil can be dealt with mentally, which is why Christian Science emphasizes the use of their own practitioners rather than physicians. It therefore deals with evil by challenging premise three of our syllogism, above, which states that evil exists.

Eddy wrongly supposes that if God is omnipresent then nothing else can exist because "all space is filled with God."[18] This makes God more like a solid than a spirit in the sense that nothing else can be where God is. Furthermore, while she correctly makes God the cause of everything she wrongly concludes that only those things that God would directly cause can exist.[19] But of course this ignores that God caused beings with free wills who themselves cause things and commit evil acts. So not only can something other than God exist because He is Spirit, but evil can exist without God directly causing it since He created free wills.

Eddy's life didn't seem to fit her teachings in two areas. She claimed that she suffered a debilitating injury from falling on ice and that she recovered only by applying the views that came to be known as Christian Science. But her claims to have been badly injured have been seriously questioned.[20] Secondly, later in life she had physical conditions that she could not treat by her own teachings. In fact, credible sources allege that pain caused her to resort to the use of morphine on a number of occasions.[21] So critics would say that the injury she said she recovered from never happened, and the pain she did have she couldn't cure.

Though she claimed the Bible as her authority,[22] it affirms the reality of evil, sin, death, and hell. It treats evil not as a figment of the mind but as a reality of the will, something that causes real guilt and requires atonement (Gal. 1:4; 1 John. 3:4; Heb. 9:27).

Various strands of such thought as Eddy's came together to form the modern New Age movement. By contrast, most people today accept some sort of realism, the view that at least some reality is outside us and it is unaffected by whatever we think. (Postmodernism is a new though different challenge to realism.)

Regardless of the debate about realism, most people would not accept that evil is an illusion. The idea contradicts everyday experience and common sense, which are backed up by general revelation (Rom. 1:18-21; 2:14-15).

Good and Evil are Equal Principles – Dualism

While pantheism considers evil an illusion, dualism supposes that good and evil are each ultimate. Zoroastrianism is an ancient Persian religion with two gods, one good and one evil. The cosmos is their battleground.[23]

Early in his life Augustine held a form of this view, but later criticized it after converting to Christianity. Rather than accept the view that evil comes from a second god, he held that it is the absence of good.[24]

Though there are scarcely a hundred thousand Zoroastrians left, Taoism is a thriving religion. It divides reality into two contrasting yet interdependent forces. Yang is strong, light, forthright, dry, sweet, and masculine. Yin is said to be dark, decaying, damp, deceitful, weak, sour, and (though it's rarely mentioned in Western books on the subject) feminine. Both forces are necessary and must be kept in balance. Much Chinese cooking aims to produce that balance in our bodies, using, for example, sweet (yang) and sour (yin). Herbal medicine has the same goal.

Supposing there are two ultimate principles in the universe seems somewhat artificial. On the one hand it seems that reality is far too diverse to be divided into just two categories.[25] There are too many different sorts of things, too many shades of gray. On the other hand, underneath all the diversity the universe seems too unified to be the product of more than one being or force. For example, gravity (the attraction of masses), explains not only why things fall to the ground but also the tides, planetary motion, and the movement of whole galaxies. That one principle accounts for much of the movement across the entire universe. Furthermore, gravity plus what is called the fine-structure constant determine the nature of everything from the smallest asteroids to the largest stars. They determine why the earth is the size it is and why bodies like the sun give off heat and light.[26] That so much in the universe should be uniformly organized around a few simple principles like these is evidence that one mind – not two or more – is behind it.

Oxford philosopher Richard Swinburne also points out that one God is a better explanation for the universe than two or more because it is simpler.[27] That is significant because simpler explanations usually turn out to be true, as science has long recognized.

There are good reasons to believe that one God exists who is a separate being. But what kind of Being is He? Some say He is not all powerful.

God is Not All Powerful – Process Theodicy, Mormonism, and Rabbi Kushner

According to Process Theology, to understand reality is to understand that everything is in process, everything is changing. That is the opposite of traditional western thinking, which has always held that at its very core, reality does not change; and at the center of that core is an unchanging God.

In Process Theology God has a side that is changing. According to the Process view, evil exists because God does not have all power. He cannot have all the power there is supposedly because creatures have some power. So He can try to persuade people to do what is right but He cannot coerce them.

Process Theology therefore focuses on premise two of the syllogism, which says that if God were all powerful He would be able to eliminate evil.

By contrast, in traditional theism God has all power but gives some to creatures as a part of granting them free will. Thus evil exists because God allows it, not because He lacks power. Furthermore, traditional theism emphasizes God's ability to work through a person as a secondary cause such that His will is accomplished through their choice.

Process Theology has been criticized for distorting the traditional view of omnipotence by setting up a false choice between God having either coercive power or persuasive power. There is no reason to think He can't have both. As well, God has powers that are entirely compatible with persuasive power. He has sustaining power, for example.[28]

There is a more difficult problem. If the God of Process Theology can do no more than persuade us, then either we are good enough to make progress by persuasion alone, or there is no hope that we will ever stop doing evil. That is because the Process God cannot fundamentally change our nature nor can He force us to do good. Philosopher Frederick Sontag says that such optimistic views of human nature require only a God who will cooperate with us. But if evil is part of human nature (as is obvious from Scripture as well as human history) then we need a different God, one who can either control us or alter our nature. Otherwise evil will never be overcome.[29] Besides its difficulty accounting for how God will overcome evil, some have also concluded that the limited God of Process Theology neither inspires our awe nor commands our worship.[30]

Like many ancient Greeks (such as Plato and Aristotle), Process Theology holds that God merely formed the universe out of eternally existing matter; He did not create it out of nothing (*ex nihilo*). This further reduces God's accountability for evil because He is limited by the material with which He must work. Because Mormonism also holds that God merely worked with eternal matter it has the same option in dealing with evil.

But there are problems with the view that matter, and therefore the universe, is eternal. An argument for the existence of God (called the kalam argument) points out that a universe that has no beginning must have an infinite series of things (causes, etc.) reaching back eternally, which is highly problematic or impossible. Furthermore, it is evident that the universe is winding down, which means it must have started at some point in time (such as a big bang) rather than going back forever. If it has been unwinding forever, it would already have been wound down. (More about the kalam argument in the chapter on answering skeptics.)

In contrast to the view that God worked with eternal matter, the biblical God created out of nothing. Biblical descriptions of God creating are different from descriptions of humans creating. The Hebrew word for "create" is used to describe people forming things from existing matter, but it is never used that way of God. In fact, "create" appears in certain Hebrew verb forms (the Qal and Niphal stems) only when used of God. That implies there is some special sense in which God "creates" which is not shared by humans. Nowhere does Genesis chapter one indicate that God merely formed the universe out of existing matter. Furthermore, a number of passages explicitly support creation out of nothing. It is said that God created by His Word, "so that what is seen was made out of things which do not appear" (Heb. 11:3), and that He "calls into existence the things that do not exist" (Rom. 4:17; John 1:3). No wonder the Jewish and early Christian traditions believed in creation out of nothing.[31]

Rabbi Harold Kushner proposes a solution to the problem of evil in terms of limits on God. His book, *Why Bad Things Happen to Good People* is without doubt the most widely read book on the problem of evil in decades. He wrote it after being sensitized to suffering by the tragedy of his son's fatal disease. He believes he made the same choice that Job had to make: "Forced to choose between a good God who is not totally powerful, or a powerful God who is not totally good, the author of the Book of Job chooses to believe in God's goodness." God wants good people to experience only happiness, "but sometimes even He can't bring that about. It is difficult even for God to keep cruelty and chaos from claiming their innocent victims."[32]

He accounts for suffering in two ways. Like Process Theology and Mormonism, he thinks of creation as merely forming order out of chaos (p. 51). Though God has brought much order in the universe, chaos still brings trouble where God's creative light has not penetrated (p. 53). Chaos operates outside the laws of nature that God set up. Suffering is its result, and it is as much outside the will of God as is chaos. As far as the future, either God will continue to produce ever more order, in which case random evil will decrease; or else He has finished His work and left us to deal with the residual chaos. If the chaos and the suffering it brings is permanent, Kushner suggests that we can take comfort in the thought that earthquakes, accidents, robbery and murder "are not the will of God, but represent that aspect of reality which stands independent of His will, and which angers and saddens God even as it angers and saddens us" (p. 55).

The second reason for suffering, according to Kushner, is that the laws of nature act impersonally, without regard to whether people are righteous or not. God never reaches in and spares anyone from the regular operation of the world. The world's regularity is what allows us to live in it. As far as the suffering it brings, "...God does not cause it and cannot stop it" (p. 58).

Though he has sincerely and seriously wrestled with the issue of suffering the explanation he developed is a little fuzzy. He forces a choice between God's goodness and His power because he is convinced that God cannot have both. A basic problem of Kushner's treatment is that there seems to be no reason why God could not or would not finish the job of bringing order to all the universe. If He is able but chooses not to, how could He be good? If on the other hand He is unable to do so, why could He bring order to most of the universe but not all of it?

Furthermore, there is irony in the fact that where God hasn't worked there is suffering from the chaos, yet where He has worked there is also suffering because natural laws operate blindly, without mercy or justice. Kushner insists that suffering is never brought about by God's justice.

It's not clear how this God is especially loving, nor why the key to the enigma of evil is understanding that He lacks the power we normally ascribe to Him. As well, most people would probably feel less comforted by the thought of a God who simply cannot control evil than they would by the traditional view that God is in total control but allows undesirable things for a purpose. At least if God is in control we can be assured that our sufferings have some higher purpose and that we are not victims of blind chaos. And the traditional view that God intervenes in the world is more comforting than Kushner's view that God always lets nature operate blind.

In contrast to Kushner's view, the biblical God works both through regular operations of natural law and also through seemingly chaotic events such as earthquakes, violent storms, drought and disease. Furthermore, He occasionally intervenes to change the course of natural events, for example, in response to prayer or faith. And He sometimes brings suffering as punishment for evil. All this is clear in the prophets (e.g., Ezek. 14) and in Moses' farewell address to the people of Israel (Deut. 31-32). Kushner's account overlooks the importance of morals and character in the problem of evil.

That said, if some of Kushner's ideas were sharpened they could fit into a viable explanation for evil. For example later in this book we shall see that, as he says, the world must be a predictable place for us to live in it; and that very predictability can bring certain types of suffering. He also explains the constructive role of pain. But some who reflect on the Holocaust hold that there can be no constructive purpose for horrific evils.

God is Not All Good – Theodicy After the Holocaust

The Holocaust deeply shocked modern humanity. It tore the veneer of goodness and perfectibility off human nature, exposing its deep flaws. Europe had become optimistic about humanity in the century of peace and progress that followed the defeat of Napoleon. Then World War I destroyed much of that optimism, and World War II obliterated what was left. Now looking back and trying to make sense of it, some regard

Hitler as a madman and the Holocaust as an historical anomaly, yet both conclusions ignore the full reality of evil. Hitler's program wasn't just insane, it was wicked. And clearly, history is strewn with evil on a mass scale.

Modern Judaism has understandably been especially shaken by these events. Its belief in a God who had chosen them – or belief in any God at all – has for some been thrown into dark doubt. Rabbi Richard Rubenstein expresses his doubts by asking, "How can Jews believe in an omnipotent, beneficent God after Auschwitz?"[33] He can no longer believe in an omnipotent, beneficent God; he finds solace in mysticism.[34]

Few things can put us more quickly in touch with the experiential side of the problem of evil than reading accounts by Holocaust survivors, especially those who wrestle out loud with the question of God. Elie Wiesel recalls the unspeakable cruelty of the death camp and how people around him struggled to hold on to faith. He tells how he himself lost that struggle,

> Never shall I forget that night, the first night in camp, which has turned my life into one long night, seven times cursed and seven times sealed. Never shall I forget that smoke. Never shall I forget the little faces of the children, whose bodies I saw turned into wreaths of smoke beneath a silent blue sky.
>
> Never shall I forget those flames which consumed my faith forever.
>
> Never shall I forget that nocturnal silence which deprived me, for all eternity, of the desire to live. Never shall I forget those moments which murdered my God and my soul and turned my dreams to dust.[35]

In later writings he seems ambivalent, seeing God as weeping over the sufferings of His people and pleased with those who continue in their faith.

John Roth, the son of a Presbyterian minister, coauthored a book with Rubenstein. In an earlier work Roth describes his "theodicy of protest." Unlike Process Theology, he affirms God's omnipotence. But therein lies the problem. Since God could have prevented evil but did not, He is not all good. For good to come of all that has happened in the world "human repentance will have to be matched by God's [repentance]."[36] He says, "Thus, in spite and because of his sovereignty, this God is everlastingly guilty and the degrees run from gross negligence to murder. Perhaps we should feel sorry for a God so soiled."[37]

So Roth would focus on premise one of the syllogism (above), and conclude that God is not good. Yet remarkably, he claims that "Scripture is authoritative in my theodicy..."[38]

In Roth's view no amount of future good or blessing could make up for the evil of the "waste" that God has allowed. Herein lies the central problem with his view. How can we, with our tiny minds, declare with such confidence that there can be no justification for what has happened? Even more audacious is the claim that no matter what eternity holds there can never be sufficient justification. (More about both these issues in chapter thirteen.) We have to view claims like his against the reality of our own ignorance: we discard and update scientific theories at dizzying speed, and our knowledge in certain fields doubles every few years. Yet the mind of an omniscient creator must be far more complex, hidden, and difficult to discover than the world around us. This is not to say that we can have no grounds for knowing the mind of God – our creation in His image suggests that we can know something of His mind. But our ignorance leaves quite a bit of space for faith that God has good and sufficient reasons for allowing evil. This book will explore what those might be.

God is Good and All-Powerful – Orthodoxy

Theodicy must face the full reality of evil while affirming an orthodox view of God. It must affirm that God is both good and all powerful. Defending the existence of a good and all powerful God despite the existence of pain and evil is known as theodicy.[39]

Orthodox theodicy's answer to the syllogism challenges premise one: God is indeed good yet has sufficient reasons for allowing evil. Some orthodox answers to the problem of evil also challenge premise two, saying that it would be a logical contradiction for God to grant creatures genuine freedom and also guarantee that no one misuses it. In other words, if God's plan includes genuine free will then it cannot exclude sin.

So we will find out in this book how, in spite of evil, God can be both good and all powerful.

GOING FARTHER

1. How can the theist find intellectual assurance for his or her faith with regard to the order in the universe? Its existence? Objective morals? The existence of the conscience? Providential care of living things?

2. What is the difference between general revelation and special revelation? Do you think this traditional distinction is found in the Bible?

3. How do the atheist's struggles with evil differ from those of the theist?

4. What is pantheism and what are some problems with it?

5. What did Mary Baker Eddy mean that evil is not real? What fundamental mistake did she make with regard to the existence of God that allowed her to claim that evil could not really exist?

6. What are some problems with the claim (made by Taoism, for example) that good and bad are two equal principles?

7. Summarize the difficulties with solving the problem of evil by limiting God's power. What are the problems with Rabbi Kushner's approach? What are the reasons for holding that the universe is not eternal?

8. What would you say to someone who says there is evil because God is not purely good?

NOTES

1.R. Baker, *Growing Up* (New York, NY: Congdon and Weed, 1982), 61; quoted in Paul C. Vitz, *Faith of the Fatherless: The Psychology of Atheism* (Dallas, TX: Spence, 1999), 146.

2. *1,911 Best Things Anybody Ever Said*, ed. Robert Byrne (reprint; 3 vols. in 1, New York, NY: Ballantine Books, Fawcett Columbine books, 1982-86), 162.

3. I realize that proving the existence of a designer does not prove that designer to be loving. On the other hand, the "design" in most design arguments is beneficial design, implying something about the goodness of the designer. In any case (as I see it), beliefs are connected, so that if we prove a designer we have made progress toward proving a good designer; if we prove a good designer, we have made progress toward proving the God of theism; if we prove the God of theism, we have made progress toward proving the Christian God. Proof of complex ideas is thus cumulative, that

is, evidence can accumulate or add up. No on expects to prove a criminal guilty with just one piece of evidence, for example. Those who use arguments for the existence of God acknowledge that they do not go all the way to proving the Christian God but nevertheless they are useful in a total case for the Christian God.

4. The argument that the universe has been fine tuned for life has been called the anthropic argument. See, for example, M. A. Corey, *God and the New Cosmology: The Anthropic Design Argument* (Lanham, MD: Rowman and Littlefield, 1993); John Leslie, *Universes* (London: Routledge, 1989); William Lane Craig, "The Teleological Argument and the Anthropic Principle," in William Lane Craig and Mark S. McLeod, eds., *The Logic of Rational Theism, Problems in Contemporary Theism*, xxiv (Lewiston, NY: Edwin Mellen, 1990), 127-153; L. Stafford Betty and Bruce Cordell, "New Life for the Teleological Argument," International Philosophical Quarterly, 27 (1987), 409-35.

5. A general treatment of the cosmological argument is in J. P. Moreland, *Scaling the Secular City: A Defense of Christianity* (Grand Rapids, MI: Baker, 1987). It also includes one of the recent forms of it, the Kalam argument, developed more fully in William Lane Craig, "The Finitude of the Past and the Existence of God," in William Lane Craig and Quentin Smith, *Theism, Atheism, and Big Bang Cosmology* (Oxford: Oxford University Press, 1993), 4-76; the latter is an updated excerpt from William Lane Craig, *The Kalam Cosmological Argument*, Library of Philosophy and Religion (London: Macmillan, 1979).

6. See, for example, Hick's response in R. Douglas Geivett, *Evil and the Evidence for God: The Challenge of John Hick's Theodicy* (Philadelphia, PA: Temple University Press, 1993), 229-37.

7. Bertrand Russell, *Why I Am Not A Christian and Other Essays on Religion and Related Subjects* (New York, NY: Simon and Schuster, 1957).

8. Lee Strobel, *The Case for Faith: A Journalist Investigates the Toughest Objections to Christianity* (Grand Rapids, MI: Zondervan, 2000), 141.

9. Bertrand Russell, letter to the Observer, 6 Oct. 1957; quoted in William Lane Craig, *Apologetics*: An Introduction (Chicago, IL: Moody, 1984), 47.

10. Bertrand Russell, "My Mental Development," in *The Philosophy of Bertrand Russell*, ed. P. A. Schilpp (Evanston/Chicago: The Library of Living Philosophers, 1944), 19; quoted in Ben-Ami Scharfstein, *The Philosophers: Their Lives and the Nature of their Thought* (New York, NY: Oxford, 1980), 313.

11. To Constance Malleson, 29 Sept. 1916; Autobiography, vol. 2, p. 75; quoted in Scharfstein, 312.

12. However, some forms of Buddhism add beliefs in supernatural beings.

13. Of course there is much more to say about this issue, such as about our fallen nature, redemption, the role of the Spirit in producing moral change, and so on. Such development is outside the scope of this book.

14. "Pantheism," Alasdair MacIntyre, *The Encyclopedia of Philosophy*, ed. Paul Edwards (New York: Macmillan, 1967), 6:34. He offers (*en passim*) problems with various other forms of pantheism.

15. Mary Baker Eddy claimed that Christian Science is not pantheistic, and is "neither hypothetical nor dogmatical, but demonstrable, and looms above the mists of pantheism higher than Mt Ararat above the deluge" (p. 2). But she went on to say of theism, "In religion, it is a belief in one God, or in many gods. It is opposed to atheism and monotheism, but agrees with certain forms of pantheism and polytheism" (pp. 3-4). This is an atypical understanding of at least one theological term. Note that

the popularity of Hegel's idealism as well as fascination with new information about Eastern religious philosophy made ideas like Eddy's more acceptable in the nineteenth and early twentieth centuries. Excerpts from Mary Baker Eddy, "Christian Science versus Pantheism," (1898), accessed Nov. 23, 2004; <http://mbeinstitute.org/Prose_Works/CSvsPantheism.html>.

16. Mary Baker Eddy, *Science and Health with Key to the Scriptures* (1875; reprint, Boston, MA: The First Church of Christ, Scientist, 1994) 71.

17. Eddy, Science and Health, 470.

18. Eddy, Science and Health, 469.

19. Eddy, Science and Health, 207, "There is but one primal cause. Therefore there can be no effect from any other cause, and there can be no reality in aught which does not proceed from this great and only cause."

20. Walter Martin, *The Kingdom of the Cults*, ed. Hank Hanegraaff, updated and expanded ed. (Minneapolis, MN: Bethany House, 1997), 253-55. Eddy's homeopathic physician, Dr. Alvin Cushing, denied under oath that he had ever claimed she was in a precarious physical condition, said instead that she had always been in robust health, and reported that he administered medicine to her four times in August 1866 (her fall and supposed mentally induced recovery had been in February). His 1,000 word statement is in Georgine Milmine, *The Life of Mary Baker G. Eddy and the History of Christian Science* (Grand Rapids, MI: Baker, 1937), 84-86. Secondly, Julius Dresser, received a letter from Eddy two weeks after her supposed recovery; in it she expressed doubt that she could continue to recover. F. W. Peabody, *The Religio-Medical Masquerade* (New York, NY: Fleming H. Revell, 1910, 80-81. Sources cited in Martin, 254. See also, Gillian Gill, *Mary Baker Eddy* (Reading, MA: Perseus Books, 1998), 158-64 (Eddy's letter to Dresser and his reply, pp. 158-59). Cushing's affidavit wasn't given until 1907, but he said he remembered clearly and was helped by his medical notes. Eddy (then Mrs. Patterson) tried to get the city to pay her for damages from the fall, claiming the streets were dangerous. She fell in early February yet the petition was submitted months later (in late summer) claiming then that she had suffered "serious personal injuries *from which she had little prospect of recovering*" (emphasis added). Yet she would later claim authority for her teachings because she had healed herself "on the third day" (Eddy to W. W. Wright, 1871; in Gill, 162).

21. Martin, 248. Martin cites *New York World*, 30 Oct. 1906; Robert Peel, *Mary Baker Eddy*: Years of Discovery, 195; Ernest Sutherland Bates and John V. Dittemore, Mary Baker Eddy: *The Truth and the Tradition* (New York: Knopf, 1932), 41-42, 151, 445. Cushing recalled that on the third day after her injury he gave her medicine. Later when it came time to move her home, he gave her 1/8 grain of morphine (affidavit in Gill, 164). Calvin Frye recorded Eddy's decline in his diary, 9 May 1910, "Mr. Adam H. Dickey last night told Mrs. Eddy that she shall not have any more morphine!.... [H]e believed she did not need it, but that it was the old morphine habit reasserting itself and would not allow her to have it" (Gill, 545). Gill concludes that Eddy used morphine only for pain but was not addicted (p. 546).

22. Eddy, 126, 497.

23. How ultimate good and evil are depends on the particular theology within Zoroastrianism. However, both early and late views have the good god judging the evil god and his followers. Niels C. Nielsen, Jr. et al, *Religions of the World*, 2nd. ed (New York, NY: St. Martin's, 1988), 61-67. Hans Schwarz, *Evil: A Historical and Theological Perspective*, transl. Mark W. Worthing (Minneapolis, MN: Fortress, 1995), 86-90.

24. Augustine, *The City of God*, xi, 22.

25. In Zoroastrianism people follow either the good or the evil god, and they are judged accordingly. In Christianity (cf. John; 1 John), people follow either God or not, however people are not viewed as pure good or pure evil. More importantly, salvation is based on grace not on personal morals. In Christianity there are two spiritual forces (God and His host, Satan and his demons) but unlike Taoism, all creation has its source in God alone; evil is not ultimate but arises from a misuse of free will.

26. The fine-structure constant is the square of the electric charge on a single electron divided by the product of the speed of light and Plank's constant (which expresses quantum energy). The fine-structure constant equals about 1/377. For an explanation of constants and their significance, see John D. Barrow, *Theories of Everything*: The Quest for Ultimate Explanation (New York, NY: Fawcett Columbine, 1991), chapter 5.

27. Richard Swinburne, *The Existence of God*, revised ed. (Oxford: Oxford University Press, 1991), 141-42.

28. Michael Peterson, William Hasker, Bruce Reichenbach, David Basinger, *Reason and Religious Belief: An Introduction to the Philosophy of Religion*, 2nd. ed. (New York, NY: Oxford University Press, 1998), 138-39.

29. Frederick Sontag [critique of David Griffin's theodicy], in *Encountering Evil*: Live Options in Theodicy, ed. Stephen T. Davis (Atlanta, GA: John Knox Press, 1981), 124-25.

30. Stephen Davis (reply to Griffin), in Davis, 127; and John Roth (reply to Griffin), in Davis, 121.

31. For more detailed treatment, see Millard J. Erickson, *Christian Theology* (Grand Rapids: Baker, 1983, 1984, 1985), 367-70; and Paul Copan and William Lane Craig, "Craftsman or Creator? An Examination of the Mormon Doctrine of Creation and a Defense of Creation Ex Nihilo, chapter 3 in The New Mormon Challenge, ed. Francis J. Beckwith, Carl Mosser, and Paul Owen (Grand Rapids, MI: Zondervan, 2002).

32. Harold Kushner, *Why Bad Things Happen to Good People* (New York, NY: Avon, 1983), 43. He made the comments in reference to Job 40:9-14. Subsequent references in the text are to his book.

33. Richard Rubenstein, in Dan Cohn-Sherbok, ed., Holocaust Theology: A Reader (Washington Square, NY: New York University Press, 2002), 41; reprinted from R. Rubenstein, *After Auschwitz* (Indianapolis, IN: Bobbs Merril, 1996), 153. Rubenstein rejects the traditional God who controls history, but accepts God as (a creative) Nothingness. *Holocaust Theology* is a good source for the diverse reaction to the Holocaust.

34. Dan Cohn-Sherbok, *Fifty Key Jewish Thinkers* (London: Routledge, 1997), 110-13 (cf. Elie Wiesel, 127-30).

35. Elie Wiesel, *Night*, trans. Stella Rodway (1958; reprinted, New York, NY: Bantam, 1982), 32.

36. John Roth, "A Theodicy of Protest," in Davis, 10.

37. Roth in Davis, 16.

38. Roth in Davis, 31.

39. The term was coined by German philosopher Gottfried Leibniz (1646-1716), from the Greek for God (theos) and righteousness (dike). In his Theodicy (1710), Leibniz said that God has good reason to bring our world into existence in spite of its evils because it is, over all, the best possible world. The evils contribute to the

good of the whole. Strictly speaking, a theodicy builds a positive case, proposing actual reasons God allows evil. A "defense" merely tries to counter atheistic arguments from evil without trying to reveal God's actual reasons for allowing evil (e.g., Alvin Plantinga's defense). The term theodicy has been used more loosely, in a way that does not necessarily assume that God is both good and all powerful.

Chapter two

WRONG EXPECTATIONS

If you think for a moment, you probably have an unspoken list of things that you assume God must do to be good. It may include, for instance, providing things you feel you need, or protecting those who are innocent or helpless. If the latter, perhaps it would make you wonder about divine goodness if a sincere Christian were to suffer a gruesome death at the hands of a criminal. Or perhaps the horrific killing of over 330 parents and children by terrorists in the Russian school in Beslan in 2004 made you wonder. Or maybe it's just the fact that so many children die each year, about 12 million under the age of five.

Many of our questions about the problem of pain and evil are really questions about God's goodness. In a moment of hurt or doubt, we may secretly muse that if God were good – in just the way we think of goodness – things wouldn't be this way. Yet many of our challenges to God's goodness would disappear if we better understood His unique nature and His relationship to creation.

What must God do to be good?

Among the many reasons we have a "problem" with evil, two stand out in relation to God's goodness. The first is that we see a difference between our idea of goodness and God's actions. We wonder how God can be good based on our standards of goodness. We perceive a discrepancy between God and some standard of goodness to which we hold Him.

What makes this awkward, though, is that it fails to grasp the relationship between God and the very standards we are using for judging goodness. If there is a God of the sort that theists say exists, then He Himself (specifically, His character) is the standard for goodness. If loving is good it is because God is loving; if truth telling is good, it is because God is truthful.

So in a way it makes no sense to ask if God is good, because He Himself is the criteria for judging goodness.

We cannot hold God to some arbitrary and imaginary standard of goodness. We cannot say that He falls short of being good because, for example, He does not make beautiful orchids bloom in the arctic, or because He does not make it possible for every child on the planet to go to an amusement park once a year. Of course God need not do such things to be good. But if a standard for goodness is to be objective rather than arbitrary or imaginary, then the theist would base it on God, who is the ultimate source of all existence, truth, beauty, goodness, and value. We start having problems when we try to hold God to what the majority thinks He must do to be good, or to our personal standard of goodness. So doing moves us in the direction of requiring Him to make orchids bloom on tundra.

Adding to the awkwardness of judging God's goodness is the fact that whatever we know of goodness is due to God's enablement. As our creator, all our abilities come from Him, even our ability to judge goodness.

In Mark Twain's *Huckleberry Finn*, Huck struggles over whether to continue trying to free his slave friend, Jim. He thinks God wants him to return Jim to his owner, but then he also feels compassion and loyalty toward Jim. He finally resolves to do what he thinks is wrong, and continue helping the runaway slave. "All right, then, I'll go to hell..." he said.[1] The reader knows Huck has made the right decision, but in Huck's mind doing what is good is contrary to what God wants. Of course the resolution is for Huck to better understand what is right, in the sense that no one can make a valid claim on another human as their property. But it also illustrates the awkwardness of separating God and goodness.

What makes us think that we as creatures are qualified to conclude that God is not good?

If we truly accepted God as the standard of goodness, we probably would not have much problem with the existence of evil. Whatever God does or does not do, or allows or doesn't allow, we would accept as right. On the other hand, that would solve the problem of evil for us only on one level, the level of faith. We would believe God is good in spite of pain and suffering, but we would not necessarily know why and how He is good. Our questions would go unanswered and the details would be left out. We would not know why God chose to make the world this way, and how it is consistent with His character and goals. In other words, we would trust that the problem of evil has a solution, but we wouldn't know how it is resolved. And isn't a major difference between mature thinking and immature thinking a matter of knowing the details? The new believer may know merely that something is the case whereas the mature Christian knows in detail how.

Those who know a lot about how are called theologians. A theologian and an astronomer met at a dinner party, and the astronomer remarked that he had studied quite a bit of theology. "Yes," he said, "I've read about sin and redemption, about the natures of Christ, the hypostatic union, and the economic Trinity. But I think it all comes down to one thing: Jesus loves me this I know." The theologian thought a minute and replied that he had quite an interest in astronomy, and had read about the big bang and the expanding universe, about dark matter, super novas, and black holes. "But," he said, "I think it all boils down to one thing: twinkle, twinkle little star."[2] The point is that there is a big difference between an elementary and a sophisticated understanding of something.

The second reason we may have a "problem" with the existence of evil is that there seems to be a discrepancy between what God sets as the standard for goodness and His own actions. We see a difference between what God says is good and what He actually does. For example, we know God says to be kind and that we ourselves should be that way, but we wonder, wasn't God unkind to allow a certain child to be hurt or orphaned?

A number of biblical saints had this kind of problem with evil. Upon being told by his supernatural visitor that Sodom and Gomorrah would be destroyed for their wickedness, Abraham asked God to spare the city for the sake of a few righteous. He pleaded, "Far be it from You to do such a thing as this, to slay the righteous with the wicked, so that the righteous should be as the wicked; far be it from You! Shall not the judge of all the earth do right?" (Genesis 18:25[NKJ]) He was reasoning that it would be unlike God to punish the righteous along with the wicked. He would not be acting according to His own standards (interestingly, it was an argument that persuaded God).

Like the first problem, we could answer this with simple faith as well. But also like the first problem, if we stop there we will not benefit from working out the details.

There are some basic reasons why God is good without seeming to be so.

God Cannot Be Morally Inconsistent

To begin with, we should never expect that God would compromise His righteous character to do "good." The point sounds obvious, but there are hidden implications.

When we expect that God always overlooks evil to show kindness we are demanding that He give up the good of justice for the good of kindness. Such a demand overlooks the fact that justice is itself a form of goodness (a subject we will explore further in chapter six). Bringing consequences upon the serial rapist or genocidal dictator is a good thing. Bringing consequences for lesser sins is also good and we cannot accuse God of failing to be good when He causes or allows pain as a just consequence.[3]

We are especially tempted to expect that God would overlook justice in order to be kind when the consequences seem remote from the sin. When years of anger or worry eventually cause an individual health problems, or when a nation tolerates gross sin and eventually suffers on a mass scale, we are tempted to see the suffering as unconnected from its cause and suppose that God has been unkind. Israel tolerated gross sin for generations, failing to heed warnings from the prophets. Eventually sin brought national disaster in the form of conquest by a foreign power. Not only did the people fail to see how their sin had led to it, they failed to grasp how God's chastening was a form of mercy, purifying them in order to prevent them sinning further.

Years ago I heard that a newborn had died, and shortly after that his mother died, leaving the husband to grieve alone. It set me wondering why God would allow such a thing. Wouldn't it have been much better to prevent such a tragedy, especially among believers? It was one of those things I could resolve only by sheer faith.

About a month later I talked to a pastor who knew the history. I found out that the man and his new wife, both professing Christians, had each been married before. They had met at church, had an affair, and despite pleadings and warnings from everyone, they left their families and their young children in order to marry each other.

When the baby died, the man saw it as an act of God's severe mercy, leading him to repentance. He concluded that God had not overlooked his brazen, public sin. He also saw it as a warning to all that would follow the couple's destructive example.

He was in church the very next Sunday, humbled and teachable. He repented, and began to exhort others not to stray from the path of righteousness.

God Cannot Be Mentally Inconsistent

While God cannot – or perhaps we should say will not – violate His moral character, neither can He or will He violate His "mental" character. Hence His actions are logically consistent. He cannot make square triangles or married bachelors. These are not things to make, they are simply nonsense, so the fact that He cannot make them is in no way a test of His omnipotence. Furthermore, the Bible assumes – and God expects us to believe – that if something is true, then its opposite is false. If it is true that He exists then it is false that He does not exist; if He is holy then He is not sinful; if He is unchanging then He is not changing. This is in contrast to some eastern thought which holds that the highest spiritual truths transcend the principle that contradictions cannot both be true (called the principle of non-contradiction).[4]

There are also times when God can bring about one thing or the other, but not both. God can bring it about that Jones is in Casablanca, or that he is in London, but He cannot bring it about that he is in both places at once.

That God cannot and does not do what is contradictory has important implications for the problem of evil.[5]

This has been related to free will and evil. According to the argument from free will, God cannot both grant free will and also guarantee that no one ever uses it to sin. So if people have free will even God cannot rule out the possibility of evil (more about this in chapter four).

God's consistency further demands that once He has made one choice, even as God He is limited (or more accurately, self-limited) as to His other choices. Once He has chosen, for example, to bring it about that human actions have consequences good or bad, and that people should have the opportunity to learn from consequences, then He cannot also continually shield everyone from consequences.[6] So the wastrel ways of a person who buys everything he desires brings financial consequences both on himself and his innocent dependents. The advantage is that seeing those consequences gives him the opportunity to understand the error of his ways and to change. Similarly, the need eventually suffered by the lazy person may force him to change.

The implications of God's consistency reach farther than we might think. Some people, for example, wonder why God gave them certain parents. Wouldn't it have been so much better, they suppose, if God had caused them to be born into a different family? I've heard people wish that they had parents who understood them better and could help them develop their talents, or parents who were more caring; or only that they had a mother or father who would not abuse them.

But we have to realize that once God has determined that people be genetically the product of their parents, it would be impossible for you to have been born to anyone else. You would not be you. To exist at all you had to be the product of certain parents, thus to wish you had other parents, is in a sense, wishing that you did not exist. So not only is such wishful thinking unproductive, it is outright contradictory. We could, of course, wish instead that our parents had made better choices. In a practical sense, those choices, good or bad, have shaped us. But how it shapes us is up to us. We can learn from their bad example and vow not to repeat it, or we can choose to be just like them. Two children in the same home can react to their environment in opposite ways. One son I know raised by an alcoholic became a drug addict and a career criminal; the other son determined never to touch drugs or alcohol. He became a very responsible and highly productive person, as well he is a dedicated father to his own children.

Pining for the impossibility of having other parents only tempts us to become bitter. So rather than regret what we can't change, we should focus on making the most of what we have experienced.

Another implication of God's consistency is that we also cannot fault Him for failing to accomplish something good if it would conflict with accomplishing something better. For example, it may be good if everything went perfectly in our lives with no problems or frustrations, but it would be better if we learned patience and persistence. If we cannot have both, God will give us the trials (cf. James 1:3).

The simple fact that in some cases God cannot bring about both what is good and what is better can resolve what might be the most common objection to God's goodness. That is that He has failed to make the world a place in which every creature is as happy as it could be. For many people, the reason evil poses a problem for the existence of a good God is that we could imagine a world so much "better" than this one, which usually means a world in which creatures are so much happier.

This world is indeed enigmatic if we assume its point is to make every creature as happy as possible. But if we allow that the greatest happiness of every creature is not the highest goal for the universe, then the existence of evil becomes far less puzzling.

For God to have made the world the happiest possible place all the time would no doubt have been a good thing – but it should not be accomplished at the expense of a better thing.[7] God should not make this world a place of maximal happiness if there is something more important and He cannot do both.

I would suggest that there is such a higher goal and that it does conflict with a world of maximal pleasure for every creature. That goal is the fullest possible revelation of God's character, traditionally referred to as His glory. As the greatest being, the fullest revelation of Him is the greatest good – He being the very ground and apex of all goodness, truth, and beauty. The glory of God includes the possibility of His character being formed in us and thereby revealed through us as moral beings (which is sometimes included in what it means to be in the image of God). Knowledge about Himself is the greatest gift God can bestow on creatures.

We can get a negative view of God's desire to glorify Himself because in people such desire is usually associated with self-centeredness. But God's desire to glorify Himself is different. I would suggest that, being the source of everything, He needs nothing (which is why His choice to create was a free one). It being impossible for Him to act out of need, it would seem that He therefore acts unselfishly.[8] For people who are right with Him, the revelation of divine glory is a great blessing (whereas in chapter eleven we will see how judgment glorifies God without blessing the recipient).

I believe that the glory of God holds the key to understanding why He would create if He foreknew the suffering that would result. That suffering is worth it because it makes possible the fulfillment of higher goals, especially with regard to those who accept God's grace and come to know Him personally. He allows some pain and suffering partly because it reveals aspects of Him that would otherwise be hidden from us (such as forgiveness, which is known only where there is sin; and mercy, which is known only where there is suffering; more about this in chapter five). As Augustine said, "For God would never have created a man, let alone an angel, in the foreknowledge of his future evil state, if he had not known at the same time how he would put such creatures to good use, and thus enrich the course of the world history by the kind of antithesis which gives beauty to a poem."[9]

We have to keep in mind that personal character which glorifies God by reflecting His character cannot be poured into us like a liquid. Rather, it is formed in us by our choices and responses to situations. Thus we learn it through experiences, some of them unpleasant, as when we learn to forgive someone who has hurt us. If the world is to provide the greatest possibilities for shaping our character, it cannot be a place of uninterrupted pleasure. Rather, it has to be a place in which we must face and overcome some difficult challenges.

According to Scripture, there is coming a new world of limitless happiness (for those who accept God's grace of forgiveness), but first there are important things that can be gained from living in this world.[10]

Does God Have a Duty to do Good?

The idea that a good God ought to have made the world differently, or at least managed it differently, is largely based on notions about His duties (since duties determine what a person ought to do). But our ideas about duties are based on our knowledge of human duties, and we cannot necessarily transfer them to God since He is unique.

For one thing, our duties are based on what is owed. We owe God obedience to His commands, and His commands are based on His character. We ought to love, for example, because God does. But what ought God to do? He does not have duties in the same way that we do. If duties are based in God Himself, His ultimate duty (if we can even speak of Him having duties) is to be true to His character. He does not have duties imposed on Him from the outside as do humans. Everything comes from Him. As He asked of Job, "Who has given to Me that I should repay him? Whatever is under the whole heaven is Mine" (cf. Job 41.11 Exod. 19:5, Job 35:7; Rom.11:35). Any duties God may have would ultimately be from Himself.

We may be tempted to think that God had a duty to make a different world, one with happier people, who have less pain or emotional difficulty, or who are so much better than the current human race. But God could have no duties toward uncreated people; they are imaginary and will never exist. For us humans it would be like a coworker scolding us for failing to do our job the way an imaginary boss would want it done, or for failing to give money to an imaginary fellow worker in need.

Many suspicions that God is not good come down to the sense that He has not been as gracious as He should have been toward us or someone else. We may wish that He had made us healthier or wealthier, or with greater opportunities for what we consider to be a good life. Yet if there is one thing clear about grace it is by definition undeserved. It is therefore contradictory to say that God ought to have been more gracious. By the very nature of grace, there can be no duty to be more gracious. Whatever we get is of grace and God does not owe us more grace than He has chosen to give us. No child can say on Christmas morning that his or her parents did wrong by not giving more gifts. Christ told a parable in which workers were hired throughout the day, and at the end of the day each was paid the same although some had worked much longer. When some grumbled about it the employer pointed out that he had wronged no one, and he could be generous to the latecomers if he so chose (Matt. 20:11-15).

There can be no doubt that whatever good things have come to us are a matter of sheer grace. God did not owe them to us. He did not give them to us in return for anything, since He is the source of everything in the first place. In fact, our right to anything was forfeited by our failure to give Him His rightful place in our lives. We went our own way, violating His principle of love. This fact is echoed by Jeremiah, who said while surrounded by horrendous suffering, "Why should any living mortal, or any man, offer complaint in view of his sins?" (Lam. 3:39).

British poet Alexander Pope (1688-1744) had his share of troubles. He was forbidden a university education because of his Catholicism, and he suffered from tuberculosis, asthma, and curvature of the spine, which limited his stature to four and a half feet. But he held to a doggedly optimistic view of suffering. He was convinced that God knows what He is doing, and, "That wisdom infinite must form the best."[11] Yet pride motivates people to want more than God gives, Pope said. They fail to appreciate God's plan, and they fail to realize that if anything, they deserve worse.

Presumptuous man! the reason wouldst thou find
Why formed so weak, so little and so blind?
First, if thou canst, the hard reason guess,
Why formed no weaker, blinder, and no less.[12]

Life's blessings are like forgiveness of sin; both are matters of grace. Whatever God gives us humans is of grace. In fact it is twice a matter of grace: we did not deserve anything in the first place, and we also forfeited any possible claim to anything on account of our sin.

Because whatever we receive from God is undeserved, we have no grounds for begrudging the fact that we did not get more. We have no grounds, therefore, for resenting the fact that our wife or child did not live seventy years, or that our ministry seems insignificant compared to someone else's, or that we have health problems, or that we are stuck in a job we don't enjoy.

When Christ told Peter he would be martyred, the apostle's response was to ask about John's fate. It seems Peter was comparing God's grace in his life to the grace given to another. Jesus' response was that Peter must not be distracted from faithfulness by how God deals with another (John 21:18-22). Nor should we.

A dear woman I know had lost, in the same year, her husband and her only child. Her teenager died in a car accident and her husband succumbed to cancer. With eyes full of hurt she asked me one day how she could deal with it. I struggled to say something that would be of help, knowing the gulf between her experiences and mine. After a pause I pointed out that there are two ways to regard such things. We can think we had a right to more and be bitter that we didn't get it, or we can look at what we got and be glad that we got it. Our attitude, not our circumstances, determines whether we are basically grateful and content, or else bitter and angry at God. I added that there's no guarantee our spouse will live a long life or that our children will outlive us. But then, if we never reach out and love in spite of the potential for loss, we will never know the joys that can come of it. I continued by saying that she could cope by focusing on the fact that she had so many wonderful years with her family and that they had enriched her life. Thinking of those years as a wonderful gift that will always be with her is the way to cope.

Reflecting for a moment, she said that she had come to the same conclusion about what her attitude should be and that she was trying hard to see it all that way. Struggling to hold back tears, she quietly walked away.

Is This the Best Possible world?

Have you ever wondered if this world is the best it could be, or if it could be better in some way? Does every detail about the world have to be as it is, or could it have turned out differently in some way and been just as good?

Philosopher Gottfried Leibniz (1646-1716) boldly claimed that this is the best of all possible worlds because God would not have created less than the best. He went so far as to claim that if there were no best world among the possible worlds God would not have created at all.[13]

To Voltaire (1694-1778), the French philosopher and satirist, the view was laughable. He poked fun at it in his story, *Candide*. In it a professor Pangloss responds to the most tragic events with what is portrayed as a pedantic and silly claim that "every thing was such as it could not be better.... All this was indispensable... and private misfortunes constitute the general good; so that the more private misfortunes there are, the whole is better."[14] The pessimistic philosopher Arthur Schopenhauer (1788-1860) not only rejected the idea that this is the best possible world, he said it is the worst possible world, and it is evidence against a beneficent creator. Nuclear scientist J. Robert Oppenheimer said, "The optimist thinks that this is the best of all possible worlds, and the pessimist knows it."[15]

Leibniz claimed not that every particular event happens in the best way, but that as a whole, the world has the best possible balance of good over evil. It is a mistake, Leibniz said, to think that the whole cannot be the best unless each part is the best; a work of art, for example, can be beautiful without each part being beautiful.[16] He believed that having some evil allows for more good, as for example when we appreciate our health (which is a good thing) only after being ill (which is a bad thing).[17] Thus a world without evil would not be the best possible world.

For him this meant that the world has to turn out one and only one way, down to the last detail, with not one evil thing missing, no matter how small.[18] I have met Christians who believed much the same thing, going so far as to say that the universe could not have had one molecule more or less than it has. Supposedly, if just one of our footsteps were a slightly different length it could radically affect our lives – our footsteps might not meet up with those of our future spouse, for example. On this view, God has to micromanage the spin of every last electron in the universe to ensure everything happens exactly right, otherwise it would not be the best.

On this view, for every freak accident or every child's death, there is a reason why it happened just then and with just that outcome. Leibniz did not think he was able – or obligated – to give reasons why specific incidents of suffering were for the best. He thought it was enough to show that a specific evil could contribute to what is best on the whole. More specific knowledge would have to wait until the next life.[19]

Is every detail of every unwanted event necessary, and do we have the one and only best possible world? It is not an easy question.

The first thing we have to do is ask, best for what? Best for realizing our personal ambitions? Best for revealing truth to us? Best for punishing moral evil? What most people really mean is the best for promoting happiness – especially theirs. But is that the highest purpose?

To really be the best world, it should be one which accomplishes the best end, and does it using the best methods. As we've said, it need not accomplish lesser goals, like the happiness of all creatures, if those goals conflict with the highest goal. If the fullest revelation of God (His glory) is the highest goal, then the best world would be the one which achieves that in the best way.

The very concept of "the best" is another issue. What does it mean to be the best? We are so used to thinking of the best in easily quantifiable terms. The best athletes have the fastest times, or the highest scores. The best companies are rated by things like profit and market share. It is not surprising that we think of the best world in the same terms, as somehow having more units of goodness than any other world.

By contrast, it has been suggested that the best possible world is as much an impossibility as the highest possible number.[20] Just as there is always a higher number so there is a world with a little more goodness. Whether or not there could be one and only one best possible world would be very difficult to know because it is extremely difficult for us to even compare worlds. That is because difficulties and even tragedies can lead to much greater good. Would it have been a better world had there been half the bankruptcies in the great depression? But what if those bankruptcies led people to realize that there is something more to life than money, or led a lot of people to have compassion on others, or led to meaningful financial reform so that for many decades to follow there was much less financial suffering? What if a child's fall out of a tree made her decide to listen to advice, which later kept her from getting into drugs or into a disastrous marriage? When we consider things like attitudes and long range consequences, we can see that determining what is "best" quickly becomes too complex to determine, at least for humans.

That means that we humans cannot easily figure out what would make this a better world. Contrary to common opinion, it is not at all obvious that the world would be a better place without a particular tragedy. It is not easy to determine, for example, that the world would have been better had a mudslide that buried fifty people buried only twenty instead, or that it would have been better had a person who died at forty years old died at sixty instead. I have known of a number of men who made disastrous decisions in their later years, leaving their spouses and children, bringing upon them a deep sense of rejection as well as poverty. Others wrecked their entire life's work in ministry or business through foolishness or sin. Had their lives ended a little earlier would it have been a bad thing?

Besides the sheer difficulty of determining which set of events would be better, hence which world would be best, the whole effort can lead to a kind of chipping away attack: no matter what amount of pain or evil exists, one can always ask why God did not prevent it. Had God prevented all but twenty deaths in the mudslide people would ask why He allowed those twenty people to die. Yet had He prevented all but one death, people would still ask why He allowed that one person to die. In fact, had the universe contained only one painful event, it could still be asked why God allowed even that when He could have prevented it and made the universe completely without evil.[21]

We can wonder on the other hand if there could be a number of equally good worlds. Our world may be no better or worse than one that is perfectly identical except that it has one extra leaf on a tree somewhere, or in which we blink one extra time in our entire life – or where one less person or one more person died in a mud slide. It may be that many possible worlds would have been the "best" in the sense that no other world would have been better.

If this is the case, God could have brought about any number of worlds and still have brought about the "best." An important consequence for the problem of evil is that we would not have to defend the exact way everything happens as necessarily better than every other possible outcome. We can simply show some good reasons why God would allow things to happen as they did. So we do not have to show why it is best that a child died exactly at the age of six and not eight or seventy-five. We can simply show why, in the broad scheme of things, God might have allowed the child to die. We could point out that a world in which someone, through no fault of theirs, was slightly injured in a traffic collision could be as good as a world in which he was not hit. The accident might prompt the driver to reevaluate his life and priorities, becoming a better person. Thus the inconvenience of the accident is balanced by the goodness that came from it. In that sense having the accident turned out to be no worse than not having it when it comes to the total sum of goodness in a possible world.

The view that there is only one best world in which absolutely every detail must be just as it is down to the last molecule, fits comfortably with Newton's theories. Even its view of God's workings and sovereignty fit. Newton's laws of motion seemed to make the universe like a giant machine in which every gear turned every other gear in a precise way. Everything seemed so locked together that some claimed if we knew enough about the beginning of the universe and the laws governing it, we could predict every future event.[22] In such rigid versions of the Newtonian worldview, nothing can be missing or out of place in the world, and there is only one right way it functions. From this view it is natural to hold that God's sovereignty and plan require that all the details be exactly right, just as a mechanical clock won't work properly if it is missing even one tooth on one gear.

The physics of this deterministic world were eroded early in the nineteenth century when physicist Werner Heisenberg claimed to show the impossibility of predicting the precise movement of sub-atomic particles. If the atomic foundation of the universe is unpredictable, the rest must be too, it was thought.[23] Events seemed undetermined, just as they had been before Newton.

In addition to the changes in physics, mathematical studies showed the difficulty or impossibility of predicting outcomes in situations where things affect other things, which in turn affect still other things. So in contrast to the Newtonian vision of perfect predictability, some complex things are now thought to be unpredictable after only a few steps in a chain of events. Making even short-term predictions turns out to be so complex that some people are now suggesting that God Himself cannot know the outcomes (supposedly even an omniscient being can't know that much!).

Because of these major changes, many who want to maintain that God controls the outcome of all events have updated their worldview, from Newtonian to quantum physics. In the quantum universe, events could turn out a number of ways, but we could still say that God controls things to produce the outcome He desires.[24]

Whatever we conclude about the physics and such, biblically it seems we have to allow that things could indeed turn out more than one way. Several passages speak of things turning out differently. When David was being sought by Saul he tried to find refuge in the city of Keilah. He asked God whether the men of Keilah would deliver him over to Saul if he were to stay there. God said that they would, so David gathered his men and left the city (1 Sam. 23:12, 13). David's question and God's answer require that things could turn out differently. If not, then David's question would not make sense, and God would not have answered it as if it did. If David, who knew so much about God and the way He operated, didn't know the most basic thing about the world (that there is only one way in which things can happen) and had asked a question that would amount to nonsense, then God would have corrected him. But apparently the question was not nonsense, and in fact, it was insightful. Far from correcting David, God confirmed his insight about the way things might turn out.

When Paul's ship was in a violent storm and all hope was lost, he announced that God had granted His prayer request to spare the lives of everyone on board. Later, he had to warn the centurion to stop some of the crew who were trying to jump ship. "Unless these men remain in the ship, you yourselves cannot be saved" he told him (Acts 27:31). Though God had determined that all would be saved, it required specific choices. Absent those choices, it would turn out a different way.

The whole biblical concept of prayer assumes that events could turn out differently. James says that the prayer of a righteous man can accomplish much (Jas. 5:16). If no event could ever turn out differently from the way it does then James could not say that. That is because the prayer of a righteous man would change absolutely nothing.

When Hezekiah fell ill the prophet Isaiah was sent to tell him to set his house in order because he was going to die. Hezekiah prayed fervently for God to spare his life. Isaiah was sent back to tell him that his prayer had been answered and that God would add fifteen years to his life (2 Kings 20:1-6). If we do not press a different worldview onto the passage, it is clear that things were going to turn out one way

– we know because God said so – and God changed them to turn out a different way.

Accepting that events can turn out different ways still leaves open the question of whether there is one and only one best world such that God guides all events toward it. There does not seem to be any biblical reason why we have to insist that the universe turn out precisely one way, down to the last molecule. Would the universe be the worse if there is one extra molecule in a distant star, or one extra grain of sand in the Sahara? Insisting that it would presses an alien worldview onto Scripture; it certainly doesn't come out of Scripture. Moreover, it would seem that if there is precisely one best world and God is (self)obligated to bring it about, then He has absolutely no choices to make. He either brings about that best world or He doesn't. And if that best world is better than no world, then God does not even have a choice as to whether or not to create. He is locked into creating that one best world with no choices to make, ever.[25] Something seems amiss.

Just what events could be different and still have an equally good universe is impossible for us humans to say. Could two universes be equally good if they are identical in every way except that in one a person dies half a second earlier? What about a month earlier? What about, like Hezekiah, fifteen years later? We can quickly see the significance for the problem of evil – do things have to turn out exactly as they do for God to be good? And do we have to defend every event, no matter how small as the best? Furthermore, whether the future can turn out differently within God's plan or not affects how we understand the way God works with us beings who have a free will (which we will explore more specifically in chapter four).

The question of whether events can turn out differently is an issue entirely separate from God's omniscience. Of course, being omniscient, God knows all possibilities as well as which of those possibilities will actually happen. God knows beforehand what we will pray and which prayers He will answer. He knew that David would ask what the men of Keliah would do, that He would answer, and David would escape. He knew that the sailors in Paul's ship would try to escape and that Paul would warn the centurion. He knew He would grant Hezekiah a longer life.[26] But the fact that God knows how things will turn out does not necessarily mean that there has to be only one way in which He could make them turn out, nor that there is only one way in which He will allow them to turn out.[27]

Whether or not we conclude that ours is the best possible world in the Leibnizian sense, fatalism and resignation are not justified (we'll look briefly at fatalism in chapter four, and at our duty to act in chapter fourteen). If there really is only one best world and God is guiding every last molecule in the universe toward it, then we still ought to strive to do what we know is best – and our efforts will become part of the fabric of that best world.

GOING FARTHER

1. What things would, if they happened, challenge your confidence that God is good? Has anything happened that made you wonder why God would do it or allow it? How did you resolve it?

2. Have you ever struggled with a difference between your standard of goodness and what God has done or allowed?

3. Has it ever seemed to you that God did not live up to His own standard of goodness? If you were to think so, what would you say to God about it?

4. If God could choose to be gracious to everyone, why doesn't He?

5. What are some implications of God's logical consistency?

6. What do you think is the highest goal of the universe? What are the implications for pleasure versus suffering?

7. What things do you think you have a right to before God? What does it mean that everything we have is of grace?

8. What did Leibniz mean that this is the best possible world? In what sense might there be a number of equally good worlds?

9. Do you think events could turn out more than one way? Do you think God guides the universe to precisely one outcome down to the last spin of every molecule, or do you think a number of outcomes are within His will?

NOTES

1. Mark Twain, *The Adventures of Huckleberry Finn* (1884; reprint, London, England: Penguin Books, Puffin Books, 1953), 283 (ch. 31).

2. I adapted this from the favorite joke of Huston Smith, the doyen of comparative religion.

3. Of course, as we will discuss later, the genius of the cross is that it joins justice and love: God graciously paid the penalty of sin Himself, allowing Him to deal lovingly with the evil doer. Justice and love are thus fulfilled. The point here, however, is that we cannot expect God to be gracious in every case. As we shall see, doing so would leave His justice unrevealed thus His character less revealed. In traditional terms it would leave Him less glorified. Since God is the highest good and His glory is the highest good, forgiving all sin would not be the highest good.

4. In the west, the philosopher Hegel challenged traditional thinking about contradictories. In his view, A and not-A can interact to form something new. This shifted the focus off the unchanging essences of things (a feature of western thought since Plato and Aristotle) and focused on processes ("becoming").

5. I will not try here to deal with the underlying issue of different types of impossibility, such as logical versus physical (e.g., it is impossible for a swallow to carry a coconut, a point argued at some length in *Monty Python and the Holy Grail*). The only point we need to make here is that even an omnipotent being cannot do some things (or perhaps we should say, is self-limited), and that has important implications for the problem of evil. For convenience I am using the principle of non-contradiction, that if A is true, not-A is false. So it cannot be both true and false that God exists, that swallows can carry coconuts, that Jones is now in London and Casablanca.

6. Here we emphasize that God is self-consistent, which limits possible outcomes of actions. In chapter five we see that God limits the possible *range* of outcomes, but there we emphasize how it is a way of shaping our character.

7. Later, in chapter six, we will add the nuance that even a world of maximally happy creatures would not be good if it is unjust. Imagine, for example, a world of Nazi's wildly happy over having exterminated those they supposed were genetically inferior.

8. It is interesting that when we see God's desire for glory, it is often one member of the Trinity glorifying another; for example, the Spirit glorifies the Son (John 16:14), the Son glorifies the Father (John 17:1, 4), and the Father glorifies the Son (Acts 3:13) in Himself (John 13:32).

9. Augustine, *The City of God*, bk. xi, ch. 18, trans. Henry Bettenson (Harmondsworth: Penguin, 1984); in Mark Larrimore, ed., *The Problem of Evil*: A Reader (Oxford, UK: Blackwell, 2001), 54-55.

10. Of course everyone need not go through difficulties; those who die at birth do not. God is also glorified through diversity (e.g., those who die at birth have never been sinned against nor have they experienced willful sin). More about diversity and the glory of God in chapter five, when we discuss plenitude.

11. Alexander Pope, An Essay on Man, i.43-44; quoted in Joseph F. Kelly, *The Problem of Evil in the Western Tradition: From the Book of Job to Modern Genetics* (Collegeville, MN: The Liturgical Press, 2002), 124. Kelly gives an excellent survey of Western thought on evil.

12. Pope, *An Essay on Man*, i.35-8; quoted in Kelly 124.

13. "Now this supreme wisdom, united to a goodness that is no less infinite, cannot but have chosen the best. For as a lesser evil is a kind of good, even so a lesser good is a kind of evil if it stands in the way of a greater good; and there would be something to correct in the actions of God if it were possible to do better.... [I]f there were not the best (optimum) among all possible worlds, God would not have

produced any." G. W. Leibniz, *Theodicy: Essays on the Goodness of God and the Freedom of Man and the Origin of Evil*, ed. Austin Farrer, trans. E. M. Huggard from C. J. Gerhardt's edition of the *Collected Philosophical Works*, 1875-90 (La Salle, IL: Open Court, 1985), bk. 1 sec. 8 (p. 128).

14. Voltaire, *Candide and Zadig* (New York: Airmont, 1966), 19-20 (*Candide*, ch. 4).

15. *The Portable Curmudgeon*, ed. Jon Winokur (New York, NY: New American Library, 1987), 211.

16. Leibniz, 212-13, pp. 260-61.

17. Leibniz, 12, p. 130.

18. "Thus, if the smallest evil that comes to pass in the world were missing in it, it would no longer be this world; which, with nothing omitted and all allowance made, was found the best by the Creator who chose it." Leibniz, 9, p. 128.

19. Leibniz, 145, p. 214.

20. See for example, Alvin Plantinga, *God, Freedom, and Evil* (1974; reprinted, New York, NY: Harper and Row, 1977), 61; Robert M. Adams, "Must God Create the Best?", reprinted in Michael L. Peterson ed., *The Problem of Evil: Selected Readings* (Notre Dame, IN: University of Notre Dame, 1992), 275; John Frame, *The Doctrine of God* (Phillipsburg, NJ: P&R, 2002), 171 (he notes that the next world is better than this one, implying that this is not the best. But philosopher William Rowe contends that if there is no best world and there could always be a better one, then there could be no morally perfect creator. That is because whatever world God created, there could always be a better world made, we could imagine, by a better creator. See Timothy O'Conner, "Freewill," *The Stanford Encyclopedia of Philosophy* (Summer 2004 Edition), Edward N. Zalta (ed.), URL=<http://plato.stanford.edu/entries/freewill), p. 9.

21. As John Hick says, "For evils are exceptional only in relation to other evils which are routine. And therefore unless God eliminates all evils whatsoever there would always be relatively outstanding ones of which it would be said that He should have secretly prevented them." *Evil and the God of Love*, revised edition (SanFrancisco: Harper, 1978), 327.

22. Not everyone thought Newton's laws led to rigid determinism. One example is philosopher Rene Descartes (1596-1650) who held that the workings of our minds are exempt from physical laws because the mind is not physical. However, in modern times as the mind came to be regarded as merely physical it too was considered to be subject to physical forces. The rigidly deterministic worldview gave birth to deism, the view that God creates the world then does not interfere with it because He does not need to do so.

23. Albert Einstein never accepted the idea of a truly unpredictable universe. He believed that it only seems unpredictable because we don't know enough about it. He said he could not believe that God "plays dice" with the universe. Nor did he think Heisenberg established freedom of the will. See Albert Einstein: *Philosopher-Scientist*, ed. Paul Arthur Schlipp, vol. 7 in *The Library of Living Philosophers* (New York, NY: MJF Books, 1970), e.g., 286. Whatever the case, the metaphysical implications of Heisenberg's principle were somewhat overdone – rather like the implications of Einstein's relativity, which were taken as justification even for ethical relativity (Einstein was dismayed and baffled by some of the uses made of his theory).

24. A general source on this subject is Ian G. Barbour, *Religion and Science: Historical and Contemporary Issues* (San Francisco, CA: HarperSanFrancisco, 1997), chapter 7, "Physics and Metaphysics."

25. Leibniz resisted this conclusion, however, most would say that he did not develop his reason very convincingly. For example, see O'Conner, p. 9.

26. Leibniz said, "Therein God has ordered all things beforehand once for all, having foreseen prayers, good and bad actions, and all the rest...." 9, p. 128.

27. For more on the best possible world issue, see for example, Robert M. Adams, "Must God Create the Best?", pp. 275-88; and Philip L. Quinn "God, Moral Perfection, and Possible Worlds," pp. 289-302, both in *The Problem of Evil: Selected Readings*, ed. Michael L. Peterson (Notre Dame, IN: University of Notre Dame Press, 1992. Adams' article was reprinted from, *The Philosophical Review 99* (1990): 131-155. Quinn's was reprinted from *God: The Contemporary Discussion*, ed. Frederick Sontag and M. Darrol Bryant (New York, NY: 1982), 199-215.

CHAPTER THREE

OUR PHYSICAL EXISTENCE

Imagine a world with no pain. Wouldn't it be ideal? Knives would never accidentally cut us, falling boards and bricks would bounce harmlessly off our heads. Anyone attempting to harm us could never succeed. Arrows and bullets would fly straight when they were shot at paper targets but when aimed at a person they would suddenly turn corners in mid-flight, or abruptly stop short of doing harm and fall to the ground. Even accidental falls would be impossible because gravity would work only when it achieved some constructive purpose.

But actually such a world would be vastly inferior to this one. It would never allow us to become even a shadow of what God designed us to be.

The reason a harmless world is not a better one has to do with two of the most fundamental truths about humanity. Both are relevant from Genesis to Revelation. The first fact is that we are a fallen race, morally imperfect by nature. We need troubles to restrain and shape our character (look at what happens to people who become dictators and have nothing to restrain their behavior).

The second fact is often overlooked in the problem of evil. To see it, consider that Genesis opens with the creation of the physical world out of nothing. Man as the crowning achievement is a *physical* being made in God's image, being both rational and moral. When he falls

God works redemption through Christ, who is a *physical* incarnation of God. The redeemed are *physically* resurrected. From creation to heavenly exaltation we are physical beings. Because as believers we normally focus on sin and redemption we miss that fact. We see the moral dimensions of the problem of evil – sin and judgment, grace and redemption – but we do not see the physical dimensions.

We have a distinct place in the biblical world view. Above us are angels, who are rational and moral, but non-physical. Below us are animals, who are physical but neither rational nor moral. We are physical as well as moral and spiritual. And that means we need a certain type of environment, especially as fallen beings. An idyllic, painless world would not do.

Why Pain is Necessary For Our Physical Life

I remember watching Andrew years ago. He was a quiet man about forty years old, who suffered constant, racking pain. It was a battle just to get through the day. He told me he was diagnosed with a rare type of multiple sclerosis that brought insufferable pain instead of the usual numbness. Several times a day the once strapping man would wonder aloud in a thin, pitiful voice why he had to suffer, why he had to have a rare disease that brought so much pain.

The most difficult part of it was that his pain seemed to serve no constructive purpose whatsoever. Sometimes he would just sit with his head in his emaciated hands and moan. For years his wife cared for him as she and her three boys watched him waste away and die gradually.

A few cases of seemingly pointless pain can blind us to the fact that most pain has a good effect. Consider a few rare cases where a genetic abnormality leaves a person incapable of feeling normal pain. One mother's suspicion that her daughter had a problem was confirmed when the girl came in from play to casually show how her arm "looked funny." Her mother gasped at the arm, which had been broken so badly it was bent like a coat hanger.

Another girl with the same untreatable condition, five year old Ashlyn, has to be watched constantly. Teachers have to put ice in her food because if it is too hot she will gulp it down regardless. She has to be watched carefully while playing and checked daily for injuries by the school nurse. Once she was taken to the doctor for a swollen eye, and tests revealed that her cornea had been badly scratched (I myself have had a mild scratch, and that was very painful). When her baby teeth came in she would chew her lips in her sleep, bite through her tongue while chewing, and she even stripped the flesh off her finger. One child with the same condition reportedly had appendicitis and no one knew it until it burst – a potentially fatal situation.

The rare condition is called congenital insensitivity to pain with anhidrosis, or CIPA. One specialist knows of only thirty-five cases worldwide.

Ashlyn's mother drew a poignant lesson from her daughter's insensitivity to pain, "Some people would say that's a good thing. But no, it's not. Pain's there for a reason. It lets your body know something's wrong and it needs to be fixed. I'd give anything for her to feel pain."[1] Absent the body's complex warning system Ashlyn has to follow a crude rule: if she sees blood, she is supposed to stop what she was doing.

When Tanya was seventeen months old her mother found her fingerpainting red swirls in her crib. Looking closer she was aghast to discover she had bitten off the end of her finger and was actually painting with her own blood. Over the months her parents could not convince Tanya to stop bitting her fingers. She laughed at spankings because she felt no pain. She quickly learned that she could get her way by threatening to bit off the ends of her fingers. Her father eventually left the family, saying they had "begotten a monster." At four years old she had serious injuries to her feet because she would not even pull out nails and tacks she had carelessly stepped on. When she injured a joint she would not shift her weight off it and so injured it more. By age eleven she was in an institution. Both her legs had to be amputated because she had refused to wear proper shoes or shift her weight off injuries. She had lost most of her fingers, her elbows were constantly dislocated, and her tongue was badly chewed. The doctor who had examined her summed it up, "Tanya was no monster, only an extreme example – a human metaphor, really – of life without pain."[2]

Pain is vital because it tells us our bodies are being damaged, and the pain prevents further damage. And in general, the more serious the damage, the more intense the warning signal. We can't ignore it; we are driven to remove ourselves from danger. Andrew's body was telling him that his nervous system itself was being destroyed (tragically, by his own immune system). Sadly for him, medicine had no way to stop his body's self-destructive process, nor had it a way to turn off the pain.

But for every Andrew whose pain seems pointless, there are millions whose pain rescues them from bodily damage or death. Pain makes us pull our finger off the hot stove, visit the doctor to see what is wrong with us, or go easy on a pulled muscle. Pain makes it possible for us to survive and thrive as physical beings.

We wouldn't need pain if God would constantly whisper in our ear, telling us what will harm us and how to navigate in the world. But even if humans were that close to their creator – which, as fallen, they are not – they would not function very well in the world. They would never mature to make good choices and to be creative, thereby reflecting God.

Why we need pain to grow to maturity

A world safe enough to be painless would be a place with few possibilities for our development, achievement, expression, or even enjoyment. Because we couldn't do much, the human race would have very little opportunity to reflect God's creativity and innovation. Consequently, our capacity to grow to reflect God and to be in His image – integral to our purpose for being – would be far more limited.

For us to really be safe without pain, God would have to directly intervene in our world constantly. That intervention would have to go far beyond what it is in our present world. It would have to extend down to minute details of the way things happen. That would make the world unpredictable, with God intervening everywhere in ways that would baffle us. We would always be mystified because God would always know so much more than us about what would harm us. Furthermore, we could never learn what would harm us because God would continually prevent harm! We would have to be coddled every moment, and our lives would not amount to much.

In a world where God's total protection would make it unpredictable to us, we could not plan and bring things about, or even function rationally. We could hardly be moral and rational beings in such a place.

Imagine, for example, trying to build something in a world that was micro-managed so as to be completely pain free. Suppose you wanted to do something as simple as make a trough that would carry water to crops so that you could have enough to eat. The tools you would work with could not be sharp enough to cut anything because then they would be sharp enough to cut you. The materials could not be stiff enough to carry water, because if they were they would be hard enough to have sharp edges, which could hurt someone. But of course, the water you want to channel is heavy, so you would have to have something stiff. So you probably couldn't build the trough.

That means you would have to water your crops with a bucket instead, and since you can't carry much water, you can't grow much food. What would baffle you is that every time you try to build a bigger bucket, it just wouldn't work. That is because God would have to prevent you from building it so that you would not hurt your back from all the weight a bigger bucket can carry. He would have to intervene mysteriously to thwart you because you would have never learned how much weight is too much to carry since you can't feel pain. While you would be protected from physical pain in such a situation, you would certainly suffer the emotional pain of frustration, living in a world where nothing seems to make sense and where you could not carry out your plans.

A world in which there could be absolutely no pain would lack a lot of things we take for granted. It would probably not have glass because the quality that makes it so clear also makes its edges sharp. We couldn't have even the simplest sharp tools so we couldn't make much. We could not even cook normally because something might burn us.

We would have trouble avoiding risks without such help because we would never see injury, never know how people get injured, and never see potential for harm. We would have a lot of trouble navigating in the physical environment we were born to inhabit. And unable to navigate, our growth would be hindered since we would have trouble making wise choices, planning, and doing things because we would have trouble taking risks into account.

Pain is part of the learning process for us, teaching us how to live in our surroundings. And pain being so unpleasant, we make sure that we don't repeat the damaging behavior. Children who have scraped their knees, for example, are much more careful about running down hills. We also learn from others' pains. When a child gets hurt climbing a tree, all the children on the block tend to be more careful. That cumulative experience of the race – what we personally suffer as well as what we see and hear of in others – comprises an awesome bank of knowledge that helps us make the most of this world's possibilities while avoiding its troubles.

So because our world allows for some physical harm it has possibilities for greater personal maturity and accomplishment through which we can reflect God in a physical world.

Had the race remained unfallen perhaps things would be different. We may have been close enough to God that He could communicate with us on a continual basis, enough that we could learn from Him how to do sophisticated things without being exposed to physical harm. But He would likely have to communicate constantly, perhaps even several times a minute if we are doing something like building, working with hazardous chemicals, or playing a sport. Fallen beings, especially those unreconciled to God, would not respond well to continual divine directions. And fallen beings, even those who are redeemed, are not that close to God. We no longer hear Him walking in the garden (Gen. 3:8), and seeing Him face to face is the rarest of events for humans (Deut. 34:10; Gen. 32:30).

Perhaps another alternative is that God could have limited the range of physical possibilities to protected us from harm. Water, for example, could still have the properties to slake our thirst yet God could rescue everyone in danger of drowning; electricity could still power things but God could ensure that no one ever got electrocuted. And while there is no doubt God sometimes does intervene to prevent harm, it is better that He not do so continually, as we shall see in this chapter.

But there may be another reason why God neither constantly tells us what to do nor constantly protects us from harm. A parent must protect a toddler from harm by, for example, removing sharp objects and hazardous chemicals from reach. But part of reaching adulthood is knowing how to navigate in the world without requiring that everything harmful be removed from your path, or even needing to be warned all the time about what is harmful. An adult knows how to navigate in the world and can accomplish something constructive in life.

Why should God treat us any differently? Had we remained unfallen, perhaps we could have become mature by God communicating with us while limiting what could happen in our environment. But that certainly would not work now and it would be a lot more problematic than it sounds, as we shall see.

Why We Need Painful Predictability

The environment we operate in can be a troublesome one indeed. On the news today, a couple was killed when an avalanche hit their vacation home in Idaho, some snow boarders were trapped in an avalanche in Utah (but survived partly because of their good planning), and a charter plane crashed in the Persian Gulf killing some one hundred forty passengers. In our little mountain town in just the past two months a store and two houses burned, one from a gas leak. A few weeks ago a car that was going too fast around our winding roads flipped over and killed the driver. Each week on our way to church, we pass near the scene of one of California's worst disasters: the Mullholland dam, which broke in 1928 sending a 100 foot wall of water speeding fifty-four miles to the sea. In its five and a half hour journey, hundreds of homes were destroyed and untold hundreds of people died.[3]

Some bad things happen simply because the world's physical processes have to operate regularly. Gravity works the same all over the world, and even all over the universe. Its force holds in the earth's atmosphere, which allows for life. It holds us and everything else down with unfailing predictability. As humans we have to understand it and work with it. And while it keeps our buildings on the ground, if we do not construct them properly they will lean or even collapse. We can work standing on a ladder, but if we are not careful we will fall. Gravity operates even if a child leans too far over a balcony. Chemicals do certain things and combine in certain ways. They have set properties which do not change. That means that an acid can clean something so it will look practically new; it can make electricity in the battery that starts our car. But it will also burn our skin. Recently I saw a notice from an animal shelter looking for a new home for a dog whose previous owner had burned its face with acid. Chemicals function the same way whether a chemist is using them to improve our lives, a horribly cruel person wants to harm an animal, or a terrorist makes a bomb to explode in a crowded market. Electricity, too, operates with blind consistency. It makes much of modern life possible, but it will also kill you in a fraction of a second. Lasers can detect smoke, be used to communicate great distances, or reproduce music. But they can also be weaponized and used to damage a pilot's eyesight.

We have seen that we need a world in which our bodies feel pain. We have seen why as fallen beings God does not prevent all harm by trying to protect us from everything. Why do we also need a physical environment that works with blind consistency?

Imagine an environment which is inconsistent because it is divinely manipulated to avoid all possibility of harm. Gravity would hold a ladder in place, but if someone carelessly leaned too far over they wouldn't fall; if they are painting it wouldn't even spill because that would inconvenience them and God would prevent that. Children could dance on the railings of third story balconies because if they lost their balance they wouldn't fall.

But then think of the problems. In that sort of world things would happen for no apparent reason. Gravity would work most of the time, but sometimes things would stay suspended in the air, or heavy objects would float to the ground. Only an omniscient God would have any idea what would happen next. Multiplied over countless times for factors such as gravity, temperature, hardness of materials, and so on, we could not function. Things would happen or not happen seemingly without reason.

Take something as simple as trying to grade a hillside for the convenience or safety of the people who live at the bottom of it. There would be no set angle at which the dirt would slide down because that would be determined not by the constant physical properties of the dirt and gravity, but by how it might inconvenience or harm someone. In some places the dirt would hold at a very steep angle. That is because the person whose house is at the bottom doesn't want dirt to slide down into their yard. But a little farther over on another part of the hill, the dirt would slide down even though the slope is quite gentle. That is because – unknown to us – the person at the bottom of that part of the hill wants a little more soil for his yard. There would be no way to draw rational conclusions about angles of soil. Hence there would be no way to plan the hillside or design it. What would happen if someone who did not want dirt in their yard moved away to another neighborhood and someone else moved into the house they left? Would the dirt slide down the hill to suit the new home owners? Would God make the dirt go away if the home owner changed his mind and no longer wanted the dirt? What would God do if the people affected disagree among themselves? Suppose the husband wanted the dirt to slide down and the wife didn't?

A world in which physical processes operate in such a way that no one ever gets hurt or troubled would be too unpredictable for us to function rationally. Compared to our world it would be a crazy place, where much planning and action would be pointless. Furthermore, it would not allow us to develop morally.

That is because morality has a lot to do with choosing outcomes. If we see someone shivering and we give them our coat, it is because we want them to be warm as the outcome. The same is true if we see someone starving and we give them food, or if they are sick and we give them medicine. But in a world where the physical processes do not work regularly there would be no way to choose outcomes. Outcomes would be unknown except to God. So we would have no reason to give someone a coat, or food, or medicine, because it wouldn't necessarily cause anything. To make moral choices we have to know how to cause things.[4] Without a reliable connection between choices and their consequences, we are really not choosing anything.

Moral choices do not demand that we have 100 per cent certainty about outcomes however. We do not have certainty even in our present world because we do not completely understand natural processes, though they are so regular. Nor do we necessarily know what other people are going to choose, which adds further unpredictability. Too, God sometimes providentially intervenes (which we will discuss, below) and we do not always understand His ways. Yet our world with these uncertainties is still fundamentally different from one in which the very natural processes have no regularity due to God constantly intervening to prevent harm of any kind.

So, to be rational and moral beings we need a consistent world, not one ordered around our personal pleasure, and not one in which God constantly intervenes to keep us from pain. To make choices and do things we need to know that – whether we like it or not – hillsides fall down if their angle is too steep, boards hold a certain amount of weight but no more, electricity flows through the path of least resistance even if that path is our finger, and so on. Only such an essentially regular world can be a character building place.

Why We Need Unwanted Consequences

Another problem with a world in which God ensures that no one gets hurt is that we would never see evil for what it is. That is because every time someone would try to harm another person, the natural processes would change to make the harm impossible.

Boards would be stiff and hard but would turn to rubber whenever they were swung over someone's head. Bullets would go straight except when aimed at a person. Even sound waves would not carry hurtful speech. No one would ever suffer at the hands of another person because God would intervene, changing the physical processes.

It also means that a person could be in a murderous rage against someone without there being even the slightest bad consequence. And that entails that we would never see the consequences of sinfulness. Extreme sinfulness would have no worse consequence than righteousness. The problem with that is we would never see the consequences of sin. So how would we see sin for what it is? How would we learn to reject it and repent of it? What incentive would we have to pursue good?

In such a world God would be less glorified since we would not fully grasp the ugliness of sin nor the contrasting beauty of His holiness. We would know His greatness to be sure, but without the benefit of the more vivid knowledge we now have because we can view God against the stark contrast of evil, against the shadows.

By constantly intervening to prevent any consequences of evil God would be undermining the most valuable things: knowledge of Himself and formation of His character in us.

How Our World Keeps Us From Selfishness

There is a further problem with a world in which God would prevent all physical pain. As imperfect beings we are continually tempted to be self-centered, and it would not help us a bit for God to constantly intervene in natural processes in order to respond to our whims and to ensure our comfort. That would only make us more self-centered, whereas we need to become the opposite.

Have you ever met a person who had gotten whatever he wanted since childhood yet became loving and self-sacrificing? I never have. In fact we usually call such a person "spoiled," because of the effect such pampering has on their character.

Imagine how most of us would turn out if no less than God Himself saw to it that we always got what we wanted. The entire planet would be overrun with Godzilla-sized egos. If we were naturally unselfish it might work out – but Adam's fallen race is definitely not that way.

After the fall, God told Adam that life would be hard. The environment would resist him such that he would have to toil and sweat in order to eat (Genesis 3:17-19). It was judgment but it seems it was also a check on the now fallen human will. A comfortable, accommodating environment suited the unfallen will, whereas the fallen will have deserved – and seems to have needed – a more difficult environment. I have noticed among a number of cases I have counseled that when a person who is troubled by a sin problem stops working and becomes idle, that problem usually gets dramatically worse. If they were eaten up with bitterness and anger, it can consume their thoughts; if they were depressed, they can struggle much more deeply; if they were tempted toward criminal behavior, they can get into much more trouble. In many ways having to work can be a blessing.

The luxury and comforts of Eden made it no place for fallen beings. Nor would fallen wills be contained and reshaped in a world where God constantly intervenes to keep humans comfortable. No, our world has to be east of Eden; and so it is.

As C. S. Lewis said, "God whispers to us in our pleasures, speaks in our conscience, but shouts in our pains: it is His megaphone to rouse a deaf world." And, "No doubt Pain [sic] as God's megaphone is a terrible instrument....It removes the veil; it plants the flag of truth within the fortress of a rebel soul."[5]

So in our world we cannot always get what we want. There are delays, frustrations, and disappointments. The world's natural processes do not bend to our will; rather, we have to accommodate ourselves to our environment. On the other hand, through hard work and diligence we can usually make progress on things (Prov. 21:5) . So while the world is not designed to cater to our whims, it is a place that can build our character.

How Godliness Prevents Some Pain

Working my way through college as an ambulance attendant, and for a time training in an emergency room, I had a lot of opportunities to see the connections between behavior and pain. What amazed me was just how many injuries were the result of foolishness and bad judgment. So often the person who got injured was doing something wrong, or was naive, or was with someone who made for bad company.

In one of many cases where all three came together, two young teenagers were driving so wildly their car rolled over and crashed into a tree. One young man's temple was sliced down to the skull, but miraculously, his temporal artery was not severed. With the tissue dissected from around it as clean as any surgeon could cut it (and closer than a surgeon would want to cut), it hung there suspended and pulsating, his life's blood held back by tissue no thicker than a rubber balloon.

Foolishness and bad company had in an instant brought him within a few hundredths of an inch of death. Hoping to drive the point home, I and another worker expressed our amazement that his artery had not been sliced with the rest of the tissue. In response to our statements, he began groping to feel the artery, and we had to quickly stop him from accidently rupturing it by the slightest touch. After we stitched and bandaged him, he left the emergency room seemingly without ever coming to grips with how close his choices had brought him to death.

While in emergency medical work I noticed that a staggering percentage of injuries involve alcohol, even if only small amounts of it. That is because even a little impairs people's reaction time, and that causes problems when they are trying to do things like operate machinery or drive a car. But what is just as dangerous, it impairs judgment. The person who would otherwise know how to steady a ladder doesn't do it properly. Or the person who should know not to try to fix an electrical appliance with it plugged in the wall forgets. I knew a very savvy person, a fine man, who worked for many years on a renown commando-like strike force. He had survived hundreds of deadly situations only to be seriously injured in his own garage when a car he was repairing slipped off its jack. When he told me what had happened, I figured right away he must have had a little to drink just before the accident. It wouldn't have been much, I thought, otherwise he would have realized his impairment. It would be just enough to throw off his judgment without it being obvious to him. I pressed him as to whether that had been the case. Surprised that I had figured it out, he asked how I knew. After seeing so many injuries, it wasn't hard.

Understanding how to work effectively within our physical environment while avoiding troubles goes far beyond a simple mechanical knowledge of things. The book of Proverbs shows how pain – physical and otherwise – is linked to our moral and spiritual life. Like the rest of Scripture, it tries to teach us the precious life skills of wisdom and prudence. Proverbs makes the point over and over that to function successfully in the world we need to live in a way that pleases God on a moral and spiritual level. To do so is to live in accordance with the way He made the world; to do less is to invite trouble.

This means that we need to know not only obvious physical things such as that sharp things cut and hot things burn, but less obvious things, such as that laziness brings hunger (Prov. 13:4), that adultery brings trouble and even death (6:32-33), and so on. It also means that in addition to heeding the warnings of simple physical pain we should heed the warnings of conscience and godly counsel (19:20, 27). We should be able to recognize such things as approaching evil, "The prudent sees evil and hides himself, but the naive go on, and are punished for it" (22:3; 27:12, 14:16). Summing up the importance of our internal life we are told, "He who watches his way preserves his life" (16:17).

Naivety about the moral dimension of our environment is dangerous. According to Proverbs, wise is the person who realizes that the physical and moral realms are linked, and that a deeper knowledge of how troubles come about can help us avoid so many of them.

Though most people figure out how to avoid physical dangers, few go on to this deeper knowledge of the moral dimension of our world. Consequently, the causes of so many of life's pains remain an enigma to most people. Only the wise know some of the hidden reasons for happiness and sorrow. That is one reason why "...the path of the righteous is like the light of dawn, that shines brighter and brighter until the full day. The way of the wicked is like darkness; they do not know over what they stumble" (4:18). The unrighteous do not know why: things go so badly (15:19), they lack basic material needs (13:25), are disrespected (18:3), are left with damaged relationships (14:1); are not trusted with more responsibility, such as a promotion at work (12:24); cannot seem to accomplish anything important (focus, 28:19; diligence, 13:4), cannot seem to get wisdom (17:16), struggle with damaging habits (e.g., sexual sin, 23:26-28; wine, 23:29-35), and so on.

The godly can avoid so many of life's deeper sorrows, which are emotional and often interpersonal. Thus this world is suited to developing good character by, in some ways, blessing those who have it while bereaving and chastening those who lack it.

Of course morals and values are part of the world's workings because of its creator. Its very operation reflects His character. Yet insofar as the actions of fallen creatures are contrary to the divine will they can be a source of trouble for the righteous, thereby reversing life's character-rewarding ways. The Bible is full of examples of righteous people like the apostle Paul suffering at the hands of the ungodly. Yet even opposition to righteousness serves a purpose, in that it provides an environment in which people pursue goodness for its own sake rather than purely for reward (more about that in chapter five).

Besides persecution we have to allow for a "Job factor" in that some suffering may be for a divine purpose that we simply cannot figure out (though we have the advantage of a perspective Job lacked during his troubles, it was to test whether he would be godly for strictly unselfish reasons).

Is Any Pain Pointless?

Physical pain has an important function in that it warns us of harm, but it comes with no guarantee that we will always be able to end the pain when the threat of harm to our bodies passes. As a sprain heals, for example, some pain lingers. (Though even that type of pain serves a purpose in that it protects us from re-injuring it before healing is complete.) There are a few cases like Andrew's, where chronic pain seems to serve no constructive purpose in that he was already warned of damage to his body and nothing could be done about it.

These are, admittedly, difficult cases. But even seemingly pointless pain has potential for good if we look beyond the physical dimension. I recently attended the memorial service of a colleague's wife who had suffered for many years with debilitating pain. Surgeons had operated years earlier in an attempt to bring some relief, but the operation caused an infection, only making it worse. Her grown daughters, one of them a missionary, spoke tearfully of their mother's humble, committed love and of its lasting effect on them and everyone her life touched. Then her husband spoke and summed it up, "Pain makes you either better or bitter; it made her better." He told how he had benefitted from her fervent prayer life and had grown from her character. Earlier he had told me that her condition had made him a much more sensitive person.

Chronic pain can have a ripple effect far beyond one life. Those immediately around the person can become more compassionate, sensitive, and grateful for God's goodness to them. It can produce compassion even in strangers. It can motivate some in society to develop cures and preventative measures. We can never know the good accomplished by seemingly pointless pain.

All things considered, it would be difficult or impossible to know for certain that a particular person's pain is pointless. Perhaps only an omniscient being could ever know such a thing.

Troublesome Natural Processes

Natural processes can be another source of physical suffering. Take the weather, for example. It is a complex thing that brings both blessings and trouble. The sun shines on our planet at different angles, bringing extreme heat to the equator where it beats down directly, and leaving the poles icy where the slant of the rays dilutes the light's intensity. The differences in temperature produce differences in air pressure, which even out through wind. Were it not for the wind a good deal more of the globe would be too hot or cold to inhabit. Wind is simply a property of all gasses whereby molecules even out pressure. While the process benefits life, it can also make things inconvenient, or even dangerous. When differences in pressure get too great, the wind speed can spoil our picnic, tear shingles off roofs, and topple trees onto power lines and houses. So, what brings a refreshing breeze on a hot day and makes so much of the earth inhabitable can also bring inconvenience and harm.

Another natural process, evaporation, puts water in the air and brings rain to crops and animals. But that means sometimes rain will come when we want to do something outdoors. The properties that make soil hold some of the rain so that plants can grow also entails that sometimes it will get waterlogged and slide down a hill into someone's backyard, perhaps even knocking down a house.

In our present world at least, we can't have the good properties without also some unwanted consequences. We might be tempted to think that God should intervene so that we have only the good aspects of the world and none of the bad. But that is a lot more problematic than it sounds. While we are hoping it doesn't rain on our local parade, the farmer down the road is hoping it will rain on his crops. God could make it rain on the farm but not on the parade, but just how far do we expect Him to customize the world? Suppose someone watching the parade likes rain, should God make it rain on him or her but not on everyone else? Or suppose the farmer needs more rain on some crops than others; should God alter the rain by the square foot? The same could be said for temperature. I like things a little on the cool side; my wife shivers when the temperature drops below eighty degrees Fahrenheit. Should God maintain our individual temperature bubbles as we move around?

Some accommodations would require even more serious alteration of the world, and some would be physically impossible. For example, for those who prefer to walk downhill rather than uphill, there seems to be no way God could make a road go downhill in both directions.

Even if God could customize the world for our greatest personal convenience, it would at times still be uncomfortable and unpredictable. That is because God's love would occasionally require that He give us what we need rather than what is pleasurable at that moment. Then, even in that world, as now in our world, we would have to deal with why God brought us inconvenience or pain. It is unlikely that God could avoid occasionally discomforting or inconveniencing us even were He to make our comfort His highest priority. Not only would discomfort come from having to do what is good for us, but at some point our personal interests are going to conflict with someone else's. And when God chooses not to customize things to meet one person's goals because of another's goals, someone will be inconvenienced or discomforted. Only in a world of complete harmony of wills can such a conflict be avoided. While heaven is said to be just such a harmonious place, this world obviously is not.

How Does God Intervene?

The need for consistency does not require that God never intervene in response to someone's desire. If that were so He would never answer prayer, which brings His intervention into natural processes. There have been popular misunderstandings on both sides of this issue. At one extreme is the view that God does not answer prayer and never intervenes in the world; at the other is the view that if only we would pray and have faith He would intervene in remarkable ways at every moment.

Deism is the view that God never intervenes into the natural realm thus never answers prayer or changes things in response to faith. The Deist believes that those who want God to intervene fail to understand how perfectly He made things. While the Deist has great respect for God's engineering, he errs by not grasping that God wants to interact with the world in order to show His character and have a personal relationship with His moral creatures. The Bible is filled with examples and admonitions to pray.

Through our prayers and actions God offers us a way to join with Him in shaping the world. In mature prayer, for example, we ask for the things that God would want in the world. As Jesus put it in His example of prayer, we ask that "Thy will be done on earth as it is in heaven" (Matt. 6:10). God invites us to have a part in bringing about a better world, as is shown by verses about the value of prayer (e.g., James 5:13-18).

So, far from being a Deistic spectator who wants nothing more than to sit back and observe the running of His perfect cosmic clock, God longs for us to interact with Him and take initiative – which is all linked to being in His image. But of course, the possibility that our actions can shape the world for good also means that we can shape it for ill (though not through prayer since God wouldn't answer prayers that are against His will). Our ability to do evil accounts for quite a bit of human, and some animal, pain.

As far as the problem of evil, we often limit our role to that of intellectually figuring it out rather than personally taking action to solve it by being compassionate and the like. While solving the intellectual problems surrounding evil is very important, we have the opportunity to go much further in that we can ourselves be part of the solution (which we will say more about in chapter fourteen).

At the opposite extreme from Deism is a form of popular Christianity that says if we would pray and have enough faith God's miraculous intervention would be commonplace in our lives. It is thought that He will supernaturally eliminate all our suffering so that we will never get sick, never get hurt, always be prosperous, and never want for anything; and we will die only once we feel that we would rather be in heaven.

As a solution to the problem of evil it falls short in two areas. First, it fails to see that God normally works through natural processes rather than apart from them. Second, it fails to see the potential value of suffering.

Scripture regards natural processes as an integral part of how God works in the world, and as a tribute to His consistency. "The heavens are telling of the glory of God," says the psalmist (Psalm 19:1). They give a message without words (v. 3) that everyone can receive (v. 4). It is the message of God's existence, sovereign control, and consistency. Paul told his pagan audience that the consistency of the natural order is a blessing to humanity because it allows us to grow food and be satisfied – a testimony to God's goodness (Acts 14:17). Psalm 104 says that God brought about the stability of the natural order (vv. 5, 9) and uses it to provide for plants (v. 16) and animals (vv. 11, 12, 17) and to bless man (v. 14, 15). When God works, He usually works through natural means, through the processes He has set up. We should not expect that He will routinely suspend the natural order to make us comfortable and grant our every desire.

On the other hand, God can and does intervene to change events. When Ahab's sins moved God to take his life, a soldier drew his bow "at random" and the arrow struck him in a joint in his armor, mortally wounding him (1 Kgs. 22:34). In this case God guided the natural order and the movement of the archer in a remarkable way. Yet even here He did not suspend the natural order, as Jesus did when He performed miracles like walking on water (Matt. 14:26).

Miracles are useful precisely because they are not normal. They give unmistakable evidence that God Himself is acting. When a person performs them, they help validate his claim to speak on divine authority. That is why Nicodemus could say to Christ, "Rabbi, we know that You have come from God as a teacher; for no one can do these signs that You do unless God is with him" (John 3:2). It is no wonder that in the Bible miracles abound when there is a need to validate a messenger and his message: when Moses was used to call out God's people, when Elijah called God's people back from apostasy, when Christ came, and when the Apostles laid the foundation of the church; and in the tribulation, such as when the two witnesses proclaim truth to a world under heavy judgment (Rev. 11:4-6).

Why doesn't God work supernaturally, or transcendently, all the time? Why do we have to practice archery to hit what we want, rather than God simply guiding the arrow every time in response to prayer? Why do we have to work for a living, get aching arms when we want to paint a room, exercise if we want to be fit, and so on? Why can't the world work like the 1960s comedy television series about a woman who could make anything happen with a twitch of her nose? When she wanted the house cleaned up, a twitch would do the whole job instantly. Getting money, cars, and other things were no problem.

Were God to intervene miraculously to always make us comfortable and give us what we want, there would be little chance to develop our character, to develop the wisdom to want to bring about the best goal by the best means, then to patiently and diligently work the plan, adjusting it to the situation as it unfolds. The whole process expresses our character as well as uses our God-given abilities, providing a way to further develop both. We thereby glorify God by reflecting Him, who Himself makes plans and brings them about. It is part of our being in the image of God.

A world where we could do anything we want by merely twitching our nose or calling on a divine genie to grant our every wish would develop none of those more valuable character qualities. We would have power at our disposal but little opportunity to grow in character. And as fallen beings we would be tempted to be self-centered. Immaturity wants my will to be done. Our environment, people, and even God become nothing more than a means to the end of getting what we want. But maturity says, "Thy will be done." The focus is not on getting God to cater to us, but conforming our character to His and getting His will done.

Whereas the world's major religions have a strong moral element, the occult differs in that it offers power without moral accountability. Occultic knowledge or power is generally used to get whatever the practitioner wants, not to improve their character or to make the world better. It's not surprising that the program in which the woman could twitch her nose and get anything she wanted had a lot of occultic overtones, and was called "Bewitched."

What Good are Disasters?

As Newton's discoveries revealed a world of regularity and magnificent design, confidence grew that even suffering must have some purpose, however hidden. Alexander Pope expressed this view in a poem that appeared in over a hundred editions and eighteen languages within a century. He wrote (1733-34),

> All nature is but Art, unknown to thee;
> All Chance, Direction, which thou canst not see;
> All Discord, Harmony, not understood;
> All partial Evil, universal Good;
> And, spite of Pride and erring Reason's spite,
> One truth is, "Whatever IS, is RIGHT."[6]

But on November 1, 1755 tragedy struck at the optimism of the age. An earthquake in Lisbon, Portugal killed perhaps as many as 60,000. For Voltaire it was another blow to his already eroding optimism. He could see no reason why God would bring such tragedy. It could not be for sin,

Will you maintain death to their crimes was due?
And can you then impute a sinful deed
To babes who on their mothers' bosoms bleed?
Was then more vice in fallen Lisbon found,
Than Paris, where voluptuous joys abound?

He could see nothing gained from the catastrophe, "Say what advantage can result to all, From wretched Lisbon's lamentable fall?" He wondered aloud why God would not be merciful. He mocked the view that some general good could come from suffering, supposing the theodicist would say that death is a good thing because it gives birth to insects that feed on bodies. He summed it up "With faltering voice you cry, 'What is, is right'? The universe confutes your boasting vain...."[7]

Natural disasters are the most spectacular of natural evils (natural evils are sources of pain not directly caused by human wrong doing). Like the rest of the problem of evil, we cannot remove all mystery from it, nor can we say precisely why God allowed specific tragedies – but we can point to some principles as to why God allows natural disasters in general.

For one thing, natural evils are largely an outworking of regularities in nature. And as we have seen, a certain amount of regularity provides an environment by which we fallen beings can be rational and moral.

That means that, for example, the qualities in water that enable it to carry nutrients to our bodies and quench our thirst also give it the properties to flood towns and drown people. The qualities that make snow pile up and drip into the ground to water plants also make it occasionally get too steep and cause avalanches. The pressure differences that produce the winds which evens out the extreme temperatures of the earth mean that sometimes the wind will get strong enough to knock things down. God could supernaturally limit those possibilities so that wind never blows hard enough to damage property and water never runs off fast enough to flood. No doubt He does prevent a lot of disasters, but it is better that He allows some to trouble our fallen race.

Though tragedy blinds us to them, there are constructive consequences to disasters. They often bind people together and force them to work together, breaking barriers of race, class, and national origin. I remember after each of the two major earthquakes in Southern California how people finally got to know their neighbors, helped each other, spoke freely to people standing next to them in grocery lines, and bonded to those who would otherwise be distant. Such disasters can break down interpersonal walls as few things can. After the Asian tsunami in December 2004 some Hindus and Muslims freely helped each other in India, and warring factions in Sri Lanka as well as in Indonesia gave each other assistance. Disasters give people the opportunity to show bravery, as when rescuers search crumbling rubble for survivors. People have the opportunity to show mercy by providing for those in need of food and shelter.

Too, the possibility that a disaster might occur gives individuals and society strong incentives to work together and to plan ways to prevent them or lessen their impact. It inspires building codes, and construction of sea walls, dams, flood channels, tornado warnings, and avalanche patrols. Cooperation and foresight are important virtues.

Disasters tend to reward character qualities like diligence and prudence. After a tornado destroyed a mobile home park in Texas, killing a number of people, one man was interviewed because his large family was entirely unhurt. He had taken the warning of tornados very seriously and for months spent his spare time building a concrete room under his mobile home. It was no way to spend evenings and weekends, and the money could have gone to a lot of other things. But it had paid off. Though shaken, his face beamed as he said he had come through the disaster with all that mattered to him in this life – his family. And they all sat around him, grateful, without so much as a scratch.

The desire to understand the world and prevent disasters motivated scientists to develop a way to predict volcanic eruptions. This provided warning that Mount St Helens was about to blow. Everyone in the area was warned and nearly all evacuated. But as with so many things, people can make unwise choices. I saw an interview with one stubborn elderly man who refused to believe that anything could go wrong in a place he had lived most of his life. Like dozens of others who failed to heed the warning, he died in the first seconds of the spectacular explosion.

Just as disasters are opportunities for developing noble character they are opportunities for despicable character. In many cases after an earthquake, flood, or fire, law enforcement personnel have to follow right behind rescue workers to prevent theft.

The losses from disasters can have a hidden moral element. In one tragedy, six brides died just hours before their weddings when a beauty salon collapsed in Egypt. It is easy to question why God would allow such a thing, but an investigation revealed a series of gross human errors. A young woman survived but was trapped in the rubble. She made a desperate call from her cell phone, but was told by the operator that cell calls could not be accepted and she would have to call back from a regular phone – which was impossible. Ambulances and rescue crews took an hour to arrive at the scene, and a local official said the lack of skill in the rescue operation caused more deaths. The main cause of the tragedy, however, was that the building had been condemned and ordered to be demolished five years earlier – yet nothing had been done about it![8]

A recent earthquake in Iran killed at least 40,000 people. But again, a deeper look reveals that sin allegedly played a part. A history of earthquakes in the region caused the government to prohibit rebuilding homes in the area. But, according to an astute middle eastern commentator, corrupt Islamic clerics took bribes from racketeers and pronounced the prohibition void on religious grounds. The government did nothing about the arrangement, and rebuilding of shoddy housing went unchecked – until this latest catastrophic earthquake. There is now concern about the safety of a nuclear power plant that is being built on the same fault line. A Chernobyl-like disaster could shut down oil transport in the Persian gulf, cutting off nearly half the world's oil supply, which would have a catastrophic effect on the world's economy.[9]

The 2004 Asian tsunami killed 270,000 people, yet it was predicted by a geologist at the California Institute of Technology, who had studied the region for over a decade. When it became clear that government officials would not listen to his warnings, he went directly to the people, distributing 5,000 posters and flyers, and speaking in churches and schools.[10] Moments after the quake occurred it was detected by U.S. monitoring centers, and officials began frantically trying to warn the nations at risk that a deadly wall of water was on its way. But most of the nations had failed to set up any public warning system.[11] Indonesian scientists themselves had tried in vain to get their government to upgrade their warning system.[12] It took an hour or more for the tsunami to reach Thailand, Sri Lanka, and Malaysia, and it was said that anyone who could have walked fifteen minutes inland would have been saved. The monumental failure prompted Rabbi Daniel Lapin to write an article entitled, "Don't Blame God for Asian Casualties." He said that western culture protects its people better because its biblical heritage directs us to value human life and to subdue the earth (Gen. 1:28), which includes controlling nature's harmful aspects.[13]

Could God intervene to prevent the damages wrought by natural processes? Certainly He could. But He allows them for higher purposes. Such higher purposes include revealing His divine qualities such as His power, mercy, protection, and justice. Events that reveal these qualities might unfold in response to prayer, or they may take place simply as the workings of His providence.

God can intervene at many levels to show His power, mercy, and the like. He can for example allow the person trapped by a flood to be rescued. Or He could intervene one step before that and allow them to escape to higher ground before they need rescuing. Or He could intervene before that and prevent them from getting close to flood waters (perhaps by giving them the discernment to leave the city beforehand). Or He could prevent the storm in the first place.

It is important to realize that we will never know how many times He has intervened on these initial levels to protect us, because of course, it never came to a crisis. But of all the possible evils, whatever few He does allow, people will always ask why He did not intervene to prevent them.

Can we say that God is less merciful or loving or just to have allowed whatever disasters He did? In answer, we first have to remember that, as we saw in chapter two, the highest value in the universe is the revelation of who God is (His glory); lesser values such as human comfort cannot always be achieved along with the highest value. So we can expect that God would sometimes choose to reveal Himself more fully at the expense of human comfort. In light of this, couldn't we say that the person who was rescued against all odds has a greater potential for seeing the hand of God than had God simply prevented the storm entirely? Wouldn't he have a better chance to know God's power and protection, to see Him more clearly, to trust Him more? This would be true even if the person suffered some permanent loss, such as loss of property.

What about those who die in disasters? There is of course the none too comforting reality that we will all have to die in some way, and for some it may be by a disaster. That is true even for devout believers, so we cannot say that God failed a person because he or she died by way of a disaster. But besides that, we have to realize further that our belief that we deserve better than we get – that God owes us something better – is mistaken. As people who have transgressed God's moral laws we have no right to something better. Anything we get is of grace, and as grace by definition is not owed, there is no way we can say God owed a better fate.

This does not mean that disasters are necessarily retribution for specific sins, or that disaster victims are more sinful than others. Jesus made that point in reference to a local disaster: "Or do you suppose that those eighteen on whom the tower in Siloam fell and killed them were worse culprits than all the men who live in Jerusalem? I tell you no, but unless you repent, you will all likewise perish" (Luke 13:4-5). The point is not what befalls us, but that each person needs to deal with the sin and salvation issue between themselves and God.

Disasters do something else for us that is important. They point us to the hard reality that life is fragile and unpredictable, and that we are not always in control of things. Disasters shatter the complacency of our settled, make-believe world in which we can rule ourselves and our destiny. They further point us to the fact that not all is well between us and our environment, and thus they can lead us to conclude that not all is well with our creator. In general, pain is a messenger calling us to our creator. Disaster is a messenger with a megaphone – its warning is nearly impossible to ignore. We are forced to stop and think about our mortality and all that is connected with it.

About natural evil in the broadest sense, Christian philosopher Eleanor Stump sums it up this way,

> Natural evil – the pain of disease, the intermittent and unpredictable destruction of natural disasters, the decay of old age, the imminence of death – takes away a person's satisfaction with himself. It tends to humble him, show him his frailty, make him reflect on the transience of temporal goods, and turn his affections towards other-worldly things, away from the things of this world. No amount of moral or natural evil, of course, can guarantee that a man will seek God's help. If it could, the willing it produced would not be free. But evil of this sort is the best hope, I think, and maybe the only effective means, for bringing men to such a state.[14]

While disasters demonstrate the puniness of mankind, they also highlight the unmeasurable power of God. One earthquake on the island of Santorini, Greece (about 1470 BC), had more power than one hundred hydrogen bombs and ejected some fifteen cubic miles of earth. One meteor in Russia in 1908 devastated 1,500 square miles and was felt 600 miles away. Disasters display only the tiniest amount of the power that created and sustains the universe.

As we have seen, God's purpose for us as physical beings made in His image, as those who can reflect something of Himself, has a lot to do with the problem of evil. If we fallen beings are to lead physical lives that are rational and moral, then the world must entail some unwelcome characteristics and consequences. Those consequences can shape us to better reflect God. Next we look at what part our will plays, and in what sense we make genuine choices.

GOING FARTHER

1. Why do we need pain to live as physical beings in a physical world? What pain have you had because of this principle?

2. What does predictability have to do with pain? How does this affect your own life?

3. How does morality depend on a regular environment?

4. What would be the disadvantages of a world in which evil behavior never caused harm?

5. How do pains and inconveniences contribute to the shaping of our character? What would we, and society, be like if God prevented all pain?

6. What examples have you seen of wise living preventing suffering, and unwise living bringing troublesome consequences?

7. What are examples of pains that appears to be pointless yet really have significant benefits?

8. What would be the problems with a world in which God diligently saw to our individual comfort?

9. In spite of the need for regularity and for problems to help us grow in different ways, why is it acceptable – even advantageous – for God to sometimes intervene? How has He done so for you?

10. What examples have you seen of good coming from natural disasters?

11. How is morality a factor in the effects of natural disasters?

12. In what way does God's prevention go unnoticed? He can prevent harm at different points, from averting it altogether (in which case no one will ever know) to rescuing someone from the midst of trouble. What are the advantages and disadvantages of God preventing trouble altogether? Of allowing trouble but intervening early in its development (e.g., shifting the wind in a forest fire)? Late in the process (e.g., facilitating someone's rescue from the midst of flames)?

13. In what way has God not failed the believer who dies in a natural disaster?

14. How do natural disasters put God and man in proper perspective?

NOTES

1. "Girl with Rare Disease Doesn't Know Pain," Nov. 1, 2004, story from Associated Press on <CNN.com>, Health section. (Emphasis within mother's quote added.) The specialist is Dr. Felicia Axelrod, at New York University School of Medicine.

2. Philip Yancey and Dr. Paul Brand, *The Gift of Pain: Why We Hurt and What We Can Do about It*, previously titled, *The Gift Nobody Wants* (Grand Rapids, MI: Zondervan, 1993, 1997), 4-5.

3. The official death toll of about 470 was based on bodies counted. Actual deaths were much higher because many transients and illegal immigrants lived on the river and low lying areas along which the flood waters traveled.

4. Saying that choosing actions has something to do with choosing outcomes is different from saying that right action is determined exclusively by choosing outcomes. Basing right action on outcomes is called teleological ethics (from *telos*, end). It competes with deontological ethics (from *deon*, duty) according to which an action is right or wrong in itself, apart from considering the outcome. And it competes with virtue ethics, according to which right action is a matter of right character. The main views of ethics assume that we can understand causality in the world – how things work so as to bring about the right results (teleological), or to do what is right (deontological), or to act within right character.

5. C. S. Lewis, *The Problem of Pain* (New York, NY: Macmillan, 1962), 93, 95.

6. Alexander Pope, "An Essay on Man," Epistle I; excerpted from, *The Problem of Evil*: A Reader, ed. Mark Larrimore (Malden, MA: Blackwell, 2001), 202-03.

7. Voltaire, "The Lisbon Earthquake: An Inquiry into the Maxim, 'Whatever is, is right,'" trans. Tobias Smollett and others, in *The Portable Voltaire*, ed. Ben Ray Redman (Harmondsworth: Penguin, 1949), 560-9; 560-2; 564-9; excerpted from Larrimore, 205-07.

8. "Six Brides Killed Hours Before Weddings," *Ananova*, 26 Feb. 2002; from <www.ananova.com/news/story/sm_530869.html>, accessed 27 Feb. 2002.

9. Amir Taheri, "Iran's Political Quake," *New York Post*, 30 Dec. 2003.

10. "Geologist Gave Repeated Alerts," *Times Online*, 2 Jan. 2005, <http://www.timesonline.co.uk/article/0,,18690-1422669,00.html>. The geology professor was Kerry Sieh.

11. "Lack of Tsunami Warning Doomed Thousands," *Seattle Post Intelligencer*, 27 Dec. 2004, <http://seatlepi.nwsource.com/national/205355_warning27.html>.

12. "Indonesian Scientists Left Helpless to Warn Neighbours [sic] about Tsunami," *Khaleej Times*, 2 Jan. 2005, <http://www.khaleejtimes.com/DisplayArticle.asp?xfile=data/todaysfeatures/2005/January...>.

13. WorldNetDaily, 3 Jan. 2005, <http://www.worldnetdaily.com/news/article.asp?ARTICLE_ID=42212>

14. Eleanor Stump, "The Problem of Evil," Faith and Philosophy 2 (1985): 409; quoted in Alston, 106..

CHAPTER FOUR

THE PRICE OF FREEDOM?

As a boy from an affluent family, Ziad Jarrah attended Christian schools in Lebanon, and eventually went to study in Germany. When a young man, he met Aysel Sengun, a German-born physician of Turkish origin.[1] Their goal was to marry and have children, after he got training as a commercial pilot. She helped him find a flight school in the United States, from which he later proudly graduated. Those who met him found him friendly and engaging. During his stay in America he missed Aysel and called her or his own family almost every day, taking no less than five trips abroad to see them. His last trip back was paid for by her, she having bought him a one-way ticket in hopes he would stay.

But Mr Jarrah was torn by another commitment, which a sinister contact in Germany urged him to keep in an emotional meeting during that last trip. He went back to America to keep it. Three weeks later he called Aysel from the east coast of the United States, as he was piloting a commercial jumbo jet. He spoke to her very briefly, telling her three times that he loved her. She asked what was wrong, but he hung up. Shortly after, the plane crashed in a field in Pennsylvania, near Washington D. C.

But two other planes flown by his associates did not fail. They completed their terrorist mission, crashing into and destroying the Twin Towers the morning of September 11, 2001.

Whether Mr Jarrah ought to fly his plane into the White House or the Capitol building had been a matter of debate between the plot's mastermind, Khalid Sheikh Mohammed, and Osama bin Laden. Some of al-Qaeda's senior leadership did not want to attack the United States at all, for fear of reprisals, but Bin Laden overruled them.[2]

Were the conspirators' actions self-determined, or were their desires ultimately the product of forces outside themselves? Existentialist Jean Paul Sartre's view that our actions are completely our own has given way in the past few decades to the postmodern view that we are the product of forces such as our social circumstances, language, and the power-seeking manipulations of others.

Christians view the issue through a theological lens. What was God's role in those dark deeds that have defined the dawning of the twenty-first century? Did He have a role in the development of the terrorists' plot, the deliberations and hesitations, and the ultimate execution of events that day? More broadly, what is His role in all human choices, good and evil? The freedom of our will is a hot topic in philosophy, and the more specific question of how our will is influenced by God is a matter of spirited debate in theology.

The stakes in the debate are high. For our worldview in general, it goes to the heart of how we understand God's interaction with free beings, and the very nature of freedom and moral responsibility. For the problem of evil specifically, it determines whether or not God ultimately ordains or even causes our actions such that we cannot do anything different from what we end up doing. For that matter, it can decide whether we speak in terms of God somehow *causing* evil for some good purpose, or merely *permitting* it and channeling its effects to some good end. In terms of how we answer the problem of evil, the question of God's influences on us determines whether we can use what is called the free will defense. Thus so much comes down to the nature of free will.

What is Free Will Anyway?

Have you ever known a fatalist? According to the view, held since the ancient Greeks, nothing we do can affect our future. Oxford philosopher Michael Demmett recalls the Nazi bombardments of London in World War II, and how some people died because they would not take cover in the bomb shelters. They reasoned that it would not matter whether they took precautions or not. If they were going to live they would live, if they were going to die they would die.[3]

Most Christians reject the idea that the future is unchanged by our actions. Even for many who hold a strong view of predestination, whether we were predestined to be blown up has something to do with whether we took cover. As seen from the divine side, if God intends to save us, He will likely give us the wisdom to get out of harm's way. Biblically, it would be difficult to make sense of divine commands if obeying them made absolutely no difference to outcomes, especially when so many commands come with promises of future benefits for those who obey and warnings for those who disobey.

Fatalism is often confused with determinism, the view that everything which happens is caused. According to determinism, the things in place before something happens are sufficient to completely determine the outcome. Thus the future has no alternatives and is as fixed as the past. French physicist and mathematician Pierre-Simon Laplace (1749-1827) claimed that if a being with a super-mind had Newton's laws and knew the location and speed of every particle in the universe, it could know every event that had ever taken place and ever will take place. Though determinists today think it would take more than Newton's laws to predict everything, the view that the future is determined by forces of nature is quite alive. Behaviorists like B. F. Skinner (1904-90) hold that humans too are determined, thus free will as we think of it is an illusion.

Besides these examples of "scientific" determinism (or causal determinism) there is theological determinism, which has direct bearing on the problem of evil. On this view, God determines everything that happens and there is no free will as we normally think of it; that is, we are not the source of our decisions, entailing that we could not chose anything different from that which we actually do chose.

Some would like to say that the question can be decided very simply: because God knows x will happen then x must happen. So if God knew yesterday that you would be reading this book today, then there is no way you could do otherwise. If God knew in the year 2000 that Ziad Jarrah would embark on a terrorist mission in 2001, then he could not do otherwise. Sometimes this is linked to God's omniscience by claiming that it is His infallible knowledge of the future that makes it impossible for things to turn out differently. Supposedly, if today we could do something different from what God knew yesterday that we would do today, then we have the power to falsify His knowledge – which is impossible. Actually, though, the same claim could be made without bringing God into it: if it were true yesterday that you would read this today, then you could not possibly do otherwise. Both have the effect of removing our free choice.

Without going too deeply into it, we have to be careful not to confuse what will be with what must be. If God knows what will happen tomorrow, it does not necessarily mean that He will *cause* it to be so, nor that He will make it such that it can't be otherwise. Therefore it would be better to say that God merely *knew* yesterday what you would freely choose today.[4] So if you choose not to read this book today, then yesterday God would have known that you wouldn't read this today. So we can see that the question of whether God determines events cannot be decided by the mere fact that He knows what will happen in advance, so we will have to look deeper for answers.

The problem is that the idea of our decisions being determined – not just influenced, but determined – by something outside us does not sit well with our intuitions about free will. Many people believe that if something or someone besides ourselves determines what we would do then we did not choose it and our responsibility for it is diminished or non-existent.

Those who agree that choices cannot be both determined and free are called incompatibilists, because they think that free will is incompatible with determination. Those who think that our choices are determined and consequently there is no such thing as free will are called hard determinists (exemplified by eighteenth century French philosopher d'Holbach, whose work shocked even Voltaire; and by some modern behavioral psychologists). Those who think that our choices are determined but that we are nevertheless free are called soft determinists or compatibilists.

Devout Christians can be found on both sides of the compatibilist and incompatibilist issue. And it is this issue that decides whether we can use the free will defense to answer the problem of evil.

The Free Will Defense

Often associated with Augustine, the free will defense has long been a standard answer to the problem of evil. It is a form of the higher good argument, which is appealed to in this book. According to the argument from higher goods, the manifestation of certain types of good requires the existence of some evils (we'll develop this more in the next chapter). The free will defense states that God deemed it better to create beings who can freely love Him and choose good; He did not want to create mere robots. But by definition free beings cannot be coerced into doing good, and thus they can do evil. So God did what was good, which is make free beings, and those beings chose evil. Thus the higher good of having free beings who can do good comes at the price of allowing some evil. The point is that to exclude all possibility of evil God would have to exclude all moral good by refraining from making morally free creatures.

When it comes to free will and evil, an obvious question is often asked: how did the first beings sin if they were created good (Gen. 1:31)? It is connected to the question, where did the first sin come from? When these questions are asked most Christians want to immediately retreat to the safe ground of mystery, but there are a few things we can say.

In answer, God did not have to create "evil" as an option for us to choose in order for evil to enter the human race. That is because evil is not something out there, independent of us as something to choose, as if we could choose between a house, an automobile, or evil. Evil is more like the misuse of our capacity. Thus the ability to do evil is inherent in free will.[5] So if there were only ourselves and God in the entire universe we could still decide not to give God His rightful place – we could choose ourselves over God. Whereas philosopher John Hick objects that this amounts to the self-creation of evil out of nothing (ex nihilo),[6] we could reply that evil is not a substance and so is not being "created."[7]

So if the first person created was part of the overall scenario that God called "good" (Gen. 1:31), how was there a fall? We could answer that God's creation of the first beings as innocent and good does not entail that they had absolute moral perfection. They were immature. Unlike God, they could be tempted (James 1:13). Even God's pronouncement that creation was "very good" does not require that the first human had absolute perfection. Whatever "good" means in Genesis chapter one, it applied to all of creation, including rocks and trees and everything else. Christian philosopher Stephen Davis says that it must mean that the creation "was a harmonious, beautiful, smoothly working cosmos rather than the ugly, churning chaos over which the Holy Spirit had moved (Gen. 1:2)."[8]

For Hick it is ridiculous to suppose that either human or angel would give up the joys of righteousness and communion with God only to become evil and miserable. To make such a choice would require that they had been created as irrational beings, and Hick says God would then be to blame for creating them that way.[9] In answer, the biblical text nowhere suggests that the first humans or angels who were tempted thought they were choosing between blessedness and misery. The choice was between keeping God in His rightful place, or usurping His authority. Misery was not an option they thought they were choosing – but it certainly was a consequence.

Augustine sought additional support for his theodicy from his idea that evil is not a positive thing but rather the absence of good.[10] Just as blindness is the absence of sight, so a sin like cowardice is the absence of bravery. This matters because if we affirm that God is the ultimate cause of everything, we do not have to say that He caused evil, since evil is not a thing to be caused but merely a lack of goodness. Rather than cause evil, God simply did not grant the grace to have more goodness – which is entirely His prerogative. No one says that God ought to give unlimited goodness. It is a clever argument.

Augustine also had an explanation for why it is even possible for humans to sin. It is because only God is perfect. Our liability to sin thus arises from our finiteness (Leibniz held a similar view).[11]

Although Augustine's idea of evil as a lack of good is ingenious, we have to say that some types of evil are easier to regard as a lack of goodness than are others. It is easy to think of a person born blind as lacking the grace given to the sighted person. But it is a little awkward to say that a genocidal dictator lacks benevolence. It certainly is not experienced by his victims as a lack of anything, but as a brutal use of his power. Perhaps in an abstract sense it is a lack of something.[12] It might be simpler to think of moral evil strictly in terms of free will: God granted free will and we misused it. (Augustine did hold that a person's lack of moral good is their own fault.)

In the modern debate about evil, anti-theists and anti-Christians used to claim that any amount of evil disproves the existence of God because a good and all powerful God would not allow it. But by skillful use of the free will defense, Christian philosopher Alvin Plantinga showed that the mere existence of any amount of evil cannot disprove the existence of a good and all powerful God. Simply put, he argued that even an omnipotent God cannot make creatures who are free but who never sin. That is because a being who is free cannot also be controlled (or determined). It would be as impossible as determining that a bachelor can also be married. Similarly, being controlled and being free are incompatible. As mentioned in this book's introduction, it was generally conceded that Plantinga was right, and the debate shifted to the evidential problem of evil – how God could allow so much evil, some of which seems pointless.

It is clear that Plantinga's argument – and the free will defense – depends on incompatibilism. It requires that to be free a being cannot be controlled. Is that the case?

Incompatibilism – Real Choice

For you to be free and responsible for what you do, the incompatibilist requires that no outside thing or person determines what you do. In other words, for you to be free to do x you have to be able not to do x, otherwise your decision was not really free and you are not responsible for it. So for you to be free to read this book you have to be able not to read it. Nothing outside of you can be making you read it. Nothing outside Ziad Jarrah could have made him decide to fly the hijacked plane. As Plantinga put it, "Now God can create free creatures, but He can't *cause* or *determine* them to do only what is right. For if He does so, then they aren't significantly free after all; they do not do what is right *freely*."[13]

For moderate incompatibilists, our decisions can be influenced by internal things like our beliefs, desires, and character; and by external things like promises, expectations, and rules. Jarrah, for example, was influenced by his sinister contact in Germany, who convinced him to leave his fiancee forever, and to fly his terrorist mission. He flew it freely, however, because the shadowy figure did not make him do it. In the end, the decision was Jarrah's.

Moderate incompatibilists who are theists believe that God can influence us in various ways that come short of making us do something, short of making us do what we do so that we cannot do anything else. However, for you to be free no one can *force* you to do something you do not want to do. For you to walk freely into a bank with bank robbers, no one can physically drag you into the bank against your will. Most would say too that the robbers cannot threaten to kill you and your family if you refuse to help them rob the bank. Were you to participate in the robbery under that kind of coercion you would not be free or responsible for what you did (and compatibilists would agree that you cannot be coerced and be free).

Radical incompatibilists require that our actions cannot be determined even by our own character if they are to be done freely.[14] We have to be able to make a decision one way or another without it being possible to predict beforehand with absolute certainty which we will do.

Science used to be against incompatibilism when it seemed that physical events were determined by natural laws within the framework of classical physics and the Newtonian worldview (as mentioned briefly in chapter two). But in the early twentieth century discoveries in quantum physics seemed to support indeterminism, and therefore also seemed to favor incompatibilism. A new challenge then arose, however. If the world is an unpredictable place, as physics seemed to be showing, then it was not clear how we could be morally responsible. That is because moral responsibility requires that things happen the way we intend them to happen. When we think, "hand the food to the hungry person," our hand has to go out so that the person can take it. We are not responsible if we intend to do one thing and a different thing happens at random. Moral responsibility seemed more assured when causes and effects were thought to be locked together deterministically.

But not everyone thinks that the quantum world is relevant to the issue of free will. For example, quantum physics has to do with atoms whereas our brains are huge masses of material. Some suggest that whatever indeterminacy there is on the atomic level would be canceled out by the trillions of molecules involved in our thought processes.[15] Others say that we can still have moral responsibility in the quantum world even if things probably happen rather than definitely happen, and that is because our actions will probably produce the result we intend.

Rather than insist that we are free only when we have a real alternative (i.e., could have chosen not to do what we did, or could have chosen something different altogether), some incompatibilists say what matters is that we must be the ones choosing the action. To be free we have to be the cause of the action, not someone or something else. So we freely chose to read this book if we did the choosing, not something else (like our genetics or natural laws) or someone else (such as a parent or even God). In theological terms, this is part of our being made in God's image. He made us to be like Him in that we can choose to initiate action. So just as God can decide to do things, He made us capable of deciding to do things, although He retains ultimate control over outcomes. On this view we reflect Him in a small and imperfect way, just as our partial knowledge reflects His perfect knowledge; as our partial goodness reflects His perfect goodness, and so on.

All this is denied by compatibilists, who claim that much less is required for us to be free and responsible.

Compatibilism – Real Desires

For compatibilists, determinism is not a threat to free will. What we do can be one hundred per cent determined by something outside us. You are reading this book freely even if there was never any possibility that you would not read it. Jarrah flew the plane freely even if there was never any possibility that he would not. Something apart from us can completely determined what we would do, yet we can still do it freely.

As compatibilists see it, we are free as long as we are doing what we want to do. Something else or someone else can determine what we want, but as long as it is also our desire we are doing it freely and are responsible for doing it. As one compatibilist said, "we can do what we want but we can't want what we want." God could see to it that we want to do a certain thing, and as long as we also want to do it then we are doing it freely – even if He is the one who made us want to do it.

Suppose a motorist stranded in the dark prays for someone to help him, and as you drive by God puts the desire in your heart to help. Even though you have things to do and you normally do not stop to help strangers in the dark, God makes you want to stop. He may bring to mind the time you were stranded and someone helped you. Or He may bring to mind the parable of the good Samaritan. However He does it, He makes sure that you have the desire so that you decide to stop. Here is where the compatibilist differs from the incompatibilist: the compatibilist believes that God determines one hundred percent that you will stop and there is no way you will do otherwise; yet you still did it freely. Why? Because you wanted to do it. It is true that God caused you to want to do it, but you are free and responsible for your actions because you also want to do it – again, because God made you want to do it.

For compatibilists, freedom is a matter of doing what you want, whereas for incompatibilists, it is a matter of being able to act differently or being in some sense the originator of what you do.

Theistic compatibilists hold that it is God who makes everyone want what they want, while non-theistic compatibilists hold that genetics, natural laws, or something else determines what we want. Compatibilists accept determinism and free will. So everything is determined such that it turns out only one way and that way could, in principle at least, be known with certainty before a person makes a decision (although in practice it may be too complicated for us humans to predict certain things). Given determinism, the future can turn out only one way, and there are no real alternatives and no such thing as chance (this relates to the question of whether there is only one best world, as discussed in chapter two).

For the compatibilist, life's road is a one-way street with no crossroads and thus no alternatives. The incompatibilist sees that road as having crossroads which present real alternatives; our decisions could genuinely change things and take us down a different path.

To add the sense that we can do something other than what we actually do, some compatibilists added that we can do other than what we do if we want to. The critic would say, however, that there is still no real choice because whether or not we want to choose differently is still decided by whatever causes our behavior (for the theist, that would be God). It was likened to a situation in which a girl absolutely cannot tolerate touching blond haired dogs. When she is offered a choice between a black haired or a blond haired dog, she is "free" to pick either, but in reality cannot pick the blond dog.[16]

In the thinking of a lot of people, freedom, the ability to choose, and the responsibility for what we do all go together. So to defend the idea that we are responsible even if we cannot choose otherwise, a compatibilist named Harry Frankfurt made up a scenario in which Mr Black wants Mr Jones to do something. He is ready to intervene in sinister ways with brain manipulation to make Jones do the deed. But he never has to intervene because Jones wants to do the deed anyway and does it. Jones did not have a choice because Black would have made him do it, but that does not matter. Jones is still responsible even though he was unable to choose not to do it.[17]

But compatibilist freedom still seems to make a human like a computer going through its motions. We can say it is doing what it "wants" to do, yet whatever it does has been completely determined by the programmer. Compatibilist theologian John Frame tries to soften this a bit. He compares the relation between God and creatures to an author and his characters. Though the author is in total control, he develops the events according to the unique personalities of the characters, which take on lives of their own.[18] God makes and carries out His plan according to what He has decided we shall be like as individuals.[19] We are part of God's creativity in that our choices reflect the choices He already made in eternity past. Through us He accepts and rejects possibilities in history.[20]

Comparing Alternatives

What drives these two competing visions of free will? Compatibilists want to ensure that God is in complete control of every detail in the universe. Incompatibilists want to make sure that humans are free and responsible for their actions, and they want to preserve God's holiness, in no way making Him the author of sin.

Reformed theologian Robert Reymond sums up the compatibilist's chief objection to incompatibilism,

> What these thinkers refuse to realize is that if there were one square inch of this entire universe not under his sovereign governance, God is neither absolutely sovereign nor omniscient since that one square inch would have equal claim to its own sovereignty to do as it willed, with the authority even to set up a sign saying to God, "Keep out!" This theological construction allows billions upon billions of these sovereign human "inches" to exist throughout God's universe, all denying by their own sovereign right his sovereignty over them.[21]

Compatibilists look to biblical verses that emphasize God's control. Ephesians 1:11, which says that God "works all things after the counsel of His will," is usually given the most expansive possible implication: not a single molecule or human thought is outside God's control.[22]

Compatibilists focus on verses that indicate God's control of evil.[23] He hardens whom He wants (Rom. 9:18), most notably, Pharaoh (e.g., Exod. 9:12); turned the Egyptians to "to hate His people" (Ps. 105:25) and sent the Assyrians (Isa. 10:6) and Chaldeans (Hab. 1:6) against them. When Samson wanted a Philistine wife, his parents objected, however they "did not know that it was of the Lord, for He was seeking an occasion against the Philistines" (Judg. 14:4). The disciples' prayer indicated a high degree of divine control over the crucifixion. Those who took part in it did "whatever Your hand and Your purpose predestined to occur" (Acts 4:28). As to those who will rebel during the end times, God will "put it in their hearts to execute His purpose by having a common purpose, and by giving their kingdom to the beast until the words of God will be fulfilled (Rev. 17:17).

God's causal relationship to evil is a delicate issue for compatibilists. John Frame says, "...it is important to see that God does in fact bring about the sinful behavior of human beings, whatever problems that may create in our understanding."[24] He would even say, albeit "cautiously," that "God causes evil and sin" (he is careful to explain what he means, saying that he wants to preserve not only God's sovereignty but also His holiness and goodness).[25]

Calvin distances God from sin by emphasizing that He is only the "remote" cause of sin, while humans are the "proximate" (or near) cause. Nevertheless, he insists that it is "frivolous" to say that God merely "permits" sins, "when Scripture shows Him not only willing but the author of them."[26] Frame offers the clarification that when God permits something, it is an efficacious permission; that is, what He permits to happen will happen. This makes permission "a form of ordination, a form of causation."[27]

Linking God so closely with evil makes incompatibilists queasy. An important verse for them is James 1:13, "Let no one say when he is tempted, 'I am being tempted by God'; for God cannot be tempted by evil, and He Himself does not tempt anyone." Incompatibilists conclude that not only does God not cause people to sin, but He is not even part of tempting them. God is said unequivocally to be "holy, holy, holy" (Isa. 6:3; Rev. 4:8), and will not even hear the person who regards wickedness in their heart (Ps. 66:18).

For incompatibilists, the idea that God determines what people do such that they cannot do otherwise makes Him something very like the author of sin. If a man kidnaps, rapes, and murders a teenage girl, and God in any way made him want to do it, then it is thought that He would be, to some extent, responsible for the evil deed.

Incompatibilists prefer to think in terms of God allowing evil rather than determining it. As free and responsible (but fallen) beings, humans originate actions, including sinful actions. God channels those actions to His good ends no matter what were the evil intentions. Most prefer not to think that God, directly or indirectly, put the crime into the mind of the rapist and made him want to do his deed such that he could not do otherwise. But God can allow the man's criminal imagination to foment into a definite plan, and allow him to carry out that plan. God can lessen the restraining influence of the man's conscience, redirect the attention of the local police so that they are nowhere to be seen at the time he attempts the crime, and so on.

God has a near endless array of ways to affect humans without determining that they will have certain desires. He can, for example, withdraw internal and external restraint, move collaborators into or out of a person's life, and allow demonic forces to work unhindered. God can exercise considerable influence without negating free will. But for the incompatibilist, He cannot make people do things such that they could not do otherwise. Incompatibilists say that if He did He would be at least somewhat responsible for evil, whereas we would be no more responsible morally than a computer program. Therefore God's influences cannot be sufficient to infallibly cause us to do something. "If they are," Norman Geisler says, "then the human agent is not the efficient cause of the action, but only the instrumental cause through which God's action is exercised. But in this case then the moral blame falls on God."[28]

Incompatibilists want to emphasize that God has a different causal relationship to good than He does to evil. He can cause good by intervening through things like conscience, law enforcement, control of nature, and so on. But when it comes to evil, He does not cause it in the same way. It does not originate from Him. Evil comes from fallen wills, human or demonic. As Norman Geisler points out, God said to Eve, "What is this you have done? (Gen. 3:13)"; and Jesus said to those who rejected divine grace, "you were not willing (Matt. 23:37)."[29] Whatever the source of action, the incompatibilist would still want to maintain that God remains in total control of outcomes.

Incompatibilists wonder how compatibilists make sense of the many verses in which God exhorts, urges, and pleads for people to do things – if God is in control of people anyway. Incompatibilists would also want to revisit verses that seem to indicate that God instigates evil. For example, before God hardened Pharaoh's heart, incompatibilists would point out that Pharaoh hardened his own heart (e.g., Exod. 8:15,32). Second Samuel 24:1 says that God incited David to sin by numbering the troops of Israel in order to bring an occasion for divine wrath. However, the incompatibilist would point out that according to a parallel passage in 1 Chronicles 21:1, it was Satan who moved David to sin. The nuance is crucial. God did not directly cause David to sin, He allowed Satan to tempt him and he fell. While the passage in Samuel gives us the overall picture, Chronicles gives us the important detail as to how God actually worked, and it was by allowing a fallen being to tempt another fallen being. Was God in control all the time? Certainly. Did it come out the way God intended? Certainly. Did God cause David to sin? No, He allowed David to sin in order to bring about His own higher purpose.

The incompatibilist would say that there is a similarly more nuanced explanation for Scripture's overall statement that the Egyptians, Assyrians, and Chaldeans turned against Israel; that Samson wanted a Philistine wife, that various individuals brought about the crucifixion, and so on. In places Scripture gives a summation rather like the passage about David in Second Samuel, but a Chronicles type account would reveal that God allowed sin and closely channeled it for good, but did not use means that decisively inclined people to sin.

Some incompatibilists[30] hold an innovative view of how God can accomplish His will infallibly while still allowing people to choose things freely. It is based on how God decides things. It deals with the kinds of knowledge God has, and specifies which kind of knowledge serves as a basis for God's choices. Simply put, it says that God decides how to accomplish things based on His knowledge of the outcome of all possibilities.

Suppose Maria is to meet her friend Susan at a restaurant at 5:30 p.m. But God would have her get there fifteen minutes late so that she will enter the restaurant just as Bob, whom she did not plan to meet, is leaving. If Bob meets her, he will hire her for her dream job. There are an array of possible situations to delay Maria. Among them, a co-worker could ask to talk with her before leaving work, or her car could break down, or her boss could ask to speak with her for a few minutes at five o'clock. God knows exactly the outcome of each of these. If her co-worker were to ask to talk to her, Maria will politely postpone it until the next day because of her appointment. If her car were to break down, Maria will be a full hour late, missing Bob altogether. But if her boss were to ask to talk to her, she will not refuse him, and he can keep her there for just the right amount of time (without his realizing his role in the divinely arranged meeting). God knows just what would move her boss to want to talk to Maria for a few minutes. God works it out, Maria runs into Bob, and gets her dream job.

What matters is that while God accomplished exactly what He wanted, each person acted freely. The boss wanted to talk to Maria, she wanted to stay late for a few minutes, Bob left the restaurant when He wanted, and ended up hiring her.

The view claims that God knows what will happen if something else happens. Since He knows every possibility, He chooses just those possibilities that will come out the way He wants. This is called "middle knowledge." It got the name in the sixteenth century from Luis de Molina, who distinguished between God's knowledge of what must be true because of God's own nature (such as truths of logic), and His knowledge of what will be true because He chooses to bring them about (that He will create, that earth will have one moon, and so on). Midway between His knowledge of what must be true and what will be true is what could be true, hence, "middle knowledge."

The idea is that God predestines based on His knowledge of all possible outcomes. So He predestined Maria to get her dream job by also predestining her boss to talk to her and Bob to hire her.

Some have objected to the very idea that God can have middle knowledge.[31] On the so called open theism view, God cannot know what people will choose because, supposedly, genuine choice cannot be predicted. Not even God knows what they will do(!) though He is still omniscient because He knows everything that could count as knowledge. The open theism view does not square with God's ability to infallibly predict the future (e.g., Deut. 18:22).

The main view that competes with the idea of middle knowledge is that God knows what will happen because he makes it happen. Middle knowledge proponent William Lane Craig, an evangelical, objects,

> But this interpretation inevitably makes God the author of sin, since it is he who moved Judas, for example, to betray Christ, a sin that merits the hapless Judas' everlasting perdition. But how can a holy God move people to commit moral evil and, moreover, how can these people then be held morally responsible for acts over which they had no control?[32]

He concludes that the view seems, "in effect, to turn God into the devil."

Just as compatibilists have to be careful when discussing God's causal connection to evil, incompatibilists have to be careful about how fallen people come to salvation. If God is the ultimate source of our salvation in that He chose us – and only for that reason we chose Him – then how did He do it? Perhaps God grants the elect grace while putting them through things that He knows will cause them to respond to Him. If that sounds like decisively inclining the will toward salvation, the incompatibilist could perhaps reply that choosing salvation is indeed different from other choices, as evidenced by the fact that no one is praised for it. It is in no way a good deed but is entirely a work of God for the elect (Eph. 2:8-9).

Whatever the challenges faced by each side, it is helpful to take a step back from the compatibilist-incompatibilist debate and see how the views are similar. Both sides agree (with exceptions among radical incompatibilists) that God knows precisely how things will turn out, and they will turn out just as He plans. His plans include things He does not desire because He has higher purposes. They both hold that forced actions are not free, and that God never forces anyone. Furthermore, to be free a person must want to do what he does, and we are responsible for sin, not God.

The difference is that compatibilists hold that God decisively determines what people do such that they cannot do otherwise and don't want to do otherwise. That is how He remains in control, even of free wills. As incompatibilists see it, humans are influenced by God and other forces, but remain at least slightly independent. That ability to make choices is a dim reflection of God's freedom, but it makes humans free and responsible, leaving God perfectly blameless for sin. He allows people to have a certain amount of independence, while remaining completely sovereign over every aspect of the universe, in spite of granting free will.

But again, consider the similarities, at least among the more moderates of each camp. As compatibilists see it, God knows and brings about what will make people want to do what is required to fulfill His plan – which includes sin where it accomplishes a higher purpose. Unlike His control of nature, He controls wills through indirect, rather than direct, means (at least for moderate Calvinists). Their will is not forced because He works by making them want to do it. John Feinberg says that God's decree includes the means to the ends He desires, "Such means include whatever circumstances and factors are necessary to convince an individual (without constraint) that the act God has decreed is the act she or he wants to do. And, given the sufficient conditions, the person will do the act."[33] God works the way we would work to "persuade" a person to do what it is we want them to do.[34] But Geisler objects that once a person rejects God's "wooing, moving or reasoning," then there is no way He can "guarantee" the outcome without forcing compliance.[35] Nevertheless both compatibilists and incompatibilists believe that forced compliance removes freedom.

Similar to compatibilists, incompatibilists see God's plan as including sin, and He works by means of what He knows will make people want to do what fulfills His plan.

Does God decisively *determine* what people want to do, and is that what makes Him sovereign over everything (compatibilism)? Or, does divine sovereignty work by *allowing* people to do things such as sin (at least to some extent), which entails that they and not God are responsible for evildoing (incompatibilism)?

For the compatibilist it comes down to what it takes for God to be sovereign. For the incompatibilist it comes down to what it takes for us to be free and responsible, and for God to be blameless.

A crucial question is, does God allow anyone to resist His workings? Compatibilists say no, on grounds that God would not be sovereign. Incompatibilists say yes, but see resistance as something worked into His plan. God allows people to resist as part of their freedom, but their resistence is included in His plan. His plan is thus never frustrated and He remains in control. So those who crucified Christ, for example, did what was wrong, but their wrongdoing accomplished precisely what God wanted. As a compatibilist would see it, God worked through indirect means to get the people to crucify Christ.

There are of course variations within each view, but this is a basic outline of the positions. The issue divides some of the best minds in theology and philosophy, and it is not entirely clear to me which of the two is correct. I lean toward incompatibilism because it seems to better ensure that God does not author sin, and I don't think the view threatens His sovereignty. On the other hand, compatibilism offers the simplest way to understand how God can be in perfect control, especially with regard to salvation.

As with so many areas of theology, here we quickly feel our cognitive limits. Whichever view we choose, we can agree with what is at least claimed by both sides: our actions are free; we, not God, are responsible for evil; and He is ultimately in control.

GOING FARTHER

1. What is the difference between a fatalist and a determinist?

2. How would you answer the view that the future is fixed and unchangeable merely because God knows what it is, in other words, x must happen because God knows x will happen?

3. What is the hard determinist view?

4. Where did the first act of evil come from? How is God not responsible for it?

5. What is the privation view and how does it try to explain how God is not responsible for evil? What do you think of the view?

6. How did Augustine and Leibniz account for our liability to sin in spite of our being created as innocent beings?

7. What is the difference between the logical problem of evil and the evidential problem of evil? Why has the debate shifted to the latter?

8. What is the incompatibilist view?

9. How have some used physics to show that acts are undetermined and random? How has that affected the overall debate about human responsibility for evil? How have some argued that indeterminism in physics is irrelevant to human responsibility?

10. What is the compatibilist view? How do compatibilists use our desire to do x as a way of defending that we are free to do x, even if God determined that we would do x?

11. What drives each view, compatibilist and incompatibilist? What does each have to be careful when explaining?

12. What is middle knowledge? How is it used to explain freewill and determinism with regard to evil?

13. What convictions do compatibilists and incompatibilists share?

NOTES

1. Rob Broomby, "Suicide Hijacker's Phone Call to Girlfriend," *BBC News*, Nov. 19 2002; accessed July 3, 2004, <http://news.bbc.co.uk/1/hi/world/europe/2493161.stm>.

2. 9/11 Commission Staff statement number 16, text as submitted to National Commission on Terrorist Attacks Upon United States, June 16, 2004; accessed 3 July 2004, <http://msnbc.msn.com/id/5224099>.

3. William Lane Craig, *The Only Wise God: The Compatibility of Divine Foreknowledge and Human Freedom* (1987; reprint, Eugene, OR: Wipf and Stock, 2000), 14.

4. This is essentially Augustine's response, *On Free Will*, bk. iv, ch. 4. Craig makes this point in chapter five of, *The Only Wise God* (pp. 67-74). Philosopher of religion Nelson Pike argued that if an omniscient God knew eighty years ago that Jones would mow his lawn last Saturday, then Jones can't do otherwise. If he could then he could make it such that God had a false belief eighty years ago. Nelson Pike, "Divine Omniscience and Voluntary Action," *The Philosophical Review*, 74 (1965): 27-46; reprinted in John Martin Fischer ed., *God, Foreknowledge, and Freedom* (Stanford, CA: Stanford University Press, 1989): 57-73 (Jones and his lawn are on p. 61). Steve Davis argues that divine foreknowledge does not cause things to happen nor rule out free will. Stephen T. Davis, *Logic and the Nature of God* (Grand Rapids, MI: Eerdmans, 1983), ch. 4, "Foreknowledge" (pp. 52-67).

5. This point is made by C. S. Lewis, *The Problem of Pain* (New York, NY: Macmillan, 1962), 69.

6. John Hick, *Evil and the God of Love*, rev. (San Francisco, CA: Harper & Row, 1978), 62f, 279.

7. R. Douglas Geivett makes this same point in *Evil and the Evidence for God: the Challenge of John Hick's Theodicy* (Philadelphia, PA: Temple University Press, 1993), 201. Hick notes Augustine's view that the willing of evil is a "self-originating act" (p. 60-61).

8. Stephen T. Davis, ed., *Encountering Evil: Live Options in Theodicy* (Atlanta, GA: John Knox, 1981), 73.

9. Hick, 69, 279. He raises the irrationality issue in connection with angels.

10. Augustine, *City of God*, bk. xi. 9; *Enchiridion* xi. Hick (p. 47 fn.) notes that a privation view of evil appeared before Augustine in *Origen, De Principiis*, ii. 9, 2; and *Commentary on St. John*, ii.13; Athanasius, *Contra Gentes*, ch. 7 and *De Incarnatione*, iv, 5; Basil the Great, *Hexameron*, homily 2, par. 4; and Gregory of Nyssa, *The Great Catechism*, ch. 7. For a critical treatment of Augustine on evil, see Hick, 37-89.

11. *Enchiridion*, xii. Leibniz observed that the ancients regarded matter as eternal and independent of God, thus the ultimate source of evil. But theists, he said, attribute all things to God. There is "an *original imperfection in the creature* before sin, because the creature is limited in its essence; whence ensues that it cannot know all, and that it can deceive itself and commit other errors" (italics in original). Leibniz further held that evil is privation. He categorized evil as metaphysical, by which he meant "mere imperfection;" physical evil, which is suffering; and moral evil, which is sin. G. W. Leibniz, *Theodicy*, trans. E. M. Huggard (1951; reprinted, Chicago and LaSalle, IL: Open Court, 1985), pp. 135-36 ("Essays on the Justice of God and the Freedom of Man in the Origin of Evil," sec. 20-21).

12. Hick (pp. 55-57) makes essentially the same points.

13. Alvin Plantinga, *God, Freedom, and Evil* (Grand Rapids, MI: William B. Eerdmans, 1974), 30 (italics original).

14. This is the form of incompatibilism that Frame criticizes. For example he says that we cannot "choose to act independently of our own character and desire;" and on the libertarian view, "the will must always be independent of the heart and all of our other faculties." John Frame, *The Doctrine of God* (Phillipsburg, NJ: P&R, 2002), 142. There are, however, a variety of incompatibilist theories. See for example,

Randolph Clarke, "Incompatibilist (Nondeterministic) Theories of Free Will," *The Stanford Encyclopedia of Philosophy* (Summer 2004 Edition), Edward N. Zalta (ed.), <http://plato.stanford.edu/entries/incompatibilism-theories/>.

15. On this general issue, see David Hodgson, "Quantum Physics, Consciousness, and Free Will," in Robert Kane, ed., *The Oxford Handbook of Free Will* (New York, NY: Oxford University Press, 2002), 85-110; Robert C. Bishop, "Chaos, Indeterminism, and Free Will," in Kane, 111-125; and Ted Honderich, *How Free Are You? The Determinism Problem* (Oxford, UK: Oxford University Press, 1993), pp. 55-67, ch. 5, "Neuroscience and Quantum Theory."

16. Told in Michael McKenna, "Compatibilism," *The Stanford Encyclopedia of Philosophy* (Summer 2004 Edition), Edward N. Zalta (ed.), <http://plato.stanford.edu/archives/sum2004/entries/compatibilism/>, p. 10. See also, Roderick M. Chisholm, "Human Freedom and the Self", in Gary Watson ed., *Free Will* (Oxford, UK: Oxford University Press, 1982), 26-27 (I am indebted to McKenna for the reference).

17. Harry G. Frankfurt, "Alternative Possibilities and Moral Responsibility," reprinted in Gary Watson ed., *Free Will*, 2nd ed. (New York, NY: Oxford University Press, 2003), 172-73. Of course this has not gone unanswered. See, for example, David Widerker, "Libertarianism and Frankfurt's Attack on the Principle of Alternative Possibilities," in the same volume.

18. Frame, 156.

19. Frame, 151. This "creaturely integrity" is "the ability of things to exist and function on their own terms, to be distinct from other objects, to play their own distinct roles in history" (p. 148). It is part of God's decree (p. 149).

20. Frame, 153.

21. Robert L. Reymond, *A New Systematic Theology of the Christian Faith*, 2nd ed. (Nashville, TN: Thomas Nelson, 1998), 189-90.

22. Of Ephesians 1:11 John Feinberg says, "The clause, then, broadens the scope of the verse to speak of God's sovereign control not only over election to salvation, but over all else." John Feinberg, in *Predestination and Freewill*: Four Views of Divine Sovereignty and Human Freedom, ed. David Basinger and Randall Basinger (Downers Grove, IL: InterVarsity, 1986), 29-30. For Basinger's answer, see p. 52-53.

23. For example, D. A. Carson, *How Long, O Lord? Reflections on Suffering and Evil* (Grand Rapids, MI: Baker; Leicester, UK, 1990), 202-12; Frame, ch. 4.

24. Frame, 65.

25. Frame, 176. Page 179, preserving divine holiness and goodness.

26. Calvin, *Concerning the Eternal Predestination of God*, trans. J. K. S. Reid (London: James Clarke and Co., 1961), 176 (Frame pointed me to this passage). Frame (p. 178 fn.) notes that "Calvin's use of the term author raises questions. He probably means that God authors evil happenings without authoring their evil character." Calvin notes that some have difficulty accepting that God can "bend or draw" the wicked to do His will, "Hence the distinction was devised between doing and permitting because to many this difficulty seemed inexplicable..." *Institutes*, I.xvii, ed. John T. McNiel, trans. Ford Lewis Battles (Philadelphia, PA: Westminster Press, 1960), pp. 228-29; see also, III.xxiii, pp. 956-57.

27. Frame, 178.

28. Norman Geisler, in *Predestination and Freewill: Four Views of Divine Sovereignty and Human Freedom*, 48. In context he said, "Likewise, God-given desires, reasoning

and persuasion can be conditions of a free choice. But they are not the cause. That is, they are not the sufficient causal condition of our action."

29. Geisler, *Predestination and Freewill*, 76. Verses in Revised Standard Version.

30. Proponents include William Lane Craig, Alvin Plantinga, Edward Wierenga, Alfred Freddoso, Thomas Flint, David Basinger, Johathan Kvanvig. Opponents include William Hasker and Robert Adams.

31. For very readable discussion of objections, see William Lane Craig, in *Divine* Foreknowledge: Four Views, ed. James K. Beilby and Paul R. Eddy (Downers Grove, IL: InverVarsity, 2001), 140-43, on the grounding objection; and Linda Trinkhaus Zagzebski, *The Dilemma of Freedom and Foreknowledge* (New York, NY: Oxford University Pres, 1991), 141-52.

32. Craig, in *Divine Foreknowledge*: Four Views, 135.

33. Feinberg, *Predestination and Freewill: Four Views of Divine Sovereignty and Human Freedom*, 26.

34. Feinberg, *Predestination and Freewill*, 25-26.

35. Geisler, *Predestination and Freewill*, 47.

Chapter five

A CHARACTER BUILDING WORLD

With some things, depth and detail are revealed only by shadows. Clouds blocking patches of light from a mountain can reveal the deep valleys and crevasses, the jagged edges and rolling land. Only painters like Rembrandt, who can skillfully use shadow, bring detail to life, turning brush strokes into visual drama. So, too, do pain and evil have a place in life, revealing what could not be known any other way, showing detail and depth in what would otherwise appear flat, leaving much undiscovered.

As we have seen, this life may not be well suited to providing the greatest momentary pleasure for every creature, but it does provide great opportunity for revealing certain depth and detail in its creator. That detail, like the rugged beauty in a landscape without shadows, would go undetected and unappreciated without pain and evil. As well, this world is suited for formulating character in humans that reflects those otherwise hidden qualities in God. The combination of knowing God in His depths and of being formulated in His image potentially provide the most satisfying happiness for creatures, even though moments of our existence along the way are by no means as happy as we would like them to be.

The Hidden Benefits of Fallenness

Years ago I could not have imagined anything that would be worth the price of so much pain and suffering. What could be so grand, of such incalculable value, as to be worth the staggering cost of attaining it? But now I realize that the fullest possible revelation of God, including humans reflecting His character, is just such a grandiose goal as to be worth the price of a fallen world.

A world never stained by sin and pain – the world of our fantasies – would leave so many of God's qualities poorly known, or even completely undiscoverable. A world without sin would, first of all, also be a world in which no one knew forgiveness. If no being had ever sinned, had ever bent its will against God's, how would we know that God could forgive, or would? For that matter, how would we even know what forgiveness is?

Any knowledge of forgiveness would at best be highly abstract, known vaguely, if at all. Not being omniscient, we have to learn things by forming a bridge from what we know to what we do not know. I can imagine streets of gold only because I know what a street is and what gold looks like. If you talk about unicorns I know what you mean because they are said to be something like horses. But how could any of us imagine a new primary color? Or how could we imagine color at all if we had been blind from birth? The more distance between a thing and what we have experienced, the harder it is to understand. By contrast, things that are close to our experience are vivid and clear, known so much more fully. A news report of a serious earthquake, for example, means far more to those of us who have lived near Los Angeles and have felt the earth roll and buckle and have seen walls and ceilings ripple like gelatin. For the same reason, a person who has never been outside the Sahara Desert would have trouble appreciating Robert Frost's poem, "Stopping by the Woods on a Snowy Evening."

So the reason we can understand something like God's forgiveness is that there exists sin to forgive. Without it, we would be two steps removed from knowledge of divine forgiveness, knowing neither forgiveness nor even what there could be to forgive. First, understanding sin and forgiveness makes clear a side of God that would otherwise be known in a vague and abstract way, if at all – like a blind person's understanding of a crimson sunset. Second, understanding forgiveness on a human level, by knowing what it is like to forgive others and to be forgiven ourselves, brings us closer still to understanding God's forgiveness. We can experience something of God's nature when we forgive others, and we can understand how God forgives us when we see others forgive us. Certainly this fallen world provides plenty of opportunity to forgive, and our own fallen natures provide plenty of opportunity to be forgiven.

The view that God can, in this way, bring a good result from sin is not what Paul meant when he condemned those who advocated doing evil so that good may come (Rom. 3:8). He was condemning the belief that sin itself is justified on the grounds that it makes possible the blessing of forgiveness. He was forbidding people from approving someone's sin or from sinning themselves in order to bring about a good result, such as forgiveness. Paul was not condemning the view that God brought good out of something bad such as our sin (which is our misuse of His blessing of free will). Augustine said that God allowed evil because it reveals the depths of His wisdom to bring about greater good. And saying that evil makes possible an understanding of forgiveness does not mean that we advocate doing evil, nor that we applaud it in any way. It is only to say that from its existence God has brought good which would not otherwise have come about, namely, a deeper knowledge of aspects of His character and the possibility that people might reflect those aspects.

Affirming the good consequences which God salvages from sin differs not only from affirming sin, it differs from affirming the fall. God, being omniscient, foresaw the fall; and being omnipotent, He brought good from it. This is different from directly causing the fall in order to bring about greater good. God created the (good) conditions which made the fall possible. He foresaw the consequences and allowed it.

Some Mormon theology is an example of going a bit too far in affirming sin itself. According to Mormon Scripture, the fall made it possible for Adam and Eve to have children, thus making possible the human race. And, overemphasizing the need for opposites, Mormon theology says that the fall made possible both joy and moral goodness because it brought the experiences of misery and evil.[1] Because of opposites, the fall was necessary for salvation, according to Brigham Young.[2] Mormon theologian Victor Ludlow adds that without the fall humanity would have been like its first parents, innocent and inexperienced, "we would have been with him [God], but not like him, knowing and choosing 'good from evil.'"[3] Regarding Adam's sin, Mormon church President and Prophet Joseph Fielding Smith concluded, "This was a transgression of the law, but not a sin in the strict sense, for it was something that Adam and Eve had to do!"[4]

The first thing we want to remember (whatever Mormons believe or don't believe) is that there would have been procreation without a fall. Sex and procreation were, after all, God's idea.[5] Neither was the fall necessary for some indirect reason because sex and procreation were not dependent on any of the changes brought about by the fall. Furthermore, there is no reason to think that a person must sin in order to have full freedom of choice. God has freedom of choice without ever having sinned. So whatever "knowing good and evil" means (Gen. 3:22), it cannot require sinning. It implies authority to set up one's own standards of conduct, an authority that is rightfully God's, but which was usurped by man in the fall.

What the fall has done is make obvious the ugliness of sin and provide a stark contrast to holiness. Kahlil Gibran, occasionally profound, said, "I have learned silence from the talkative, toleration from the intolerant, and kindness from the unkind; yet strange, I am ungrateful to those teachers."[6]

Any benefits of the fall did not reduce the seriousness of the transgression. That God brought good out of the sin of the first humans is entirely different from the idea that their sin was unavoidable. Human sin is not excusable merely because God, in His wisdom and grace, brought good from it.

This greater good that God has brought – the fuller understanding of forgiveness and other attributes – depends not only on the presence of sin, but also on some pain on the part of creatures because sin results in genuine harm to both sinner and victim. When others sin against us we can suffer emotional and even physical pain, and losses of all types. Our own sin can bring a wounded conscience, the pain of a damaged relationship, and a sense of lost opportunity. Yet by God's grace and power, it can also bring about a fuller, experiential knowledge of God's forgiveness.

A world such as ours not only reveals qualities in God, it is the only environment in which we can develop some of those qualities in ourselves. Only in a sinful world can we develop forgiveness, for example. So we see God's virtues not only through His actions, we come to see them by developing those virtues in ourselves, thus further glorifying God by reflecting Him.

The Cost of Suffering

A young man I knew, Tim, worked at a market in a rather rough part of town to pay his way through college. One afternoon another checker appeared to be having trouble with a customer, so Tim went over to see if he could help. When he walked up, the customer suddenly pulled out a gun and shot him through the heart, killing him instantly. When the killer was caught, I wondered how his parents would handle it emotionally. But his father, a pastor at my church, went to the jail and told the man he forgave him, and that God offered him forgiveness too.

For all the tragedy that father faced, I envied him a little for his sharing in God's awesome power to forgive. But like anything else of value, it came at a high price.

Not everyone, though, is willing to forgive. In World War II, the Japanese defended a rock fortress against a fierce American onslaught. As the battle turned hopeless, the corridors of the fortress piled up with the bodies of Japanese soldiers determined to defend it to the end. Finally, the few remaining survivors surrendered. After the war, one of the survivors visited a house near his neighborhood where there lived a mother whose son had died in the same battle. But she refused to forgive the survivor for what she regarded as a betrayal of her son's honor. He never gave up seeking her forgiveness, going back to her house sometimes every day. But to the day of her death nearly twenty years later, she refused.

Sometimes forgiveness comes only with great struggle. Corrie Ten Boom, who was imprisoned in a Nazi concentration camp for her efforts to rescue Jews, recounted meeting one of the prison guards after the war. He had become a Christian, and she met him in a church. When he reached out to shake her hand, it took all she had to reach out and clasp it. A member of the Ten Booms' church later told how other Dutch Christians faced a similar struggle to accept German Christians into their fellowship after the war.[7]

Sometimes forgiveness is hard because sin wounds us so deeply; sin robs us of something. But when we forgive we accept the wound, refusing to make the guilty pay, not wounding back. When we forgive we come to know God a little deeper, we reflect His character a little better, and thus we allow others to know Him better too.

To get through graduate school, I worked for an airfreight company, loading and unloading cargo planes. A person who worked there had a way of imagining that people had wronged him, then mentally justifying his harming them in "retaliation." He would tamper with their cars by pouring water or sand in the gas tank, loosening clutch adjustment screws, and the like. Along with a number of other employees, I fell victim to his vicious imagination. Besides a rash of engine trouble, I had four tires slashed, and my brakes failed while I was driving (I was never sure whether it was sabotage). At the time I was dating Donna, my wife, who was also working there. Her car had trouble too, once leaving her stranded at rush hour in the busiest intersection in the city.

The cost of all this was mounting, and things were getting a little dangerous. Some friends in law enforcement told me how difficult it would be to do something about it legally. I concluded there was really nothing I could do. Some Christian friends offered some ethically unorthodox solutions, such as catching him alone and teaching him a lesson he would never forget. They themselves were eager to help. One of the more creative suggestions was to simply have someone follow him around for a few days to scare the wits out of him.

I had to conclude there was nothing I could do.

At that point I really felt the cost of forgiveness. I could not prevent him ravaging my precious time and money, nor jeopardizing my safety and Donna's. I had to forgive and simply do nothing. Furthermore, as I thought over my biblical responsibilities, I concluded I should treat him as kindly as possible, even pray for his good (Matt. 5:44). To show kindness and personal concern, I started to ask him every day how things were going, how his family was doing, and so on. It was hard to do, I admit.

As it turned out, God intervened in an ironic way because of my kindness. The employee somehow saw my innocent questions as veiled threats. When I asked how his day had gone, he thought I was trying to find out if a sinister plot against him had succeeded. When I would ask how his mother was doing, he suspected that I was plotting to harm her.

The first hint I got of his fears was that he began to shake when I asked innocent questions. Then one day, by coincidence (perhaps divinely ordained), I was across town and saw him driving next to me on the freeway. I waved and smiled, and he veered sharply to an off-ramp, nearly crashing into a concrete barrier and colliding with the car behind him. He told our employer that I had been following him and was trying to harm him. I was threatened with being fired if I did not leave him alone. I tried, without success, to explain that I had no intention of hurting him and had not been following him. Anyway, the incident scared him into leaving me alone. I took it as God intervening on my behalf because I had done it all by His rules.

The Varity of Virtues Revealed

The Bible predicts a future state when we will no longer know the pain of sin. Those who chose in this life to reflect God's forgiveness will forever know Him in a special way because they shared a part of His character – a part that would have been forever unmanifested had creation never been tainted by sin. Forgiveness is just one of the many facets of God that is known best, or at all, in a world with sin and pain. It is also just one of the virtues that people can develop only in a fallen world like ours.

So much of what we can now know of God would have gone undetected in a "perfect" world. Longsuffering, the ability to patiently endure repeated harm, can only be shown in a world where people harm others. Mercy can be shown only in the presence of suffering, both that aspect of mercy which desires to bring inner comfort as well as the aspect of mercy that shows willingness to intervene in order to improve the circumstances that caused the suffering. As well, compassion and sympathy can be expressed only in response to people's suffering.

Now and then I like to read a book or watch a documentary on war. As a microcosm of the darker side of our fallen world, war is horrible, but also fascinating. Seemingly ordinary people are put in situations in which they can do extraordinary things. Some people call on every ounce of their abilities, enduring unimaginable hardships, endangering their lives, and in some cases dying for a great cause. For others, war reveals weakness of character, cowardice, overbearing egos, and eagerness to profit from crisis and tragedy. In a "perfect" world, none of these unique opportunities to glorify God would exist, either by imitating His character in doing good, or by contrasting it through doing evil.

Besides virtues like forgiveness that would be all but unknown in a sinless world, there are other virtues that would be known but not as well. In a "perfect" world, we would still need patience to wait for something good; however, it would not take the same strength of character as waiting in the face of loneliness, depravation, hunger, pain, anguish over the well-being of a loved one, or other experiences that can make waiting so difficult.

Diligence would also be needed in a "perfect" world because there would still be good things to bring about, yet there would be no chance for suffering loss if we fail (unless perhaps it is the "loss" of achieving less than the very best). Our fallen world makes diligence all the more crucial, and thereby reveals its great value.

Kindness would still exist, but it could not be contrasted with cruelty, and there would be no pain resulting from the failure to be kind. Kindness in a fallen world is all the more gracious, all the more welcomed, all the more beautiful.

Self-control might exist, but there would be no tempting circumstances to overcome, and no disastrous consequences for us and others if we fail. Self-control in a fallen world is enhanced by a deeper understanding of the true nature of sin and righteousness, an understanding that sin is not worth it and is not what it seems. It takes sheer determination to be obedient and not cross the boundaries God has set for our lives even when we cannot see the reasons He has set those limits.

Some special qualities are virtues in us only in an indirect way. For example, faith is not so much a virtue in us as it is our willingness to acknowledge virtue in God: that He is reliable, truthful, and unfailingly holy. An otherwise sinful person can have faith in God because faith is merely a matter of recognizing and acting on God's righteousness. In this sense faith is unlike other character qualities, such as diligence, which you must have within yourself because it is not merely acknowledging a good quality within another person (some qualities, like longsuffering, even require that you acknowledge the sin of another). It is no surprise that God ordained that faith should be the hand that accepts salvation because it requires no other virtue on the part of the sinner. It simply points to God's virtue, giving Him all the glory (Eph. 2:8-9). Of course, faith can also exist in a godly person, alongside other virtues (and usually that is how it is found).

Humility is another quality that is a virtue only in an indirect sense. It is merely an awareness and admission of our true abilities and place. A humble person has a grasp on his sinfulness (though perhaps no one can ever know its depths) and limitations. But he also realistically grasps his abilities. For example, to be humble, the best pitcher in the sport need not regard himself as less than the best. But he should not think of himself as the best if someone else is better. And he must recognize God as the giver of all talent.

These special, indirect virtues would still exist in a "perfect" world, but they can be honed in a unique way in our sort of world, where for instance lack of faith can bring serious consequences, as can pride. Presumably, in a perfect world, faith takes less will-power because God's presence is obvious (as it was to Adam). In the case of heaven, we shall know God more immediately, the way we now know others. The chance to grow strong in faith when God is not so obvious will by then be gone. A world where God seems hidden is the best place for growing the strongest in faith. Presumably, too, humility will be easy to manifest where God is so clearly known – but it will be even easier for us to exercise humility having gone through this world, where our weaknesses and failings were made so obvious.

Our world, then, is a good place for growing strong faith and true humility.

We could add that even divine attributes that would be well known in an unfallen world can be known better in a fallen one. In a sinless world we would see, for example, omnipotence in the process of creation; but we see more facets of omnipotence in a fallen world, where God's power to deal decisively with evil is also revealed. John Milton captures this in Paradise Lost, where Satan and his angels rebelled in part because they did not fully realize God's power: "...his strength conceal'd [sic], which tempted our attempt, and wrought our fall. Henceforth his might we know..."[8]

Though God is glorious in an unfallen world, He is more clearly so in a fallen one.

In Defense of Fallen-World Virtues

It might be objected that if the world had none of the flaws we know so well, there would be no value in developing such virtues as forgiveness and mercy, since there would be no need for them – that they are needed only where sin exists. On this view, it would have been better had God not allowed a fall so that we could have skipped developing these virtues altogether. The view depends on the idea that these virtues have little or no intrinsic value, that they are not good in and of themselves, but only insofar as they produce something else that is good (in this case, the ability to live successfully in a fallen world). So, it is said, developing them is not worth the price of God allowing a fall.

But is it really the case that virtues that are displayed only in the presence of sin have no intrinsic value? As we have seen, they do show us facets of God's nature that would otherwise be undiscovered (or known only vaguely, in the most abstract terms). And if the fullest possible revelation of God is the highest value of the universe, it is worth the loss of good things of lesser value, such as the greatest moment by moment happiness of every being.

So the losses resulting from sin are more than worthwhile because of the preeminent value of knowing God so much more fully. Paul makes this point when he compares the gain of knowing God with the loss of things most people would value. Paul said, "I count all things to be loss in view of the surpassing value of knowing Christ Jesus my Lord, for whom I have suffered the loss of all things, and count them but rubbish in order that I may gain Christ" (Phil. 3:8). He had no regrets whatsoever over the price he paid for knowing God better. If God is Himself the nexus of highest value, and knowing Him is our highest good, then that is what will bring us the greatest fulfillment. It will far surpass the lesser, fleeting pleasures of a world without pain and evil.

The Benefit of Variety

A long tradition in theology holds that there is value in greater variety, in "plenitude." Aquinas said that because two natures are better than one, a universe that contains angels as well as other kinds of things is better than one containing only angels.[9] Of course, this does not mean that variety of any kind is valuable, otherwise we would have to say that greater varieties of evil are good in and of themselves. But variety is good where it results in fuller revelation of God, and in bringing about other good things, such as the formation of God's character in man.

Some virtues that can be cultivated only in a world such as ours have no exact counterpart in God. It may appear that they have no value in revealing God or molding us to be like Him. It may appear that we therefore can do without them. But a closer look reveals that they too have value and are worth the price of a fallen world. Courage, for example, consists of commitment to duty despite threat of loss, harm, or death. God, of course, can experience no such threat. Being the owner of all, He can experience no loss; and being immaterial and eternal, He can suffer no physical harm or death. Yet courage is based on another quality: the willingness to sacrifice for the good of another or for what is right in principle. In that broader sense God the Father showed a willingness to sacrifice for the salvation of people. And it is not surprising that Christ incarnate, who existed in a form in which He could experience loss and death, was a man of great courage.

Virtues such as frugality and prudence are valuable only in a world with limited resources. It could be objected that there is no intrinsic value to such virtues since God need not have made a world with the sort of limits we have in ours. Suppose, for example, that He supplied inexhaustible resources of water, food, clean air, fuel, and so on. It might seem that the cost of developing these virtues is unnecessary. To see that these virtues, too, are worth the price, we can consider that in a finite universe no physical thing could be in limitless supply without God's continual intervention. He would have to create resources, such as food, on the spot. But this would have the undesirable effect of robbing the world of its predictability, and predictability is essential for developing any virtue. But there is another benefit to limited resources.

Human Limitations, God's Limitlessness

The limited resources in a world such as ours forces us to formulate priorities and live by them. At the heart of priorities are judgments about what is more and less valuable. This gives us the opportunity for another layer of virtue: having priorities that reflect God's. Although He does not have limited resources, He still has a hierarchy of values (He values human life over animal life, for example).

We are forced to prioritize wherever there are limits, which means we need to have priorities for just about everything. Every individual and every organization has to decide how to use money according to what is most important. Our community has been through some droughts in the past decade, which has required them to set some priorities on uses of water. In severe drought years washing cars and watering gardens is restricted because water is needed for drinking. To emphasize the need to have proper priorities with respect to time, an academic dean at a Christian school displayed a cartoon of a young man watching television until the wee hours of the morning. From a mess of tipped cans and spilled popcorn, he looked up, eyes bloodshot, and said, "I sure wish I knew the Bible better!"

Some of God's attributes, such as omniscience, omnipotence, and omnipresence, could never be attained by a creature in any world, whether that world has evil or not. They are the very things that separate His nature from ours, and unlike other divine qualities, we are never commanded to imitate them. But a world such as ours (as well as many worlds unlike ours) provides the backdrop against which to understand and appreciate the vastness of God. The limited aspects of our own existence enable us to understand the limitless nature of His. Because we can bring about some things that we desire, we can understand in a very small way His omnipotence. We can also understand God by contrast, realizing that His power has none of the limits of our power. And though we will never approach omnipotence, we can expand our abilities and power and use them to do good. So the limited nature of our power helps us to understand God, both by its faint reflection and by its contrast.

The same holds for omniscience in that we as humans can understand truth in a limited way, providing both a faint reflection of His knowledge and a contrast to its limitlessness. And we can use that knowledge to glorify Him by understanding the world and appreciating its creator, as well as by using knowledge to act as He would, fulfilling our role as image bearers, thereby glorifying Him.

Omnipresence is unique in that we cannot imitate it by growing in our spacial presence. We exist in a limited space, and in that our nature provides a contrast to God's. We can expand our presence only indirectly, by expanding our influence.

Our limits as they relate to these three attributes (limits that are unavoidable for any creature in any world, fallen or not) can be a source of frustration, a type of pain. By nature, we cannot bring about anything we choose; we will always have a sense of our limits, and a need to submit our will to God's. We will always have less-than-perfect knowledge, consequently less-than-perfect ability to understand our circumstances, our future, and the results of our actions. We will always be dependent on God's complete knowledge.

The frustrations arising from these limits of our nature are overcome, at least as a source of irritation and unwanted consequences, by dependence and trust in One with an infinite nature. Insofar as the frustrations arising from our limits are intensified in a world with pain and evil, our world can be a good environment for driving us to submit to God and depend on Him. Without the possibility of bad consequences arising from such things as acting apart from divine aid, from only our finite powers and mere human knowledge, we would not be driven to God for the advantages of His limitless abilities. We can never replace God or prosper without Him, and if we try, this type of world is a good one for making our failure to depend on Him painfully obvious.

Making Wise Choices

In practical terms, we must realize that a world of pain and evil presents to us merely the opportunity to benefit; whether we actually benefit depends on our attitudes. Being morally free, we can make the wrong choices, and lose the chance to gain what can be gotten only in a fallen world. We can fail, for example, to forgive someone who has sinned against us. That failure limits, even if slightly, our knowledge of God and the chance to reflect His character. So it is with other virtues, such as mercy, sacrifice, diligence, patience, kindness, gentleness, and self-control. A string of such failures can add up to a great loss indeed.

I once knew a man who suffered one setback after another, for years. One of the things he had to deal with was a medical condition that left him with serious pain continually, requiring him to use a cane and sometimes a walker. I asked him how he responded to all of it. His main concern and prayer was that he learn what he needed from each setback, so that God wouldn't have him repeat the lesson. Needless to say, he grew a great deal, and when I met him years later, he was as kindhearted and giving as he was longsuffering. He and his wife were using all their resources to care for a child whose own parent could no longer deal with the boy's paralyzing nerve condition.

To me, one of the saddest passages in Scripture depicts the future for those Christians who have failed to benefit from this life's unique opportunities. It pictures our life's work being tested by a fire that burns up everything of no value. For some, it will be a time of great loss. We are told, "If any man's work is burned up, he shall suffer loss; but he himself shall be saved, yet so as through fire" (1 Cor. 3:15). Salvation, being a gift, is secure; but rewards depend on what we have done. For some it will be like coming home to a dream house they spent a lifetime building only to find it burned to the ground, nothing left. It is frighteningly possible for a true Christian to waste much of his or her life on worthless things, such as personal comfort, selfish ambitions, and mere temporal goals. What should be a time of rejoicing over efforts that last into eternity may instead be a time of experiencing some level of awareness of wasted opportunity.[10] (Some think that we will be unaware of any loss of reward.[11]) Even if we are aware, however, that sense will no doubt fade in the glories of heaven and God's presence.

Paul says, "we must all appear before the judgment seat of Christ, so that each one may be recompensed for his deeds in the body, according to what he has done, whether good or bad" (2 Cor. 5:10). The "bad" deeds are those that are essentially worthless, or good for nothing (φαῦλος; also committed by the unsaved, John 5:29), as opposed to those which are good through and through (ἀγαθός).

Those who make good use of this life, including its pains and evils, will find great reward. Part of that reward, as valuable as precious metal purified by fire, is a deeper knowledge of God gained by a life focused on Him. It requires such things as forgiving those who wrong us, having mercy on the suffering, being diligent and faithful, trusting God, and having an accurate view of ourselves. Through all this we shape our own character while gaining deeper insight into His, thereby glorifying Him.

What we need in order to gain these precious virtues, James tells us (James 1:2-4), is endurance, the ability to keep on keeping on, without getting bitter or giving up. And that comes, he says, through successfully dealing with life's trials. When we keep bearing the hard things, we develop other virtues. If anyone cannot see how endurance produces virtue and its fruits, or cannot see the value of maturity itself, James tells him to pray for the wisdom to be able to see it (v. 5).

In the context, he makes clear a crucial point about a fallen world: even though good things may result if we respond properly to trials, the source of inner solicitation to do evil never comes from God (v. 13). The inner pull to do evil comes from ourselves (v. 14). God, however, can allow us to be tempted in order to give us the opportunity to choose rightly and to grow thereby, glorifying Him. Jesus Himself was impelled (Mark 1:12, ἐκβάλλω) into the wilderness by the Spirit to be tempted by the devil (Matt. 4:1; Mark. 1:13). But in light of the very real possibility of our failure under temptation, He later included in His example of a disciple's prayer the petition to "lead us not into temptation, but deliver us from evil" (Matt. 6:13).

A Divine Enablement

God is working with us, and in us, to enable us to make moral choices. He is causing us to want to do and enabling us to actually do His will

(Phil. 2:13). Of course His action does not eliminate our part. He gives direction and power, but to some extent we can switch off His power. Such habitual disobedience grieves the Spirit (Eph. 4:30), the source of power in our lives (Gal. 5:16). Yet God can apply outside pressure, through discipline in all its forms, to encourage us to obey.

He has not allowed the world to become a place of pain and suffering while remaining distant and uninvolved, hoping some good will come of it all. One thing He has done is use processes on various levels to bend the human will, ultimately allowing us to benefit if we respond positively. Divine confrontation of our will is itself the source of a good bit of pain in this world.

The Gift of Conscience

The first divine road sign warning us to turn off the path of sin is our conscience. We all know only too well that built-in awareness of wrongdoing. Our conscience does not come perfectly formed, but is a product of what we put in, and how we respond to its leadings. Consequently, it can be less than perfect. There are people who feel guilty when they do things that are not wrong, like stepping on cracks in the sidewalk. Over the years a few students at the college where I teach have told me that they feel it is wrong to allow any book to lie on top of the Bible because it is disrespectful to God's Word, in that it implies that there is some authority higher than it. My own view is that there is really nothing wrong with having a book on top of the Bible (I sometimes quip that if I had any such view I would say the Bible should be on the bottom of every stack of books as the foundation of knowledge!). A conscience that makes a person feel guilty over something that is not really wrong is underdeveloped in that it is making inaccurate judgments.

In the early church, some with overly sensitive consciences did not want to eat meat sacrificed to idols. Paul said that doing so was not really a sin, but that those who realize that have to make allowances for those who do not (Rom. 14:15, 21).

More typically, though, our consciences are not sensitive enough. When we wander into sin we are unaware of it. Others who are more mature, can perhaps see our mistake, but our conscience gives us no warning.

To grow a conscience that accurately reflects God's ideas of right and wrong, we have to give close attention to biblical and moral instruction, listen to godly counsel, and do everything we currently know to be right. I find it helps to spend devotional time thinking over some simple moral principle, such as kindness, or diligence. As I do so, I realize there are things I can do better. At the end of the day I'll reflect on how I did, the things I said, my attitudes, and how I used my time, opportunities, and spiritual gifts. For me, such frequent reflection helps me to draw the guidelines of right and wrong closer to where God has them, though I'm sure I am still off in a lot of places.

The Provision of Counsel

If we continue down the road of disobedience by ignoring warning signs from our conscience (assuming we know something is wrong), then we may cross another warning sign, put there by someone who can see that there is a problem. We can avoid needless mistakes and the suffering they bring by making sure we are close to one or more mature persons who can point things out to us. The book of Proverbs warns that someone who has only shallow friends will come to ruin (Prov. 18:24). These friends add nothing of value to our life, such as reproof. When we do get reproof, even if it comes from someone we would rather not listen to for whatever reason (we suspect their motives, regard them as unnecessarily hostile, or some other reason), we must be careful to consider it and heed it if we judge it to be valid.

Proverbs also tells us that listening to good advice will bring prosperity (16:20) and security (1:33), and is both a sign of wisdom (13:1) and the way to get more wisdom (19:20; 15:31). A true friend is straight with us even if it hurts (27:6), and a wise person appreciates that (9:8; 28:23). If we fail to take reproof to heart we will get into trouble (13:13; 19:27), and eventually be ruined (1:27; 15:10; 28:9; 29:1).

Just last week I heard about three teenagers who were in a serious traffic accident in my area. Two were killed and the third is in critical condition. It sounded like another random tragedy, the sort that makes people wonder how a good God could be in control of things. Then I heard that the accident was caused by the driver recklessly speeding. So I was told that his death was, to put it bluntly, his own fault. But what about his passenger? I found out that he had disobeyed clear instructions from both his parents not to be in a car with that driver. Had the driver obeyed the law, or had the young man obeyed his parents, the outcome would have been very different.

Farther down the road, past the warning signs of conscience and counsel, we are likely to encounter a road block in the form of some troubling circumstances. Disobedience brings trouble because God set up the world that way (Prov. 11:19, et al.)

The Restraining Influence of Laws

Laws can offer the next level of restraint. In a just society, those who commit grosser sins get punished, and hopefully, they reform because of it. Besides criminal laws, various codes prevent irresponsibility and abuses of all types, from shoddy construction to unhealthful storage of food in restaurants. In addition, the civil courts allow for private redress of wrongs.

On a spiritual level, God can abandon those who stubbornly choose to ignore all warnings and consequences. This can come either as a final form of chastening aimed at bringing repentance (1 Cor. 5:5), or as purely judgment. A chilling description of this moral God-forsakenness is found in Romans chapter one. Lacking any restraint (something rooted in God's grace), sin becomes rampant in the abandoned person's life, and the sin brings its own damage. Therefore, wrongdoing receives some kind of punishment even if only internal.

While discipline has reform as its primary aim, punishment does not. Those who have accepted God's forgiveness by accepting His sacrifice for sin are special objects of His love, and therefore get His correction (Heb. 12:7, 10, 11). Nevertheless, they too will get the consequences of what they have done. Paul warned the Thessalonians, whom he did not doubt were Christians, not to engage in sexual immorality because "God is the avenger of all such" (1 Thess. 4:6).

Divine justice and willingness to punish sin are part of the nature of God which can best be known only against a backdrop of sin. Had no being ever sinned, this significant part of God's nature would have remained obscure. Like forgiveness, it would have been known only abstractly, if at all. In a fallen world, divine righteousness can be seen more clearly because of its stark contrast with evil, divine love and forgiveness are put on brilliant display, and God's determined opposition to evil can be more fully revealed as well.

Turning from Shadows to Light

Understanding the unique benefits of our imperfect world helps us a great deal, but still, living in it is not easy. Sickness still drains vitality and even life itself, sin still causes real harm, and we still grieve over our own failings. Often, godfearing, productive people die young, while the wicked are allowed to carry on for years. Missionary David Brainard died at age thirty, chaplain Peter Marshall died at forty-seven, Oswald Chambers at forty-three, and German theologian and pastor Dietrich Bonhoeffer at thirty-nine. On the other hand, Manasseh, one of the wickedest rulers of Israel, began to reign at twelve years old and continued for the next fifty-five years. He led the nation disastrously astray, building altars to an idol, burning his own son to death, and filling the city of Jerusalem with innocent blood (2 Kings 21).

We cannot always draw obvious correlations between suffering or evil, and the good things they produce. That is partly because people do not always respond as they should and therefore they do not always benefit from the opportunities presented by suffering and evil. Two recent news reports remind me of a number like them I have heard over the years. A woman was kidnaped, fighting and screaming, from a busy mall while no one tried to help her. She was taken to a field and repeatedly raped, then stabbed. Only much later did someone decide to get involved enough to report what they had seen, and the victim's body was found. In another report, a private plane crash-landed on a golf course, and a crowd gathered to look. The people all stood around merely watching, except for one person who desperately tried to free the victims, all the while calling to the bystanders to help him. Working alone, he succeeded in pulling both people from the wreckage just before it burst into flames. He alone had acted heroically.

A couple of weeks ago at our church I met the mother and stepfather of a young man, Chris, whom I had heard about in the news several years ago. He was participating in a science experiment at school which was supposed to shoot a tennis ball out of a pipe and into the air. In the procedure, highly flammable liquid was to be poured into the tube and lit, but the person pouring it did not know there was already a flame in the tube. The liquid exploded, splattering several students. Chris was badly burned from the waist up. Fortunately he instinctively closed his eyes in time to save his sight. For several days it was unknown whether he would ever be able to talk again, as his vocal cords were burned by the flash of searing heat. What followed was years of reconstructive surgery, in which even what was left of his nose had to be cut off and reconstructed using skin from his scalp.

Yet his mother told me that through it he never complained, never said he wished it hadn't happened, and never fell into self-pity or depression. He just kept dealing with life as it came, and pushed ahead. Once he said, "It wasn't the end of the world; not even close." Six years and thirty-five surgeries later he is now well along in college, and determined to make a contribution. I have no doubt this remarkable young man will do just that.

Along his difficult journey, Chris met a young man who had been similarly burned about the same time at another school, by the same experiment. I was told that he, however, has (understandably) had a very difficult time emotionally.

This fallen world abounds in opportunities for determination or capitulation, forgiveness or bitterness, sacrifice or self-centeredness, heroism or cowardice, and a thousand other choices. Only in a fallen world can we grow to reflect God's own character in these special ways, or, by failing to do so, can we glorify Him by contrast. And only in a fallen world can we see those parts of His character which would go unrevealed were it not for the shadows – shadows which will someday disappear in the bright light of His presence.

GOING FARTHER

1. What qualities in God do we know only because of the sin, falleness, and limitations of this world?

2. What qualities in God do you cherish most? How do you know them better because of this fallen world?

3. Which character qualities can be developed only in a fallen world?

4. When have you personally had the chance to further develop character qualities that cannot be formed without the presence of sin?

5. What character qualities can we develop in a fallen world that have no counterpart in God?

6. How do the limited resources of this world help us form character?

7. In what sense are the conditions of this life only opportunities?

8. How has God guided you through conscience, counsel, and laws?

9. Why is it difficult to see a correlation between suffering and the good things it can produce?

NOTES

1. 2 Nephi 2:23. "And they would have had no children; wherefore they would have remained in a state of innocence, having no joy, for they knew no misery; doing no good, for they knew no sin." Eve supposedly says, "Were it not for our transgression, we never should have had seed, and never should have known good and evil, and the joy of our redemption, and the eternal life which God giveth unto all the obedient" (*Pearl of Great Price*, Moses 5:11). Regarding opposites, "For it must needs be, that there is an opposition in all things. If not so, my first-born in the wilderness, righteousness could not be brought to pass, neither wickedness, neither holiness nor misery, neither good nor bad. Wherefore, all things must needs be a compound in one..." (2 Nephi 2:11).

2. *Discourses of Brigham Young*, 2nd. ed., pp. 157-8; quoted in Joseph Fielding Smith, *Doctrines of Salvation: Sermons and Writings of Joseph Fielding Smith*, Compiled by Bruce R. McConkie (Salt Lake City: Bookcraft, 1954), 112-3.

3. Victor L. Ludlow, *Principles and Practices of the Restored Gospel* (Salt Lake City: Deseret, 1992), 186.

4. Joseph Fielding Smith, *Doctrines of Salvation*, 1:115. Regarding J. F. Smith's authority, McConkie refers to his teaching as having the "authoritative finality of the oracles of God" (ibid., Preface, v.).

5. J. F. Fielding Smith did not believe that Adam's transgression [note his use of the term] involved sex (*Doctrines of Salvation*, 1:114-5).

6. Kahlil Gibran, "Sand and Foam," quoted in Langenscheidt's *Pocket Merriam-Webster Guide to Quotations* (New York, NY: Langenscheidt, 2002), 128.

7. Hans Poley, *Return to the Hiding Place* (Elgin, IL: LifeJourney Books, 1993), 193. On his own struggle to forgive, see pages 192-5.

8. John Milton, *Paradise Lost* 1.641-43

9. *Summa Contra Gentiles*, III, 71; cited in, Arthur O. Lovejoy, *The Great Chain of Being: A Study of the History of an Idea* (New York: Harper Torchbooks, 1936), 77.

10. G. G. Findlay, "St. Paul's First Epistle to the Corinthians," in *The Expositor's Greek Testament*, ed. W. Robertson Nicoll (reprint; Grand Rapids, MI: Eerdmans, 1979), 2:792. He quotes with apparent approval, J. A. Beet's *St. Paul's Epistle to the Corinthians* (1882), "He rushes out through the flame, leaving behind the ruin of his work...for which, proved to be worthless, he receives no pay."

11. For example, Millard J. Erickson, *Christian Theology* (three vols. republished as one; Grand Rapids, MI: Baker, 1983-85), 1234.

Chapter six

A JUST WORLD

The topic of God's justice has been unpopular since the nineteenth century, when it was thought that God is too loving to punish people. It was held that the desire to punish is a weakness, an impulse born of revenge. God must be above that sort of thing. It was said that the idea of God punishing people comes from projecting our weaknesses on Him. Instead, He must be the most perfectly loving father, and all humans must be in His family. The Fatherhood of God and the brotherhood of man became something of a slogan.

As the concept of divine justice was fading from society a similar fate was befalling the notion that right and wrong is objective. In May 1919, astronomers photographed a solar eclipse, and in the process they confirmed Albert Einstein's prediction about the way light would bend. Other experiments confirmed his theory of relativity, and in the popular mind that confirmed that everything – including ethics – is relative (a conclusion which dismayed Einstein).

About that time Freud was reinterpreting the conscience, which had always been regarded as a sure source of knowing right from wrong. He regarded the conscience as the product of inner turmoil and forces that even the individual himself cannot understand. He further claimed that we cannot untangle our motives for wanting to do what we think is right.

Marxism burst into power in Russia, preaching a similar message. The world is not as it seems, but is the product of hidden, largely economic, forces that engulf society and the individual, controlling how we think and act, including how we view right and wrong.

The loss of objectivity sent shock waves through culture. Even novels were no longer about responsible living and its consequences. Art, too, revolted against objectivity in the Dada movement and Surrealism, which featured, for example, Salvador Dali's watches melted over landscapes.

In earlier eras – more barbaric to modern thinking – God was seen as not only an objective reality but also just, a father but also a judge who upholds a universal moral code. Accordingly, we should do what is right if for no other reason than that God sees all and will punish the wicked. It's not surprising that the twentieth century, which spawned regimes that abandoned any ultimate basis for justice, was mankind's bloodiest by far.

So much of mankind now lives in tension. People want to condemn things like racism and genocide, but lack a transcendent basis for doing so (that is, they lack a basis that goes beyond the temporal world of material objects, human opinion, and so on). They would like to think that their sense of justice amounts to more than mere preferences of theirs or their culture's, yet their worldview won't permit it. Without affirming a holy God, sin amounts to little more than a violation of public opinion, transgressing whatever the majority says is wrong. Or, for those bent toward pragmatism and survival, sin is something that jeopardizes the stability of society and thus the survival of the race, or at most, the survival of all living things (although they have no transcendent reason for preferring survival to extinction).

C. S. Lewis observed that removing objectivity from sin and its punishment, turning sin into something like an illness rather than a immoral choice, destroys human dignity. It also exposes society to the manipulations of a self-appointed elite who want to mold behavior into what they consider ideal.[1]

For those who deny the existence of a righteous God but still want to ground morals in natural law (the view that right and wrong is dictated by the way things are rather than something else, like opinion), immorality can be little more than a lack of prudence, that is, living in a way that is harmful to one's self or one's society.

It is interesting to see the shift in thinking reflected in films. In films made about the time of World War II, for example, the main character would often make a speech about how it was worth fighting for values like equality and freedom. These essential principles were regarded as something bigger than the character, bigger even than society. The implication was that they are the grounding for society – even though by then the idea that the values themselves are grounded in God had largely faded. The hero often made it clear these values are worth dying for, and that conviction is partly what made the person a hero.

Most modern films, however, lack any sense of something transcendent. Characters in war films for example, are frequently motivated by personal things rather than universal things. Often it is an emotion. In *Rambo* that emotion is the desire to avenge the death of a friend. In *Uncommon Valor* a grieving father organizes a desperate search for the son he believes is still held captive in Vietnam after the war.

In films of the 1990s some principles appear, but for the most part they are vague and disconnected from a worldview. Rather than being something transcendent, the principles are essentially a personal matter and therefore a likely source of conflict with other characters who happen to prefer different principles. Forrest Gump, for example, is an individual who operates on simple kindness – but not because it is a duty or transcendent moral obligation; it's just his nature. His ways at times lead him into conflict with others, who have different personalities. Kindness does win out, but it is not a victory for any ultimate values; it's just that Gump is so nice. In *Saving Private Ryan*, the official military policy of saving a family's sole surviving son becomes a matter of contention among the characters.

What is missing from the modern mind is any sense that there are principles that transcend human feelings, opinions, or conventions, that morals and ultimately life are grounded in something higher than ourselves. The modern worldview lacks a God who not only loves and forgives, but also judges. His character is the ground of right action, and He sees to it that eventually people get what they deserve, good or bad. That means some people suffer because they deserve to suffer. No wonder suffering is especially baffling to the modern mind. Rare indeed is the pop-culture hero who champions a great cause that is grounded in something more than whatever happens to provide an advantage to the human race.

As the objectivity of right and wrong have faded from the culture, a clear sense of justice has also faded from the minds of many Christians. No wonder few Christians appreciate the complexity of divine justice.

A further problem is that we Christians fall into a universal human tendency to make everything as simple as possible, yet so often it is complexity and nuance that make the world decipherable. Consider the subtleties of divine justice. It can be immanent, working through natural processes, or it can be transcendent, something God does more directly. It can be swift, or delayed for years in order to give a person time to repent. If delayed, the wrongdoer can go on hurting others. Meanwhile, the righteous can suffer, which in some cases God allows in order to prevent them from falling into sin, as well as to make them more mature. The timing of deliverance or punishment can be linked to the hidden timetable of God's dealings with individuals, families, groups, nations, or the whole human race.

When we oversimplify God's ways we are like the man whose wife asked him what the sermon was about that Sunday. "It was about sin," he said. "Well... what did the pastor say about it?" she probed. After a brief silence, the man said, "He was against it."

Going deeper to grasp the nuances of God's justice, while not removing its mysteries, will give us confidence to face the world's harsher realities from the perspective of faith.

The Hiddenness of Divine Justice

God's justice is not always easy to detect. We tend to expect justice to come from on high, apart from normal natural processes. The classic image of justice is a lightening bolt. It is sudden and dramatic, seemingly from heaven, but above all it is unconnected to the normal workings of things.

God can indeed work apart from natural processes. Miracles are the most extreme examples, where God works outside the natural order of things. But God also works in a wide range of ways, from those unconnected to normal natural processes to those entirely in and through natural processes (what theologians would call immanently). Take healing, for example. In the New Testament we see God healing in miraculous ways, giving sight to a person immediately, or making a handicapped person suddenly walk. But God can also heal through medicine and the body's natural processes. When God heard Hezekiah's plea to extend his life, he was healed through a fig poultice that God told him to put on his boil (2 Kings 20:7). It was a common ancient treatment for such things. Both can be considered the workings of God. The same range of divine action can be seen in His justice.

Immanent Justice

God can bring justice in supernatural, obvious ways. Herod was speaking to a crowd which began flattering him, calling him a god. The Bible says, "he did not give God the glory, and he was eaten by worms and died" (Acts 12:23). Those who rebelled against Moses' leadership were suddenly killed when the ground opened up and swallowed them, then two-hundred and fifty of those who should not have been burning incense were burned up (Num. 16:31-33, 35). Ananias and Sapphira were also judged instantly for their sin (Acts 5).

People somehow think that if God is working it will be obvious in that extremely unlikely things will happen. When I used to work as an ambulance attendant, I noticed that the sight of an ambulance affected people very differently. For some, it represented help and was a comforting sight. But it struck fear in the hearts of others. I remember one person who shook uncontrollably when he saw us parked. Being curious, I struck up a conversation with him and asked about his obvious strong reaction. The ambulance made him think of sudden injury and the inevitability of death. After a little probing, he admitted that he related this fear to a vague sense of a righteous God who will hold him accountable for his sins, and who might strike him down at any time.

Divine actions are obvious when God works through things that would not normally happen. But He can also work more subtly, and more often does. Since this is harder to recognize, it is common to think He is not working at all. Hence people do not see much of God's justice. As we have seen, a major theme in Proverbs is that God has woven justice into the fabric of the world. In general terms, the righteous are rewarded and the wicked suffer. Yet it takes discernment to see such things.

I knew a man in law enforcement who struggled because it seemed to him that so many criminals get away with doing incalculable harm to people. I pointed out though that the human justice system is only a small part of divine justice. Those who harm others, I suggested, typically suffer internally with such things as an accusing conscience, inner turmoil, a very negative view of themselves, and a constant fear of prison or of retribution from those they have harmed. Thinking a moment, he agreed, recalling his surveillance on criminals and the glimpse it provides of their often tortured minds. He found them typically nervous, suspicious, and fearful. Some have trouble carrying on relationships or even getting a good night's sleep. And some can't so much as make a routine trip to the store without doubling back, careening down alleys, and doing other bizarre things to avoid being followed.

I have met people who gave up a life of crime, never having been caught though committing a number of felonies each month. They had escaped the criminal justice system yet it was obvious to me that they had not escaped the internal damage their actions caused (though the ones who turned to God experienced slow inner healing). The results of doing evil can be hardened self-centeredness, lack of inner peace, insensitivity to good, and an perpetual awareness of being evil and guilty.

Of course criminal activity is only a very small category of all possible wrong doing. Other sins, too, have their consequences – which further shows that the universe is the handiwork of a just God. A number of sins have physical consequences, as the Bible has long attested and as modern medicine has discovered. Fear and anxiety, anger, jealousy, bitterness, and loneliness are some of the emotions that can take a heavy toll on our health. David spoke of the high cost of hiding his sin, probably referring to his adultery with Bathsheba and bringing about her husband's death: "When I kept silent about my sin, my body wasted away through my groaning all day long.... My vitality was drained away as with the fever heat of summer" (Ps. 32:3-4).

There are also consequences for specific sins, such as the sin of lack of self-control. For Americans, the most common health problems and leading causes of death can be brought on in some cases by eating habits. Heart attacks, the leading killer, account for nearly one third of all deaths. Strokes are the third leading cause of death, and diabetes is the seventh.[2] Weight reduction is recommended for over half the population,[3] and obesity related health problems are said to cost $117 billion dollars a year.

In the United States, about one in twenty deaths, and about 40 per cent of hospital admissions are alcohol related (incurring medical costs of $116 billion a year).[4] Half of all cigarette smokers will suffer disability or death from their habit, amounting to 440,000 deaths in the United States each year (one in five deaths), and costing $150 billion.[5] Smoking deaths worldwide amount to four million a year, which is expected to reach ten million by 2030.[6] Illicit drug use in the U.S. alone can kill over 19,000 in one year.[7]

In the world there are about a third of a billion new cases of the top four sexually transmitted infections (there are more than twenty such infections). Fifteen percent of all infertile women became that way because of a sexually transmitted infection.[8] There are about forty million cases of AIDS worldwide, two and a half million of which are under the age of fifteen. There are five million new cases a year, or about 14,000 a day.[9]

Sins can have external as well as internal consequences. Prolonged anger, for example, can damage our bodies but it also has serious consequences on our relationships. A problem with anger can destroy a marriage, damage children emotionally, cause us to lose our job, and can ruin a church.

I knew of a pastor who struggled with his temper. Try as he might to encourage his flock, meet with leaders, finesse the church budget, support the youth group, or whatever, he could not get past the damage caused by his temper. Had his struggle been in any number of other areas he would not have damaged his ministry nearly as much. Had he been depressed, for example, few would have even known about it. But raising his voice at elder's meetings, and at a mild-mannered church woman in a busy parking lot worked to erode the credibility he needed to lead and to solve the church's challenging problems. Attendance dwindled and he eventually left.

It is very difficult for someone else to step in and buffer such a person from the damage caused by his actions. In the case of a problem temper, for example, Proverbs warns, "A man of great anger shall bear the penalty, for if you rescue him, you will only have to do it again" (Prov. 19:19).

Proverbs warns of specific consequences of many sins. For example, a number of sins are said to lead to poverty: laziness (10:4, 13:14), drunkenness and gluttony (23:21), love of pleasure (21:17), and doing useless things instead of working (28:19). Gains made deceitfully will vanish (21:6), and ignoring instruction will lead to poverty and shame (13:18). The mouth of the wicked can destroy a city (11:11), but in turn the unfaithful are destroyed by their duplicity (11:13). The wicked will bow before the righteous (14:19), they are trapped by their own sinful talk (12:13), their own ways lead them astray (12:26), they are filled with fearfulness (28:1), what they fear will overtake them (10:24), calamity will destroy them (14:32), and their "house" will be destroyed (14:11). The person who refuses continual reproof "will suddenly be broken beyond remedy" (29:1). Rebellion against parents is also terminal, "The eye that mocks a father and scorns a mother, the ravens of the valley will pick it out, and the young eagles will eat it" (30:17).

While laziness has consequences, usually leading to poverty, there are exceptions. Occasionally we hear of a person who doesn't want to work winning the lottery. I remember hearing of one man who found out he had won the lottery while he was betting at the race track, where he could spend much of his time because he was living on welfare. All of this can baffle anyone who expects God's justice to always be swift and obvious.

We can learn a lot about God's timetable from what He revealed to Abraham about His just dealings. After telling him that his descendants will be afflicted in Egypt for four hundred years, He says that judgment will come on the oppressors and that Israel will come out with great wealth (Gen. 15:14). However, the deliverance must wait because "the iniquity of the Amorite is not yet complete" (Gen. 15:16). In the words of commentator Keil, they were "not yet ripe for the sentence of extermination."[10] God would wait four more centuries in order to give the people either more time to repent or to do enough evil to warrant crushing them. In the meantime, God would not be deaf to the sufferings of His people, but would deliver them in due time, making up for their having been slaves by allowing them to plunder their Egyptian oppressors. This is a glimpse of God's long term planning on just one issue.

We can only imagine what it would have been like to live during those four hundred years without understanding God's grand plan. Had I lived then, I'm sure I would have been tempted to doubt the goodness or the wisdom of God's plan. It takes great faith to experience or even witness unjust suffering, especially long periods of it, and to believe that God is longsuffering rather than uncaring. Some of God's most sanctified people have had just such a struggle. It is even said that those in heaven martyred during the tribulation will cry out to God, "How long, O Lord, holy and true, until You judge and avenge our blood on those who dwell on the earth?" (Rev. 6:10[NKJ]).

When the Bible, and especially Proverbs, talks about the results of human behavior, it describes what is normally the case; but it allows for exceptions. As a general rule violence takes away the life of those who practice it (1:19) and "all those who take up the sword shall perish by the sword" (Matt. 26:52). But sometimes there is a Carlo Gambino, allegedly one of America's most powerful organized crime figures ever. After entering the United States illegally he quickly rose up the ranks of the Mafia. By age forty-five he had made his first million dollars, largely in illegal liquor, it was reported. He married his first cousin, sister of a another crime figure. Then he had the head of his crime family murdered, it was widely believed. So by age forty-seven he was the boss of his crime family. On the deaths of two other bosses, Gambino was made head of the Commission, which ruled the entire Mafia. It was said that he controlled the New York waterfront and garbage collection, and an important division of the trucker's union, an alien smuggling ring, and more. He was arrested once, but the case was thrown out of court. The U.S. government tried to deport him, but he developed health problems, which stalled the proceedings. While in his summer home, he died quietly in his sleep, at the age of seventy-four. It was said that the Mafia don in the movie, *The Godfather*, was modeled after Gambino.[11]

Those who struggle with God's seeming inaction could benefit from realizing that even small details fit a much grander plan. Job was one who could see no farther than his own personal situation. He was unaware of God's greater plan to demonstrate that some of His people, including Job himself, do good for its own sake and not merely for the advantages it brings them (Job 1:7-12). Nor did he realize the comfort and faith his sufferings would bring others for several thousand years. Mary and Martha thought only of the loss of their brother Lazarus, being grieved and frustrated at Jesus' seeming failure to do what they knew by faith was in His power. Jesus, however, had a much greater purpose, to show His power by resurrecting their beloved brother (John 11:44). When we struggle with God's ways, we need to realize we are part of a grand divine plan.

God's Universal Grace

The world is all the more puzzling, and justice is all the more hidden, because to some extent God's immanent workings are gracious to everyone, righteous and wicked alike. His sun shines on the wicked and the good, and rain waters the crops of the godfearing and God hating alike (Matt.5:45). Injuries heal, refreshing breezes blow, and sunsets are beautiful for everyone. In fact, in some cases the wicked seem to have more of this "common grace" (as some theologians call it[12]) than the righteous. The drug dealer may have a stronger, healthier body, enabling him to work longer each day than the missionary doctor. The atheist may be blessed with a sharper mind than the apologist. The lazy person may inherit a fortune while the generous, hardworking person remains relatively poor.

These apparent inequities are another source of challenge for the faithful. Asaph, the writer of Psalm 73, tells how even he looked at the apparent prosperity of the wicked and became embittered: "For I was envious of the boastful, when I saw the prosperity of the wicked." In spite of blatant sin against man and God (oppressiveness, violence, pride) they seem strong (v. 4) and blessed with the world's goods (v. 7). They even seem to avoid the normal share of life's troubles (v. 5) and they die peacefully (v. 4).

Considering all this strained his faith: "my feet came close to stumbling" (v. 2), he admitted. It even tempted him to give up the quest for a righteous life: "Surely in vain I have kept my heart pure, and washed my hands in innocence; for I have been stricken all day long, and chastened every morning" (vv. 13-14). But as he thought it through (v. 17) he gained a deeper perspective; seeing the not so obvious things renewed his faith. "I perceived their end," he said (v. 17). Their well-being is unstable and fleeting (vv. 18-19). They will be destroyed utterly (v. 18) and forgotten entirely (v. 20).

Contemplating all this he realized how foolish it is to envy the wicked. Besides, he admitted, he really wants nothing in this life but God anyway (v. 25). Like Paul, he realized that the blessings of this life pale in comparison to the richness of knowledge of God (Phil. 1:21; 3:8). So it doesn't matter, really, how blessed the wicked seem to be.

God's Patience

The wicked can be tempted to misinterpret God's forbearance and think He is not there, doesn't care what they do, or is impure like them in that He tolerates evil. God says to those who do wicked things, "These things you have done and I kept silence; you thought that I was just like you" (Ps. 50:21; cf. Isa. 42:14). When justice doesn't come, it is easy to conclude that God is complacent, but Paul warns that His kindness is leading them to repentance (Rom. 2:4).

Far from being a sign of complacency, the fact that punishments and rewards are not given out with mechanical regularity serves God's higher end. A world where justice is always instant – where good and evil actions obviously and unfailingly received their reward – would be a place where people would be far more likely to do good and shun evil for merely selfish reasons. It would be difficult for people to love good and do it for its own sake. And clearly, it is much better that people do good for pure motives. Doing good for its own sake better reflects the character of God, and thus better fulfills mankind's purpose as the image of God. But a world such as ours where actions are not infallibly connected to rewards means that doing good will sometimes bring unwanted consequences, even harm; and doing evil will sometimes bring prosperity.

Such a world can advance other aspects of God's will, such as mercifully giving the ungodly time to repent, and allowing the innocent who suffer at the hands of the wicked to develop a longsuffering spirit, to continue to trust Him, and to love their enemies.

Clearly, God's justice can be a complex process, full of different goals and priorities, each pursued in their proper time. It can be baffling at times. But the believer is never commanded to understand it all, only to trust that God is good, that He knows what He is doing, and that it will all come out right in the end. Sometimes this can take more than a little faith.

Justice and the Secret Things

We can trust that God will eventually bring to light the hidden things, good and bad; some in this life, the rest in the next. As Paul said, "The sins of some men are quite evident, going before them to judgment; for others, their sins follow after" (1 Tim. 5:24).

On the positive side we can take comfort in the fact that our good deeds, however unappreciated by people, will be rewarded eventually. Christ promised that, "...your Father who sees what is done in secret will reward you" (Matt. 6:6, regarding secret prayer). Conversely, sinful deeds done in darkness will be revealed openly (Matt. 10:26; Luke 12:2).

I knew a detective who tried to solve a difficult murder case. Through the investigation he eventually figured out who had committed the crime. He tried to gather enough evidence on the man and interviewed him several times, but he knew there was just not enough to charge him with the crime. Faced with seeing the murderer go free, he told the suspect very frankly that it is possible to beat the human justice system and that some people have done it. But, he said, you will never escape God's justice. He knows what each person has done, and someday everyone – including you – will face Him, all alone. A few days later he got word that the man wanted to confess to the murder he would otherwise have gotten away with. In court when the judge, a bit puzzled, asked why he confessed, the man pointed to the detective in the front of the court room and said, "It was that man. He told me that someday I would face God with the things I have done, and that really scared me. And I would rather face God having confessed to this already." The man realized something few people come to terms with in this life, that as radio preacher J. Vernon McGee used to say in his Southern drawl, that you may think no one sees you, but God knows just what you've done, and "no one's gettin' away with a thing!"

When God punishes those secret sins in this life, it can be disturbing to those who do not understand. It seems that tragedy has struck a person undeservedly. When David sinned secretly by committing adultery with Bathsheba, God took the life of the son born of the affair (2 Sam. 12:14, 18). For a time virtually no one had known of David's sin and its connection to the death. The prophet Nathan also foretold that the sword would never depart from his house and that evil would arise against him from within his own house (2 Sam. 12:10-11), which were tragically fulfilled in the deaths of David's sons, Amnon and Absolom (2 Sam. 13:28-29; 18:15), some of which had to do with the rape of David's daughter, Tamar (2 Sam. 13:1-33). God also told Solomon that his spiritual defection would result in nearly the entire kingdom being wrenched away from his son (1 Kings 11:9-13).

Someone watching these catastrophic events without knowing of the sins and their punishments might be tempted to wonder at God's ways. A glimpse at hidden workings like these can help us to realize that we do not always see the whole picture – but God does. It is not unreasonable to conclude that judgements like these happen around us.

A nurse told me that she had felt badly earlier that day when a man with a wife and young children had suffered a heart attack. The family was in the room trying to comfort him and deal with it. Then another woman and her children approached the nurse looking for the man's room. She said she was his wife. Taken aback the nurse asked her to repeat what she had said. For an instant she considered getting the man out of the extremely awkward situation, but then decided, no, she would let him face it. So she said, "right this way!" For the first time the man's two wives and two sets of children met, discovering that he had secretly been leading a double life for years.

Justice and Generations

Jesus revealed an aspect of divine justice that is virtually forgotten today. Wrath can build up over generations, as people spurn God's patience and keep on sinning. Christ's warning to the religious leaders of His day hearkened back generations:

> ...I am sending you prophets and wise men and scribes; some of them you will kill and crucify, and some of them you will scourge in your synagogues, and persecute from city to city, *that upon you may fall the guilt of all the righteous blood shed on earth*, from the blood of righteous Abel to the blood of Zecharia, the son of Berechiah, whom you murdered between the temple and the altar. (Matt. 23:34-5; italics added).

God had sent messengers to His people and they had persecuted them. Wrath had built up over generations which would overflow in their day. Christ used a common image of filling up a measuring cup to overflowing, where finally the adding of one more drop would make it spill (Matt. 23:32; cf. 1 Thess. 2:16, regarding those who hindered Paul's ministry). The abuse of yet more messengers would finally bring about the overflowing, "upon this generation," as Jesus foretold (Matt. 23:36).

Does God punish one generation for the sins of another? In Ezekiel's day the people tried to maintain that they were innocence in spite of obvious divine judgment. They claimed that their sufferings were not for their sins, but for those of previous generations. In answer God declared that,

> The soul who sins shall die. The son shall not bear the guilt of the father, nor the father bear the guilt of the son. The righteousness of the righteous shall be upon himself, and the wickedness of the wicked shall be upon himself. (Ezek. 18:20)

Moses had stated the same principle (Deut. 24:16) but added that iniquity – and thus its punishment – is passed from one generation to another. In Exodus 20:5 God said that He visits "the iniquity of the fathers upon the children to the third and fourth generations of those who hate Me...." Yet He also added the parallel principle that those who act uprightly will also be treated accordingly, "...but showing mercy to thousands, to those who love Me and keep My commandments."

Jesus elaborated on the principle that people can experience judgment for carrying on the sins of previous generations, "...You bear witness against yourselves," He told them, "that you are sons of those who murdered the prophets" (Matt. 23:31). Since they themselves fully participated in the persecutions carried out by past generations, they would in effect be filling the cup to overflowing: "Fill up then the measure of the guilt of your fathers" (23:32). But He told them that He would rather have been merciful, that He had often wished he could gather them together "the way a hen gathers her chicks under her wings" (23:37). Yet they were "unwilling." He added the astounding prediction that not one stone of the magnificent Temple would be left upon another (Matt. 24:2). His words came literally true when the Romans wiped out the city in AD 70. According to the New Testament, with the persecution of Christ's followers, the cup had been filled to overflowing.

Corporate Guilt and Punishment

The idea of corporate guilt, of participating in the sins of a group, is common in the Bible but is rarely grasped these days, especially in our individualistic Western society. Yet God holds us responsible not just for the way in which we act alone, but for whatever group sins we participate in.

On Nations

One of the most prominent themes of the prophetic books of the Old Testament is God's judgment of the nation of Israel. Much of the book of Isaiah is filled with the subject. Other nations besides Israel are held accountable too, and judgments include famine (Isa. 14:30, Philistia), civil war (19:2, Egypt), conquest by a foreign power (23:15, Tyre), and complete desolation (13:20, Babylon).

God reveals some of His penetrating insight into the national sins for which He judges nations – insight which our modern nations would do well to heed. God condemned Israel's general spiritual degeneration, citing such things as failing to honor Him in their words and deeds (Isa. 3:8), growing weary of Him (43:23), turning worship into empty ritual through hypocrisy (29:13), and ignoring the Jewish Sabbath (58:3-5).

Their society's morals sank, and there was widespread lying (59:13), drunkenness (5:11; 28:7,8), pride (2:11; 5:21), greed (5:8), violence (59:7), lack of compassion and abuse of the downtrodden (3:15; 58:7), seduction (3:16), and political corruption (1:23). Their moral judgment became perverted such that they regarded evil as good and good as evil (5:20). In such moral darkness, the brazenly wicked person ("fool") who scoffs at religion and thinks himself enlightened is regarded by society as great and given respect.[13] The crafty person is mistaken for being generous (32:4).[14]

The corruption was evident not just on a religious and social level, but also throughout the entire judicial process. Those who enacted the laws and recorded them were willing to rob people of their rights for personal gain, victimizing even widows and orphans (10:1; 5:23). People were willing to employ worthless arguments and accusations, such as someone might use to argue a sham case before a judge (29:21). Furthermore, it was common[15] for people to pursue fraudulent law suits using lies and other morally corrupt means (59:4). So justice had been perverted and used as a tool for selfish gain through any available means. And this included those who made the laws (in our society, politicians), judges, those who argued cases (today, lawyers), and the citizens who pursued cases. The prophet summed up God's view of it all, "Now the Lord saw, and it was displeasing in His sight that there was no justice" (59:15).

God revealed a few of His creative ways of chastening societies. He said, "I will make mere lads their princes and capricious children will rule over them" (3:4). This may have included not only literal children (Manasseh became king at age twelve) but incompetent rulers guided not by wisdom and law but by their own childish urges, such as lust, desire for personal gain, and cruelty.

Oppression can come not just from the top down, but from all around as "the people will be oppressed, each one by another, and each one by his neighbor" (3:5). This is illustrated by youths storming against elders, and by the most debased people showing barbaric insolence[16] toward those who should be respected (3:5). Economic ruin comes, and with it starvation, such that anyone who has food and clothing is thought to be qualified to be the nation's leader, but no one has even such meager resources, or no one wants the job (3:7).

In spite of such a vivid and severe picture of divine judgment, God also made it clear that His plan is precise in that it is no harsher than what is needed to bring about righteousness. He compares Himself to a farmer who carefully chooses the right method of growing and harvesting each crop so as to get a full yield without damaging it (28:23-28). While he scatters cummin seed he plants wheat in rows so that it will grow strong. At harvest dill and cummin are beaten out but the grain is crushed, yet not enough to damage it.

Throughout the prophesies we see some of the divine wisdom in choosing just the right form of judgment to bring repentance. For instance, the women who dressed fashionably so as to seduce men would lose their physical beauty and be stripped of their finery, being made to wear the roughest of garments (3:16-24). Those who sought wealth by grabbing other people's land and building on it would have to abandon it all because of crop failure (5:8-10).

When so many of the judgments Isaiah foretold finally fell upon Israel, Jeremiah reassured the people that God indeed had a purpose for it, though it seemed to be the worst possible circumstances. Many had been slaughtered, and the conquered ones were herded like animals off to Babylon. God told them it would last for seventy years, and then they could return. In words that can now offer hope to a broad scope of people, God said, "'...I know the plans that I have for you, ...plans for welfare and not for calamity to give you a future and a hope'"(Jer. 29:11). In their case He knew that the chastening would accomplish its purpose and spoke of the time when it would be over,

> "Then you will call upon Me and come and pray to Me, and I will listen to you. And you will seek Me and find Me, when you search for Me with all your heart. And I will be found by you," declares the Lord, "and I will restore your fortunes and will gather you from all the nations and from all the places where I have driven you," declares the Lord, "and I will bring you back to the place from where I sent you into exile." (Jer. 29:12-14)

We can take comfort in the fact that Isaiah shows God to be loving toward not only Israel but the other nations. He is planning their good as well. Speaking from the perspective of the millennium, He says,

"... Blessed is Egypt My people, and Assyria the work of My hands..." (Isa. 19:25). He is not just the God of Israel.

Abraham Lincoln reflected privately on the purposes of God during one of the darkest days of the American Civil War. He wrote, "...it is quite possible that God's purpose is something different from the purpose of either [warring] party." He said also, "God wills this contest, and wills that it shall not end yet."[17] Why might God want such a horrific conflict to continue? His second inaugural address seems to shed light on it. He suggested that God may continue the war as retribution for the injustice of slavery, "until all the wealth piled by the bond-man's two hundred and fifty years of unrequited toil shall be sunk, and until every drop of blood drawn with the lash, shall be paid by another drawn with the sword, as was said three thousand years ago, so still it must be said "the judgments of the Lord, are true and righteous altogether[.]"

On Families

Nations are nearly the largest groups that God holds corporately responsible (He considers allied nations, and even the whole human race as a unit in the most general sense). Families are one of the smaller groups God deals with as a unit.

When the jailer asked Paul and Silas how to be saved, they replied, "Believe in the Lord Jesus, and you shall be saved, *you and your household*" (Acts 16:31, emphasis added; cf. 11:14). I've heard some Christians say while referring to this verse, that if they can just get a father to believe then his whole family will be saved even if no one but him believes. That view ignores not just other Scripture on salvation, but the context of the verse, which says that Paul preached to the jailer's whole house, that all believed, and were baptized (16:32-34). What this shows is a certain amount of family solidarity (especially in that society), and the potential influence of a father (in any society).

We see the same principles but in the context of judgment upon the negligent parenting of the judge and high priest, Eli. His adult sons were known to be "worthless" men (1 Sam. 2:12), to greedily defile the sacrifices in the temple, to be violent (2:16), and to be sexually involved with the women who served at the temple (2:22). Eli's rebuke of them as adults, being so long overdue, was pathetic and ineffective (2:23). God held him accountable for his and his sons' part in abusing the sacrifices (2:29), and for failing to rebuke his sons for behavior that brought a "curse on themselves" (3:13). God told him that nearly all his priestly family would be killed, that for all generations his other descendants would die young (2:31-32). As a sign to these future judgements Eli would see his two sons die the same day (2:34). His sons died when the Philistines defeated Israel in a slaughter and captured the ark. Because of sinfully eating the fat of the sacrifices instead of burning it, Eli was a heavy man (2:16, 29); so on hearing of the calamity, he fell off his seat, broke his neck, and died (4:18). The other judgments were eventually fulfilled when Saul ordered eighty-five priests killed for being sympathetic with David (22:18), and then later when Solomon dismissed Abiathar, the last priest from Eli's family, for his part in a plot against him as king. Solomon then transferred the priesthood to the family of Zadock (1 Kgs 2:26-27, 35).

This shows the frightening consequences of a father's failure, and how God judges sin within an immediate and an extended family. God's judgment on Eli and his sons, as well as on Abiathar, was according to their own sins. Because sins run in families the accompanying judgment does as well.

I once talked to a Christian man whose father had committed adultery when raising him and his brother. Acutely aware of how sins are passed from parents to children, and abhorring his father's sin with its tragic consequences for the family, the man and his brother were utterly determined not to repeat that moral failure. They diligently cultivated faithfulness to their own wives, and stayed as far as possible from any situations and attitudes that might even remotely be connected with adultery – down to the jokes they would laugh at and the entertainment they would accept. As well, they made very sure their own children grew to share their moral values and lifestyle. "My brother and I are determined that my father's sin will stop at his generation," the man told me. I have little doubt that the sin they so hated will stop at their generation. We would all do well to be so careful about our generational vulnerabilities.

On Churches

The Book of Revelation reveals how closely God scrutinizes churches and holds them accountable. They were variously commended for things like "toil and perseverance," and sound doctrine (Rev. 2:2-3, Ephesus). But they were rebuked for things like tolerating false teachers (2:14-15, Pergamum) immorality (2:20, Thyatira), and for lack of heartfelt zeal for God (2:4, Ephesus; 3:16 Laodicea). Christ warned that disciplinary action would be taken where necessary. False teachers and those influenced by them would be appropriately punished (2:22-23); churches that were dead (3:3, Sardis), lukewarm (3:16, Laodicea), or that had lapsed into loveless orthodoxy (2:4, Ephesus) would be disciplined and would perhaps cease to exist.

They are sobering words for the churches of any age. God still scrutinizes churches, which should make us wonder what He thinks about the church we go to and how we can help it become, or remain, pleasing to Him.

Corporate Versus Individual Guilt

Individuals share different degrees of responsibility for the sins of their groups. For example, Israel's political, religious, and cultural leaders no doubt had a greater responsibility for its sins than many of its citizens. But influence is not all top down, and private individuals – even individual members of churches – determine to some extent what kind of leadership they will follow. That is why to some extent people share in the guilt of what their leaders do. The reverse is also true. Leaders influence their followers and thus share some of the blame (or praise) for what their people do.

Though God as the omniscient judge can see exactly what level of responsibility each person has, when judgment falls on a group it usually affects everyone in the group, but not always exactly according to their level of guilt. When a country experiences famine, for example, those with the fewest resources suffer most though they probably had the least to do with the national policies that brought judgment. And those who care the most about people are likely to be in the most anguish over the starvation, though because of their character they are least likely to have caused it. So corporate judgment, by nature, is not always exact. But sometimes God fine tunes it to protect the innocent, as when Elijah, the widow of Zarephath, and her son were supplied with oil and flour throughout the famine God had brought (1 Kgs 17:14-16).

In spite of the general inexactness of group judgment, God shows concern about justice toward individuals. For example, God listened to Abraham's plea to spare the wicked city of Sodom because of the suffering it would bring on the righteous people there (Gen. 18:23-32). However, we cannot ignore the fact that everything does not always appear to be fair. Daniel, for example, survived and prospered during his captivity whereas Jeremiah died tragically. Sometimes God's ways of rewarding and punishing are hidden from us, and we have to remember that they do not end in this life.

Living in the Light of Corporate Responsibility

Living in the light of corporate responsibility requires that we take a sober look at our relationship to the groups of which we are a part. We have to realistically assess both how they are affecting us and how we are affecting them. What sins or strengths characterize the group? Which are affecting us? Which do we contribute to?

National sins can affect believers in insidious ways. In the United States, for example, materialism has influenced a fair number of Christians. Also, some Christian's attitudes toward church resembles unchurched persons' attitudes toward entertainment.

We have to take a hard look at these areas and work overtime to be sure we have not allowed ourselves to be molded into the image of our culture where we should have been molded into the image of God. It takes a concerted effort to swim against the current.

As to our relationship with our family, we would do well to think about the strengths and weaknesses of our parents and extended family. Have we imitated their strengths and avoided their weakness? If they are diligent and savvy, are we? If they have weak marriages, do we? The brothers whose father had committed adultery wisely avoided certain of their father's sins, but perhaps more importantly, they worked in positive ways to cultivate strong marriages.

We have to face the fact that insofar as we are part of a group, we ourselves make it what it is to some extent. Do we have a constructive influence on our church, for example? Or is our contribution one of complaining, or of contributing to division? One way to gauge our impact is to ask ourselves, if everyone in the church were like me, what kind of church would it be? We can ask ourselves the same questions about our relationship to our workplace, our family, and any other group of which we are a part.

What does Justice Have To Do With Love?

We can conclude that one reason a loving God can indeed allow pain and evil is because He is just in addition to being loving. And, unpopular as the notion is these days, justice requires not only allowing some types of pain but causing them. God's purposes are remedial, to bring about in His creatures the highest good by which they will also experience the highest fulfillment, which entails freely choosing the good. That fulfills their purpose to know God and reflect His character, which is the greatest value in the universe. But what about the pain that He inflicts (or allows) that He knows will never result in moral improvement or in the knowledge of Himself? Is such justice loving?

In theology as well as philosophy (specifically, ethics) there is a long-standing discussion about whether or not justice is an aspect of love. Some say that one is reducible to the other such that all virtues are really some form of love. On this view God would seek justice because He is loving. There seems to be something to this since moral laws are said to be summed up in love (Matt. 22:37-40; Gal. 5:14). As part of this view, punishment could be regarded as God's reaction to people's failure to be loving; its aim is to make people repent and be loving, which is for their own good. In some sense justice is God's way of confronting a lack of love and applying pressure to make a person loving.

The contrasting view is that justice is not reducible to love, that they are essentially two different attributes and not aspects of one another. This view better explains why, out of justice, God allows or inflicts suffering that will never produce repentance. Even if the experience will not reform the sinner, he may suffer solely because he deserves it.

The only way we can consider punishment to be good for the suffer is if we regard their sufferings as giving them more knowledge of God than they would have without the sufferings. That knowledge would be of God's uncompromising righteous nature and willingness to punish unloving behavior. Insofar as the unrepentant sinner is aware of God's mercy on others who do repent, his sufferings may also cause him to better understand the meaning of God's grace even if he does not experience it himself. Yet in spite of the possibility of this somewhat indirect benefit to the unrepentant sufferer, it is still possible that he will learn nothing and care nothing about who God is, and that he will only curse God for his sufferings. If we still say that God would be just in punishing that sinner even though it would do him no good at all (not even giving him knowledge of God's righteousness through his deserved sufferings), then we cannot really say that justice in his case is loving. And if that is so, justice is not an aspect of love.

The cross helps us understand the relationship between justice and love. On it God, through Christ, paid the penalty due to the sinner.

His love fulfilled His justice such that in place of our sin we have the righteousness of Christ (2 Cor. 5:21), adoption (Rom. 8:15), and all His spiritual riches (Eph. 1:3). However, the unrepentant sinner has put himself outside God's ideal plan, in which love and justice come together in salvation through Christ. It seems that for those who are unrepentant, justice and love remain forever disconnected. Their sufferings do not necessarily do them any good, and they suffer solely because they deserve it. That has to be the most tragic end of a moral being.

Conclusion

God's justice is a complex and often hidden thing. Though its reality has been largely suppressed in modern times, we will see it operating around us if we take a long-term view of things, realizing that He is longsuffering and desires that people repent, but He is also determined to give people what they deserve. In all, seeing the part divine justice plays in the problem of evil is partly a matter of insight and partly a matter of faith.

GOING FARTHER

1. What evidence have you seen that the subject of God's justice is unpopular in modern culture?

2. How is justice woven into the fabric of the world?

3. Give some examples you have seen of God's immanent justice.

4. How is it harder to see God's justice because of His universal grace?

5. How do people's secret sins make discerning God's justice more difficult?

6. How does punishment involve more than one generation?

7. Although it is difficult to determine, do you know of events in the history of any country where you think God was bringing justice on a national level (e.g., prosperity, security, peace; or poverty, instability, conquest)?

8. Can you think of examples where the sins of a parent are passed onto the next generation?

9. In light of God's strict evaluation of churches in the Book of Revelation, what do you think God would say to your church?

10. What groups are you a part of, and how do you think God views them? How have you influenced these groups, and how have they influenced you?

11. What do you think is the relationship between love and justice? What difference does their relationship make?

NOTES

1. C. S. Lewis, "The Humanitarian Theory of Punishment," reprinted in *God in the Dock* (Grand Rapids, MI: William B. Eerdmans, 1994). For a discussion of these issues, see, Murray R. Rothbard, "Punishment and Proportionality," accessed 27 Nov. 2004, <http://www.mises.org/rothbard/ethics/thirteen.asp#_ftn18>,

2. From the National Center for Health Statistics, 1998, table in *The World Almanac and Book of Facts*, 2001 (Mahwah, NJ: World Almanac Education Group, 2001), 875. Heart disease causes 31 per cent of deaths. Of course for diabetes, as for the other health problems listed here, not all cases are the result of personal choices.

3. From the National Institutes of Health, 1998, *World Almanac*, 2001, p. 728. The exact figure is 55 per cent of the population. The risk is measured by body mass index.

4. "Alcohol Dependence: Diagnosis, Clinical Aspects, and Biopsychosocial Causes." Joseph R. Volpicelli, M.D., Ph.D., University of Pennsylvania Health System, accessed 8 Jan. 2004, <www.uphs.upenn.edu/recovery/pros/dependence.html>.

5. "Targeting Tobacco Use: The Nation's Leading Cause of Death," Center for Disease Control, Chronic Disease Prevention, accessed 8 Jan. 2004, <www.cdc.gov/nccdphp/aag/aag_osh.htm>.

6. "US Recreational Drug Deaths," Special News Release of *BBS News* Faqlet#1 (98) July 2002, accessed 8 Jan. 2004, <http://bbsnews.net/drug-deaths.html>.

7. *BBS News*, op cit.

8. Institute of Medicine, Committee on Prevention and Control of Sexually Transmitted Diseases, *The Hidden Epidemic: Confronting Sexually Transmitted Diseases.* Eng TR and Butler WT, eds. Washington, DC: National Academy Press, 1997; cited in "Sexually Transmitted Diseases Statistics," NIAID Fact Sheet: NIAID. Accessed 12 Jan. 204, <www.wrongdiagnosis.com/arctic/sexually_transmitted_diseases_statistics_niaid_fact>... The top four sexually transmitted infections are, gonorrhea, chlamydial infection, syphilis, and trichomoniasis. Based on 1997 figures.

9. "HIV/AIDS Statistics," January 2004, National Institute of Allergy and Infections Diseases (NIAID), a division of the U.S. Department of Health and Human Services. Accessed 12 Jan. 2004, <www.niaid.hih.gov/factsheets/aidstat.htm>.

10. C. F. Keil and F. Delitzsch, *Commentary on the Old Testament in Ten Volumes*, Vol. 1, *The Pentateuch*, three volumes in one (reprinted; Grand Rapids, MI: William

B. Eerdmans, 1991), 1:216. He observes that the Amorites were the most powerful tribe of the Canaanites and their name is used for all the Canaanites (cf. Joshua 24:15). Moses delivered judgment to Og, king of Bashan, and to Sihon, king of Heshbon. Joshua fought the five Amorite kings (Joshua 10:1-43) and others (11:1-14).

11. Accessed 7 Sept. 2004, <http://www.geocities.com/hollywood/academy/5854/netgambino.htm>. For hundreds of pages of FBI documents on Gambino, see listing, <foia.fbi.gove/alpha.htm>.

12. L[ouis] Berkhof, *Systematic Theology* (Grand Rapids, MI: 1939), 434-446.

13. The "Fool" is *nabhal* and "is a scoffer at religion, who thinks himself an enlightened man, and yet at the same time has the basest heart, and is a worthless egotist." C. F. Kiel and F. Deilitzsche, *Commentary on the Old Testament*, vol. 7, Isaiah (reprint, 2 vols. in 1, Grand Rapids: Eerdmans: 1991), bk. 1, 50.

14. The context describes the Kingdom, during which such scandalous lack of discernment will be corrected. It is likely that people in Israel were making these kinds of errors in judgment, prompting its mention by the prophet.

15. Kiel and Delitzsch note that the abstract infinitives which follow in verse 4b "express the general characteristics of the social life of that time...." ibid., bk. 2, 396.

16. "Ferocious insolence," Joseph Addison Alexander, *Commentary on the Prophecies of Isaiah*, revised ed. (1875; reprinted, Grand Rapids: Zondervan, 1978), 111.

17. Sept. 2, 1862. Ronald C. White, Jr., *Lincoln's Greatest Speech: The Second Inaugural* (New York, NY: Simon & Schuster, 2002), 122. Lincoln's secretary, John Hay, kept it and named it, "Meditation on the Divine Will." News had come that the North had lost 16,000 men and been pushed to the outskirts of Washington D. C. itself.

CHAPTER SEVEN

THE SUFFERING OF INNOCENTS – Animal Pain

Atheist philosopher Quentin Smith told how he was sleeping in a mountain cabin when the cries of an animal awoke him. He could hear the thing scream in agony as it was slowly being eaten. After a few emotionally wrenching moments there was silence. The horrible experience confirmed his atheism. He reasoned that a good and powerful God would not allow the torture of an innocent creature when nothing good could have been accomplished through it – much less would a good God make such an event the normal workings of nature.[1]

Theistic answers to the existence of pain and evil have, for the most part, said little about animal pain specifically. Yet there has been a growing concern for animals. This may be in part because they seem closer to us since research into their brains, social structures, and communication has shown that in many ways they are more like us than we once thought. Ironically, society has come to value animals more while at the same time valuing humans less – atheistic evolution has made man just another animal anyway. At the other extreme, some in the New Age movement say that consciousness is not unique to humans and everything is conscious to some degree, which makes us essentially the same as animals from a spiritual perspective. Environmental concerns about pollution and overpopulation have recently focused on consequences to animals. Some people would go so far as to claim that a person's life has no more value than an animal's. Many people say they would rather risk people being harmed by a product or medicine than have it first tested on animals. Vegetarianism too is on the rise, and even some Christians are joining in.

Christians ought to give more attention to the question of animal pain if for no other reason than there is so much concern about it. But apart from current interest, the question itself begs for an answer. The first step is to put the problem in perspective so that it does not appear bigger than it is.

The Limits of Animal Suffering

When most people think of suffering in the animal world they consider the total suffering of all creatures. It adds up to an enormous amount because the number of creatures is so large. We tend to think of human suffering the same way, as a staggering sum. We naturally wonder how God can justify the totals.

Yet if we look at it another way, we realize that with animals, as with humans, no one creature experiences the whole. Each experiences only its own pains, not those of any other creature. So if millions more individuals suffer, it does not increase the amount of suffering each creature feels.[2] In that sense pain does not accumulate from individual to individual to form an enormous experienced total. If five billion creatures experience a pin prick, the amount of pain experienced is still only a pin prick, not a total of five billion pin pricks because each person feels only one prick. So as far as experience is concerned, the question is not why God allowed the enormous total, because each individual suffers only its infinitesimal part of it. We are faced with the much smaller question of why God allowed the sensation of a single pin prick.[3]

When we consider the problem of predatory behavior in the animal world, we are tempted to think in terms of billions of creatures being eaten. It helps a little to realize that creatures which are eaten suffer only one brief experience. I live in the mountains, and like Quentin Smith I awoke one night to the sound of an animal screeching as though it were being eaten. But unlike Smith, I thought about how remarkably short that moment was for the animal compared to its years of life that doubtless had included many wonderful experiences. And if their experience of significant injury is anything like ours, their bodies may mask the first few minutes of pain, which would be enough to cover their entire experience of death. Furthermore, it is likely that their experience is only one of being harmed, not of being killed. Death as personal extinction is an abstract concept that is probably beyond the mental capability of animals.

Christian philosopher Richard Swinburne goes so far as to suggest that it would be wrong to regard predatory behavior in animals as a natural evil. Death by another animal is no worse than death from another cause such as accident or disease, and it is not evil since actions by animals are not moral anyway. As he sees it, death by another animal is not something evil but simply the end of something good.[4]

Whether or not we regard predation as a natural evil, the problem of animal pain is greatly reduced by realizing how much we project our human capacities onto animals. Much of our suffering as humans comes from capacities and perspectives which just don't exist in the animal world.

Unless a person has some special physical condition, most of his or her sufferings are non-physical. For most people, the deepest hurts are intensely interpersonal. A person may have felt abandoned or abused as a child, rejected by a spouse or family member, or betrayed by a friend. Or he may suffer because of something that happened to someone else, such as his child. Perhaps a person hurts for people he doesn't even know, such as refugees or impoverished children.

But these examples of pain are emotionally and neurologically complex and are therefore mostly or entirely outside the experience of animals. First of all, nearly all of those experiences involve highly developed memories. As humans, most of our emotional hurts have to do with things that are not happening in front of us at this moment. They happened before today, and perhaps many years ago. But it takes a fairly sophisticated brain to retain such complex memories over a long time. Not even the human brain can hold permanent memories for the first several years of life. It is doubtful that very many of even the highest animals can experience anything like the sort of emotional suffering of which a mature human is capable. And lower animals probably do not have enough memory to realize even that a physical pain they are currently experiencing has gone on for a long time. They know only that they are experiencing something painful now.[5]

Secondly, even most of the emotional pain we as humans experience as happening now is not happening right in front of us. In that sense, much of our capacity to suffer comes from our ability to think abstractly. The parent, for example, who is hurt over the way her child is teased at school is aware of something happening some distance away. Likewise for the person concerned about the health of a parent or friend. But thinking about things not happening in front of us now is a highly sophisticated ability. Dogs in a neighborhood may howl in sympathy when one of their own sounds hurt, but they stop as soon as that dog stops sounding hurt. They do not go on howling for days because they suspect the dog's master is abusive. Considerations of that sort would require abstract thinking of which even the highest animals are incapable. Even the relatively sophisticated brain of an infant has difficulty thinking about the simplest abstraction. They may have difficulty realizing, for example, that things exist when they go out of view. I once saw a chart on the wall of a pediatrician's office which recommended that parents make a game of hiding an object from their infant then revealing it in order to help them realize that things keep existing even when they are no longer visible.

If this seems like a minor point with regard to animal pain, consider further how much of our suffering depends on abstract reasoning. Besides thinking about things in the past or some distance from us, much of what we worry about concerns things that might happen in the future. Worry also requires a degree of abstract reasoning. Another source of human suffering concerns what could have been: lost opportunities, personal capacities and resources unexpectedly reduced, relationships with spouses or family that are not all they could be. These experiences can crush us yet they are neurologically very complex and probably have little or no parallel even in higher animals.

What appears to be abstract thinking in animals is probably not. A monkey can learn to move a toy car forward on seeing a green light, and to stop it when the light turns red; but that does not mean it understands the abstract concept of "stop" and "go." If you put a spot on an animal's forehead and let it look in the mirror most would have no idea it is on themselves because that would involve a concept of self. Certain primates are among the few animals that try to rub it off, recognizing that it is on themselves. Up to a certain age even human infants cannot pass that simple test.

I saw a documentary about a woman who worked extensively with an orang-utan to find out its capacity for abstract thought. Over a long period she taught him a number of hand signals through which he could communicate, for example, that he wanted a hug or certain foods. He learned to get a key from a box and use it to open another box with food in it. Eventually those in charge decided that she should not continue the experiment and she was not allowed to see him for a couple of years. When she was finally allowed back for a visit, he avoided her at first, as if angry over being abandoned. But after awhile he warmed up and communicated a few signs. The story was touching, and the abilities she developed in the animal were remarkable (as was its memory), but even these abilities are far from the complexity of human thought – and this was from one of the most sophisticated of all animal brains that had been trained intensively for a long time.

Dogs also illustrate the limits of animal brains. After thousands of years of domestication, the brightest and best trained dogs can understand at most a few hundred words. The smartest dog on record was trained to do 469 tricks, including "playing the piano" and getting a tissue when someone sneezes.[6] Yet many dogs cannot pass even the simplest abstract thinking test. If their leash is fastened to one peg in the ground and then wrapped around a second peg such that it is too short to reach some object the dog wants, many dogs cannot figure out that it has to move away from the object in order to unwrap the leash and get to the object. Though my dog's intellect shines in many areas, this isn't one of them. I've often had to unwrap her from a post she has managed to wind herself around.

With capacities of even the highest animals so low it is easy to mistakenly suppose that they suffer a good deal more than they actually do. We think about the life of a deer, for example, and suppose that its alertness shows that it is constantly fearful of death in the way we would be if we were hunted by some predator. We suppose that it understands what it means to exist versus not to exist, and that it is capable of carrying deep emotional scars as would occur if some deer it knew was lost to a mountain lion years ago. We suppose it would wish that its companion were there to taste the fresh spring growth. We further suppose that it worries for the lives of its offspring the way we would for our own children. But most likely the deer experiences little or none of these emotions (though it no doubt experiences some loss). It is primarily aware of what is immediately before it. Its responses are rather mechanical, largely a matter of response to stimulus. Certainly it experiences pain and can be aware of danger, but anything much deeper is probably a projection of our own experiences onto the animal.

Given the level of animal consciousness, their experience probably parallels a human's most closely during dreamless sleep. When asleep we still feel pain, move to make ourselves comfortable, hear things, and perhaps even unconsciously communicate something. Like animals, we are reacting but have little if any abstract thought. We can see from this that their capacities for suffering are much smaller than ours.

We do not, however, want to dismiss the sufferings which animals do experience. No doubt the more developed the creature's nervous system, the greater its capacity to feel things like pain, fear, and grief; and to recall bad experiences. But then too, the more developed they are, the greater their capacity for enjoying such things as play, courtship, and satisfaction of curiosity.[7] Why does God allow whatever sufferings animals do experience?

Building a Spiritual Perspective

To begin with, there is no question that God cares about animals. Psalm 104 describes His providential working for all creation. He makes springs in order to "give drink to every beast of the field" (v. 11), and grass to feed cattle (v. 14). The animals wait for God, "to give them their food in due season" (v. 27). Proverbs associates righteousness with concern for animals"(Prov. 12:10). And when God told Jonah that He wanted to spare Nineveh, He said that the city had more than 120,000 people who could not tell their right hand from their left, "as well as many animals" (Jon. 4:11). God is concerned not merely for masses of life but for individual creatures, down to the single sparrow (Matt. 10:29).

Some of the same principles that apply to human suffering also apply to animals, as we saw from the fact that sufferings do not add up to an experienced total. Another example is that, as with humans, we cannot apply our own ideal of what we think a good life would be for an animal and then regard God as unfair simply because its actual life fell short of our ideal. Anything God gives a creature – animal or human – is of grace and undeserved. He owes them nothing. If a dog lives five years we cannot fault God that it did not live twelve years, any more than we can find fault with a human living thirty years instead of seventy. Again, this does not diminish the real pain that animals do experience. And as with humans, we can still ask why the lives of animals are not somehow "better."

Answers to the problem of animal pain can be divided into three categories. One explains animal suffering in terms of humans, accounting for it either as a consequence of human evil or as a benefit to human existence. The second approaches it from the standpoint of possible benefits to animals themselves. Finally, we can consider the issue in relation to God.

Animal Suffering as Secondary to Human Good

The most obvious (though not the most common) reason for animal suffering is human evil in that people deliberately abuse animals or simply neglect them. Dogs are beaten and kicked, cats are neglected, unwanted pets are abandoned to starve in the wild, farm animals are mistreated, and the list goes on. I recently heard of a doctor who owned a beautiful show horse that one day was slow to obey him. In a drunken rage he shot it in the knee, permanently crippling it.

Occasionally police uncover a dog fighting or cock fighting operation in which the cruelty of the sport is typically made all the more deplorable by the unhealthy conditions in which the animals are kept. Others harm animals without meaning to, as when a person leaves a pet in a car on a hot day, or tries to care for animals without adequate resources. A woman in Los Angeles kept over two hundred stray cats in unhealthful conditions (why God would allow so much suffering on the part of her neighbors – odors wafting through the neighborhood and all – is a problem of evil question all its own!).

From the standpoint of humans, animals form part of the environment for human experience. They provide opportunity for us to reflect God's character by showing divine traits such as compassion and love. They form part of the greater environment in which human dominion is played out. That dominion over the earth has the possibility of reflecting God's dominion over the universe. It is thus part of the background for man's creation in the image of God (Gen. 1:26, 28). But as with all human behavior, the freedom and capacity to do good entails a proportional capacity to do evil. Animals certainly provide the opportunity for humans to do both. In the case of the doctor who shot his horse, someone got it to a ranch in Texas whose mission is to take care of animals that would otherwise have no chance to live. The disabled horse will live out the rest of its life under the loving care of the ranchers.[8]

Some animal suffering due to human sin is on a large scale, such as when a careless camper starts a forest fire, burning many animals and destroying the habitat of survivors for years. In the last couple of weeks fires in two areas of the United States have burned nearly a million acres of forest. Two people have been arrested for starting them, one was a fire fighter who allegedly wanted to ensure that he had work through the summer. There are also problems caused by pollution and by mismanagement of resources. Whole forests have been eliminated by clear cutting, wherein every tree is cut to the ground for timber, leaving no animal habitat.

On the other hand people also have a great capacity to care for God's creation. I live in a national forest where specialists care for the forest and its fauna. Weak trees are cut to produce stronger stands, and animal populations are watched for signs of large scale problems.

In Romans 8:19-22 Paul characterizes the whole creation as anxiously longing for human redemption, having been subjected by God to "futility" because of the fall of humanity. Like so many other aspects of creation, humanity's dominion was a good thing turned bad by human choice. Though fallen, God still allows man dominion over creation, permitting creation to suffer the sinful exercise of human power. Paul pictures creation groaning – yet as in childbirth – because the eventual redemption of man will bring sanctification of his powers over creation and a reversal of the curse (Rev. 22:3, contra. Gen. 3:17-18). Thus someday creation will be set free from its "slavery to corruption" and will itself experience a glorious transformation.

The future transformation is described poetically by Isaiah (11:6-9; 65:25), who says that the lion shall eat straw like an ox, the wolf will dwell with the lamb, and the nursing child will play by the hole of the cobra. God declares, "They will not hurt or destroy in all My holy mountain, for the earth will be full of the knowledge of the Lord as the waters cover the sea" (11:9). God's reign will be characterized by peace (9:6, under the Prince of Peace) and harmony. So to those like Quentin Smith who conclude that a good God cannot exist because animals experience pain, we can say that the world in this age is indeed far from its ideal state.

For now all is not well, and this provides a silent warning to mankind that something is not right between creator and creation, similar to the warning that natural disasters provide to a human race in rebellion. Our inborn ability to look at creation and conclude that God exists (Rom. 1:18-20), and our intuitive knowledge that God has moral standards (Rom. 2:14-15), help us realize that something is wrong with our world. In effect, the problems of suffering that surround us shout out that a serious problem exists. If we do not turn a deaf ear to the dissonance between the world as we find it and the world as we know it could be, then the groanings of creation can turn us toward our creator.

Much is made these days of the suffering caused by people eating meat, a practice regarded by some as abusive. A Christian once told me that he had become a vegetarian because he thought it was wrong to make animals suffer for the sake of our appetites. Curious, I asked why he thought God had explicitly given animals to us for food (Gen. 9:3) and if he thought Christ was wrong to eat meat and fish (Passover lamb, Matt. 26:21, Luke 22:14; fish, Luke 24:42-43). He replied that eating such things is an option we can choose not to exercise. That's true, but even he would admit that it is not wrong if someone chooses to eat meat.

If people want to eat only vegetables because they think it will limit animal suffering that is certainly up to them. But like the animal suffering issue in general, we have to put it in perspective. First, for the most part, animals that are used for food are killed humanely, and given their lack of awareness, they have scant knowledge of what is happening. Second, animals that are raised for food typically get far better care, feeding, and protection from predators than they would have living in the wild. As well, they have been selectively bred so they are born strong and healthy, enjoying good lives. Furthermore, billions of animals would never have had a life at all had they not been raised for food. It is the fact they are raised for food that causes them to be born, live well, and experience any life at all.

Once when driving by a field with cows my wife said, "They sure don't know what they are in for; someday they're taking a one-way trip to the slaughter house." But I thought for a moment and replied with a faint, perverse smile, "Well, so are we humans; they're no different from the rest of us. Our end is as sure as theirs, the only difference is that we choose not to think about it, whereas they are incapable of thinking about it." Of course death doesn't end all for us, but like them, we each get a relatively few earthly years.

Animal Suffering in Relation to the Created Order

Even through its fallen state, nature still bears testimony to order and thus to a creator. As a whole, the vast order of nature has beauty and value even though in the present age it must be sustained by the birth and death of its many individuals. Augustine explained how creation as a whole exists through this ongoing process:

> ...they are so ordered that the more infirm yield to the firmer, and the weak to the stronger, the more impotent to the more powerful.... But to things falling away, and succeeding, a certain temporal beauty in its kind belongs, so that neither those things that die, or cease to be what they were, degrade or disturb the fashion and appearance and order of the universal creation: as a speech well composed is assuredly beautiful, although in its syllables and all sounds rush past as it were in being born and in dying.[9]

The beauty of leaves dying in the fall, and the process of their becoming new soil that yields new life is part of the ongoing creation. So too is the dying of animals to feed other animals. To focus solely on the death of individuals is to miss the bigger picture of their part in sustaining the creative whole, Augustine maintained. Is it so bad that an animal should die benefitting another animal by feeding it, rather than dying of old age? In cases where predators catch older creatures because they are slower, the life span may be about the same anyway. From our modern perspective, we could add the fact that predators often catch weaker members of a species, which ensures that only stronger individuals breed, leading to a better life for future generations. In Scandinavia, herds of migrating reindeer swim a channel of open water, losing quite a few of the herd in the ordeal. Local people began ferrying them across yet stopped after a few seasons when it became apparent that the herd was becoming weaker.

Animal Suffering in Relation to Animals Themselves

It seems there should be more to say about why God allows animals to suffer. Philosopher of religion John Hick objects to the view that the purpose of animal suffering is merely to provide an object lesson for humans. The view, he says, "implies a strikingly different conception of God from that of the heavenly Father who cares for the birds and flowers, and without whose knowledge not a sparrow falls."[10] Is there some reason God allows their suffering for their own good?

The most obvious reason is that God allows some of their sufferings for the same sorts of reasons that He allows certain human sufferings. If they, like us, are to have a physical existence, it helps them maneuver through the world if they have a certain amount of pain as a warning of harm. They must feel pain when they fall, or rub against sharp objects so that they will learn not to hurt themselves. To some extent they can learn from the experiences of other animals, such as knowing to avoid a bog by seeing another animal stuck in it.

Like us, animals must have some vulnerabilities in order to function effectively. For example, if their bones were so strong they could not break they would also be too heavy to allow easy movement. And like us, they must have capacities to do things if their lives are to have any significance, and those very capacities can be used in destructive ways. Just as they can work together to get food, they can kill each other; they can raise their young or neglect them (which is all too true of humans as well).

Animal Suffering in Relation to God

We have seen that in addition to traditional thinking that animal pain is for human good, animal suffering is part of the entire created process and can benefit the animals themselves. In what sense does animal suffering also relate to God?

Animal suffering can provide another way for God to be glorified, that is, for His attributes to be revealed. Though as we have seen, even higher animals lack a sophisticated mental and emotional life, they seem capable of some level of mutual care, help, sacrifice, and so on. On our property I often see quail shepherding their little offspring to food and safety. An adult stands watch while others feed. If there is a threat, one may try to draw a predator away by acting injured so as to look like an easy kill. Many dogs are great examples of loyalty. When our children were young they were protected by our fiercely loyal Siberian Husky, who gave no thought whatsoever to her own safety. She also protected me as we jogged many hundreds of miles a year together. More than once she put herself in harm's way against two or more dogs bigger than herself. If parents and spouses were as loyal and caring as some animals the world would be a very different place! Of course, as with humans, animals can also act in a way that is cowardly, selfish, treacherous, and so on. And the more sophisticated the creature, the more complex its behavior can be.

It is paradoxical that we talk about animal behavior in moral terms, such as loyalty or sacrifice, yet most Christians regard animals as non-moral beings that are unaccountable to God.[11] There is no doubt that higher animals act in ways we can describe in moral terms even though we do not know how much is based on instinct, stimulus response, and the like.[12] Can something done by instinct rather than moral choice reflect the character of God? Perhaps it has moral significance only if a moral being observes it and values it.

Conclusion

Subtracting the sufferings that we mistakenly project onto the animal world is helpful but it still leaves a difficult issue. If suffering has ultimately so much to do with the consequences of sin, and if animals cannot sin because they are not moral beings, why does God allow them, as innocents, to suffer? We have seen some answers, but like other aspects of the problem of evil, we cannot account for everything perfectly. John Hick said it well,

> It may very well be that the material universe, and the ranges of sub-human life within it, have further significance for their Maker than simply as an environment for personal life. We can set no limit whatever to the possibly multi-dimensional complexity of the divine purpose. It may be that God fulfils many different intentions at once and that innumerable strands of the divine activity intersect in the universe in which we live. But if there are any such further meanings of our environment, they are unknown to us. We can glimpse only that aspect of God's purpose for His world that directly concerns ourselves.[13]

GOING FARTHER

1. In what ways is animal pain limited? How do we often project onto animals sufferings that they do not experience?

2. Why does Swinburne think that predation in animals is not a natural evil? Do you agree?

3. In what sense can we misconstrue the "sum total" of suffering when it comes to animals and people?

4. How is some animal suffering related to human sin or righteousness (thus to the question of human free will)?

5. Viewed in the larger context, how does animal death contribute to the broader issue of life on earth?

6. In what way is some animal suffering a part of their physical life?

7. How would you summarize Hick's view of animal pain?

NOTES

1. Quentin Smith, "An Atheological Argument from Evil Natural Laws," *International Journal for Philosophy of Religion* 29 (1991):159-174. Cited in John G. Stackhouse, Jr., *Can God Be Trusted? Faith and the Challenge of Evil* (New York: Oxford University Press, 1998), 43.

2. C. S. Lewis, *The Problem of Pain* (reprint, New York: MacMillan: 1962), 129.

3. Of course there still may be senses in which it is useful to talk about total amounts of suffering, such as why God would allow an environment in which such things as pin pricks are possible and even universal. Moreover, the more suffering there is in the world, the more acute is the problem of pain: it is a worse problem if billions suffer than if only one creature in the entire universe suffers. Yet from the important standpoint of the pain experienced by individuals, we have to remember that it does not add up to an enormous total.

4. Richard Swinburne, *Providence and the Problem of Evil* (Oxford: Oxford University Press, Clarendon, 1998), 172.

5. This same point is made by Richard Swinburne, 174.

6. *Guinness World Records: 2002* (New York, NY: Bantam, 2002), 161.

7. Swinburne, 175.

8. Called the Black Beauty Ranch of Murchison, Texas, <fund.org>; the story was told by Jack Hanna, animal specialist at Bush Gardens <www.jackhanna.com>.

9. *Concerning the Nature of Good*, viii. See also, *Enchiridon*, iii.2.15; *City of God*, xii.4; xii.5; *On Free Will*, III.xv.42-43. I am indebted to John Hick (pp. 82-7) for his work on Augustine and the problem of evil. John Hick, *Evil and the God of Love*, rev. (San Francisco, CA: Harper & Row, 1978).

10. Hick, 85. He was remarking on Augustine's view that animal death bears witness to the desire for "bodily unity," but his objection could be applied to other views of animal pain.

11. It is thought that they have no direct awareness of God because they lack a soul or spirit by which to survive death. Scripture gives no indication otherwise.

12. An animal's apparent sense of guilt, for example, may be mere anticipation of punishment rather than any moral sense of wrongdoing. And an animal can have little sense of the finality of death, which must alter our assessment of its courage.

13. Hick, 317.

CHAPTER EIGHT

ILLNESS – Proof of Our Weakness

In October of 1347 a ship arrived in Messina, Sicily, with dead men at the oars. Those still dying groaned from boils oozing blood and pus. Along with cargo from the Black Sea the ghastly crew brought a plague that would grow to apocalyptic proportions.

So lethal was it that some people went to bed well and died in their sleep. There were reports of doctors catching it at a person's bedside and dying next to their patient. Within a couple of years it had spread to northernmost Europe. In Norway a ship arriving with a cargo of wool drifted offshore, ghostlike, its crew all dead.

In some areas mortality reached ninety per cent and whole towns disappeared. With people dying so fast bodies were merely dragged out of houses and left on front doorways. When the graveyard in Avignon, France filled up, bodies were dumped into the Rhone river. No one knows how many died, but the rough figure of one third of Europe was used partly because it fit the plague in the Book of Revelation.

The terrified population struggled to understand the combination of respiratory and blood born strains of Bubonic plague. The death of so many, especially the young, shook people's faith in God, and some wondered if life could be understood rationally at all. It seemed that life itself was nothing more than brief preparation for death. In Kilkenny, Ireland, a monk sat writing, alone and surrounded by the dead. The whole world seemed to be "within the grasp of the Evil One," he wrote. He recorded events in case "any man survive and any of the race of Adam escape this pestilence...."[1] Then he too died.

Theories about the causes of the plague abounded, and suspicion fell on Jews, who had been forced to the fringes of society. They attracted attention because it seemed that the plague did not ravage their communities as badly. It may have been because they kept cats, and that kept down the number of rats, and the fleas that transmitted the plague. The rest of the population did not have cats because they associated them with witchcraft.[2] Whatever the case, confessions induced by torture provided supposed evidence of an international conspiracy to wipe out Christian society by poisoning its wells. In the ensuing hysteria several hundred Jews were herded into a specially built house on an island on the Rhine, and burned. Two thousand were taken to a burial ground in Strasbourg and all but those who converted on the spot were burned. In Worms, 400 Jews burned themselves in their homes rather than be killed. Pope Clement tried to stop the slaughter and condemned any blaming of Jews as the work of the Devil.[3]

Though that was a particularly bad outbreak, it was only one of many that swept Europe periodically. The scourge of illness has always been something of a mystery. While the medievals saw illness as the chastening of God, many today have the opposite view, supposing that it cannot be from God and can have no divine purpose in the life of the believer. I've watched a few television preachers proclaim that you don't have to be sick if you don't want to be, and that you should be the one who decides when and how you will die. If you ever get sick, they say, it's only because you lack faith. Furthermore, death should come only when you are good and ready, as supposedly evidenced by Paul's pondering whether he should go and be with Christ or remain to continue in fruitful labor (Phil. 1:22). These views are akin to those which claim that God's will is for every believer to be wealthy every day of his life, and that the only reason our whims don't get fulfilled is that we lack faith.

Several people have told me that they had a much harder time their first few years as Christians because they were told that coming to Christ would solve all their problems. They became surprised and confused when they found it wasn't so. I've often wondered how many believers who accept such views find their faith severely tested when they get cancer or even a common illness, when they have financial troubles, or when a loved one suffers an untimely death. On such a view the explanation for any suffering must be that the person just did not have enough faith, since the event could never have been part of God's ideal plan.

The people who teach these views are a little like Job's three friends. They thought the only reason for suffering of any sort was sin, and they spent their time trying to get their suffering friend to realize that. In a similar way, these modern-day friends of Job claim it's all a lack of faith.

If we fail to see that God's dealings in this age are more complex than that, we will miss out on the lessons to be gained from suffering. Let's not forget too that God did not appreciate Job's three friends misrepresenting Him and His methods with regard to pain and evil. He said, "My wrath is kindled against you...because you have not spoken of Me what is right..." (Job 42:7).

The Roots of Misunderstanding

The view that illness or adversity of any type cannot come from God misunderstands one or more subtle scriptural principles. Such misunderstandings can lead to the view that the believer, in this life, should experience no illness whatsoever. As one preacher put it, the Christian should experience "...not even a headache, sinus problem, not even a toothache – nothing!"[4]

Misapplying all Israel's Blessings to the Church

Most of the verses promising God's people temporal blessing come from the Old Testament and are given to Israel. We have to realize that God's covenant with them was largely focused on this life. Moses summed it up in his speech to Israel at the end of Deuteronomy: if Israel would obey God they would inhabit the promised land, their children would be healthy, their animals would multiply, their barns would overflow, they would have plenty to eat, and they would defeat all their enemies (Deut. 28:1-14). In short, they would "abound in prosperity" (28:11). But if they would disobey, they would get the opposite of all those blessings – plague, starvation, suffering, conquest, and death (28:15-68).

God was dealing with Israel as a nation, in temporal ways. He was revealing Himself through them, in accordance with ancient beliefs about gods. Ancient peoples largely judged a god's power and personality by the way he dealt with the nation that worshiped him. If he won wars, he was powerful. If his people were blessed, their god must be pleased with them, and so on. The God of Israel intended peoples to understand Him through His dealings with His people, and we still benefit from that revelation today by looking back on Israel's history in the Bible.

In contrast to Israel, the church has no national or ethnic identity; it is promised no land, for example. The New Testament believer reflects the life of God within and through the culture in which he or she lives rather than through a unique (Jewish) national identity. The Christian's national citizenship is of no spiritual significance because their spiritual citizenship is in heaven (Phil. 3:20).

Being typically a minority within their country, the Christians' spiritual condition is not necessarily the main factor in determining how God deals with the entire country. In that sense Christians who invoke 2 Chronicles 7:14 (that if God's people will repent He will heal their land) are taking it slightly out of context. Since it was promised to Israel, "My people" it implied a whole nation in repentance. That is not the same as repentance on the part of, say, 2 or 3 per cent who are Christian out of an entire nation. The point is that the temporal blessings of a nation today are not necessarily promised on the basis of the spiritual condition of its Christian population. So obedient Christians are not necessarily guaranteed the temporal blessings promised to Israel.

The New Testament does not lead us to expect that righteousness will necessarily lead to temporal blessing. In contrast to God's promise to keep an obedient Israel safe from its enemies, the New Testament warns the obedient believer that there will be spiritual persecution (e.g., Mark 10:30). God led Paul through troubles that did not sound at all like the blessings promised to Israel (2 Cor. 11:23-27). And far from expecting prosperity as a reward for his obedience, Paul said that he had learned to deal with need (Phil. 4:12). In contrast to Old Testament guarantees of protection for an obedient Israel, tradition has it that the apostles died violently.

One television preacher was applying all Israel's blessings to the church, concluding that we should never suffer illness or want of any sort. When he came to God's promise that His people would possess the land he obviously could not apply that to Christians. So he pointed to his body and said, "This is the land, it is your body. God promises you will possess your body so that only what you want to happen to it will happen." Needless to say, that's quite a stretch, and it won't close the gap between Israel's theocracy and the church.

God does promise to meet the material needs of the obedient Christian (Phil. 4:19). He may heal in response to prayer (James 5:15), and He may choose to protect the believer (cf. Acts 5:19). But in contrast to God's promises to Israel, such temporal blessings are not the centerpiece of the New Covenant, where instead the primary emphasis is the blessings of the next life (1 Pet. 1:13, "fix your hope completely on the grace to be brought to you at the revelation of Jesus Christ."). He may give the obedient Christian a long, healthy, and prosperous life...but then again He may not. For the Christian such blessings are a matter of grace rather than birthright.

Regarding Miracles as Normal

God has performed miracles most noticeably during three periods in the past: through Moses, in order to call out God's people and initiate the covenant; through Elijah, when apostasy had become so bad that the people of Israel were not even sure which was the true God; and through Christ and the apostles in order to validate the Messiah and His message. In the future, the two witnesses in Revelation will do great miracles to validate their message (Rev. 11:6). In each period miracles are the divine credentials of the messenger and his message.

Christ's ministry contained remarkable miracles, some of which He did out of sheer compassion and not just to validate His message (Matt. 8:4, Luke 8:56, Christ told people not to publicize a miracle). For a time His apostles continued to work miracles. But there is no indication that miracles were to be normal for all ages such that all suffering and want could be removed entirely in this life (even Christ did not remove all suffering from people's lives). This is evident in the New Testament, where the ability to work miracles was associated with the apostolic band and did not become normal for every Christian. Working of miracles was said to be the mark of a true apostle (2 Cor. 12:12), so it could not have become normal for every Christian. Secondly, we know that miracles were not everyday solutions to suffering even for the apostle Paul. He told Timothy, for example, to deal with his frequent health problems by taking a little wine (1 Tim. 5:23), which was a way to purify unhealthful water in those days. Paul said that he had to leave Trophimus sick at Miletus (2 Tim. 4:20), and Epaphroditus nearly died from an illness (Phil. 2:25-30). There is no indication that either of them were in sin or lacked faith.

That is not to say that today God would never do something remarkable, even miraculous, or heal in response to prayer – Scripture has not ruled out that He might do so. But saying that God acts today in response to prayer is different from saying that He necessarily wants to routinely solve every problem through a miracle, and that only our lack of faith prevents Him from doing so. Some see it as the difference between providence, by which God acts through natural process, and miracle, by which He acts counter to natural processes.

Healings in the Atonement

One basis for the view that the believer should be free from all sickness and pain in this life is the notion that the atonement guarantees it. One popular preacher said that when the Devil began to give him symptoms of the flu, he told himself, "I'm redeemed from the flu! Immediately I began to confess God's Word that I'm healed by the stripes of Jesus. I rebuked Satan and refused his lying symptoms."[5]

The conviction that physical wholeness comes with redemption is based partly on a passage in Matthew. It says of Christ's healing on a particular day, "...He cast out the spirits with a word, and healed all who were ill in order that what was spoken through Isaiah the prophet might be fulfilled, saying, 'He Himself took our infirmities, and carried away our diseases'" (Matt. 8:16-17).

Matthew was referring to a verse in Isaiah chapter fifty-three dealing with the effects of Christ's ministry (Isa. 53:4) Verse five says, "And by His scourging ["stripes," KJV] we are healed." It is supposed from this that healing comes along with forgiveness and in the same way – it can be claimed in this life by faith. But it is not quite that simple.

The first thing we notice is that Matthew was talking most directly about what Christ did while He was alive, as part of His earthly ministry, and not while He was on the cross. However there is a deeper connection between bearing of sickness and bearing of sin. In the biblical (and ancient Jewish) view sickness is ultimately rooted in sin and its effects, there being no place for it in a perfect world. So the atonement removes the taproot of sickness. But while the atonement deals directly with sin, and forgiveness is thus granted immediately on accepting the work of Christ, sickness is only indirectly connected with sin. Health does not necessarily follow immediately upon accepting forgiveness.

Death, too, is rooted in sin (Gen. 2:17) and like sickness it is not immediately eliminated from the life of the Christian. No one claims that becoming a Christian immediately makes one immortal! The Christian is still subject to death just as he is subject to illness.

Scripture is explicit that physical perfection awaits the next age and is not to be had in this life. Only heaven eliminates pain, tears, and death (Rev. 21:4). Surely God can graciously speed our recovery from an illness or prevent it entirely, but immunity from all illness in this life is not promised.

The Curse of the Law

Another misunderstanding about believers and illness comes from Paul's reference to the curse of the law. Galatians 3:13 says that "Christ redeemed us from the curse of the Law." And Deuteronomy 28 (regarded as part of the "law") includes illness among its curses. So, it is thought, Christ redeemed us from illness.[6]

As we saw above, the context in Deuteronomy contains God's warning that He will either bless or curse Israel based on their morals and spirituality. Illness is just one of those cursings (28:27, 35, 59-61). And as we saw above, all the specifics of God's covenant dealings with Israel do not necessarily apply directly to the church. The curse Paul is referring to is made clear in the context, in Galatians 3:10. It is not the curse of illness, but the burden of having to obey all the law while coming under condemnation for falling short of absolute perfection. Furthermore, the law cannot justify us, because justification comes not by works but by faith (3:11-12).

Paul's point is that Christ, by becoming a curse for us while hanging on the cross (v. 13), relieved us from the law's curse and established justification by faith (v. 24). So Christ rescued us from condemnation rather than illness.

Idealist World View

Many of those who teach that sickness can be cured by right thinking or by "confessing" health seem to hold at least a mild form of the worldview called idealism. According to idealism, reality is more like a mind than a thing. Theists who are idealists generally regard God as the supreme mind over the universe. Some idealists hold that reality is composed of ideas and thus our minds can influence reality. Therefore, if we want something to happen, we should think it, or visualize it. I have heard television preachers associate visualization with prayer. Supposedly, in prayer we visualize something and make it happen.

Some further suppose that just as God can control reality through His words as an extension of His thought, so we can control reality through our thoughts. This leads them to give great attention to the words that we speak, which, along with our thoughts, supposedly control reality. As one influential teacher put it, "Every circumstance – the entire course of nature, is started with the tongue."[7] With regard to health then, if we believe that we are healthy and say that we are healthy, then we will be healthy. It implies that our mind controls physical reality.

Due partly to German philosopher Hegel, the idealist view was popular from the nineteenth century up until the early twentieth. A number of sects sprang up during that period, some of which have strong tendencies toward idealism. They claim that illness can be controlled completely through the mind (this is different from the modest claim that some long-term attitudes such as anger or happiness can have an affect on our body). Christian Science founder Mary Baker Eddy taught, "When the first symptoms of disease appear, dispute the testimony of the material senses..."[8]

Some believe that the similarity between New Thought and Christian Science type themes, and elements of the modern healing movement is not coincidental. Hank Hanegraaff of the Christian Research Institute (founded by cult researcher Walter Martin) believes that preacher Essek William Kenyon (1867-1948) was influenced by the teachings of such unorthodox groups and that he greatly affected the media preacher who has had the greatest influence on Christian health and wealth preachers.[9] In a scholarly work, Dale Simmons agrees as to the extent of Kenyon's influence, but shows that the primary influence on Kenyon was the Higher Christian Life movement. New Thought and the like had a part, however, and the two movements shared some interesting similarities (Kenyon condemned New Thought and Christian Science, but thought they had grains of truth).[10]

In the early twentieth century realism replaced idealism as the dominant worldview in Western society. Realists believe that things exist independently of minds; minds cannot directly determine what things are, instead they know things for what they are. Typically for the theist with a realist worldview, life's challenge consists of knowing what things are and dealing with them accordingly, not controlling reality directly through our thoughts or confessions. Prayer within a realist view would consist purely of asking God to change the reality over which He is sovereign; and if it is His will, He will do it. But we don't imitate God's direct control of reality through our minds and words.

Medicine and the Believer

One popular teacher recounted how he was at a convention when he felt "sharp pains" around his heart; "It seemed to quiver and stop. It even felt as if my breath were being cut off."[11] Rather than seek medical help (or even to ask for prayer) for what appeared to be classic symptoms of heart trouble, his response was to rebuke the devil for, as he put it, trying to "get me to believe the symptoms and go by my senses." He said that he refused to "permit a doubtful thought to enter my mind." He took it as a spiritual victory when the pain went away (which it would anyway if it were a heart attack and was not too severe; however a heart attack can leave the heart permanently damaged).[12]

Another popular preacher holds that medicine is only for the spiritually immature: "If you need a crutch or something to help you along, then praise God, hobble along until you get your faith moving to the point where you don't need the crutch."[13] A mature person who can "stand on the promises of God" doesn't need it, "That's the reason I don't take medicine," he said.[14]

Would God rather work through faith than medicine? Are the two necessarily opposed? Certainly it would be a spiritual problem to seek medical help as an alternative to trusting in God. Asa had that attitude during the last six years of his life, when he had lapsed morally. His feet became diseased and it was said that he "did not seek the Lord, but the physicians" (2 Chron. 16:12). It is possible that these "physicians" used nothing more than pagan magic, but whatever the case, he sought them as an alternative to trusting God. The treatment did no good, and eventually he died.

Scripture regards the use of medicine as normal and responsible, even though some ancient methods were perhaps only marginally helpful. Jesus accepted recourse to physicians as normal practice (Matt. 9:12). Of course, the gospel writer Luke was "the beloved physician" (Col. 4:14) and nothing suggests that his profession was anything but legitimate. In fact, the Bible shows that God expressly worked through medicine of the day: when He answered Hezekiah's plea to be spared, he was healed only after Isaiah's order was carried out to put a cake of figs on the boil (2 Kings 20:7). In Jesus' parable, the Samaritan poured wine and oil on the beaten man's wounds, a practice of the day (Luke 10:34; cf. Isa. 1:6). The mild antiseptic qualities that made wine useful for wounds also purified water, which is why Paul recommended it for Timothy's stomach problems (1 Tim. 5:23).[15] Jesus used an eye salve in healing (Mark 8:23; John 9:7), and the church of Laodicea was told to use eye salve for its blindness, which is significant even though metaphorical (Rev. 3:18).

The inability to accept that God would work through medicine misunderstands how God normally works in the world. God works through natural processes because it is He who set them up. This is what we called in a previous chapter His immanent action. God's justice is working imminently, for example, when a person contracts a sexually transmitted disease while committing adultery. On the other end of the scale, God can work in a way that has little connection to the normal flow of natural processes, or what we call transcendently. He could, for example, cause an otherwise healthy man to suddenly suffer a massive stroke as a way of dealing with some sin, or cause lightening to strike him. (As was previously pointed out, the most transcendent actions – those least connected to the flow of events and the natural laws that cause them – are miracles.)[16]

God's action could be described in the same terms with regard to healing. He could work immanently, using natural processes, or He could work more directly (even miraculously). He could, for example, heal one cancer patient through chemo-therapy and another patient apart from any medical procedures (where they go into spontaneous remission, for example). The first follows the more likely outcome of natural processes. The second is less likely and it seems therefore that it requires God to act more directly; consequently, it seems clearer that God has acted. Yet we have to realize that God is behind both recoveries, whether He worked through normal processes or more directly. The point is that contrary to the preacher who thought it more spiritual to trust God to deal with his heart attack without medical aid, it is not more spiritual to expect that He will work apart from the processes He created.

We don't typically expect God to work transcendently regarding non-medical issues in life. For example, we don't think it's unspiritual to work for a living rather than trust God to supernaturally put money in our bank account. We don't think it is more spiritual to let our car run out of gas and trust God to make it go. (I have, however, met a Christian who thought it more spiritual to trust God to supernaturally guide him while driving, so he would close his eyes for a few seconds, until his "lack of faith" would cause him to reopen them and look at the road.) I suppose those who expect God to limit His actions to more supernatural means can be commended for their faith, though not for their theology.

Many who expect God to work only in supernatural ways look to the gift of healing to cure all illnesses. Even in apostolic times it was never a solution to all illnesses. James, even though writing very early in the life of the church when miracles were prevalent, advocated that the sick call for the elders, who would anoint the person and pray (James 5:14). No mention is made of calling for someone with the gift of healing. And as mentioned above, three people were not healed though they were close to Paul himself: Trophimus, Epaphroditus, and Timothy.

Without getting into the issue of whether certain gifts have ceased, we can say that healing as Jesus and the apostles practiced it is not typical of today's faith healers. One difference appears to be that today their basic method is usually to pray and trust that God will heal. By contrast, healing in the Gospels and Acts was to a greater degree under the control of the healer. The apostles, for example, did not pray for the crippled man at the gate – or even check to see if he had the faith to be healed (Acts 3:6). They just told him to get up and walk; and he did.

They were following Jesus' example, as He was often the one who took the initiative to heal. For example, He initiated healing while teaching in a synagogue (Luke 13:10-13, crippled woman; Matt. 12:9-13 man with withered hand) and while at a feast (John 5, paralyzed man).[17] As New Testament scholar D. A. Carson points out, Jesus saw healing as part of His messianic work (Matt. 8:16-17; 11:5-6), but almost always His teaching and preaching were emphasized (e.g., Mark 1:15, 21, 35-39; 2:2, 13; 3:14, 22-23; 4:1; 6:1-2, 34; 7:14; 8:31, 34; 9:30-31; 10:1; 12:1, 35).[18]

Secondly, healing in the first century was instantaneous, not the result of a divinely shortened convalescence where people gradually got better. Thirdly, they included the most difficult cases and there could be no doubt of either the problem or the miraculous cure. Included were things like long-term blindness, deafness, or lameness since birth. Thus, on at least two occasions it is said that Jesus healed everyone who came to Him (Luke 4:40; 9:11). Even the most hardened critics could not dispute that the healings were miraculous. They may have attributed them to Satan, but they did not doubt the person had been healed (Matt. 12:24; cf. John 3:2). By contrast, even the best known modern faith healers, some of whom devote most of their ministry to healing, do not claim to be able to heal everyone.[19] One well-know minister who gives healing a very prominent place in his ministry estimates that his "success" rate is about two per cent.[20]

While no believer should doubt that God can grant remarkable answers to believing prayer in any age, we can conclude at the very least that first century style healing is not God's plan for every sickness today nor for the daily life of every Christian. So, contrary to some popular thinking, sickness sometimes figures into God's plan for this life, even for the obedient Christian. But why?

God's Purposes for Illness

There is no doubt that God's ideal is health and that illness and disease are part of the entrance of sin into the world. Christ's ministry is one source of evidence that God's desire is for people to be healthy.

Illness is not God's Desire

Teaching and healing were two major emphases of Christ's ministry. Healing was a sign of the Messiah, a sign which Christ offered to John the Baptist as he languished in prison, struggling with doubts (Matt. 11:4-6). Furthermore, His disciples' first mission was to "Heal the sick, raise the dead, cleanse the lepers, cast out demons..." (Matt. 10:8). He healed even though it motivated His enemies to kill Him (Matt. 12:14). And He said that when He sits in final judgment, one evidence that a person belongs to Him will consist of whether they visited the sick (Matt. 25:36).

While healings formed part of Jesus' divine credentials, there was nothing impersonal about it. Nine times it is said that He was motivated by compassion.[21] And He was patient with those who came for healing, even when they were something of a disruption (e.g., Mark 2:4). Furthermore, He allowed lepers and others who were unclean to touch Him; He also reached out with His healing touch. This was done in a culture that had limited compassion for the sick because they associated it so closely with judgment.

All this shows that healing is close to the heart of God.

Illness that Punishes or Chastens

While there can be no doubt that health is the ideal, neither can there be any doubt that God allows – and even causes – illness and disease.

The most obvious reason God brings illness is to punish sin. When Miriam rebelled against Moses' leadership, God's anger burned against her. As the cloud of His divine presence lifted from them, she was white with leprosy (Num. 12:9-15; she was healed later when Moses and Aaron prayed). King Uzziah suffered with leprosy for life due to overstepping his bounds by usurping priestly authority in the temple (2 Chron. 26:19, 21). Azariah, too, was struck with leprosy until his death (2 Kings 15:5). Jesus connected sin and illness when He told a man after healing him, "do not sin any more, so that nothing worse may befall you" (John 5:14). Paul told the Corinthians that many of them were weak and sickly because they had dishonored God by mistreating the Lord's supper (1 Cor. 11:30).

God visits whole nations with sickness because of their sins, but He can also abruptly end such judgement (Num. 16:47-48). On the other hand, He can deliver a whole nation, keeping its people in health. He forewarned Israel that His blessing and punishment would be carried out in the arena of their health (Lev. 26:16; Deut. 7:15; Exod. 23:25).

It is sometimes difficult to separate punishment from discipline. In principle, punishment delivers what is deserved without regard to the good of the sinner. Discipline (chastisement) on the other hand aims at the person's good and therefore brings only enough discomfort to bring repentance. In a general sense, God punishes those who have refused atonement for their sins, but He disciplines those whose punishment has already been-paid on the cross. Yet in a practical sense those categories may be hard to distinguish, for example, in the case of the believer who contracts Aids from sexual sin – the result lasts for life regardless of whether the believer repents and mends his ways. Many consequences of sin are similarly permanent. There are major health problems, for example, which are consequences of bad life-style choices. As mentioned in the chapter on justice, this can be the case with strokes, heart attacks, diabetes, certain types of cancer, and of course, sexually transmitted diseases.

Yet even the permanent results of sinful behavior can be a blessing in disguise if it helps keep us from ever repeating it. I've known a number of people who began a more disciplined, responsible life-style after a mild heart attack, or after developing diabetes due to poor diet, overweight, and lack of exercise. The scourge of an incurable sexually transmitted disease can have the same beneficial effect. I have known of single Christians who, after contracting an incurable but non-fatal sexual disease became much more devout, vowing never to fall again. I have also known of a number of more tragic cases of Christians who sinned and contracted Aids. Even some of them responded well and led much more committed lives, albeit more complicated because they were married with children.

As with so many types of evil in this world, whether or not it produces good in us is up to us. Illness or disability can soften us, producing repentance, humility, and godly priorities; or it can harden us into bitterness and anger. Suffering is only an opportunity, and like all opportunities, they are only what you make of them.

David's wisdom showed in his response of faith in the face of sufferings: "I know, O Lord, that Your judgments are righteous, and that in faithfulness You have afflicted me" (Ps. 119:75). He knew that troubles were designed to bring about his maturity: "It is good for me that I was afflicted, that I may learn Thy statutes" (119: 71). The writer of Hebrews exhorts us to remember God's loving motives for chastening, "My son, do not regard lightly the discipline of the Lord, nor faint when you are reproved by Him; for those whom the Lord loves He disciplines, and He scourges every son whom He receives" (Heb. 12:6; Prov. 3:11-12). These truths moved the Renaissance poet John Donne to plead,

> Batter my heart, three-personed God; for you
> As yet but knock, breathe, shine, and seek to mend;
> That I may rise and stand, o'erthrow me, and bend
> Your force to break, blow, burn, and make me new.[22]

In response to illness, especially frequent or protracted illness, we would do well to search our heart to be sure that we have not overlooked some sin. If God is indeed chastening us, we should not take it "lightly," yet neither should we become despondent. During the process we should keep uppermost in our mind that God's motive is love (Heb. 12:6) and that His goal is a righteousness that brings true peace (Heb. 12:11). These attitudes will help give us the strength to move on in the right direction and prevent more serious damage to our lives (Heb. 12:13).

Illness that Keeps us in Spiritual Power

Being prone to sinning as we humans are, some of us can benefit from a limitation that keeps us humble and dependent on God. God in His wisdom gave Paul a particular difficulty to keep him from exalting himself on account of the "surpassing greatness of the revelations" he received (2 Cor. 12:7; cf. 1 Cor. 8:1, "Knowledge makes arrogant"). Whether the problem was with his eyes,[23] recurring malaria, a demonically inspired person,[24] or something else, it prompted him to earnestly pray three times that it be removed. Yet God knew what was best and turned down his request, revealing to him that "power is perfected in weakness" (2 Cor. 12:9).

From his "thorn" and his other struggles, Paul gained a clear and constructive view of his personal weakness (2 Cor. 12:10) and inadequacy (2 Cor. 3:5). He came to see that although our lives hold divine treasure we ourselves are merely plain clay pots (2 Cor. 4:7). More than anything else, it was this humility that kept him strengthened with God's power, enabling him to be used in ways that few humans ever have.

He made a point of telling the Corinthians of his struggles – no doubt because, like our society, they were so taken with spiritual glitz and status. They were seeking spiritual power and pedigree, whereas Paul focused on his sufferings and humiliation. Similarly, Jesus had told people who wanted authority that they had to become as slaves (Matt. 20:26, 23:11). Paul made it clear to the Corinthians that real power comes from God, but through weakness (2 Cor. 12:9-10).

It's hard to imagine Paul attracting many people to a modern mega-church growth seminar with that message! These days, it seems that so many Christians (especially in America) search endlessly for the latest method that will ensure spiritual success. The idea of focusing on our weaknesses and inabilities in order to maintain God's power doesn't sell. Yet as Paul reveals, such is the paradox of spiritual power. He found real spiritual power and could hold onto it because his struggles constantly reminded him that his own strength wouldn't do.

A few years ago I got sick with a particularly bad strain of flu, and I came down with it not long after getting over some other virus. I was back at school struggling to continue teaching while still enduring quite a bit of misery. As I walked unsteadily across campus I was regretting how much time had been pointlessly wasted in all this when I came across a South American student who had always impressed me with his spiritual outlook. He asked how I was doing, so I told him honestly, and I'm sure I did not come across as excessively cheerful. He thought for a moment and said, "Well, I know that sickness always forces me to see my weakness; that's what sickness does for us, it helps us to remember our weakness."

I've thought of that very brief conversation many times over the years and it has reminded me that illness can serve to impress upon us our true condition and the source of our power.

A few months ago I got very ill from serious bacterial food poisoning and could not eat for six days. Losing nearly ten pounds in the ordeal (which I could not really afford to lose), I had absolutely no trouble remembering my weakness. But I was also impressed with the divine help that kept me going. So I would add to the student's insight that sickness not only reminds us of our weakness, but it also makes us look to God's power and depend on it.

Illness that Forms our Character

Charles Spurgeon suffered with bad health for years, partly because of painful gout. Looking back he concluded, "I am certain that I never did grow in grace one-half so much anywhere as I have upon the bed of pain."[25] Though he died when he was only age fifty-seven, he became one of the most powerful preachers of his day, and is the most widely read preacher in history. There was obviously a supernatural quality to his ministry, and it has been bearing fruit for over a century.

James encouraged his readers with the fact that trials produce endurance, which gives us the chance to become a complete and mature person (James 1:2-3; he was probably talking about trials from persecution, but his mention of "various" trials shows that the benefits can come from a wide variety of troubles; cf. 1 Peter 1:6-7). Remembering that clouds have their silver linings can keep us from being overwhelmed by grief and discouragement. James goes on to warn us that if we fail to persevere the opportunity for growth will turn into a temptation and then an occasion to sin (James 1:12-13).[26] So to maintain the perspective that it is all for our good and to thereby maintain our strength, we need to pray in full faith (James 1:5-7). And if we can keep a right perspective, we will not only come through it but benefit greatly from it.

During trials it can comfort us to remember that God may bring suffering in order to form our character and not necessarily because of some great sin in our life. The writer of Hebrews reminds us that even Christ learned obedience by the things He suffered (Heb. 5:8).

Illness that Glorifies God

Christ healed some people without regard to whether they had faith, or even a relationship to God at all. The Syrophoenician woman's daughter, the centurion's servant, and demoniac boy were all healed because of the faith and pleas of a third party, not pleas of their own (Matt. 8:5; Mark 7:25, 9:17-18).[27] This suggests that healing is not always a matter of forgiveness, which we normally associate with faith, contrition, and the establishment of a relationship between the person and God.

It is natural – but incorrect – to always connect illness with sin and healing with forgiveness. This classic error was made by Job's three friends. Christ's disciples also reflected that thinking when, on seeing a blind man, they assumed that either he or his parents must have sinned. Jesus corrected them, saying that neither had sinned (John 9:2). Thus while He did not deny some general connection between sin and illness, He rejected the idea that personal acts of sin are always the cause. In this case, He told them, the purpose was to reveal the "works of God." At the very least, the blind man provided an opportunity for God to show His great power by healing him. And God could conceivably show Himself in other ways through people's deficiencies (which we will discuss when we look at birth defects).

I knew a man who told me he had spent his youth bound to a wheel chair. He completely recovered the use of his legs, which he attributed to God answering his prayers. In his late fifties the event still energized his daily life in that he continually thanked God and took opportunities to tell others about Christ. Sometimes too he would run for the sheer joy of being able to use his legs and to remind himself of what God had done. But, conceivably, God could also be glorified through those who never recover from illness or disability. Who can doubt that God's character, purposes, and grace have become better known through the lifelong disability of Joni Erickson?

Illness that Prepares us to Serve

Paul told the Corinthians not only that his sufferings helped him maintain a vital sense of dependence, but they made him usable in the lives of others who suffered. God comforted him and his ministry companions in their trials, Paul told them, so that "we may be able to comfort those who are in any affliction with the comfort with which we ourselves are comforted by God" (2 Cor. 1:4).

When someone is suffering, it helps a great deal if we can connect with them on a heart to heart level. A person who knows Bible verses without knowing personal suffering will probably be of limited comfort to others. Paul thus recognized that affliction added an important dimension to his great spiritual insight: it made him usable in the lives of real people with real hurts. We can master concepts and biblical content, but suffering makes them real to us in a way that can help us make God real to others.

Paul recognized a further benefit to suffering: it allows us to know God as a comforter. He referred to God as, "the Father of mercies and God of all comfort, who comforts us in all our affliction..." (2 Cor. 1:3-4; how evil of various types helps us to know God is developed in chapter 7, above).

Illness and Evil Spirits

For much of the twentieth century scientific naturalism[28] held sway, and the idea of supernatural beings was ridiculed, especially the idea of evil supernatural beings. That attitude seems to be changing as the popular thinking flirts with the New Age, wherein everything is seen as spiritual, or even divine.

In any case, in the biblical world there are fallen spiritual beings who choose to afflict humans. Satan afflicted Job with boils (Job 2:7). Demons caused muteness (Matt. 9:32), seizures (Mark 1:26; 9:26), seizures along with deafness and muteness (Mark 9:18, 25), blindness and muteness (Matt. 12:22), and spinal problems (Luke 13:11). Just which types of medical problems or which individual cases today have some demonic dimension to them is perhaps impossible to know. It may be that the best way to proceed is to simply treat any physical component of a problem with medical remedies while still being alert to spiritual issues (psychiatric issues are more complex). However we deal with it, we should recognize that in the biblical world view, demonic activity is an important source of human suffering.

Though fallen spirits are in rebellion against God He uses them for His purposes, which is one of the highest testimonies to His wisdom and power. Satan's buffetings had a special purpose in Job's life, to show the loyalty of a godly person and to emphasize that a sovereign God has legitimate yet sometimes hidden purposes for what He does. God uses demons to test and toughen the faithful (Matt. 4:1, Jesus; Luke 22:31, Peter), and to keep them humble (2 Cor. 12:7, Paul). He also uses them to punish the stubbornly sinful (1 Sam. 16:14, Saul; 1 Tim. 1:20, Hymenaeus and Alexander), perhaps turning them to salvation (1 Cor. 5:5).

We can take comfort in the biblical fact that though evil spirits cause trouble, their activities are woven into the fabric of God's good purposes.

Illness that is a Mystery

A major part of Job's trial was that he had no idea why God allowed him to be afflicted in such a way. The fact that it was a mystery provided him the opportunity to grow in faith, patience, and humility. So unique was the cause of his suffering that had the book of Job not revealed it we probably could not have figured it out from the rest of Scripture.

What is significant here is that there is no reason to think that Job was the only one in history with a veiled and special divine purpose behind his sufferings. If that is so then we cannot rule out a Job factor today, perhaps even in our own lives, whether with regard to a health issue or some other difficulty (we'll develop this further in chapter fourteen). So if we can find no answer for our situation after long and diligent searches of our hearts for sin and the Bible for answers, it may be that it is not for us to know, at least not at this time. The very mystery of it may be a vital part of the whole experience, as it was for Job.

Illness, with its complex causes and divine purposes, reflects the greater problem of pain and evil. And like other aspects of that greater problem, whether it benefits us depends on our response. Illness – like all pain and suffering – is at the same time tragedy and opportunity.

GOING FARTHER

1. How can some of God's promises to Israel be mistakenly applied to the church?

2. What would you say to someone who regarded miracles as normal and routine for every Christian today?

3. What does healing have to do with the atonement?

4. How would you reply to the view that illness is a curse which was removed by the atonement?

5. How has idealism affected thinking about healing?

6. How do healings in the New Testament differ from most healings today?

7. Practically speaking, how can we avoid being chastened for sin?

8. What sufferings in your life have kept you dependent on God?

9. In what areas has suffering helped to form your character?

10. In what ways might suffering glorify God without being the result of sin?

11. Who are the people you are most likely to go to for counsel? What difficulties in their lives have made them humble, approachable, and wise? (If you don't know, you might ask them some time.)

12. Do you think there is a demonic dimension to illness?

NOTES

1. Barbara W. Tuchman, *A Distant Mirror: The Calamitous 14th Century* (New York: Alfred A. Knopf, 1978), 95.

2. Justo L. Gonzalez, *The Story of Christianity* (reprint, two volumes in one; Peabody, MA: Hendrickson Publishers, Prince Press, 1999), 1:328.

3. Tuchman, 113, 115. Papal Bull of September 1348.

4. Benny Hinn, *Rise & Be Healed!* (Orlando, Fl: Celebration Publishers, 1991), 32; quoted in Hank Hanegraaff, *Christianity in Crisis* (Eugene, Or: Harvest, 1993), 242.

5. Jerry Savelle, *If Satan Can't Steal Your Joy...*(Tulsa, OK: Harrison House, 1982), 9-10; cited in Hanegraaff, 243.

6. Hanegraaff, 251. He explains and criticizes the view.

7. Kenneth Copeland, *The Power of the Tongue* (Fort Worth, TX: Kenneth Copeland Ministries, 1980), 22; quoted in Hanegraaff, 268. This is not to say that Copeland necessary has idealist leanings.

8. Mary Baker Eddy, *Science and Health with Key to the Scriptures* (1859; reprint Boston: First Church of Christ, Scientist, 1971), 390; I was made aware of this reference by Hanegraaff, 246.

9. Hanegraaff, 32-33 The preacher whom Hanegraaff says was influenced by Kenyon is Kenneth Hagin, who even adopted Kenyon's statement, "Every man who has been born again is an incarnation, and Christianity is a miracle. The believer is as much an incarnation as was Jesus of Nazareth." Kenyon coined the phrase, "What I confess, I possess," now commonly used by health and prosperity preachers. Hanegraaff says (p. 33) that Hagin influenced virtually every major "faith" teacher. (Of course whether or not there is a connection between Kenyon and Christian health and wealth preachers, the latter would reject most of the beliefs of groups like Christian Science, and most of the philosophy of idealist thinkers like Hegel.)

10. Dale E. Simmons, *E. W. Kenyon and the Postbellum Pursuit of Peace, Power, and Plenty, Studies in Evangelicalism*, No. 13 (Lanham, MD: The Scarecrow Press, 1997), xi-xiv. Simmons finds that Hagin was heavily influenced by Kenyon, without acknowledgment (x), and that New Thought and Higher Life were "birds of a feather" (xii). Simmons finds that Kenyon's strong emphasis on positive confession is his closest link to New Thought, though even such confessions are in line with Higher Life teaching (p. 304).

11. Kenneth E. Hagin, *Right and Wrong Thinking* (Tulsa, OK: Kenneth Hagin Ministries, 1966), 20-21; quoted in Hanegraaf, 245.

12. Nothing I say, quote, or refer to is intended as medical advice and should not be construed as such. For medical advice one should seek the help of a qualified professional.

13. Frederick K. C. Price, *Faith, Foolishness or Presumption?* (Tulsa, OK: Harrison House, 1979), 93; quoted in Hanegraaff, 248.

14. Price, 88; quoted in Hanegraaff, 248.

15. Also, wine and myrrh were thought to be a sedative (cf. Mark 15:23).

16. There is a debate as to whether miracles are violations of natural law or merely the divine operation of natural laws in ways we do not understand and therefore find remarkable. See for example discussions in R. Douglas Geivett and Gary R. Habermas eds., *In Defense of Miracles: A Comprehensive Case for God's Action in History* (Downers Grove, IL: InterVarsity, 1997).

17. For these cases I am indebted to D. A. Carson, *How Long, O Lord? Reflections on Suffering and Evil* (Grand Rapids: Baker, 1990), 125.

18. D. A. Carson, 125.

19. See for example, the investigation of physician William Nolen, *Healing: A Doctor in Search of a Miracle* (New York: Random House, 1974); "In Search of A Miracle," McCall's (September, 1974), 107. Also, researcher James Randi, *The Faith Healers* (Buffalo: Prometheus, 1987). Both authors cited from John MacArthur, *Charismatic Chaos* (Grand Rapids: Zondervan, 1992), 205-209. Though Randi (a magician turned researcher) aims to debunk supernatural claims and is not favorable to Christianity, he could generally be regarded as fair in his methods. He asked scores of faith healers to provide him with evidence that could be objectively examined. He

concluded that each case could be explained by natural convalescence, psychosomatic factors, or outright fakery. While we need not accept his conclusion at face value, it at least shows that the work of modern healers do not offer the sort of irrefutable evidence that came with first century healings. Though His source of power (Matt. 12:24) or obedience to the Sabbath were debated (Matt. 12:13-14), no one could doubt that Jesus had healed – or that the apostles had, for that matter (e.g., Acts 3:9-11).

20. John Wimber; cited in D. A. Carson, 124.

21. R. E. O. White, "Heal, Health," *Evangelical Dictionary of Biblical Theology*, ed. Walter Elwell (Grand Rapids: Baker, 1996), 328.

22. John Donne (1572-1631), "Holy Sonnet" no. 14, in Mark Larrimore, ed., *The Problem of Evil*: A Reader (Oxford, UK: Blackwell, 2001), 145.

23. He reminded the Galatians (4:13) that he first preached to them because of a "bodily illness" that might have tempted them to despise him (v. 14). From this some have concluded that his weakness might have been something like malaria, which would have made him very sick. Others believe the problem had to do with his eyesight because he said that at the time they loved him enough to have plucked out their own eyes for him (v. 15). Furthermore, he closed the epistle by showing them "what large letters I am writing to you" (6:11). It was his custom to have a scribe write for him, but he would also include something in his own handwriting as evidence that the epistle was his. Large writing might indicate a problem with his vision.

24. *The MacArthur Study Bible*, ed. John MacArthur (Nashville, Word, 1997), 1783 (2 Cor. 12:7), points out that "messenger" (ἄγγελος) is likely a personal agent rather than a medical problem since 180 of 188 NT uses refer to angels. Furthermore, "buffet" always refers to bad treatment from other people (e.g., Matt. 26:67; 1 Cor. 4:11). And, in the OT Israel's opponents are referred to as thorns (e.g., Num. 33:55; Josh. 23:13). Yet Hodge rejects the idea that a person was the problem because Paul says that the thorn was in his "flesh" (σάρξ). As the Bible indicates that demon spirits often trouble the body, a messenger of Satan might well use a medical problem. Charles Hodge, *An Exposition of the Second Epistle to the Corinthians* (1859; reprinted, Grand Rapids: Baker, 1980), 287.

25. Mary Ann Jeffreys, "Sayings of Spurgeon," Christian History, 10, 1 (1991):12a; quoted in Hanegraff, 267.

26. The word translated "trials" in James 1:1-12 is also translated "tempted" in verse 13. "James' point is that every difficult circumstance that enters a believer's life can either strengthen him if he obeys God and remains confident in His care, or become a solicitation to evil if the believer chooses instead to doubt God and disobey His Word." MacArthur Study Bible, 1927 (note on James 1:13).

27. Millard J. Erickson, *Christian Theology* (Grand Rapids: Baker, 1983-85), 838.

28. Naturalism is the view that everything is "natural" and can be studied through the methods of science. It excludes the possibility of such things as souls and spirits.

CHAPTER NINE

THE SHADOW OF DEATH

In my late teens, after working awhile as an ambulance attendant, it struck me one day how much our society avoids facing death. When someone dies, "arrangements" are made – just one of the many euphemisms that help us avoid the unpleasantness of it all. Florists make the surroundings beautiful, and special make-up artists ply their craft to remove all appearances of death from the deceased. In a few days, the whole thing is over and the person is in the ground, out of sight and largely forgotten by all but a few.

On the other hand, those who are rescued and recover are thought of as somehow avoiding death rather than merely postponing it. Yet everyone – absolutely everyone – will succumb to death. It is one of the very few experiences we will all share. But it is so hard to face it. Perhaps that is one reason why billions are spent on things like hair dye, skin creme, and herbal supplements in order to hide or slow the aging process. But as we get older, the mirror reminds us we won't live forever.

Death as Just

Although we don't like to think of it this way, at the very root of it, death is no accident. It is God's just sentence on sin. Other ancient traditions regarded mankind as having lost eternal life by trickery (the

Adapa myth) or theft (the Gilgamesh epic),[1] but the Bible represents it as the Creator's decree to end this mode of existence.

The central message of Christianity, the Gospel, is the solution to this universal problem of death. Sin brings separation between humanity and a holy God thereby cutting humans off from the only source of life (Rom. 6:23) and immortality (1 Tim. 6:16). Being therefore dead spiritually, physical death inevitably follows. The fear of death haunts us (Heb. 2:15). Christ paid sin's penalty by dying on the cross, making possible the establishment of our connection to God, who is the source of life. Those who accept forgiveness by accepting Christ's payment for sin are made spiritually alive. Being still human, those who are saved from the penalty of sin are still subject to physical death (1 Thess. 4:16) but they will not experience the sting of separation from God (1 Cor. 15:55). Thus while the believer's physical body must die, death brings the believer into the presence of a loving Father. In that sense, they "never see death" (John 8:51, cf. 5:24). Those who refuse forgiveness remain forever cut off from the life of God. So for the unsaved, death is the great divider; for the saved, it is the great uniter.

Death as Teacher

The central message of Christianity, then, is that God has graciously made a way to reestablish life. Death is transformed from being an endpoint to being the start of life as it was intended. The believer has no need to avoid thinking about death, but can face it squarely and use it to remind him of life's priorities and limits. As Solomon said, the heart of the wise is in the house of mourning (Eccles. 7:4).

We should also realize how fleeting and unstable life is, like a vapor (James 4:14) or a flower that withers in the desert sun (Isa. 40:7-8). Realizing that our days are numbered will help us to live wisely (Ps. 90:12) while making the most of our time (Eph. 5:16). Far from grimly watching the hourglass of our life, we should live each day to the fullest, enjoying all we can (Eccles. 3:12, 9:9). Therefore, rather than be an ominous threat, death can be our great teacher, helping us improve the quality of our lives, getting the very most out of every day.

Occasionally I am reminded of the passing of life, perhaps by the death of someone I know, or the realization that my children are growing up all too quickly. I take it as a reminder to not be dominated by life's oppressive trivia, but rather to make sure I fully enjoy the blessings of marriage, family, health, ministry, and the silent beauty all around us. Life's blessings pass so quickly they have to be grasped each day and enjoyed. They cannot be thrown away by continual complaint, anger, or bitterness. The very shortness of life should remind us of that.

Coping with Loss

Although it is legitimate to feel loss when someone close to us passes (Phil. 2:27), we need not have a sense of hopeless grief if we have the confidence that the person was reconciled to God (1 Thess. 4:13). But if they were not reconciled we can trust them to the God who judges righteously. Depending on the circumstances, it may not be unrealistic to allow for at least the slight possibility that an individual came to God in his or her final moments. Who would have thought that a hardened criminal who was bent on blaspheming Christ even while being executed would then repent in the very final moments of his life and be received into heaven? Yet that was the experience of the thief on the cross (Luke 23:40-43; cf. Matt. 27:44)

Dealing with death can be difficult enough, but it is especially puzzling and faith-testing when we regard it as untimely. Perhaps the most difficult in this regard is the death of a young child or infant. Why would God take someone when seemingly they have their whole life ahead of them?

The first thing we have to remember is that any good thing we receive from God is of grace and is not owed (as mentioned in chapter three). We cannot say that God should have given more. God has not been unfair to anyone who lives less that seventy-five years. Rather than be bitter over a perceived loss, we should try to be thankful. But granted, being thankful in the face of sorrow can be a struggle.

We can still be left with the question of why God didn't graciously grant us more years with a person. We know that our loved one could have been such a blessing on earth here with us and with the people who needed him or her. It is good that they have gone to a better place, but we can't help wondering why that couldn't have been postponed for the sake of the good they might have done here?

While the question is understandable it assumes that they have left the only place where they can be a blessing to others, serve God, and accomplish good. It assumes that in heaven there are none of those things, only rest and personal blessing. Though the glimpse we get of heaven in Scripture is very limited, I would suggest that it is anything but a place of inactivity. Certainly we no longer suffer the unpleasantness of this life with its pain, sin, and toil; but we still serve God in worship and through the use of our unique personality and gifts. And we can conclude that our relationships there will be far better than they could ever be here on earth. The only things absent are sin and its consequences.

To see that a perfect state is one of activity, we can look to the Genesis account of Adam before the fall. He was not inactive, but worked in the garden (Gen. 2:15). No doubt it was pleasant and self-fulfilling, like the effort we expend on a favorite hobby or sport. Too, we are told that the unfallen angels use their varied abilities in service, and not just in resisting evil (e.g., Isaiah 6:2-3). This shows that fruitful effort is part of a perfected state and that people in heaven will not spend eternity staring blissfully at clouds.

What this means is that God may have greater purposes for our loved one elsewhere; He did not just take them out of our lives for no good purpose. In light of the things He has for a person to do on earth, His timing is perfect as to when they are born. It is reasonable to suppose that the same is true of the timing of His plans for a person entering heaven. We see only a person's departure from this life, and knowing how much they are missed, we are tempted to doubt God's timing. What we don't see is what God is doing in the greater picture beyond this life. Besides, when it comes to the death of a young child or infant, is it so bad that His plan for them is to never experience the sorrows and ravages of sin and its consequences, but instead to take them directly to a pristine place, a place of perfectly loving relationships, and into His wonderful presence?

Keeping these things in mind can soften our understandable sense of loss and puzzlement.

In God's Immediate Presence

We can be assured that our believing loved one is indeed in the presence of God, not in a state of unconscious "soul sleep," awaiting a future resurrection. Scripture sometimes refers to death as falling asleep (e.g., John 11:11; Acts 7:60), but the metaphor is based on the body's appearance. If the soul slept, Moses and Elijah could not have appeared on the mount of transfiguration (Matt. 17:3), the parable of Lazarus and the rich man would make no sense (Luke 16:19-31), and

Jesus could not have told the thief on the cross, "today you will be with me in Paradise" (Luke 23:43). Furthermore, Paul would not have felt a tension between wanting to depart to be with Christ versus remaining on earth in order to continue in fruitful labor (Phil. 1:23-24). There is such tension only in the face of two good options, laboring or being in God's presence. There would be no tension if the choice were between laboring and being unconscious for untold centuries. Such a choice would not present a dilemma since laboring longer would in no way delay his departure to heaven.[2] He could labor for many years and lose nothing. Clearly, he preferred to be, "absent from the body and to be at home with the Lord" (2 Cor. 5:8).

Death as Judgment on Believers

Though it is not common in Scripture, it is possible for a believer's death to be caused prematurely by his own sin. Annanias and Sapphira (Acts 5:5, 10) received this ultimate discipline for lying about the portion of their goods that they had given to the church, a sin that Peter identified as in reality lying to God. The penalty was so serious probably because God was impressing on the young church the need for obedience and purity, similar to His taking the life of a man collecting sticks on the Sabbath in the early days of Israel (Num. 15:32-36). The Corinthians were told that a number of them had died because their lives had dishonored God (1 Cor. 11:30). It appears that John is talking about these sorts of cases when he mentions "sin leading to death" (1 John 5:16).

The church can respond to serious sin by putting the sinner outside the blessings and protection of Christian fellowship. Paul delivered Hymenaeus and Alexander to Satan "that they may be taught not to blaspheme" (1 Tim. 1:20). Hymenaeus was named as teaching the false idea that the resurrection had already taken place and was upsetting some believers' faith (2 Tim. 2:17). Paul urged the Corinthians to "deliver to Satan" a man in their church who was sexually involved with his stepmother. It was to be done "for the destruction of his flesh, that his spirit may be saved in the day of the Lord Jesus" (1 Cor. 5:5). Such destruction indicates ruin, and could entail sickness and possibly even death. The severe action was successful as the man did repent (assuming he is the one Paul later urged should be brought back into full fellowship so as to avoid any more damage to the man; 2 Cor. 2:7-8).

Years ago one of my theology professors who had a lot of ministry experience made the point that God did not stop carrying out these judgments on believers in the first century. Someday in heaven, he said, we will realize that God has been doing these things in our midst all along.

Death by Choice

For those who find the emotional or physical pain of this life unbearable, or who merely find life not worth the trouble, there is the temptation of ending their own life. One in five adults say that they have seriously thought about committing suicide, and one in fourteen have actually attempted it. It is a matter of some concern that 29 per cent of people over the age of sixty-five believe suicide is acceptable given certain circumstances.[3]

Suicide

Suicide was almost unheard of in Israel probably for a number of reasons. In the Old Testament giving and taking of life is regarded as the prerogative of a sovereign God. It depicts life as a great blessing, and focuses more on possibilities of this life than the one to come. Saul and Ahithophel killed themselves, but only because they faced certain death at the hands of their enemies (1 Sam. 31:4; 2 Sam. 17:23). In the New Testament, it is reported without comment that Judas killed himself (Matt. 27:5).

Though directed toward one's self, suicide is still the wrongful taking of life. It violates the scriptural emphasis on God as the author and Lord over life and death. (Exceptions are capital punishment, which was initiated to punish murder, according to Gen. 9:6; and just wars, which prevent wrongful taking of life by foreign powers.) Even Job did not commit suicide though it was said that Satan himself tormented him horribly. Nor did any scriptural writer consider it an option even though they contemplated and even witnessed every conceivable suffering.

Suicide is the final and ultimate removal of one's earthly life from God's control; as such it is a lack of submission and faith. Christian philosopher Richard Swinburne points out that in allowing us to choose between life and immediate death through suicide, God has given us one of the most significant of all choices. Suicide is wrong because it amounts to "throwing back a very good gift in the face of the giver."[4]

Insofar as suicide denies others the good we could do them, it can be an act of selfishness. As a way of avoiding troubles, it can be weakness. As a way to avoid facing personal disgrace, it can be rooted in pride (even in Japan where it can be regarded as an act of "sincerity"; the mother who kills her children before killing herself is praised because leaving them motherless would supposedly be cruel).[5] Nevertheless, who can help feeling deep sympathy for the struggles that drive a person to such a tragic end? I've seen several dozen attempted suicides and a few that were successful, and I felt deeply for every one of them. I have also felt no less deeply for the many people who have told me they were contemplating suicide.

I've known a couple of people that I am sure were Christians but who committed suicide. One fine man, for example, developed a terminal illness and was told in very realistic terms by his doctor what was likely ahead for him in his few remaining months. Unable to face it, he went home and killed himself, which was discovered by his wife of some thirty years. One friend, fellow student, and coworker felt overwhelmed by two areas of personal struggle. A number of his friends, myself included, and several pastors tried to help him through it, but privately he fell deeper into despair. At one point I thought he had resolved it because he seemed unburdened and at peace. Everything was okay, he told me. I found out later that he had merely resolved to end his life. In the aftermath of his suicide was a massive court battle lasting years and costing hundreds of thousands of dollars, over whether churches could be held responsible for "clergy malpractice." It was based on the accusation by the family that the church had not done enough to help him. Eventually the courts decided that a church could not be sued over such things.[6]

Another person, whom I barely knew, was a coworker at a ministry. In a time of great despondency he drove to a remote location and shot himself in the chest. He immediately regretted it and asked God for help. Seemingly from nowhere a person came by and heard calls for help. He was rushed to the hospital and survived. He later explained to shocked coworkers what had happened, and people worked to help him through issues that were now made far worse by his tragic attempt on his life. Though people thought things were getting resolved, I heard that some months later he made a second attempt on his life, that one successful.

There is no reason to think that their acts were any less forgivable than any other sin. The idea that suicide cannot be forgiven because it is impossible to confess it afterwards rests on a faulty view of 1 John 1:9, "If we confess our sins, He is faithful and righteous to forgive us our sins and to cleanse us from all unrighteousness." The verse does not hold that only those sins which are confessed are forgiven. Rather, it characterizes the Christian as a person who continually confesses sin (a present tense verb, denoting continuous action), thereby acknowledging his need for forgiveness – which God continually grants. Furthermore, Scripture affirms that salvation is ultimately a matter of God's grace, it is therefore not lost by individual acts of sin (e.g., Eph. 2:8-9; although a lifestyle of sin can indicate that a person is not saved).

Euthanasia

Society's growing emphasis on personal autonomy brings with it increasing pressure to allow deliberate ending of life for the person who desires it. Already, one in five people say that a person's choice to commit suicide must be respected no matter what the circumstances.[7] This pressure will mount as society looks for ways to solve the growing healthcare burden of the aging baby boomer population (currently about one third of the work force in the United States).

Could euthanasia be an acceptable solution to the problem of pain for some people? Derived from words meaning "good" and "death," euthanasia is the deliberate act of ending a person's life painlessly, usually in contrast to death by incurable disease or injury. Active euthanasia is generally recognized as directly taking a person's life, as with lethal injection. Passive euthanasia avoids prolonging the dying process by not starting, or else by withholding, some treatment or life support. In active euthanasia the cause of death is something administered by a person, such as a lethal injection. In passive euthanasia, the cause of death is the disease, which is allowed to take its course more quickly because the means to stop it have been withdrawn or were never begun. One amounts to death by commission, the other by omission.

Some recognize another option called "letting die," which focuses on intentions. Unlike either form of euthanasia, there is no intention to use death as a means to end suffering. So unlike passive euthanasia, it does not permit withholding or withdrawing treatment or life-support if those offer any chance of continued life. It does allow withholding or withdrawing them where they are useless so that the focus of treatment can shift to relieving pain. An example would be choosing not to perform painful surgeries on a hopelessly burned patient and instead concentrating on making their final hours as painless as possible. If further treatment would likely be useless it may not be worth whatever pain and expense it entails. No one can fault the person who decides against treatment that would at best postpone inevitable death for a few days, especially when forgoing it would lighten the stress on loved ones and possibly avoid their having to carry a financial burden the rest of their lives. But if there is any hope that treatment would indeed save the person's life, the letting die position would begin the treatment, even if doing so would be more difficult and painful than allowing them to die sooner.

I know the chaplain at a very large county hospital who is often called in by the medical staff to help with very difficult situations. In a number of severe burn cases he has been the one to discuss the treatment options with the patient. At times he has had to explain, gently and frankly, that no one has ever survived burns as extensive as theirs. He says that the doctors will work hard to save them if that is their desire, but the process will be uncomfortable or painful, and without the equivalent of a miracle, it will fail. Or, if they choose, the doctors can work to make them as comfortable as possible in their final hours. None of them has chosen the treatment.

There has been some dissatisfaction over the distinction between active and passive euthanasia. One group objects that it promotes the idea that passive euthanasia is acceptable but that active euthanasia is not; these critics accept both. The other group fears that calling them both euthanasia will minimize what they see as a crucial difference between them, thus encouraging people to accept active euthanasia, which they regard as immoral.

Back when I was in ambulance work, I remember that "no heroics" (or, "do not resuscitate") was sometimes written on a patient's chart. That meant that in the event of a medical emergency, extraordinary life saving measures should not be started. Such requests typically came from the doctor by way of a patient who was terminal and near death. Some of the ambulance staff debated just what their responsibilities would be in such a situation.

In a few cases I saw a medical worker make his or her own decision – not by the patient's request – to perform only a token effort to save the life of a terminally ill person. I was transporting an unconscious patient whose papers revealed that he was in very serious condition because of degenerative and possibly terminal conditions. Just as we arrived at the other facility, he went into cardiac arrest. We started resuscitating him, but when we brought him to the nurse in charge, she quicky assessed his problems and told us to discontinue all procedures. We made it very clear that she was making that decision on behalf of what was now her patient, and that if it were up to us, we would choose differently. She agreed to those conditions and told us to "just put him in the corner." We left him there, under her care, his life quietly ending in the hallway.

Some fear that euthanasia is a slippery slope and acceptance of it in any form will inevitably lead to acceptance of more and more radical forms. I talked to an elderly Christian woman in Holland who was concerned that if she went into a Dutch hospital for treatment a medical decision might be made to not only deny her treatment, but to end her life. Consequently, she made regular trips to the United States for treatment. A lot of her elderly friends had the same fear. Just last week the Dutch were discussing guidelines for euthanasia of those "with no free will," including children and the mentally retarded. In the process it was revealed that they have already been euthanizing babies.[8] In Germany a doctor is being investigated because 250 people died at her clinic in four years. According to a BBC News report, "She has said she was assisting seriously ill patients to die – after consultations with them and their relatives, for compassionate reasons."[9] In the United States, a male nurse plead guilty to murdering thirteen hospital patients in two states.[10]

The argument for merely letting die is the easiest to defend biblically since it advocates making every useful attempt to save the patient's life. When further intervention is for all practical purposes useless, it is committed to helping the patient cope with whatever remains of life. The more aggressive the approach to ending life (such as by lethal injection), the more it usurps the authority of the life giver and thus the harder it is to justify biblically. The ancient world of the biblical writers was filled with at least as much suffering as we have today – all faced without modern methods of controlling pain – yet they did not accept killing a person to end pain any more than they accepted suicide.

We have to remember that God is fully able to take a person's life in an instant or to change their circumstances, including eliminate their pain, in an instant. Actively ending life, even if it's our own, is outside the range of our biblical options for solving a personal problem.

None of this means that we cannot sacrifice our lives for the sake of a good cause or for another person, such as the teacher who died getting students to safety in the 1999 Columbine High School shootings in the U.S., where two students conspired to kill a number of their classmates.

A biblical view of ethics would have us endure certain experiences because God allows them, though some of them may seem unbearable. Through them we can, for example, face our limits and weaknesses, learn to depend upon God, trust Him for things we don't understand, develop inner strength, and gain a clearer understanding of life's priorities and values. Those witnessing the suffering can benefit in similar ways, as well as develop compassion and a determination to eliminate suffering wherever possible.

We have to realize that the lessons we gain from suffering – what we learn about ourselves, faith, and God – can be gained only in this life. After this life the believer can never suffer again (Rev. 21:4). For the unbeliever, suffering at the end of life may provide the best opportunity to face personal limits and weaknesses, turning them to their Creator. Euthanasia would eliminate their last and best opportunity for that. And if eternal punishment awaits the unrepentant, is it really merciful to eliminate their relatively brief earthly sufferings – which could bring them to accept God's grace – only to send them to their eternity?[11]

Defining Life

Suffering and end of life issues get even more complicated when considering brain damage. We have an upper brain, which makes us conscious, and a brain stem, which keeps us alive by controlling the functions of our heart and lungs. Traditionally, death was considered a matter of cessation of the heart and lungs. But now that machines can keep them functioning, it is accepted that death occurs when the whole brain dies (upper and lower brain). It is all but universally accepted that withdrawing treatment ("pulling the plug") is an option in cases of brain death.

A controversy is growing, however, over a group of patients whose upper brain has been severely damaged or destroyed but whose brain stem remains alive. Consequently, their body continues to function, almost as though a machine keeps it alive. The condition is known as a persistent vegetative state (PVS). The person can show sleep and waking patterns, and even grasp, yet they have no thought or emotions,[12] and it is debated whether they can feel pain. With a feeding tube they can live for years (thirty-seven years in one case),[13] though two to five years is more typical. Their situation is different from a person in a coma, because unlike a coma, there is increasing evidence that the PVS patient can never get better.[14] It is estimated that the numbers are between 10,000 to 25,000 adults and 4,000 to 10,000 children. At a healthcare cost of $97,000 to $180,000 per year for each patient, the total is between one and seven billion dollars each year in the U.S. alone.[15]

There is a crucial debate over whether the PVS patient is even alive. If they are not and feeding them need not continue, then it would relieve thousands of people who are burdened with their care and allow limited health care dollars to be spent elsewhere. Is our allowing them to die by not feeding them God's way of reducing suffering, or is it immoral? Would God forbid ending such suffering?

How we resolve the issue could have far reaching effects, intentionally or unintentionally. It could affect many classes of people including those at the beginning of life, such as the unborn, as well as those at the end of life, such as those with extreme forms of dementia. This is a pivotal debate today and lies at the heart of two very different visions for society, each based on contrasting views of how we decide who is alive.

The traditional view is based on mere biological criteria for determining who is alive, and thus who has rights. Simply put, on this view anyone who is alive has all the rights of a human. And being alive is nothing more than a matter of having a heart beat, or as judged more recently, brain waves.

If settling the debate about PVS patients amounts to nothing more than refining the traditional biological criteria for life then it has no radical implications for society. We could decide that to be alive a person's upper brain has to be alive, or, we could decide instead that only the lower brain has to be alive. Thus the decision could be seen as merely refining what it means to be brain dead.

On the other hand the discussion can bring us uncomfortably close to a very different way of deciding who is alive, judged by who meets certain value criteria. According to this view, the question of whether someone is a human is not settled by whether they are physically alive or dead, but whether they meet some other criteria. These can be based on a person's usefulness, or whether they have a life "worth living." On some proposals, the value criteria might be as complex and vague as having the ability to benefit from social interaction and to attain self-fulfillment (I've met quite a few people who might not qualify as human under those standards!). Joseph Fletcher, who for years taught ethics at a medical school, initially laid out twenty criteria for being a human. They included concern for others, curiosity, balance of rationality and feeling, and idiosyncrasy.[16] In a futuristic nightmare scenario political elections could be decided by ethics committees which have the power to declare one candidate less than human!

If applying the value criteria to elections seems a little far fetched, applying it to ordinary people is not. A child born retarded or an elderly person who develops Alzheimer's disease could be considered not a human being. As such their existence could be terminated since they would have no more right to live than a weed in a flower garden.

It has been the Christian position that to be human is to be in the image of God, based on God's intentions when He made mankind (Gen. 1:26-27). Some believe that image consists of abilities we have as humans that are not found in animals, such as self-consciousness and the ability to reason. In other words, this views the image of God as something we are (called the substantive view). A contrasting view holds that our ability to relate to God is what makes us in His image (the relational view). A third view holds that it is a matter of what we can do, such as dominating the earth (the functional view).

While it seems possible that the image could involve aspects of all three,[17] there is no doubt that the latter two views demand far too much mental ability to be exercised by those who are in a vegetative state, comatose, extremely retarded, or senile; or even the unborn. Appeal solely to those views of the image of God as a grounds for being human would seem to leave the door open to a Huxlian brave new world in which some people decide that others have no right to live.[18]

But a second look at the image of God shows that whatever it consists of, there is no biblical grounds for the idea that some people can be denied the right to live because they do not have enough of the image of God. A person's right to live does not come in degrees – they have it simply because they are human. This is clear from the context of Genesis 9, where God says that animals can be killed for food but that killing a person amounts to murder (v. 6), which demands capital punishment. It is important to notice that there is no requirement to have a sufficient amount of something unique to humans. For example, it does not forbid killing only people who are in touch with God, or those who are fulfilling their role as dominators of the earth. This suggests that merely being human gives a person the right to life. That the image of God is something basic to our existence and cannot fall below some value threshold is also suggested by James 3:9. Here cursing is forbidden on the grounds that they are made in the image of God; no qualifications are given. This too fits the view that the image of God is something that we are as humans, rather than a capacity we have or something that we do.

So basing a person's right to live on whether their life would be useful or "worth living," is mistaken. Rather than basing it on the judgment of a person's value, it seems appropriate to base it on the more fundamental biological question of whether a person is indeed alive.

Christian ethicist Robert Rakestraw bases an individual's right to life on whether they have the image of God or will develop it. So an unborn child has a right to live because he or she will develop into the image. A comatose person has a right because he or she might regain the capacity to image God. But a person in a persistent vegetative state does not because their ability to bear the image of God is forever gone. In biblical terms, he says, they are dead though their bodies are alive. For him it justifies pulling out their feeding tube and allowing their condition to take its course such that, absent a miracle, they die.[19]

Rakestraw is trying to solve some difficult problems in a distinctively Christian way, with reference to the image of God. It appears that he is trying to maintain some reference to a biological criteria for human life.

There is as yet no clear consensus within the church as to how to resolve the persistent vegetative state issue. Some would want to resist such use of persistent vegetative states to "define" personhood, even if it is done with reference to the image of God.[20]

The issue of how we define human life deserves our attention. Leo Alexander, who served with the Office of the Chief of Counsel for War Crimes in the Nuremberg trials, recounted in the *New England Journal of Medicine* how in Germany between the two world wars there was a rapid change in criteria for determining who had the right to live. Traditional values were replaced by the criterion of "rational usefulness," he said. Soon the right to life was withdrawn from the chronically ill so as to save "useless" expenses to the community. The right was withdrawn from the racially and ideologically unwanted, and from those who were considered disloyal to the ruling group. All this was done at the hands of the medical profession.[21]

Aside from those in a persistent vegetative state, what could be the purpose of allowing people to live in spite of their severely diminished capacity? The comatose patient, for example, is not conscious of any of life's benefits. Yet even if they do not benefit, others can exercise compassion, as well as grow in selflessness and the appreciation of the mental capacities they themselves and others have. Professor of medicine and ethics, Dónal O'Mathúna, recounts how his neighbor's four month old boy, Ryan, stopped breathing. He was resuscitated but his cerebral cortex died, making him a virtual vegetable. His parents still regard him as their son, just like his twin, and they bring him home from an institution most weekends. They praise God for Ryan, and for the way he has helped them make family and people more of a priority. His mother became a Christian because of Ryan.[22]

This is not to minimize the considerable burden such a patient can place on family members and the health care system. In many cases a family member has to make enormous sacrifices to care for the patient. Careers or education have to be put aside in order to feed, clean, and move the person every few hours to prevent bed sores. Meager family finances can be turned into debt in the process – all for a person who can never know the sacrifices that are being made. But O'Mathúna would say, these are the hard cases that force us to decide what is really important in life. It is easy to slide into the view that the convenience and happiness of the many takes precedence over the rights of a few, especially when those few are completely helpless. Only a firm commitment to principle will prevent such a slide.

Nowhere is the battle for the helpless more apparent than in the issue of abortion.

Abortion

In the view of many today, abortion offers the possibility of preventing a certain amount of suffering, such as the suffering of a parent who does not want a child, the suffering of a child who is unwanted, and sufferings caused by birth abnormalities. What is the biblical view?

The Bible does not mention abortion, possibly because it was unthinkable to the Jewish community. Life and children were always considered a blessing; death and childlessness were associated with judgment. Too, in primitive agrarian societies, children provide nearly free labor as well as a means of being cared for in one's old age.

Infanticide, the killing of infants, served the same purpose as abortion in the ancient world. That is because lack of medical technology made abortions so risky for the mother. It is significant that God condemned infanticide in the strongest terms (e.g., Jer. 32:35).

Evidence for the humanity of the unborn, thus their right to life, is traditionally found in biblical statements that refer to the unborn as human rather than potentially human. David referred to God as forming him in his mother's womb, not merely tissue that would eventually become him (Ps. 139:15). He also traced his sinfulness all the way back to his conception (Ps. 51:5).[23] John the Baptist was called a "baby" and was said to leap for joy at the arrival of Jesus, while both were yet in the womb (Luke 1:44; though leaping for joy could be figurative[24]). It was also said that he would be filled with the Holy Spirit while yet in the womb (Luke 1:15). Only persons can have joy and be filled with the Holy Spirit. It is also worth noting that in Hebrew as well as Greek the same word designates both a fetus and a child (Hebrew *yeled*; Greek βρέφοζ). Had this been misleading, we would expect that the biblical writers would have clarified the difference between the born and the unborn; but they did not.

A crucial passage for determining whether or not abortion is a sin is Exodus 21:22-25. It determines the punishment in case of injury to a pregnant woman. If two men fight and a pregnant woman becomes injured such that her fetus "departs," but there is no further injury, the guilty person pays a fine. According to one interpretation this refers to a miscarriage where there is no injury to the mother ("miscarriage," NASB). That would mean that the unborn is not a human since its death is not seriously punished.

A better interpretation regards the event as a premature birth where there is no injury to either the child or the mother ("gives birth prematurely," NKJV). The noun (*yeled*) is the word for an ordinary child, and the verb (*yatsa'*) is used of a normal birth, never of a miscarriage (Gen. 25:25-26; 38:28-29; Job 1:21; 3:11; Eccles. 5:15; Jer. 20:18).[25] Furthermore, if a miscarriage had been meant the Hebrew word for it (*shakhol*; Exod. 23:26; Hos. 9:14) would have been used.

The verse (Exod. 21:23) says that if there is any further injury then the penalty shall be "life for life." It seems that if either the mother or baby suffer injury, there shall be serious punishment, including capital punishment. If this interpretation is correct, the unborn is treated as a human being since taking its life is no different from taking the life of a born child.

The early church prohibited abortion. Written within memory of the apostles' teaching, The *Didache* and The *Epistle of Barnabus* both contain the command, "Thou shalt not murder a child by abortion nor kill them when born"[26]

Over forty million abortions have been performed in the U.S. since 1973 when the Supreme Court made it legal in Roe v. Wade. It is estimated that there were forty-six million abortions world wide in 1995 alone, including a million and a half in the U. S.[27] But abortion is hard to justify even apart from appealing to the Bible.

First, as to whether the unborn is a human, there is no grounds for saying that the unborn becomes human at some specific point. There is smooth development from beginning to end. Birth is an arbitrary point for granting human rights, and so is ability to live apart from the mother (which gets pushed back continually as technology develops). Secondly, it does no good to argue that a woman can do what she wants with the fetus because it is her body: it has its own genetic code, blood type, circulatory system, and (even early on) brain waves. Clearly, one person's freedom's are restricted by another's right to live.

Claims that abortion is a way to reduce suffering are weak indeed. The claim that abortion prevents unwanted children ignores the large number of couples that want to adopt, as well as the fact that many parents who at first don't welcome a pregnancy later want the child. Also, the vast majority of abused children are wanted (90 per cent according to one study). According to Christian ethicist Robertson McQuilkin, in the first decade of legalized abortion, fifteen million were aborted yet child abuse rose 400 percent.[28] As to preventing suffering by preventing birth abnormalities, less than one percent of abortions are performed for that reason. Those who are born with abnormalities seem to be as happy as other people anyway. They do not seem to have unusually high suicide rates, and often report that they are satisfied with life.[29]

So these are good reasons to conclude that abortion is not a God-given way to limit human suffering any more than is suicide or active euthanasia.

Why would God allow people to have abortions? Humans have been given significant freedom, which entails that they be able to do genuine good or harm. Just as He allows humans the awesome power to bring a life into this world, so they have the equally awesome power to end it (though both are under God's sovereignty). But God does not grant individuals, groups, or societies the power to harm forever and commit injustice on a limitless scale. As we saw in the chapter on justice, He draws the line with whole nations just as He does with individuals.

Conclusion

Death is the divine limit on a race that rebelled thereby causing harm to itself. But the end of this existence can be the beginning of a new one in which real life is recovered in a wonderfully renewed state. However, for those who reject God's gracious plan, death leads to the bitter experience that God sacrificed His Son to avoid. Because God's sovereignty over the end of life should be respected, we should be careful not to overstep our bounds even if God's gift of significant freedom entails that we have the power to do so.

GOING FARTHER

1. How can death have a constructive role in our lives?

2. What are some ways of dealing with an "untimely" death?

3. How do we know that the believer who departs is in the immediate presence of the Lord?

4. Do you think a true Christian can commit suicide?

5. Under what conditions would your recommend that medical treatment be stopped for a critical patient?

6. What is at stake in how we define a human being?

7. How is the interpretation of Exodus 21:22-25 crucial in the biblical debate about abortion?

8. What are other biblical reasons for prohibiting abortion?

NOTES

1. Paul Ferguson, "Death, Mortality," *Evangelical Dictionary of Biblical Theology*, ed. Walter A. Elwell (Grand Rapids: Baker, 1996), 155.

2. For more, see E. F. Harrison, "Soul Sleep," *Evangelical Dictionary of Theology*, ed. Walter Elwell (Grand Rapids: Baker, 1984), 1037-8. And see Millard J. Erickson, *Christian Theology* (Grand Rapids: Baker, 1983-5), 1176-78.

3. The Harris Poll #28, May 7, 2003, "Seven Percent of U. S. Adults Say They Have Attempted to Commit Suicide," by Humphrey Taylor. Accessed 25 July 2003. from <harrisinteractive.com/harris_poll/printerfriend/index.as?PID=376>. Survey of 2,715 adults conducted March 17-24, 2003. It has a margin of error of plus or minus 3 per cent. Twenty-one percent have considered suicide; 36 per cent of 18 to 24 year olds have considered it, and 12 per cent of the same group have attempted it.

4. Richard Swinburne, *Providence and the Problem of Evil* (Oxford, Clarendon, 1998), 147, 146.

5. Kenshiro Ohara, leading authority on suicide in Japan, *The New York Times,* April 30, 1973, p. 10; cited in Vernon C. Grounds, "Suicide," *Baker's Dictionary of Christian Ethics*, ed. Carl F. H. Henry (Grand Rapids: Baker, 1973), 652.

6. Of course nothing I say constitutes legal advice. For that one should seek a qualified professional.

7. The Harris Poll #28, May 7, 2003, "Seven Percent of U.S. Adults Say They Have Attempted to Commit Suicide". Accessed 25 July 2003. From <harrisinteractive.com/harris_poll/printerfriend/index.as?PID=376>. Survey of 2,715 adults conducted March 17-24, 2003. It has a margin of error of plus or minus 3 per cent.

8. "Netherlands Hospital Euthanizes Babies," by Toby Sterling, Associated Press; in Newsday.com, Nov. 30, 2004; <wwwnewsday.com/news/nationworld/world/wire/sns-ap-netherlands-child-euthanas...>

9. "German Doctor Faces Deaths Probe," *BBC News* , March 2, 2004.

10. "Ex-Nurse Pleads Guilty in Patient Deaths," *My Way News*; April 29, 2004.

11. We are talking here from the human side, and this is not meant to deny the view that God ultimately decides individual salvation (e.g., Eph. 1:4-5).

12. "Personality, memory, purposive action, social interaction, sentience, thought, and even emotional states are gone. Only vegetative functions and reflexes persist." Report of the President's Commission for the Study of Ethical Problems in Medicine and Biomedical and Behavioral Research, "Deciding to Forego Life-Sustaining Treatment: A Report on the Ethical Medical, and Legal Issues in Treatment Decisions"(Washington, D. C.: U.S. Government Printing Office, 1983), 174-5; cited in Rakestraw, 120.

13. The survivor was E. Esposito, who remained in the condition from 1941 to 1978; D. Lamb, *Death, Brain Death and Ethics* [Albany: SUNY, 1985], 6; cited in Rakestraw, 118.

14. Rakestraw (p. 124), points to scientific evidence that PVS is permanent. He references work by Fred Plum of Cornell (who with Bryan Jennet was the first to describe PVS after brain damage).

15. The Multi-Society Task Force on PVS, "Medical Aspects of the Persistent Vegetative State," parts 1 and 2, *New England Journal of Medicine* 330 (May 1994): Part 1, 1503; cited in Dónal P. O'Mathúna, Ph.D., "Responding to Patients in the Persistent Vegetative State," reprinted in *Philosophia Christi* 19.2 (Fall 1996): 55-83. The journal is by the Evangelical Philosophical Society. The article is also on-line, <http://www.xenos.org/ministries/crossroads/donal/pvs.htm>.

16. Joseph Fletcher, "Four Indicators of Humanhood – The Enquiry Matters," in Stephen E. Lammers and Allen Verhey, eds., *On Moral Medicine: Theological Perspectives in Medical Ethics* (Grand Rapids, MI: Eerdmans, 1987), 276; reprinted from The Hastings Center Report 4 (Dec. 1975):4-7. He said his list of twenty traits of humanhood previously published in The Hastings Center Report (Nov. 1972) was "intended to keep the investigation going forward" (p. 275). In the "Four Indicators" article he (obviously) discussed only four.

17. See for example Erickson, who holds the substantive view but recognizes the importance of a relationship with God and exercise of dominion (p. 515-16, sections 3 and 4, respectively).

18. Of course, a person could advocate the relational or functional view of the image of God yet hold on some other grounds that merely being physically alive entitles a person to the rights of a human.

19. Rakestraw, 128.

20. In contrast to Rakestraw, see for example Dónal P. O'Mathúna, Ph.D., "Responding to Patients in the Persistent Vegetative State," reprinted in *Philosophia Christi* 19.2 (Fall 1996): 55-83.

21. *New England Journal of Medicine* (14 July 1949); quoted in Robertson McQuilken, *An Introduction to Biblical Ethics*, 2nd. ed. (Wheaton, IL: Tyndale House, 1995), 313.

22. Dónal O'Mathúna, loc. cit.

23. Erickson (p. 553) does not take the pronouns as good evidence that David referred to himself as a person in his pre-birth state.

24. Erickson, 554.

25. In Numbers 12:12 it refers to a stillbirth, but this is different from a miscarriage. As Erickson points out (p. 555), that it was a stillbirth is indicated in the context by the description of the fetus, not by the verb.

26. *Didache* 2:2, *Epistle of Barnabus* 19:21, trans. J. B. Lightfoot. See Michael J. Gorman, "Why Is the New Testament Silent about Abortion?", *Christianity Today*, 11 January 1993.

27. Stanley K. Henshaw, Sushela Singh, Taylor Hass, "The Incidence of Abortion Worldwide," *Family Planning Perspectives*, vol. 25, supplement Jan. 1999; accessed 10 Mar. 2004, <agi-USA.org/pubs/journals/25s3099.html>.

28. McQuilken, 323.

29. Dr. and Mrs. J. C. Willke, *Abortion: Questions and Answers*, rev. (Cincinnati, OH: 1988), 212. The authors cite, for example, P. Cameron, "Though it may be both common and fashionable to believe that the malformed enjoys life less than normal, this appears to lack both empirical and theoretical support," Univ. Of Louisville, Van Hoeck et al., Wayne State Univ., "Happiness and Life Satisfaction of the Malformed," *Proceedings, Amer. Psychologic Assn. Meeting*, 1971.

Chapter ten

SPECIAL PROBLEMS – Birth Defects, Poverty, and War.

Some experiences of suffering are virtually universal. We almost can't be human without experiencing some physical pain, being emotionally hurt in different ways by people, or suffering regrets or unrealized hopes and ambitions. Other types of suffering are special in that not everyone goes through them.

The three special problems discussed in this chapter have complex causes, and a great deal of modern effort is spent trying to understand and eliminate them. Ironically, some of those efforts make the problems worse. But for those who are alert to the possibilities, these sources of suffering present opportunities to do good.

Birth Defects

Since it was commonly believed in the ancient world that the direct cause of suffering was some personal sin, birth defects posed a problem: how could a person be afflicted from birth, before they had done anything wrong? The natural conclusion was that it must be judgment on the parents. But that raised the further question, why should most of the punishment for a sin be borne by someone else? The disciples posed this problem to Jesus when they came across a man who was born blind (John 9:2).

Jesus answered by correcting the assumption that suffering is always linked to some personal sin: "It was neither this man that sinned, nor his parents; but it was in order that the works of God might be displayed in him" (9:3). So while not denying that God's judgment can work itself out in hidden ways, Jesus introduced a whole new way of thinking about the problem. Rather that look backward to find some specific sin[1] that would merit a certain misfortune, Jesus focused on the fact that God may allow a person's suffering for a constructive purpose. God's glory would be manifested in this special case by providing an opportunity for a spectacular healing. No doubt God can have a higher purpose for other cases of suffering, and not just that of the blind man.

Although birth defects and other serious physical problems are not a part of God's ideal plan, He does not remove Himself as a cause of them. When Moses claimed to lack the necessary eloquence for his calling, God replied, "Who has made man's mouth? Or who makes him dumb or deaf, or seeing or blind? Is it not I, the Lord" (Exod. 4:11). Whatever natural processes are involved in birth defects, God is their ultimate cause and is in control of them.

The natural causes for abnormalities are complex and not always entirely understood. The major part of it, though, has to do with our genetic blueprints, which are extremely intricate. At the risk of oversimplifying, some people can carry the gene for a problem without having it themselves. It can be manifested in their children depending on the genetic background of the person they marry. There is technology to screen for some recessive disorders (such as hemophilia) so that parents with family histories of the disease can find out if there may be a problem in their children. Some genetic disorders are especially high in certain groups. Sickle cell anemia, which affects hemoglobin, occurs in Sub-Saharan Africans and one out of 400 black Americans. Tay-Sachs results from lipids on the brain, causing mental deficiency and blindness in infants. It affects one in 3,600 Ashkenazi Jews and French Canadians, but only one in 400,000 people generally.[2]

Besides problems that are passed down over generations, there is also an increasing likelihood of a problem as the mother ages. A mother of twenty has a one in 1,667 chance of giving birth to a Down's Syndrome baby, and a 1 in 526 chance of having a baby with any genetic abnormality. By age forty-three that increases to a one in fifty chance for Down's and one in thirty-three for any abnormality.[3] Besides the aging process, genetic data can be damaged from outside influences, such as radiation.

Other problems can arise during the development of the fetus. If the mother contracts certain illnesses, such as Rubella, or is exposed to any number of chemicals during a crucial phase in the pregnancy, abnormalities can develop.

As far as personal responsibility for defects, it runs the whole range from being no one's fault to being directly caused by drug or alcohol use during pregnancy. There is also the possibility of ignorance, as when a mother uses certain medications at specific stages of pregnancy. Whether she bears some responsibility for her ignorance depends on such things as her diligence to find out what is harmful and how readily the information was available.

To the extent that the cause of an abnormality is sin, the issue goes back to the fact that God gave us significant free will, which entails the power to do good or harm. The freedom which gives a woman the choice to love God and her children also enables her to abuse alcohol during her pregnancy. Yet that freedom also makes it possible for others to sacrifice years of their lives adopting and caring for the unwanted children whose brains and bodies were damaged for life by mothers who would not give up alcohol or drugs for even a few months. I've had the privilege of knowing several couples who provide the most loving care for children who have been damaged during their prenatal development by substance abusing mothers. One woman gave up her career as a veterinarian and the couple has spent thousands of dollars giving special care to a baby girl they adopted with multiple health problems. It has been wonderful to see progress that doctors never thought possible as she has grown into a very special girl. For that and for their commitment to several other children I've often told them they are angels of mercy. I can think of no clearer expression of God's love and compassion than to sacrifice for a helpless person when there is no hope of reward other than seeing them blessed.

Love and compassion can also be expressed by an entire society, such as in the way they care for those with abnormalities, and the way they support research into its causes and cures. Contrast countries with laws giving the handicapped access to public places, jobs, and education, with Nazi Germany's extermination of the them. (Nevertheless there is a faint but disturbing similarity between the Nazi quest for a better society through genetic perfection, and those in modern societies who seek genetic perfection by aborting those with detected birth abnormalities; some allege that the connection is not entirely coincidental[4]).

Birth abnormalities that are not caused by human irresponsibility seem to be a case of God allowing imperfections in a system He created. Like natural disasters, it would be an example of His broadening the range of possible states of affairs after the fall, allowing those that bring suffering. We have been investigating why He would do that, and some of the reasons that apply to other conditions also apply to genetic disorders: it provides opportunities to grow character and do good, some of which would not exist without suffering; it provides a sense that this world is not in an ideal state, and so on.

Without trivializing the difficulty of living with birth abnormalities, we can recognize some specific benefits. They showcase the marvels of God's design in that we realize the value of abilities we often take for granted. Blindness, for example, helps us appreciate the wonders of sight. Defects, especially in senses, can motivate a person to compensate by developing one or more other senses to heightened levels, such as the blind person who never forgets a voice, or the deaf person who is good at understanding people's thoughts and feelings from their facial expressions. Thought processes can be developed differently, too. A friend of mine with very little hearing is an outstanding editor of Christian books, and I am convinced his difficulty hearing has stimulated a heightened sensitivity to written communication. Another friend has dyslexia, which gives him difficulty reading, but he is one of the highest profile corporate pilots in the business and has developed a personality that works exceptionally well with all types of people. Erik Weihenmayer realized his dream of climbing Mt Everest even though he is blind! While sighted climbers can see which ice is safe and which is unsafe, he has learned to tap it to decide where to step. He says it is useless to wish for an ability you do not have. It is better to ask, "How do I do as much as I can with what I have?"[5] His friend Hugh Herr lost both his legs in an ice-climbing accident. Herr became an engineer and developed prosthetic limbs out of rubber. Now he is a better climber than ever, Erik says.

Because we focus on the few people who have deficiencies we can easily forget that each of us has very different abilities anyway. Some have great physical strength or agility, others high verbal or musical abilities, others sophisticated social skills. We even develop our thought processes differently in that some of us are creative whereas others are analytical. As well, our personalities suit us for different things. So, there may be a few people who are a little more obviously different in that they perhaps lack a sense of hearing or are unable to walk, but are they really more different from the rest of us than we are from each other? Probably not. You would probably have more in common with someone at your job or school who was born with a clubbed foot than you would have, say, with a three hundred pound Sumo wrestler, whose body is "normal" but is so different from yours in many other ways.

Many people in modern society resist as unfair the idea of inherent differences between people, especially where those differences give one person or group an advantage. Our public education, for example, spends little or nothing to develop the mentally gifted though it spends millions to help underachievers. The attitude extends to money and possessions as well. In the United States there has even been talk of a special tax on those who drive larger vehicles (sport utility vehicles, or SUV's). On the view that fairness consists of everyone being essentially the same, God is bound to look unfair for creating those with less than average capability in some area. This is made worse by the fact that quality of life is often judged by such things as how much money a person can make, how attractive they look, or how popular they can become. A person lacking some ability, such as would require them to use a wheel chair for example, is likely to seem badly disadvantaged – and thus their creator seems to be very unfair.

But differences between us, even major inborn ones, are not unequivocally bad. Besides, we must not forget that as with other areas of life, whatever we get is of grace; and since by definition grace is not owed, it makes no sense to fault God for failing to be more gracious. The person who is not tall enough to be a professional basketball player or coordinated enough to be a concert pianist cannot say God has been unfair – nor can the person who has one of his senses impaired or who must walk with a cane.

The point is more obvious when we compare ourselves as humans to other creatures. Eagles have at least four times our visual acuity, bats hear much higher sounds and use sonar (they can hear up to 200 kilohertz, whereas we can hear up to only 20 kilohertz), whales hear much lower sounds and can communicate over many miles (several hundred, some think), cheetahs can run over sixty miles per hour, chimpanzees can have the strength of six or seven men, bees can see ultra-violet, mosquitos can sense carbon dioxide (and may even be able to hear a human heart beat),[6] and it is thought that dogs can sense odors at concentrations nearly a hundred million times lower than humans (a keen sense of smell would actually be a great disadvantage to people who live in most big cities!). The strongest creature in proportion to its weight is the rhinoceros beetle, which can lift eight hundred times its weight. If humans had that kind of strength we would be able to lift sixty-five tons. Even the lowly snapping shrimp can wield its claw in three thousandths of a second (as fast as a bullet), which is nearly a hundred times faster than the human recordholder for drawing and firing a gun.

I've never met anyone who feels God cheated them because He did not make them with the capability of some other creature. But I've met plenty of people who feel God cheated them compared to some other person. Rather than compare our capabilities with someone else or something else, our focus should be on developing and using our own abilities – whatever they are – to the fullest.

It is amazing how little correlation there is between abilities and happiness, contrary to so much popular thinking. Athletes and actors, for example, whose abilities bring them fame and fortune, seem as a group to be rather less happy than average people. On the other hand, surveys of people born with handicaps show that as a group they are at least as happy as the general population. One study surveyed 150 spina bifida patients and found that not one of them said life was not worth living.[7] Another study concluded, "Though it may be both common and fashionable to believe that the malformed enjoys life less than normal, this appears to lack both empirical and theoretical support."[8]

The combination of our abilities and inabilities help make us what we are. Those with an abnormality often develop wonderful qualities such as humility, sensitivity, and compassion. I would rather spend an evening with the typical person who has struggled with a disability than with someone who is famous because of their money, or ability in sports or acting.

Though a handicap can be an important part of a person's life, helping to shape who they are, it is not an essential part of them. In other words, they would still be who they are without it, even if they might not have become what they are in terms of character. Consequently, God can remove that handicap in heaven and they would be the same individual. On a traditional understanding of heaven, He will do just that.

Poverty

When society's focus shifted from heaven to earth during the Renaissance, there began a corresponding shift in focus from our spiritual condition and future heavenly life to our material condition and the possibilities of earthly life. By the time Marx wrote his philosophy in the nineteenth century, he interpreted everything, including politics, sociology, and religion, in substantially economic terms.

Since the days of Marx and the sufferings brought on by the early industrial revolution, much popular thinking has romanticized the plight of the poor. The poor are often regarded as necessarily the hapless victims of a selfish wealthy class and a corrupt system. For sheer simplicity the view is a little like a low-budget western movie in which the good characters in white hats can do no wrong and the villains in the black hats can do no right.[9] Such a view contributed to the rise of the idea that social justice demands that the state use its power to take from the person with more goods and give them to the person with fewer goods, turning the state into a bureaucratic Robin Hood. The view that fairness is a matter of redistributing wealth reversed the view that social justice consists of the state guaranteeing each person the right to his or her own property (not someone else's), a view championed by British philosopher John Locke (1632-1704), whose views were generally influential among the American founders.[10]

Unrighteous Poverty

The biblical view of poverty is far more complex. To begin with, in contrast to Marxism it views sin not as a class issue between oppressor and oppressed, but as an individual issue whereby sin exists in every human heart. Consequently, some poverty can be attributed to laziness (Prov. 6:10-11; 10:4; 20:13; 24:33-34), lack of discipline (Prov. 13:18), or idleness (Prov. 14:23; 28:19). It can also come from a "get rich quick" motivation that shuns things like diligence, patience, and planning (Prov. 21:5; 28:20). Financial ruin can come from an uncontrolled desire for luxuries and pleasure (Prov. 21:17), or from gluttony or substance abuse (Prov. 23:21, alcohol).

Groups, too, can find themselves in poverty because of demanding ever more pay for their work. Industries where workers demand higher and higher pay may find themselves out of a job when companies find it cheaper to automate or out source the work to a foreign country.

Poverty is sometimes the result of the sins of another person or group, as in the case of a family with an irresponsible breadwinner. The impact of an absent breadwinner is seen in United States, for example, where households headed by single mothers are over five times more likely to live in poverty.[11] Nearly two-thirds of children considered poor in America live in single-parent homes. According to one study, "if poor mothers married the fathers of their children, almost three-quarters would immediately be lifted out of poverty."[12]

Another major factor in poverty is government. Like everything else in the world governments are run by sinners. They can cause impoverishment on a national scale through tyranny or incompetence. Stalin tried to speed the communization of Russian farming by confiscating the property of private farmers and even executing them, though they produced a significant amount of the nation's food. In the resulting famine of 1932 to 1933 five million people starved to death, even while police guarded huge stockpiles of grain. Similarly, Mao Tse-Tung's efforts to industrialize China reached a reckless pace during the "Great Leap Forward" (1958-62). To provide steel for industry, for example, simple farm tools were melted down, leaving farmers with no way to work the land. In the ensuing chaos some thirty million people died. As Proverbs says, "Abundant food is in the fallow ground of the poor, but it is swept away by injustice" (13:23).

Where poverty is rooted in sin, it is a moral issue and its existence can be explained by the freedom God has granted us to do good or evil. That freedom allows us to squander our resources like a prodigal son (Luke 15:13) or use them in the service of God (2 Cor. 8:2), such as by meeting the needs of others (Acts 4:34). On a governmental level, the power by which government officials can protect the innocent and punish the guilty (Rom. 13:4) can be wielded as an instrument of abuse to trample the rights of their citizens.

The most compassionate response to a person who is irresponsible or otherwise sinful is to help them to change. We can see God doing this from the opening chapters of Genesis all the way to Revelation. Believers are expected to follow His example by offering loving reproof at least to other believers who go astray (Gal. 6:1; cf. Matt. 18:15). In some cases the most loving thing we can do is to allow sin to have its consequences, such as by allowing a lazy person to experience some hunger. Paul said that a person who is unwilling to work should not eat (2 Thess. 3:10). Trying to shield the unrepentant sinner from consequences is generally useless anyway. As Proverbs warns (regarding the sin of anger), if you rescue a person from consequences "you will only have to do it again" (Prov. 19:19). The only solution is reform.

We should therefore not expect God to remove all suffering from those who have brought troubles upon themselves. The back stabber with no friends, the drug addict with constant health problems, the alcoholic without a job, and the impoverished sluggard cannot blame God nor expect Him to work miracles so they won't have to change their life style. Allowing consequences – which means allowing suffering – is the compassionate thing to do. I heard a broken father tell how he discovered that his son was responsible for the worst arson attacks in American history, in which a number of people died. Looking back he realized his mistake as a father: he was always rescuing the boy from the consequences of his wrong doing such that he never learned from his mistakes. In the end the father had to face the fact that he could not rescue his son from the sentence of life in prison without the possibility of parole.[13]

Righteous Poverty

Many people, perhaps most, are poor through no fault of their own. A few willingly live in poverty or at its edge in order to better serve others spiritually. Jesus and Paul were certainly in that category (Matt. 8:20; Phil. 4:12), so are many of today's missionaries and pastors of small churches.

The causes of righteous poverty are varied. Entire nations can be impoverished simply because of geography. They lack the assets that tend to bring wealth, such as good soil and weather for farming, minerals and energy sources, rivers and ports. But as far as whether God is to blame, He cannot be faulted for not making all the world's land equally rich. The earth's spherical shape produces intense heat at the equator and leaves the polls cold. Mountains like the Sierra Nevada in California collect snow which waters the rich valley on the west side while creating a desert in the rain shadow on the east side. When peoples chose to settle a region they accepted certain advantages and risks for themselves and their descendants. In some regions poverty is all but inevitable.

Other nations are poor even in spite of great natural resources because of incompetent or corrupt government. Scripture recognizes this as simply an unfortunate consequence of the leaders' choices (Prov. 13:23) or in some cases as divine chastening for national sins

(2 Chron. 6:26). The blameless individual caught in either situation can take comfort in knowing that God can grant special grace by alleviating their situation or helping them to endure it, as He did with the poor widow in Zarepheth (1 Kings 17:14: cf. Ps. 68:10; Ps. 146:9).

In any case, being poor is not necessarily bad if it drives a person closer to God and the real purpose of life – which is not personal comfort.

Most people are far more aware of the troubles and risks of poverty than of wealth. Yet one of the clearest spiritual patterns in the Old Testament is people's tendency to forget God when things were going well. For Israel it often took dire need, in the form of poverty or a threat from their enemies for example, to bring them back to God.

The Bible recognizes that both poverty and wealth have their unique temptations. The writer of Proverbs asks God to spare him from poverty because it brings the temptation of wrongful gain, and to spare him from wealth because it tempts a person to feel he doesn't need God (30:8-9).

For a number of years while going to graduate school I lived on the edge financially, concentrating much of my time and effort on finishing my academic preparation. I remember a time when the soles of my shoes had holes clear through so that I felt the heat of the pavement and the wet from the rain. A couple of times I had no food in the cupboards and less than twenty dollars to my name. Yet I never missed a single meal and the bills always got paid on time. It was difficult at times but I wouldn't trade the experience for anything because I learned just how much I can depend on God's faithfulness. Never once did He let me down.

Perspectives on Poverty

Poverty is a relative condition in that everyone is poorer than someone and richer than someone. What is considered poor in an industrialized country can be regarded as normal in a poorer country. In one country a person can be considered poor in spite of having several changes of clothes, a roof over his head, three meals a day, a television, and an automobile. A study by the Heritage Foundation revealed the characteristics of the thirty-five million people classed as poor by the U.S. Census Bureau:

> Overall, the typical American defined as poor by the government has a car, air conditioning, a refrigerator, a stove, a clothes washer and dryer, and a microwave. He has two color televisions, cable or

> satellite TV reception, a VCR or DVD player, and a stereo. He is able to obtain medical care. His home is in good repair and is not overcrowded. By his own report, his family is not hungry and he had sufficient funds in the past year to meet his family's essential needs. While this individual's life is not opulent, it is equally far from the popular images of dire poverty conveyed by the press, liberal activists, and politicians.[14]

This would be considered comfortably off by the standards of some other countries. I've been in rural parts of Central America where it was normal to live in a house made of mud, sticks, and pieces of scrap wood. Families with ten to twenty children live off whatever could be grown on about an acre of land. The breadwinner worked from sun up to sundown with only three or four hours off each week. Even they have a stable existence compared to a million or more in India where, from birth to death, they make their home on a few feet of sidewalk. And there are still places in the world where people fight off not just malnutrition, but outright starvation.

To distinguish between these degrees of want, we could say that the destitute are those who lack essential food, clothing, or minimal shelter; while the poor lack only less vital necessities, such as adequate medical care.

The drive to make life ever more comfortable and secure from all misfortune is virtually universal, and materialism was a common theme in Jesus' teachings. He warned, "Beware, and be on guard against every form of greed; for not even when one has an abundance does his life consist of his possessions" (Luke 12:15; 16-34). Poverty seems to be such an evil partly because we mistakenly see prosperity as vital to the good life. Yet the Bible tells us to be content with basic necessities (1 Tim. 6:8), and assures us that we can trust God to supply us with those (Luke 12:25-31). Contentment and faith will free us to focus on enriching our spiritual life (Luke 12:31) and finding that deeper divine source of abundance – which is free and available to all.

So a good deal of what we consider to be suffering is rooted in a misplaced perspective of life. Those who lack what are not necessities can still be very happy.

Reflecting God's Heart for the Poor

This is not to say that God turns a deaf ear to material want. He is deeply concerned for the plight of those who are not to blame for their destitution or poverty. He listens to their cry (Exod. 22:27; Ps. 69:33). He delivers (Ps. 40:17), provides for (Ps. 68:10, and rescues them (Ps. 35:10). He blesses those who care for them (Deut. 24:13, 19; Prov. 19:17) and judges those who oppress them (Deut. 24:15; Prov. 21:13). He commanded that they be treated with a certain respect for them and their needs, such as when taking collateral for a loan (Deut. 24:10-13), and that they be paid wages promptly because of their immediate needs (vv. 14-15). Furthermore, they could not be charged interest (Exod. 22:25) and were allowed to collect gleanings left after the harvest (e.g., Lev. 19:9-10; 23:22; Deut. 24:19-22). In the New Testament, James identifies true godliness with effectively helping the poor (James. 1:27; 2:15-16) and treating them impartially (3:1-4). What is true today was more so in ancient times, that the poor are more vulnerable, being without resources for protection or getting justice. God takes a special interest in the downtrodden.

The needs of the innocent poor and destitute provide an opportunity for us to show the heart of God. We are to be instruments of God's desire to relieve this kind of suffering. And while it is not wrong to enjoy God's blessings (1 Tim. 6:17), we should live sufficiently within our means so that we are able to meet the "pressing needs" of others (Titus 3:14).

This requires some thought and sometimes more effort than merely handing out money – the flawed approach of so many government programs.[15] In an industrialized society the typical homeless person's problems, for instance, are not solely financial. Consequently, merely giving them money will do little. (In America at least, a high percentage are substance abusers and many have serious psychological problems.) Sending aid to a foreign country's leaders will not necessarily help the starving there if their government's corruption and mismanagement are at the heart of their troubles. This is where private Christian compassion can do so much more than blind government aid or welfare.

Like so many aspects of the problem of evil, we are tempted to be mere observers, in this case musing over why God allows such poverty. Instead we should be trying to alleviate some of the suffering it has brought, thereby glorifying God by revealing His heart in a tangible way.

All the while, though, we have to maintain a spiritual perspective in spite of our materialistic age. The Bible says a lot of things are worse than poverty. For example, it is better to have a poor but harmonious home than wealth with strife (Prov. 17:1). Being poor is also better than being foolish (Prov. 19:1), crooked (Prov. 28:6), a liar (Prov. 19:22), or wealthy but proud (Prov. 28:11).

So the causes of poverty are varied. It may be the fault of the person who suffers, as would be the case from laziness or substance abuse. In that case the consequences can lead the person to change his ways. A degree of poverty may be the righteous choice of a person who values something like ministry or the needs of an aging parent over their own material comfort. Or, poverty may be the result of someone else's irresponsibility. Where there is moral failure the ensuing harmful results are part of the necessary web of consequences that lead us to repentance. As with other aspects of the problem of evil, poverty can reveal attributes of God that we would not otherwise see, as well as provide opportunities for others to manifest godlike qualities such as mercy, compassion, and sacrifice.

War

War certainly ranks among the most serious of the world's evils. Unlike a lot of other evils, technology has made the problem worse not better. The sufferings from such things as natural disasters, diseases, and starvation have been reduced, yet the instruments of warfare have become much more lethal. Medieval clashes between knights had comparatively limited consequences. But with the modern concept of total war and the proliferation of nuclear biological, and chemical weapons, humanity has the capability to obliterate whole societies, or even all life.

Other major evils are also different in that everyone works together to eliminate them. But war is by nature a matter of society against society. It is for the most part a large scale manifestation of the sin that exists on an individual level within the human heart.

One of the few positive advancements has been the advent of so called smart weapons. Developing pinpoint accuracy has cost millions of dollars, but it has spared lives and property. Who can forget seeing news coverage of the people of Bagdad apparently so confident of the accuracy of American munitions that they walked and drove down the streets as bombs blew up specific government buildings?

As far as evil and the biblical view of war, God's seemingly harsh war directives to Israel have been a special problem. Some answers are found in the historical context. If an enemy surrendered without a fight, they would all be enslaved, but if they had to be conquered all the men were to be killed (Deut. 20:11-14). It is possible that the two different kinds of treatment were calculated to encourage surrender and thereby avoid bloodshed. It is possible too that those who would put up a fight in spite of Israel's reputation for military victory would probably be troublesome later and so would have to be dealt with more harshly.

The exception to these two guidelines applied to Caananite cities within Israel's future borders. These were to be utterly wiped out, "in order that they may not teach you to do according to all their detestable things which they have done for their gods, so that you would sin against the Lord your God" (Deut. 20:18; 7:2). God knew that Israel would be influenced by them and that the result would be disastrous. The religion of the Canaanites, for example, was essentially a fertility cult which at times used temple prostitutes and practiced human sacrifice.

As to military activity, the Bible does not condemn it out of hand. God sanctioned certain wars in the Old Testament, and both Deborah the judge and Jeremiah cursed those who refused to participate (Judg. 5:23; Jer. 48:10). Jesus regarded war as inevitable until God's future reign (Matt. 24:6). The New Testament does not condemn soldiers for their profession (Luke 3:14; Matt. 8:5, 10; Acts 10:1) and even counted them among the heros of the faith (Heb. 11:32-33). Furthermore, the epistles use a number of military metaphors to describe the Christian life (2 Cor.10:3; Eph. 6:12; 1 Thess. 5:8; 1 Tim. 1:18). The New Testament makes it clear, however, that force is not to be used to advance a spiritual agenda (Matt. 26:52; John 18:36).

It is often said that Jesus forbade self-defense (and therefore wars of self-defense) when He said that we must "turn the other cheek" (Matt. 5:39). But we have to realize that a slap on the cheek is only an insult, not a physical threat. He was not telling us how to respond to someone trying to hurt or kill us, so He was not saying that it is wrong to defend yourself. Nevertheless, war is never ideal. David was prohibited from building the temple because of his extensive military exploits (1 Chron. 22:8), and Isaiah makes a special point of saying that in the future Kingdom there will be no war (Isa. 2:4).

For these reasons most of Christianity has endorsed the view that some wars are just, especially wars of self-defense or in defense of an ally.

Wars – tragic though they are – can manifest or even build character, especially qualities like bravery, selflessness, creativity, and teamwork. On a broader level, a war can force a whole society to decide what matters most, what is worth fighting for, and what matters more than life itself. World War II for example presented many opportunities for good on both a personal and societal level, and thousands rose to the challenge. Not surprisingly, the generation that won the war had grown up under the hardships of the depression, and later went on to win the cold war. As a generation they developed a remarkable sense of duty and sacrifice for great causes.

We cannot deny that good can emerge even from the evils of war. Too, God can have hidden purposes in war, as Isaiah reveals. Regarding Babylon, God said, "The Lord of hosts is mustering the army for battle.... to destroy the whole land (Isa. 13:4, 5). He identified the specific instrument, "Behold, I am going to stir up the Medes against them" (13:17; they came in 539 BC, cf. Dan. 5:30-31). Moab was rebuked for "arrogance, pride, and fury" (Isa. 16:6), and warned that judgment would come within three years (Isa. 16:14). God would bring judgment on Damascus and Ethiopia (Isa. 17, 18). Egypt would experience civil war (Isa. 19:2) and be delivered into the hand of a "cruel master" (19:4; Esarhaddon of Assyria conquered in 671 BC). God also reveals the future troubles of Babylon (21:1-10), Edom (21:11-12), Arabia (21:13-17), Tyre (23:1-18), and Assyria (33:1-24).

When God uses one nation to bring judgment on another, He in no way excuses the aggressor. He explained to Habakkuk that after using the cruel Chaldeans to punish Israel, He would hold them accountable as well (Hab. 1:11).

So while war is a product of human sin it allows for development of human character and the display of the divine attributes, especially justice. As with so many types of suffering and tragedy, it can also provide an opportunity for human good – including working to prevent war in the first place.

We can see some of the reasons behind even the worst evils of this life. But to more fully understand God's workings, we have to look beyond this life.

GOING FARTHER

1. What are some of the known causes of birth abnormalities? Which are caused specifically by human irresponsibility?

2. If God could prevent abnormalities, why do you think He doesn't?

3. In what extreme ways do people without abnormalities differ? How do we humans compare unfavorably when measured against the abilities of some animals? How can the differences between persons, and between people and animals, change our perspective on abnormalities?

4. What are some of the moral causes of poverty? How should we respond to poverty that is caused by irresponsibility?

5. How might someone be in poverty for righteous reasons? Do you know anyone in such a situation?

6. In what sense are poverty and wealth relative? Compare your own financial situation to someone much wealthier and much poorer.

7. What is God's attitude toward poverty in general?

8. What is God's attitude toward war? How does God use war?

9. Does the Bible prohibit self-defense?

NOTES

1. That the disciples considered the cause to be a specific sin is indicated by the fact that their question, "Who did sin?" uses the aorist tense. R. C. H. Lenski, *The Interpretation of St. John's Gospel* (Minneapolis, MN: Augsburg, 1943), 675.

2. Simpson, J. L., and Elias S.: "Prenatal Diagnosis of Genetic Disorders," in *Maternal-Fetal Medicine: Principles and Practice*, ed. 2, edited by R. K. Creasy and R. Resnick (Philadelphia, PA: WB Saunders Co., 1989), 99-102; cited in *The Merk Manual of Medical Information*, Home Edition (New York, NY: Pocket Books, 1997), 1237.

3. Based on information in Hook E. B.: "Rates of Chromosome Abnormalities at Different Maternal ages," *Obstetrics and Gynecology* 58:282-85, 1981; and Hook E. B., Cross P.K., Schreinemachers D. M.: "Chromosomal Abnormality Rates at Amniocentesis and In Live-born Infants," *Journal of the American Medical Association* 249 (15):2034-38, 1983; cited in Merk, 1235.

4. At the center of a hot controversy is Margret Sanger (1879-1966) who founded the organization that became Planned Parenthood (the world's largest supporter of abortion). Everyone agrees that she believed society could be improved by controlling who produces children (eugenics). "More from the fit, less from the unfit," she would say. Part of the controversy is that she associated with other eugenicists, some of whom held highly questionable views on race. Ernst Rudin, who wrote an article in Sanger's *Birth Control Review* (April, 1933), was Hitler's director of genetic sterilization and

the founder of the Nazi Society for Racial Hygiene. Her defenders point out that she resigned as editor of the *Review* in 1929 and that she later condemned Nazism. Sanger's most controversial statement was in a letter to her associate, Clarence Gamble, outlining what she called the "Negro Project." "We do not want word to go out that we want to exterminate the Negro population..." (Dec. 10, 1939). Defenders say that she was merely trying to prevent the wrong impression that their efforts were aimed at extermination of the black population, and that she never promoted race based policies regarding birth control and the like. Criticism of Sanger is in George Grant, *Killer Angel*, rev. ed. (Elkton, MD: Highland Books, 2001). A defense of her is "The Sanger-Hitler Equation," #32 of "The Margaret Sanger Papers Newsletter", <http://www.nyu.edu/projects/sanger/sanger-hitler_equation.htm>; accessed 23 June 2005.

5. "60 Seconds With Erik Weihenmayer," *Fast Company*, May 2004, p. 40.

6. One effective mosquito trap incorporates a sound pulse that mimics the human heart. American Mosquito Control Association <http://www.mosquito.org/MosqInfo/Traps.Htm>, accessed 8 April 2004.

7. W. Peacock, Pers. comm. to D. Shewmon in "Active Voluntary Euthanasia," *Issures in Law & Medicine*, 1987; cited in [Jack] Willke and [Barbara] Willke, *Abortion: Questions and Answers* (Cincinnati, OH: Hayes, 1985), 212.

8. P. Cameron, et al., "Happiness and Life Satisfaction of the Malformed," *Proceedings, Amer. Psychologic Assn. Meeting*, 1971; quoted in Willke and Willke, 212.

9. In contrast to some of his followers, Marx himself seemed to hold a more nuanced view. One of the left's few improvements in recent decades is to realize (with the help of Michel Foucault, 1926-84) that human corruption is far more complex than Communism claimed.

10. Locke held that a basic function of government is to protect each individual's natural right to life, liberty, and property. The American Declaration of Independence lists the inalienable rights as "life, liberty and *pursuit of happiness*" (emphasis added). But note that Locke uses "property" in a broad sense. He said that people form societies "for the mutual preservation of their lives, liberties and estates, which I call by the general name, 'property.' (Locke's Second Treatise of Government, 9, 123;) I am indebted to Frederick Copleston, *A History of Philosophy*, volume 5, Hobbes to Hume (reprint, 3 vols. in 1, New York, NY: Image Books, 1985), p. 132.

11. In 2001 26.4 per cent of all households headed by females qualified as poor under the government definition. Only 4.9 per cent of families where males were present were poor. Note that the government definition of poverty excludes non-cash assistance from government programs. Institute for Research on Poverty, <http://www.ssc.wisc.edu/irp/faqs/faq3.htm>, 27, Aug. 2003, page 1.

12. Robert E. Rector and Kirk A. Johnson, "Understanding Poverty in America," Backgrounder #1713, a study by the Heritage Foundation, 5 Jan. 2004 <http://www.heritage.org/Research/Welfare/bg1713.cfm>; accessed 8 April 2004.

13. The account was dramatized in a movie entitled, *Not My Own Son*.

14. Rector and Johnson. The study also notes, however, that two percent of families classed as poor say they "often" do not have enough to eat.

15. See Marvin Olasky, *The Tragedy of American Compassion* (Wheaton, IL: Crossway, 1995).

Chapter eleven

VIEW FROM THE END – Heaven and Hell

It is sometimes supposed that there are evils so great that no good could ever make them worthwhile. We occasionally hear in the news about cases of tragic evil, such as children who are abused or become victims of a natural disaster. Too, there are evils on a mass scale, such as the holocaust. For others, life's more common troubles become overwhelming, leading them to depression or suicide.

Could any good, present or future, ever wipe away what Hamlet called "the slings and arrows of outrageous fortune"? Could it be that a person suffering such evils might someday look back and say that in spite of horrendous experiences, life was worth it?

Even if an individual's earthly existence does not seem to compensate them for whatever they have suffered, heaven certainly can. It is the place where all past anguish will be comforted, either causing it to fade or to gain new significance. As Sir Thomas Moore said, "Earth has no sorrow that heaven cannot heal."[1]

The Ecstasy that Displaces all Pain

Scripture describes heaven in the grandest terms. To begin with, it is the end of all suffering, sorrow, pain, and tears: "God will wipe away every tear from their eyes" (Rev. 7:17). Physical suffering and even discomfort will cease, "they will hunger no more, nor thirst anymore; nor will the sun beat down on them, nor any heat" (Rev. 7:16). And "there will no longer be any death; there will no longer be any mourning, or crying, or pain" (Rev. 21:4). It will be the end of the age of pain and evil in that "the first things have passed away" (Rev. 21:4, 5; cf. 22:3).

The redeemed will be there having been made completely righteous in God's eyes as a gift of His grace (2 Cor. 5:21), crowned with His righteousness (2 Tim. 4:8), and standing "in the presence of His glory blameless with great joy" (Jude 24).

There will be rest (Rev. 14:3) but it will be a rest of joyful service (Rev. 22:3, 6) and spontaneous worship (Rev. 7:11-12). As Baptist preacher Alexander MacLaren said, "The joys of heaven are not the joys of passive contemplation, of dreamy remembrance, of perfect repose; but they are described thus, 'They rest not day or night' [Rev. 7:15; cf. 4:8]. His servants serve him and see his face."[2]

The people of God are said to reign forever (Rev. 22:5). It is described as a wedding (Rev. 19:7-9; 21:2), a banquet (Matt. 8:11), and a vast assembly of "the spirits of the righteous made perfect" (Heb. 12:23; 12:2).

It will be a place of great activity, but not toil. Gone is the resistence of the world, the flesh, and the devil. The activity will engage us and require effort, but it will be enjoyable, like the effort spent on a hobby or sport.

Of course the center of heaven is God Himself, who is said to reign over it (Ps. 11:4; Isa. 66:1), fill it (Jer. 23:24), and be its very light (Rev. 22:5). Our current vague understanding of God will take a quantum leap forward. As Paul describes our future understanding, "For now we see in a mirror dimly, but then face to face; now I know in part, but then I will know fully just as I also have been fully known" (1 Cor. 13:12). Early and Medieval theologians regarded this "beatific vision" (*visio Dei*) as the ultimate fulfillment of life.

At the center of the revelation of God is Christ, in whom dwells "all the fullness of Deity" (Col. 2:9; cf. 1:19). This includes "all the treasures of wisdom and knowledge" (Col. 2:3).

Heaven will be so fulfilling because God is ultimately the source of everything: "For from Him and through Him and to Him are all things" (Rom. 11:36). And there will be a "summing up of all things in Christ, things in the heavens and things on the earth" (Eph. 1:10). The believer will live face to face with the source and ground of all truth, goodness, beauty, and life. Thus in heaven we will continually experience the fulfillment of the age-old quest for ultimate value.

At that time believers themselves will be perfected in their nature and behavior (not just in their position before God, as they are at conversion in earthly life). As John says, "We know that when He appears *we will be like Him*, because we will see him just as He is" (1 John 3:2; emphasis added).

This does not mean that God must take away our free will in order to ensure that we never sin in heaven. By perfecting our nature He confirms our earthly choice of Him and of righteousness. On earth we long for God and righteousness, though our longing is imperfect, and our righteousness is mixed with apathy, self-centeredness, and failure. However in heaven, with our fallen nature removed, we will be strengthened to be what we have longed to be. And we simply will never want to choose evil. Renewed and unhampered, we will be freer than we have ever been.

What makes this all the more wonderful is that unlike all earthly pleasures, heavenly ones will never fade or lessen (1 Pet. 1:4; Matt. 6:20; Luke 12:33). They will last forever, from moment to unending moment.

We can see that heaven's joys are at root all spiritual and God-centered. Those who have refused God's overtures would not fit there. In Milton's *Paradise Lost*, Satan after his fall reviews with the other fallen angels the prospect of repenting and returning to heaven. His attitude epitomizes that of all who refuse to bow their knee to God. As he sees it, those in heaven would have to:

> Stand in his presence humble, and receive strict laws imposed, to celebrate his throne with warbled hymns, and to his godhead sing forced hallelujahs.... This must be our task in heaven, this our delight; how wearisome eternity so spent in worship paid to whom we hate.[3]

To the spiritually unrenewed heaven's joys are no joy at all. It would be like someone who hates classical music having to listen to it endlessly. Only classical music lovers would enjoy such a thing; for everyone else it would be a terrible fate. George Bernard Shaw said, "Heaven, as conventionally conceived, is a place so inane, so dull, so useless, so miserable, that nobody has ever ventured to describe a whole day in heaven, though plenty of people have described a day at the seaside."[4] Echoing that, Evelyn Waugh once said "that every creed promises a paradise which will be absolutely uninhabitable for anyone of civilized taste."[5]

The unregenerate would not experience heaven merely by being there because it is much more than a place. It is a spiritual perspective, an attitude – a desire for God and all things pure.

God will exclude the spiritually unrenewed from heaven (Gal. 5:21; Eph. 5:5; Rev. 22:15) for other reasons, not only because they cannot fully benefit, and not only because He must judge sin. But as well, those who continually choose sin would turn heaven into something less. Heaven would not be heaven with Hitler still trying to persecute Jews, dictators trying to force people to submit to them, and former slave owners trying to enslave others. Imagine what it would be like even with more common sins like gossip, divisiveness, outbursts of anger, jealousy, and so on. Heaven is heaven only where there are renewed relationships because sin, by definition, is what harms others (Matt. 7:12; Gal. 5:14). Of those who would not live for God, Dante says, "Heaven, to keep its beauty, cast them out."[6]

Perhaps the most enticing thing about heaven is how difficult it is to describe. In the book of Revelation, John seemed to struggle to find metaphors to describe what he saw. Even he was so awestruck he fell down to worship an angel and was gently corrected (Rev. 19:10; 22:8). In his vision of heaven Paul saw things he was not even allowed to mention (2 Cor. 12:4).

If heaven is so great that it defies description and is hard even to imagine, how can anyone say that no future experience could make up for certain types of suffering, however horrendous? Could suffering that lasts an hour, a month, or even years outweigh an eternity of heaven? Do we even have to wait until we experience a few trillion years of heaven to answer the skeptic, or can we already conclude that such a place could indeed compensate for anything suffered on earth?

Because God offers free forgiveness the gates of heaven stand open. But surprisingly, not everyone is interested. In a sense existentialist philosopher Jean Paul Sartre was right, the door out of hell is locked from the inside. Someday the door to heaven will close and people's choices will be finalized. The unrepentant will then be locked out forever. And from then on the door out of hell will be locked from outside.

The Agony of the Loss of all Good

The problem of the suffering of this life pales in significance to the problem of the sufferings of hell. The misery it portends is captured by

Dante's inscription over its doors, "Abandon every hope, all you who enter."[7] Of that hopelessness he says, "...these wretches have no hope of truly dying, and this blind life they lead is so abject it makes them envy every other fate."[8] Most troubling of all is that our destiny, whatever it may be, is only a heartbeat away. As Pascal says, "Between us and hell or heaven there is only life, the most fragile thing in earth."[9]

Some have concluded that a God who would send people to hell would not only be unloving but unjust. Not even the most cold hearted person would want their worst enemy to suffer forever, it is thought. It is supposed that the idea of such a vengeful being must be a holdover from viewing God as an oversized medieval ruler rather than a loving father; or it is the result of seeing Him as a kind of infinitely large human with an infinitely large appetite for revenge.

In recent decades even some who interpret the Bible literally have come to reject the idea of everlasting punishment. One alternative is annihilation, which claims that the wicked cease to exist. This makes God kinder in that He doesn't allow the lost to suffer forever. One problem is that annihilation does not carry justice beyond death in that those who sinned little (such as those who led average lives and died young) get annihilated along with those who sinned horribly (such as those who carried out mass genocide). To correct this inequity, one variation of the annihilation view holds that God punishes each person according to their sins, then annihilates them.

Another alternative to the traditional view of hell is universalism, by which everyone will eventually be saved. It turns hell into a redemptive experience. A third alternative, the view that there is a purgatory, holds that even the faithful must be purged if they are not yet fit to fellowship with God (on this view, those who are completely outside God's grace will suffer hell).

Those who regard the Bible as in any way authoritative must look to what it says to resolve the question of hell.

Is Hell a Literal Place?

About three quarters of the population believe that hell exists, but roughly the same number think they themselves will go to heaven. Only one per cent of people believe they will go to hell![10] As to the nature of hell, 31 per cent believe it is a place of torment, another 37 per cent that it is not a literal place, but a state of separation from God.[11]

There are good biblical reasons to think that hell is a literal place, and one from which there is no escape.

First of all, hell is said in the Bible to be eternal. The word that describes hell as eternal is also used of God (Rom. 16:26; 1 Tim. 1:17; Rev. 4:9; 5:13; 11:15; 22:5). So we could say that hell lasts as long as God does. Furthermore, it is said that the smoke of the torment of the lost lasts forever (Rev. 14:11; cf. beast and false prophet are tormented forever, 20:10; Babylon, 19:3). While it is true that the word for eternal (αἰώνιος) can mean a long time rather than forever, usually the context indicates it as such – and there is nothing in contexts involving hell to make us think it is anything but eternal.

Other passages show that hell is eternal. The Bible contrasts the fate of the lost with the fate of the saved. The lost will "go away into eternal punishment, but the righteous into eternal life" (Matt. 25:46; αἰώνιος). There the fire is "unquenchable" (Mark. 9:43, 48) and their "worm" does not die (Mark 9:48). It is a place of "eternal destruction away from the presence of the Lord and from the glory of His power" (1 Thess. 1:9).

That torment is said to be conscious, a place of weeping and gnashing of teeth (Matt.13:42; 50; cf. 22:13; 25:30), and "disgrace and everlasting contempt" (Dan. 12:2). Echoing this, Christian philosopher Marilyn Adams says, according to Christianity, "The best good is intimacy with God and the worst evil is his absence." She says that unbelievers find it hard to accept that the absence of God can be that bad, but that is because

> the whole earth is full of the glory of God. When we appreciate a beautiful mountain scene or immerse ourselves in Mozart or are lost in a Cezanne painting, we are experiencing God shining through the mask of his creatures. When humans share deep, satisfying intimacy, part of the joy they taste is God in the middle of it. And this is so whether or not he is recognized there. Since ordinary human experience is thus "God-infested", we are in no position to imagine the horror of a creation in which he was entirely hidden from view.[12]

Baptist theologian Millard Erickson reminds us that not even God is free to do the self-contradictory. As he sees it, just as God cannot create a square triangle so it may be that He cannot create beings to have fellowship with Himself who do not also experience anguish if they are eternally outside His presence.[13]

Hell is described as both "darkness" (Matt. 8:12; 22:13; 25:30; Jude 13) and "fire" (Matt. 3:10, 12; 5:22; 18:8-9; 25:41; Mark. 9:43, 48; Luke 16:24; James 3:6; Jude 7; Rev. 19:20; 20:10, 14-15; 21:8). Some believe these are literal descriptions; others believe that they are metaphorical, while the torment is literal.[14]

Whatever the case, the fate of the lost is not mere annihilation, but everlasting punishment. In contrast to the eternal life of the saved, the lost are said to perish (ἀπώλεια; John 3:16; 10:28; 17:12) "not merely in the sense of the extinction of physical existence, but rather of an eternal plunge into Hades...."[15] Thus, on his death Judas went to "his own place" (Acts 1:25, τόπος), he did not cease to exist. This is in contrast to believers, who are said to go to a heavenly dwelling place (John. 14:2-3, τόπος).

Some who want biblical support for the idea that the lost are annihilated say that when the adjective "eternal" (αἰώνιος) is used with a noun of action it means that something has eternal results, not that it goes on eternally.[16] So they say that "eternal punishment" happens once (when the person is annihilated) and only the results of it last forever; the punishment does not. But against this view, professor Timothy Phillips argues that the parallel expression "eternal salvation" refers to something ongoing in that the sustaining and perfecting work of Christ lasts forever, enabling us to be forever "in Christ." So in eternal salvation it is the process of salvation – and not just its results – that go on forever. That supports the idea that eternal punishment goes on forever as well.

Also supporting the idea that punishment lasts forever is the fact that Christ uses the same terms when talking about the eternally saved and the eternally lost (Matt. 25:46). So punishment lasts as long as heaven does. And it has to last because God's wrath is said to remain on the one who rejects the offer of forgiveness through Christ (John 3:36). The fire does not consume the lost such that they cease to exist.[17] If they ceased to exist there would be no reason for the fire to go on burning forever.

That the fate of the lost is not extinction but utter ruin, as is shown by the two uses of the word "destroy" (διαφθείρω) in Revelation 11:18, where it is said that God will "destroy those who destroy the earth." Those who "destroyed" the earth did not make it go out of existence, they ruined it. And that will be their own fate – ruin not extinction (cf. Luke 11:33, when moths "destroy" garments they ruin them, they do not make them cease existing entirely).

The Bible gives no indication of a second chance for salvation after death. Death is the end of any chance of our responding to God: "...it is appointed for men to die once and after this comes judgment" (Heb. 9:27).

If the saved are truly forgiven and made righteous before God by His grace (Rom. 8:1; 2 Cor. 5:21), then there is no need to purge away sin in purgatory. Furthermore, what the Bible calls the flesh, that part of the believer which holds him back from perfection in this life, is gone at death (1 Cor. 15:52-54; Gal. 5:16-19). As a renewed and purified person, after death there is no need for further purging. Therefore the believer goes directly to heaven.

But if hell indeed lasts forever, how could God possibly be good in the face of such incomprehensible suffering?

How Could God Punish Forever?

One of the most common objections to the existence of hell is that punishment cannot be justly eternal if the sins being punished were committed for the relatively short period of earthly life. Even if a person sinned for ninety years it would never warrant eternal punishment, it is said. There have been several answers to this.

The traditional response is that even a finite amount of sin against a perfectly holy God warrants unending punishment. To say otherwise underestimates either the seriousness of sin or the holiness of God.

Since the mid-twentieth century it has been more popular to emphasize that hell is a matter of God allowing the creature to make a final refusal of fellowship with Him.[18] God merely finalizes that decision at death. Along similar lines is the emphasis that hell is such a horrible place because by nature it is the absence of God. As such it is a place devoid of all truth (Deut 32:4), beauty (Ps. 24:4), goodness (Ps. 25:8; 119:68), compassion (2 Kings 13:23), comfort (2 Cor. 1:3-5), love (1 John. 4:8), joy (Neh. 8:10; John 15:11); and everything good, perfect (James 1:17) and worthwhile (Phil. 3:7-8).

One overlooked reason that punishment is endless is the fact that lost sinners never stop sinning. Since there is no reason to think that people become sinless once in hell, then they continue to sin. So it is not the case that the lost commit sin only in their earthly life and are punished eternally. They go on sinning forever and are punished forever.

The sin that people can go on committing seems to be internal in nature. Their internal experiences. sinful to various degrees, include weeping, gnashing of teeth, and shame. But there is no Scriptural reason to think that people will be able to harm others. A Hitler forever damned would not be able to persecute Jewish people, nor would a Stalin be able to send political enemies to the gulag, nor would anyone be able to enslave another.

When we wonder how God can allow people to inflict pain on others we have to remember that they can do so for only a short time. After that, they go to their destiny. In that sense hell is part of the solution to the problem of evil insofar as it justly ends the sinner's ability to do harm.

Does God Send People to Hell?

It matters what God's attitude is toward the lost. Does He *send* people to hell because it pleases Him, or does He merely *allow* them to go there as sinners deserving punishment?

One relevant issue is double predestination, the view that God predestines specific individuals to heaven and specific individuals to hell. It was suggested in the ninth century by a monk named Gottshalk.[19] Ironically, for questioning God's love he was beaten and sentenced to life in prison (which was a relatively happy ending considering that some theological disputes were settled at the stake). Critics say that the double predestination view misrepresents God's attitude toward the lost. It is better to regard God as choosing some people for special grace and passing over others ("preterition") rather than specifically choosing them for destruction. This views their condemnation as a consequence of their sin rather than as purely God's choice that they suffer, without reference to their sin.

A closely related issue is how God, in eternity past, decided precisely who would be saved and who would be lost. Did He choose between people as people – before considering them as sinners such that they are condemned purely by divine choice (a form of what is called the supralapsarian view)? Or was His choice based on their being sinners, such that He chose some sinners for special grace and others He left to the fate they deserved (the sub-lapsarian and infralapsarian views)? Simply put, the former makes condemnation purely a matter of divine choice, the latter makes it a consequence of sin.

In either view God chooses the individuals who will be saved. This fits the biblical view of man's inability to choose God since he is unable to please Him (Rom. 8:8), he is enslaved to sin (John 8:34), spiritually dead (Eph. 2:1-2), and the like.[20] Since he is incapable of so much as reaching out the hand of faith to take the free gift of salvation, even that faith must be given by God (Eph. 2:8,9; "that not of yourselves" refers to saving faith). God then predestines (Eph. 1:5) those He foreknew in eternity past, and ensures that they are saved and get to heaven (Rom. 8:29-30; cf. 8:38-39). But deciding that the saved have been chosen does not completely settle the question of how the rest have not been chosen.

Without trying to settle the very complex theological issues involved, a number of verses speak of the mind and heart of God toward the lost. He takes "no pleasure in the death of the wicked" but would rather that the wicked would "turn from his way and live" (Ezek. 33:11). Paul says that "God desires all men to be saved and to come to the knowledge of the truth" (1 Tim. 2:4). Over the lost of Israel Paul himself had "great sorrow and unceasing grief," going so far as to wish that he could somehow give up his own salvation if it would mean they would be saved (Rom. 9:2-3). Peter says that God does not wish that any would perish but that all would "come to repentance" (2 Pet. 3:9). God's attitude can be seen graphically in Christ weeping over Jerusalem (Matt. 23:37-38). And when God banishes those who are spiritually alien to Him, He sends them "into the eternal fire which has been prepared for the devil and his angels...." (Matt. 25:41). He does not say it was prepared specifically for unredeemed people.

This does not seem to fit the image of a God whose overarching priority is to have some in hell as well as in heaven, then decrees the fall in order to bring that about (not every supralapsarian would agree that this characterizes their view, however).

But this leads us to another issue. If God wants all to be saved why doesn't He just choose everyone? Though the question could be left as a mystery we can go farther and suggest that somehow it must be better that He does not choose everyone. It must be better or God wouldn't do it that way. It seems that the only way it could be better is if there is a higher good than the happiness of every creature. According to a tradition in Christianity, that higher good is the glory of God, that is, the fullest possible revelation of His character. And where a higher good is incompatible with a lesser good, the lesser good has to be sacrificed – a being who would not do that would not be morally perfect.

This brings us close to the idea that God wants some in heaven and some in hell because it glorifies Him – the view of supralapsarians. The difference is we have to emphasize the (non-supralapsarian) insight that God condemns in reference to the fall and personal sin. So some people get what they deserve because of their choices, while others are given grace. The result is that both the justice and grace of God are fully revealed.

So if God does not choose everyone, doesn't He send people to hell? Yes and no. He does as judgment, but on the other hand, people choose to commit the sins for which they are justly condemned. Furthermore, viewed from the human side, they have refused God's gracious forgiveness and thereby forfeit an eternal relationship with Him in heaven. So there is some sense – a real sense – in which people send themselves to hell. God does not grant them special grace, yet as they go to their destiny there is a tear in God's eye.

How could God have both a passion for justice as well as sorrow over consequences He could have prevented? It is not hard to see how when we consider the way in which our own emotions can be mixed. We can be simultaneously angry over the harm someone deliberately caused while being disappointed that they did not act differently – yet also saddened that they are going to be punished, but also sympathetic because of the pain they will feel. And we could feel all of that even as we set in motion the very process of justice that will bring on the consequences, for example, by calling the police. If we as humans are capable of such complexity why would we insist that God must have one, and only one, attitude toward the lost, such as pure wrath?

Are Many Going to Hell?

Christ said that "the way is broad that leads to destruction, and many are those who enter through it" (Matt. 7:13). It seems from this that few are going to be saved.

But what if God extends His mercy to those who are unable to accept His grace? That would include those with extremely limited mental capacity, and more significant in terms of numbers, young children. The number could approach one quarter to one half of the human race when we consider infant mortality rates (still significant in less developed countries[21]), deaths of young children, pregnancies that end in a miscarriage (most of them unknown to the mothers), and a million and a half abortions each year in the U.S. alone. That adds up to a very significant number of human beings. If they all go to heaven that would soften the problem of hell somewhat.

The numbers are even larger if we add the traditional Christian (and Jewish) idea that God does not hold children responsible for their sins until they are able to grasp what they are doing morally. The idea is found in law and fits with common sense. Can we really say that the selfish act of a two year old is as culpable as the selfish act of an adult? Generally speaking, we hold people accountable in proportion to how much they are aware of what they are doing. If a four year old child picked up a loaded gun left lying around and shot someone, we would not hold him or her as accountable as an adult. The idea is that God does not hold children morally responsible – and thus punishable eternally – before they are some age. That age could be different for each child, depending on their moral awareness. Though controversial, it is the majority view in Christianity.

There is some Scriptural support for such an age of accountability. The basic idea that accountability is linked to degree of awareness is found in Christ's illustration of the master who put his slaves in charge of his household. The slave that knew his master's will and did not do it "will receive many lashes" (Luke 12:47) whereas the slave who "did not know it, and committed deeds worthy of a flogging, will receive but few" (Luke 12:48). Awareness is linked to age in Isaiah, who prophesied of a child, "He will eat curds and honey at the time He knows enough to refuse evil and choose good" (Isa. 7:15).

It is clear that God holds children less accountable than adults, as is seen in the guilt of the people in the wilderness. He made a distinction between the adults, who knew better than to grumble and disobey Him, and the children, who did not. He said, "your sons, who this day have no knowledge of good or evil, shall enter there, and I will give it to them, and they shall possess it" (Deut. 1:39). Only the youths would someday inherit the land because they were not held accountable. Those twenty years old and up who sinned would die in the wilderness (Num. 14:29).

Besides the issue of accountability, there is God's attitude toward children. Christ showed special concern for children and seemed to regard them as examples of those who will inherit the kingdom. In Matthew 18:2-14 He used children as examples of kingdom humility (vv. 2-5) and said those like them should neither be made to stumble (vv. 6-9) nor be looked down upon (v. 10). The Father is not willing that any such be lost (vv. 12-14). Christ said, "Let the little children alone, and do not hinder them from coming to Me; for the kingdom of heaven belongs to such as these" (Matt. 19:14, cf. Mark. 10:14).

The evidence for the view that God extends grace to children comes short of being conclusive. It has been suggested that had God made it absolutely clear that those who die very young are saved, some misguided people would have welcomed or even caused deaths of children as a way of ensuring their entry to heaven. Given some of the bizarre behavior in history, the suggestion is not so far fetched.

If in fact God does extend grace to those incapable of accepting it then hell will not be nearly as populated. While not eliminating the problem of hell's existence, it lessens it.

Will Everyone Get the Same Punishment?

I've often heard the objection that God is unjust because in hell everyone is punished equally, and that punishment is as severe as possible. If hell is that way, the person who dies after a short and relatively good life (humanly speaking) gets the same punishment as the genocidal dictator responsible for millions of horrible deaths.

While it is true that God can see serious sin even in the life of someone who seems virtuous to us, surely some people do sin less than others. And if the sin is less shouldn't the punishment be less? The problem of hell would be less severe if eternity will not be as horrible as it could be, at least for some people, and if people are punished exactly as they deserve. There are good reasons to think that is so.

God clearly distinguishes between greater and lesser sins in His moral guidelines. The law of Israel everywhere differentiated between more and less serious wrong, and punishments ranged from fines to death. Jesus too talked about "the weightier matters of the law" (Matt. 23:23).

The point applies to sin and punishment in the next life. Jesus said that future punishment for some sins would be so severe it would be better had the person never been born (regarding Judas: Matt. 26:24; Mark. 14:21). In describing future judgment, He said that of two disobedient servants, the one who knew his master's will and did not do it would be punished more than the one who sinned not knowing his will, as we saw above (Luke 12:47-48). Similarly, judgment on the people in the cities which witnessed Christ's "mighty works" will be worse than the judgment on such cities as Sodom, Tyre, and Sidon (Matt. 11:21-24).

God is said to be the supreme and perfect judge, who "judges impartially according to each man's work" (1 Pet. 1:17) and who gives "to everyone according to his ways and according to the fruit of his deeds" (Jer. 32:19). The role of a judge is to discern guilt and meet out punishment that fits the wrongdoing. If everyone got exactly the same punishment an important part of a judge's job would be unnecessary. We would consider it a travesty if the person who did something as minor as driving a little bit over the speed limit got the same punishment as a mass murderer. Conversely, there would be understandable outrage if a mass murderer was fined only a few dollars. To be fair, punishment in this life must be proportionate to the sin. Why should it be different for the next life? It isn't. The Bible closes with a promise from Jesus as the coming judge, "Behold, I am coming quickly, and My reward is with me, to render to every man according to what he has done" (Rev. 22:12).

One way that a person's punishment would match their level of guilt is if hell includes a deeply psychological element. Daniel brings out this neglected aspect of hell, saying that the lost are resurrected to "disgrace and everlasting contempt" (Dan. 12:2). Apologist Norman Geisler says,

> Torment is living with the consequences of our own bad choices. It is the weeping and gnashing of teeth that results from the realization that we blew it and deserve the consequences. Just as a football player may pound on the ground in agony after missing a play that loses the Super Bowl, so those in hell know that the pain they suffer is self-induced.[22]

No doubt everyone in hell will be miserable, but God as the perfect judge will ensure an appropriate judgment for each person. Hell will be anything but unjust.

Can God be Good if there is a Hell?

Our fundamental question is whether God can be good in the face of pain and evil.

Though we have not softened the reality of hell's existence, it may exclude the significant number of people who die before birth or die very young. Although people go to hell because God did not choose them for special grace, it is also true that they themselves have chosen to reject God's grace. Tragically, they are getting what justice demands. And each person's punishment is neither more nor less than what is deserved.

As we pointed out in chapter two, a missing piece of the puzzle is that love is not the only form of goodness. Justice is also goodness. So God is good even if punishment never results in the betterment of those being punished. The unrepentant mass murderer who tortures and kills his victims should be punished even if it does not make him a better person.

Part of the problem of evil is that the wicked seem to get away with causing harm. Some are outraged that God does not give the wicked what they deserve. For that, hell is the ultimate solution. So God is good because He is just, and the revelation of that form of goodness – the revelation of that part of His glory – is itself good.

GOING FARTHER

1. One description of heaven is uniquely comforting to those struggling to live in the desert, "they will hunger no more, nor thirst anymore; nor will the sun beat down on them, nor any heat" (Rev. 7:16). How would that same principle be worded for your situation (no more traffic, deadlines, office backstabbing, financial struggles)?

2. What is the worst thing you have experienced? What do you consider to be the worst thing someone else has experienced (known to you either personally or from history)? Do you think an eternity in heaven could compensate for your suffering? Could it compensate for the worst that another person has suffered?

3. Think of someone you know who is uninterested in God or spiritual things. What would heaven be like for them? What would it be like for the redeemed if millions of unbelievers were in heaven?

4. Why would God make hell last forever rather than for a finite time?

5. What do you think God's attitude is toward the lost?

6. Do you think God would be just to punish everyone equally in hell?

7. In what sense is hell part of the solution to the problem of evil?

NOTES

1. Sir Thomas Moore, *Come, Ye Disconsolate*, quoted in 12,000 Religious Quotations, ed. Frank S. Mead (Grand Rapids: Baker, 1989), 218.

2. Alexander MacLaren (1826-1910), quoted in Mead, 217.

3. Milton, *Paradise Lost*, Bk II. I have updated the spelling.

4. George Bernard Shaw, in Leo Rosten's *Carnival of Wit* (New York, NY: Dutton, 1994), 219.

5. *The Portable Curmudgeon*: *Redux*, ed. Jon Winokur (New York, NY: Dutton, 1992), 134.

6. Dante Alighieri, *The Divine Comedy: Inferno*, III.40, *The Portable Dante*, ed. and trans. Mark Musa (New York, NY: Penguin, 1995), p. 15.

7. Dante, *Inferno*, III.9, Musa, p. 14.

8. Dante, III.46-48; Musa, p. 15. Dante referred specifically to the fate of those who had been lukewarm, having lived "with no blame and with no praise" (III.36).

9. Blaise Pascal: *Pensess and Other Writings*, trans. Honor Levi, intro. and notes by Anthony Levi (Oxford, UK: Oxford Press, 1995), section 185, p. 58.

10. The Harris Poll #52, Sept. 13, 2000; Humphrey Taylor, "No Significant Changes in the Large Majorities Who Believe in God, Heaven, the Resurrection, Survival of Soul, Miracles and Virgin Birth," accessed 20 July 2003 from <harrisinteractive.com/harris_poll/printerfriend/index.asp?PID=112>. The poll of 1,010 American adults has a margin of error of plus or minus 3 per cent and was conducted by telephone in August 10-14, of 2000. Exact figures are, 73 per cent believe in hell, 75 per cent believe they will go to heaven. Six per cent believe they will go to purgatory.

11. *Maranatha Christian Journal*, April 22, 1997; cited in "Religious Beliefs of Americans," accessed August 20, 2003 at <religioustolerance.org>. See also "Beliefs: Heaven and Hell," barna.org, from the Barna Research Group of Ventura, California.

12. Marilyn M. Adams, "Redemptive Suffering: A Christian Solution to the Problem of Evil," in *The Problem of Evil*: Selected Readings, ed. Michael L. Peterson, vol. 8, Library of Religious Philosophy (Notre Dame, IN: University of Notre Dame Press, 1992), 182; reprinted from Marilyn McCord Adams, "Redemptive Suffering: [A] Christian Solution to the Problem of Evil," in *Rationality, Religious Belief and Moral Commitment*, ed. Robert Audi and William J. Wainwright (Ithaca, NY: Cornell University Press, 1986).

13. Millard J. Erickson, *Christian Theology*, three volumes in one (Grand Rapids, MI: Baker, 1983-85), 1239. Erickson's point that God cannot do the self-contradictory is widely accepted by theists in general and Christians. Self-contradictions are not things that test God's omnipotence, they are simply nonsense.

14. John Walvoord holds that the fire is literal, "The Literal View," *Four Views on Hell*, ed. William Crockett (Grand Rapids, MI: Zondervan, 1992), 28. Norman Geisler holds that the torment is real but is essentially psychological and self-inflicted (he argues that literal flames would not harm spiritual bodies), "Hell," *Baker Encyclopedia of Christian Apologetics* (Grand Rapids, MI: Baker, 1999), 312.

15. A. Oepke, TDNT I:396; cited in H. C. Hahn, "Destroy, Perish, Ruin," *The New International Dictionary of New Testament Theology*, ed. Colin Brown (Grand Rapids: Zondervan, 1975), 1:464.

16. For example, E. Fudge, *The Fire that Consumes*, cited in Timothy R. Phillips, "Hell," *The Evangelical Dictionary of Biblical Theology*, ed. Walter A. Elwell (Grand Rapids: Baker, 1966), 340. Phillips gives the rebuttal of the view.

17. As John Stott holds, John R. W. Stott, *Evangelical Essentials*: A Liberal-Evangelical Dialogue, ed. David L. Edwards (Downers Grove: InterVarsity, 1988), 317; cited and rebutted in Lewis and Demarest, 3:487-88.

18. Adrian Hastings, "Hell," *The Oxford Companion to Christian Thought*, ed. Adrian Hastings et al (Oxford: Oxford University Press, 2000), 292. His point relates to Catholic theology but the trend is no doubt broader.

19. The term "double predestination" was first used by Isidore (c. 560-636) but Gottshalk was the first to develop the view.

20. In contrast to this Calvinistic view, Arminians solve the problem of human inability through what is called prevenient grace. It is thought that God graciously counteracts the effect of the fall in each person's heart so that they can make a genuine choice to accept or reject salvation. Foreknowledge, on this view, is merely His knowing beforehand who will choose Him.

21. *World Almanac and Book of Facts 2001* (Mahwah, NJ: World Almanac Books, 2001), 37. The figure is 63 deaths per 100,000 births.

22. Geisler, 312.

Chapter twelve

GOD AS WILLING SUFFERER – Suffering without Victimhood

In World War II, a German teenager named Jurgen Moltmann went off to fight in the army, like nearly every young man his age. In Belgium he was captured by the British and held as a prisoner of war until 1948. He later wrote,

> In the camps in Belgium and Scotland I experienced both the collapse of those things that had been certainties for me and a new hope to live by, provided by the Christian faith. I probably owe to this hope, not only my mental and moral but physical survival as well, for it was what saved me from despairing and giving up.[1]

Moltmann was devastated by the destruction of his homeland and the realization of its role in the holocaust. After the war he also saw the world confronted with Marxism, which seemed to offer hope while Christianity offered only a God who appeared aloof from even the worst suffering. Moltmann began to rethink the traditional doctrine of divine impassibility, which is the view that God cannot be affected by anything in the world. He was one of the loudest voices in a chorus that began in the nineteenth century, when people in Britain supposed that God must be feeling the sufferings of those harmed by the early excesses of the industrial revolution (which brought such things as child labor, unsafe working conditions, and urban blight).

The horrendous sufferings of the twentieth century have motivated a lot of people to rethink the idea that God is unaffected by anything in the world. Many have concluded that the God of the Bible is not impassible and that early Christian thinkers were too influenced by Greek thought.

Is God unaffected by suffering, or is He deeply affected by it? In creating a world in which there is so much suffering, did He know that He would never feel any of it, or instead did He know that He would share something of its sorrow? Many people today reject the idea of a God who would create a world of suffering yet sit on high never experiencing a tear of it. For centuries Christian thought held that God is beyond the reach of our pain, but in the last century most have come to regard Him as sharing in it.

Impassibility in History

The idea of divine impassibility was common among Greek philosophers who sought an unchanging reality behind this world of flux. Aristotle identified God as that unchanging reality because he thought that any change in a perfect being would have to be away from perfection. Furthermore, since Aristotle supposed that reasoning, not feeling, is the highest activity in humans, it must be so in God. Therefore God must be a being who thinks rather than feels. And, God must think about only the most worthy object, which is Himself. So He is absorbed in Himself, completely untouched by the outside world.

Later the Stoics added to this type of thinking when they said that maturity is having the personal strength to remain peaceful regardless of what happens around you. They concluded that God must have this quality to the fullest and so cannot be affected by anything.

Christian thinkers seem to have adapted the same basic idea. Anselm said that we experience God as compassionate yet He has no feeling. Addressing God, he said, "For when you see us in our wretchedness, we experience the effect of compassion, but you do not experience that feeling."[2] Similarly, John Calvin said that all talk of emotion in God is metaphorical and is simply God's way of communicating to us in a way that we can understand ("accommodation," he called it).[3] Thomas Aquinas held that some divine emotions are metaphorical while others are literally in God. Because he thought that God cannot be affected by anything outside Himself, emotions like anger and sadness must be metaphorical. On the other hand emotions like joy and love really are in God because they proceed from Himself and are not a response to something in the world.[4] Those who followed this thinking emphasized that love is not a matter of emotion but of will: God determines to do what is best for those He loves – He does not have feelings for them.

Others thought the problem with divine emotions is not that it would mean God can be affected by something outside Himself, but that emotions themselves are so often linked to weakness, even sin. God could not have emotions like greed, lust, fear, or anxiety. Augustine held that God has emotions, but they are unlike ours in that they are pure: "...He is jealous without any envy, is angry without any perturbation, is pitiful without any grief...."[5]

Those who want to limit or eliminate emotions in God seek to preserve His transcendence (e.g., Isa. 55:9; 57:15), emphasizing that He is different from creation and apart from it. They also want to preserve His immutability, that He does not change (Mal. 3:6). Thomas Weinandy defends the view that God is impassible, saying, "The absence of suffering in God actually liberates God from any self-love that would move Him to act to relieve His own suffering. The absence of suffering allows God's love to be completely altruistic and beneficent."[6]

One solution to the problem of divine suffering has been to suppose that God does not suffer in Himself but that Christ suffered in His humanity. Just as Christ could become tired, hungry, or thirsty as a human (John 4:6; Matt. 21:18; John 19:28) but not as God (e.g., Isa. 40:28, God "does not become weary or tired), so He could have emotions as a human only. As the Son, God experiences something new and fully enters into human suffering.[7]

The Bible and God's Emotions

The best place to begin resolving this issue is with the Bible itself. We can hardly miss the fact that it speaks of God as having remarkably deep emotions; in fact it is hard to imagine terms that could be deeper. For instance, God's love for His people is compared to that of a mother for her infant, "Can a woman forget her nursing child and have no compassion on the son of her womb? Even these may forget, but I will not forget you" (Isa. 49:15). It is also put in terms of a parent's love for a child: "'Is not Ephraim my dear son, the child in whom I delight? Though I often speak against him, I still remember him. Therefore my heart yearns for him; I have great compassion for him,' declares the Lord" (Jer. 31:20). The foundational image of the New Testament is also rich in emotion: a father sacrifices his only son to save those estranged from him and make them his adopted children.

As the ultimate revelation of divinity, Christ is the exact likeness of God (Heb. 1:3), and in fact very God Himself (John 1:1). It is significant therefore that Christ has a full range of emotions. For example, He experienced joy (Luke 10:21), grief (Luke 19:41), and anger (Mark 3:5).

It is not as simple as saying that Christ had emotions only in His humanity but not as God. That is because God generally – and not just Christ specifically – is said to have a whole range of emotions. God is said, for instance, to have joy (Isa. 62:5), grief (Ps. 78:40, Isa. 63:10), anger Jer. 7:18-19), hatred (Deut. 16:22), wrath (Ps. 106:15-42; Isa. 63:3), jealousy (Ps. 78:58), love (John 3:16), and compassion (2 Kings 13:23).

The Holy Spirit too has emotions in that He can be grieved (Isa. 63:10; Eph. 4:30). And when someone is controlled by the Spirit the results are described in emotionally rich terms, "love, joy, peace, patience, kindness, goodness, faithfulness, gentleness, self-control" (Gal. 5:22).

Therefore emotions are ascribed to all three members of the Trinity.

Such emotions do not seem to be mere anthropomorphisms[8] (i.e., non-literal expressions which reveal something of God by speaking as though He were a human). In Hosea 11:8-9 God says, "My heart is changed within me; all my compassion is aroused. I will not carry out my fierce anger, nor will I turn and devastate Ephraim. For I am God, and not man." It seems that here a figure of speech is used to make a literal point. His contrast between limited human compassion and His own much greater compassion demands that He indeed has compassion. If anything He has more of it.

Divine Emotions are Unique

If it is really the case that God has a dimension to His being that we could call emotion, how does it differ from human emotion? For one, He is in complete control of Himself. We may be able to get a glimpse of this from scriptural exhortations to be in control of our own emotions. Those carrying out justice, for example, are commanded not to pity the guilty (the murder who lies in wait, Deut. 19:13; false witness, Deut. 19:21; a woman who unjustly interferes when two men are fighting, Deut. 25:12). As well, many times we are commanded not to allow ourselves to fear (e.g., Isa. 41:10). We can infer from God's command to control our emotions that He certainly is in control of whatever emotions He has.

It is also certain that God is completely in control of what influences Him from the outside. He told Ezekiel that when He is determined to bring judgment no one can dissuade Him: "...even though these three men, Noah, Daniel and Job were in its midst, by their own righteousness they could only deliver themselves,' declares the Lord God" (Ezek. 14:14). Their pleas would not even deliver their own children (14:16, 18, 20). He told Jeremiah that even his prayers would avail nothing for his people (Jer. 7:16), nor would the prayers of Moses and Samuel (Jer. 15:1). On the other hand, when God has determined to show compassion, not even a vengeful Jonah could dissuade Him (Jon. 4:9-11). Thus whatever there may be of divine emotions, God remains completely sovereign.

Normally, however, the Bible emphasizes that God is willing to be affected by prayers – which is a form of outside influence. The psalmist addresses Him as, "O You who hear prayer" (Ps. 65:2). Prayer moves God to change things, in that "the effective prayer of a righteous man can accomplish much" (James 5:16). Jesus went so far as to make the point that even when it appears that prayer is not moving God we should not give up praying. He told the disciples the parable of the widow and the unjust judge to make the point that "at all times they ought to pray and not to lose heart" (Luke 18:1).

So there is no doubt that God can be affected by things outside Himself, but only because He wants to be and only as much as He wants to be. If He is moved to pity or compassion over suffering it is because He permits Himself to be so moved. No one can inflict emotional harm on Him, and He is never a victim. This deals with a major concern on the part of those who believe that God is impasssible (i.e., unaffectable).

Another reason some people want to hold that God is impassible is to preserve His constant blessedness. God is said to be "blessed forever" (cf. Rom. 1:25, 9:5), and some believe that would be impossible were He to be emotionally affected by suffering.[9] But we need not suppose that in order to be forever blessed God must be untouched by suffering. The redeemed will be forever blessed in spite of the fate of the lost (Rev. 21:4). If they can be, why can't God? Blessedness seems to be more a matter of perspective rather than imperviousness to outside influences.

Closely related to the argument from blessedness is the more traditional emphasis on God's immutability, or unchangeableness. If God undergoes changes in emotions, how can He be unchanging?[10] The answer depends on our definition of "immutable." As typically defined, "God is unchanging in *nature, desire, and purpose*" (emphasis altered).[11] That does not rule out His having emotions. As evangelical theologian Gordon Lewis points out, "Change that does not deny any of God's essential attributes is in harmony with a biblical view of God."[12]

Anglican scholar Gerald Bray believes that a misunderstanding has caused the conflict between the traditional view that God is impassible and the modern view that He suffers.

The ancients regarded suffering as mostly physical, so in their view God could not suffer whereas Christ in His humanity could. By contrast, in the modern view suffering has a lot to do with mental suffering. Thus today, empathy and compassion are viewed as a kind of suffering. The church Fathers believed that God indeed empathizes with us, but they considered empathy a part of His love, not a form of "suffering."[13] Nevertheless, Bray agrees with the more traditional view that any suffering on God's part is external to the Trinity and not within it. Suffering has to do with the relationship between God and humanity, not between Father and Son.[14]

In What Sense does God Suffer?

Where does all this leave us as to whether God is touched by the suffering of His creatures? As we can see, it is a very complex subject and we can do no more here than scratch the surface.[15]

One well known and useful way of understanding God is by analogy. It has been a more or less standard view since Aquinas used it. When we say, for example, that God knows John is at the lake, we do not mean "knows" in exactly the same way as when we say, "Mary knows John is at the lake." That is because, in contrast to human knowledge, God's knowledge is infinite and infallible; He didn't gain it through experience or reflection, nor can He forget it. But on the other hand, when we say that God "knows" we do not mean something entirely different from Mary "knows." God's knowledge is in some sense the same, and in some sense different from human knowledge. We can say that God's knowledge is analogous to human knowledge.[16]

One way to fill in a little more detail is to say that "knows" has a meaning that fits the nature of the one who knows. If we say that "Mary knows" then the knowledge is subject to human limitations: it is was gained by experience, can be mistaken, and so on. If we say that Fido the dog knows, his knowledge fits his dog nature: it can't be highly abstract or formed through symbolic reasoning, and so on. So then "God knows" fits God's nature.

This will help us pull together what we have said about God's emotions. Whatever they are, they have to fit the divine nature. It rules out certain types of emotions altogether, such as fear, greed, lust, or self-pity. Other emotions He could have only in a purified form. If God really does have anger, it must be righteous anger not selfish anger. Jealousy cannot mean that He wants something He does not have. Grief could not be anything like depression, nor could it include a sense of defeat.

How much can we know of God's knowledge, emotions, or any other attributes? It would seem, only as much as we know of His nature. And when we compare the capability of our puny little minds to all there is to know – to how much God knows of Himself – what we can know of God isn't all that much.

I like to think in terms of the difference between how much I know and how much my dog knows. While my dog is very intelligent, and made it through almost the entire five-months of intensive training to be a guide dog for the blind, she can know only a fraction of what I can know (except when it comes to how things smell!). That fraction that she does know is true; however, I know much more. She may know, for example, that there is a man standing next to a building. I know that too but I also know much more, for example that the man is a police officer investigating a robbery at a bank.

Whatever distance exists between me and my dog is nothing compared to the distance between me and God. I may know truly that God has compassion, yet know very little of what it is like. That said, however, we should strive to understand God as much as we can.

Some Christians have thought that it is wrong to try to push the limits of what we can know about spiritual things. On one version of this view, original sin was the desire for too much knowledge. It is true that it would be undiscerning to strive for certain types of knowledge.

Exactly how to abuse drugs or pick up a prostitute would not be something the average person needs to know (unless they are a vice officer). And knowledge of some things would be a waste of precious time, such as learning the exact length of every blade of grass on a randomly chosen lawn. But it is hard to imagine any reason to limit our inquiry into spiritual truth, especially about God. It is impossible for us to find out things about God that He does not want us to know. Besides, the real problem is that we quickly run out of the cognitive horsepower needed for understanding an infinite God. Still, we can push it to the limits.

In our effort to understand whether God is moved by suffering, we can conclude at the very least that God knows our suffering through Christ. Most people in recent decades would go farther and add that God as a divine Being – not just Christ in His humanity – knows our suffering. The view is suggested by the most natural interpretation of a number of verses. However God is affected, it is in accordance with His pure and limitless divine nature. And He is affected only in the way He wants, as much as He wants, and because He wants it. But that makes whatever He feels all the more significant: He doesn't have to feel our pain but He wants to. And being omniscient and omnipresent, He has the potential to see all pain, and all suffering. We, by contrast, see only an infinitesimal amount of the total. God could be aloof and untroubled by it all, but He chose to be deeply affected, caring, and compassionate.

If the message of Christianity and the cross is about anything, it is about a God who cares more than we could ever comprehend.

GOING FARTHER

1. What emotions can God not experience?

2. If God indeed has emotions, or is affected by things outside Himself, in what ways are His experiences different from ours?

3. Have you ever been more pained by something than you wanted to be? How was your experience different from God's?

4. Have you ever chosen not to be affected by someone's suffering? For example, have you ever chosen to be unmoved by someone who was getting the punishment they deserved, or who was warned against doing the very thing that eventually harmed them? Have

you ever been so exhausted by grief or compassion that you could not function unless you refocused your emotions or shut them off altogether? How were your experiences like or unlike God's?

5. Which person do you think is more compassionate, the one who cannot stop himself from being emotionally moved by something, or the one who chooses to be moved? Explain.

6. If you could choose to know all the sufferings of every creature, would you do it?

NOTES

1. Jurgen Moltmann, "Autobiographical Note," in Conyers, *God, Hope, and History: Jurgen Moltmann and the Christian Concept of History* (Macon, GA: Mercer University Press, 1988), 203; cited in Stanley J. Grenz and Roger E. Olson, *Twentieth Century Theology: God and the World in a Transitional Age* (Downers Grove, IL: InterVarsity, 1992), 173.

2. Anselm, "Proslogion", quoted in Alister McGrath, *Christian Theology: An Introduction* (Oxford: Blackwell, 1994), 215.

3. Accommodation was an important theme in Calvin. With regard to divine suffering, God accommodates His communication to us, "in order to move us more powerfully and draw us to himself." Calvin, "Commentary on Isaiah 63:9," trans. W. Pringle for the Calvin Translation Society, Edinburgh, 1853, pp. 346-47; quoted in Paul S. Fiddes, *The Creative Suffering of God* (Oxford: Oxford University Press, 1988), 18.

4. Thomas Aquinas, *Summa Theologica*, part I, question 9, article 1; part II, question 25, article 1; *Summa contra Gentiles*, part II.25.

5. "On Patience" 1; quoted in Erickson, *God the Father Almighty*, 147.

6. Thomas G. Weinandy, "Does God Suffer?" *First Things* 117 (November 2001): 35-41; <FirstThings.com>, accessed 15 April 2003.

7. A concise statement of this view is in John C. Cavadini's review of Weinandy's book, *Does God Suffer?* The review is,"No, Not Exactly," Commonweal (March 9, 2001); accessed 7 Sept. 2004, <www.findarticles.com/p/articles/mi_m1252/is_5_128ai_75445619>.

8. An anthropomorphism that is a human emotion is called, more technically, an anthropopathism.

9. Robert Duncan Culver, "The Impassibility of God: Cyril of Alexandria to Moltmann," *Christian Apologetics Journal*, vol. 1, no. 1 (Spring 1998), p. 4 of online version. Culver believes divine blessedness was the primary reason for the patristic consensus that God is immutable, and he himself accepts that reasoning. Accessed 7 Sept. 2004, <http://www.ses.edu/journal/issue1_1/1.1Culver.pdf>.

10. Thomas Weinandy, who defends the traditional view of impassibility, says, "From the dawn of the Patristic period Christian theology has held as axiomatic that God is impassible that is, *He does not undergo emotional changes of state, and so cannot suffer*." (Emphasis added.) "Does God Suffer?" *First Things*, 117 (November 2001): 35-41. Accessed 7 Sept. 2004, <http://www.firstthings.com/ftissues/ft0111/articles/weinandy.html>.

11. G[ordon]. R. Lewis, "God, Attributes of," *Evangelical Dictionary of Theology*, ed. Walter A. Elwell (Grand Rapids, MI: Baker Books, 1984), 453. The original emphasis was, "God is *unchanging* in nature, desire, and purpose." Note that Lewis also holds that God is passible.

12. Lewis, "Impassibility of God," *Evangelical Dictionary of Theology*, 553.

13. Gerald Bray explains, "The modern theologians are not talking here about brute physical force, but about compassion and 'empathy,' which the ancients supposedly ignored. That is not strictly true of course--ancient Christian writers categorized such notions under 'love,' rather than 'suffering.' Once that shift of perception is made, it is quite clear that the fathers of the church believed in God's compassion just as much as any modern theologian." From, "A Vale of Tears: Suffering As A Mark of This Age," *The Theologian: the Internet Journal for Integrated Theology*, March/April 1999; Alliance of Confessing Evangelicals. <http://alliancenet.org/pub/mr/mr99/mr9902.toc.html>.

14. Gerald Bray, *The Doctrine of God, Contours of Christian Theology*, ed. Gerald Bray (Downers Grove, IL: InterVarsity, 1993), 194-95.

15. See the section on further reading at the end of the book. Another dimension of the problem is God's relationship to time. The view that He is timeless in the sense that He exists completely outside time (such that no moment of history or the future is closer to Him or more real to Him than any other moment) fits more easily with the traditional view of impassibility. On the other hand, the view that God is eternal and exists within time (such that the present moment is the present moment for Him as it is for us, albeit He knows the past and future perfectly) could fit with either the passibility or impassibility view.

16. A term that has an identical meaning is called univocal, and one that is completely different is called equivocal. Analogical is in the middle, being in some ways the same and in some ways different.

Chapter thirteen

ANSWERING SKEPTICS

Pain and suffering is widely – and no doubt correctly – considered to be the main reason for skepticism about the existence of God. Because God is so great we will never remove some mystery as to His ways; and because our intellects are so limited we will never remove at least some need for faith (we cannot even understand the common cold – how can we hope to understand God's ways?). However, to those who are struggling to hold onto their faith, and to those who profess skepticism, we can offer various answers which believers have given.

The Problem of Evil and Reasoning

Belief is a complex thing. It is a network of assumptions, convictions, and conclusions. What we take to be knowledge, together with our judgments about such things as values, morals, and aesthetics, comprise our worldview.[1] Hence the problem of evil need not be considered as an isolated issue as if it alone could decide the question of God's existence. So for those struggling with doubt or already committed to skepticism, we can appeal to other reasons for believing in a good and all powerful God.

To begin with, let's see how a conclusion can be used to actually tear apart the argument in which it appears.

How We Reach Conclusions

Reasoning is a matter of accepting a conclusion if we accept another statement or statements as true (those we call premises). Several things have to come together for us to feel compelled to believe a conclusion. For example, we have to accept that the premises are factually true. We have to accept that the relationships within and between the premises are what the argument says they are. And we have to accept that the premises lead us to believe the specific conclusion in question.

There's more. We may have grounds, completely apart from the argument, for rejecting the argument's conclusion – grounds we find to be more credible than the premises of the argument.

Suppose your neighbor comes to you distraught because while cleaning out her family's car she finds a suspicious looking bag of white powder. Your friend who is with you makes the following brutally frank argument to your distraught neighbor, voicing her worst fears:

> If there was a bag of white powder hidden in your car then your spouse is secretly a drug addict.
> There was a bag of white powder hidden in your car.
> Therefore, your spouse is secretly a drug addict.

Since the distraught spouse found the bag herself, she does not doubt that it was in the car, so she does not doubt the truth of premise two. But in order for her to accept the conclusion she has to also accept that its being there means that her husband is a drug addict; in other words, she has to accept premise one. She may reject that idea on grounds that she knows her husband would never do such a thing. She may even have an alternate explanation for the bag being there (he may have given a ride to someone who left it there; or someone may have put it there to frame him). Furthermore, the conclusion of the argument also depends on the powder in fact being a drug, not something that merely looks like a drug.

So your neighbor believes the conclusion to be false more than she believes one of the premises to be true. On that basis she has every right to reject the conclusion. This is sometimes called the G. E. Moore shift, after the famous twentieth century British philosopher.[2]

We can see that a conclusion to an argument cuts both ways. We may accept a conclusion if we accept the premises that argue for it. On the other hand we may hold the conclusion to be false because of things we know apart from the argument, and that may lead us to believe that the argument is flawed. It may be flawed because, for example, one of the argument's premises are false, or a relationship within a premise may be incorrect ("*if* there is a bag of white powder *then* the spouse is a drug addict"), or the relationship between premises may be flawed, or the premises together may not be enough to justify the conclusion.

Now let's see an important way that this applies to the problem of evil. Consider a very basic form of argument against the existence of God (here evil includes both moral evil as well as suffering):

> If there is evil in the world a good and all powerful God does not exist
> There is evil in the world
> Therefore, a good and all powerful God does not exist

Like our friend who found the bag herself, we know there is evil in the world; that is not in doubt. Nevertheless we may well reject the conclusion because we are convinced for other reasons that God exists. This is like the friend believing her husband to be innocent because she knows so much about him regardless of finding the bag in the car. In life beliefs are like that, connected and complex. What we believe about the existence and character of God can be based on much more than the presence of evil in the world. Belief in God is part of a whole worldview. In actuality it is not as simple as entirely dismissing the argument against God from evil merely because we have independent reasons for belief in God. Instead, we may want to think through an answer to the problem of evil, as we have tried to do in this book.[3] So far this book has investigated why we should reject premise one on grounds that there are reasons a good and all powerful God would allow evil in the world. Now we will briefly suggest some reasons believers have offered for believing in God's existence entirely apart from the issue of evil.

Christian philosopher Douglas Geivett echoes Augustine's and Aquinas's approach to the problem of evil, which begins by demonstrating through various arguments that theism is the correct world view. That allows Geivett to approach the problem of evil from the standpoint of already accepting the existence of God. In effect, he argues that God does exist, so there must be some reason why He allows evil.[4]

Whether or not we use the approach that begins by proving God's existence, believers have given a lot of reasons for their conviction that God exists. It is the subject of thousands of books, articles, and scholarly papers. We can only scratch the surface here. First we have to consider how anything is proved. Correctly understanding that issue can resolve certain types of doubt and skepticism.

How We Reason

There are different ways to reason, and how we go about it determines how certain we can be about a conclusion. Deduction offers absolute proof whereas induction offers only a high degree of certainty. Confusing one with the other can lead to unnecessary skepticism.

The examples above about the distraught friend and about God are cases of deduction.. Deductive arguments offer total, air tight proof for their conclusions. Successful deductive arguments work because everything we need to draw the conclusion is included in the premises. If a person argues, for instance, that (1) every chair made by the Ever-Strong chair company can hold at least 500 pounds, and (2) this chair is made by Ever-Strong; then we have to agree with the conclusion that this chair holds at least 500 pounds.

Although deduction is very powerful, in a practical sense it is still difficult to have an absolutely convincing argument about something in the real world. First, for simple deductive arguments, those who agree with your conclusion are typically those who already agree with your premises. Could you imagine two intelligent people agreeing that every Ever-Strong chair holds 500 pounds, that a particular chair is made by Ever-Strong, yet still debate whether it holds 500 pounds? Not likely.

The second problem is that deduction tells us only what follows if we accept the premises. It gives us the structure of an argument but we still have to verify that the premises are factually true. Proving premises to be factually true has plenty of challenges of its own because proof itself is complex ("proof" here means something like "establish" or "demonstrate"). Proof typically is constructed out of such things as what we consider to be self-evident, data from our senses, testimony of experts, conclusions from other arguments, and so on. In the case of the argument about Ever-Strong chairs, what would it take to prove the premise that every one can hold at least 500 pounds?

The answer is that it depends a lot on what we mean by "prove." If we mean "reasonably sure" then we could satisfy the requirement by, for instance, showing the quality of materials, workmanship, and the inspection process. But if we mean something like "prove 100 percent," with no possibility of doubting the conclusion under any circumstances whatsoever, then it is hard to imagine what would satisfy the requirement for proof. No matter how much evidence we offer, the objector could always raise one more challenge: what about flawed materials, an error in the machinery, an inattentive quality inspector? The defender could offer, for example, that the machines are calibrated once a week; but the objector could ask further, what if it gets out of calibration in less than a week? Making objections and offering answers could go on endlessly. Objections made to any argument can range from the merely unreasonable to the outright bizarre. Someone could even go so far as to doubt that a famous person such as Winston Churchill ever existed, claiming that photographs were faked, stories were invented, that all those who say they knew him are lying, and so on. The odds of such objections being valid are one in millions or more.

We can see that it is relatively easy to demand an inappropriate level of proof. Part of being rational is knowing when we can be convinced of something.

So there are not many things in life for which we can have absolute, airtight proof with no possibility of doubt. As most people would admit, that level of certainty is limited to a few things in mathematics, such as geometrical proofs (e.g., "triangles have three sides"), some things in formal logic, and not much more. Even at that, it is generally recognized that such proofs are dependent on the assumptions of their specific context, so that even those arguments would not be true in all possible contexts.

To demand absolute proof where the subject and the nature of the argument do not allow it is naive and in some cases absurd. It is to misunderstand the nature of proof. In everyday life we consider things to be certain which are only highly probable. We are "certain" that our car is on the parking lot because we just parked it there ten minutes ago (yet it could have been stolen within those ten minutes), we are "certain" that our spouse loves us (though we could be mistaken), we are "certain" about what we had for breakfast (though our memory could be wrong).[5] We are right to be certain about such things even though there is a logical possibility we are wrong.

The threshold for proof has to be suited to the issue. Proof in history, for example, is limited by the interpretation of documents, artifacts, and the like. Sciences like physics and chemistry have a higher standard because experiments can be repeated. To demand that an historical event be repeated would be absurd. Courts, where people's freedom and even their lives can be at stake, require not absolute, 100 percent proof, but only proof "beyond reasonable doubt." That is not as high a threshold as "any conceivable doubt," or "any possible doubt." Prosecutors often discuss such differences with juries because it is crucial. On a personal level, each of us routinely has to stake our well being, and even our lives, on things we cannot prove 100 percent. The threshold of proof has to be appropriate to the issue, whether it is the safety of an airplane or a car, the competence of a doctor or pharmacist – and even how safely food is prepared in a restaurant. (If you are alive to read this then your reasoning has been successful so far!)

The point of this is that it is not appropriate to demand complete, absolute, indubitable proof that God is good notwithstanding the existence of evil. It cannot be proved to the level of certainty that triangles have three sides, that gravity acts on all objects, or that water is made of hydrogen and oxygen. If someone demands such a level of certainty regarding the question of God that means they do not understand the nature of proof – rather like the person who demands mathematical proof that Europe exists.

But that does not mean that we have to settle for less than complete certitude, our inner confidence that something is true. We can have complete confidence in something that we cannot prove 100 percent.

There is no reason to think that our level of inner certitude must never be higher than our level of proof. In fact, we quite rightly believe lots of things that we cannot prove very well. For example, we believe that the world has existed for more than five minutes. Yet we would have difficulty proving it did not just now come into existence in a way that appears to have age, in other words, with memories intact, rings in trees, history books written, and so on. We have no doubt about what we had for breakfast yesterday morning, but how could we actually prove it now that the dishes are washed?[6] We are sure that the person or persons who raised us were who they said they were, our biological parents for example. But all we can offer by way of hard evidence is a birth certificate, which we have to admit could easily have been faked. I have known of a number of persons who found out as adults that their "parents" were not their parents (two of them discovered that their "sister" was really their mother).

We typically are (rightly) certain of a lot of things based on our memory, the authority of others, and various ways of knowing that do not lend themselves to public types of proof.

Though we lack complete proof for some of our beliefs we can and should feel certain of them. We needn't entertain kinky doubts about our parentage for example. We just have to realize that our level of inner certainty doesn't always have to be limited to what we can prove to others.[7] And we can't expect that what we believe can be demonstrated to others 100 percent.

While deduction is very powerful and useful, in daily life we often reason inductively. An inductive argument offers less than complete proof essentially because the conclusion goes beyond what is given in the premises. I could say that I've examined ten Ever-Strong chairs and each one holds 500 pounds, therefore this Ever-Strong chair that I have not examined will also hold 500 pounds. I'm not 100 percent sure of the conclusion because I have not tested the chair in question, but I have good evidence that it will hold the weight. The more chairs I test and the more this chair is like the ones I tested, the surer I can be of the conclusion. I can be 99 percent sure, yet not 100 percent sure without actually testing the chair.

We have less than absolute proof for so much of what we believe. It is due to our being mere creatures. On virtually everything, only God knows with perfect certainty. For us, when it comes to spiritual things, it seems there's always room for at least some faith. That faith gives us certitude beyond the level of proof we can offer publically.[8] So we may be able to prove something to a level of 98 percent, but our faith gives us 100 percent certainty.

We have to remember too, that 98 percent proof for most things is full proof. In those cases it is all the proof we can have and it is all we need.

To summarize what this means for the problem of evil, we can offer strong reasons to believe in a good and all-powerful God, but it won't necessarily amount to the 100 percent proof associated with things like mathematics. Yet there is nothing wrong with having less than complete proof for most things we hold to be true. If the skeptic does not accept that then he does not understand the nature of reason and proof.

How We Explain this World

Another method of reaching a conclusion is reasoning to the best explanation. Using this method, we look at a situation and choose the most plausible explanation for it. Suppose we are at the beach and see two parallel strips about six feet apart, disappearing down into the distance. We look closer and see that each strip is about eight inches wide and made of small ridges. We immediately conclude that a car drove down the beach. Although it is possible that people produced the long patterns using small hand tools, it is unlikely because it would be an enormous amount of pointless effort, and we've never seen anyone do it. Besides, the car hypothesis easily explains it, and we've seen people drive in the sand leaving marks just like the ones in front of us.

The best explanation does not have to be flawless nor answer all possible questions and objections. It just has to be better than any other explanation (it's rather like surviving a bear attack; you don't have to be the world's fastest runner, just faster than the person you're with).

Is a good and all powerful God the best explanation for the world? In this book we've discussed some reasons why such a God would allow a world like this one. It is time we connect some of the dots we have been drawing throughout the book so we can see the picture more clearly ourselves and so we can show it to the doubter or skeptic.

To begin with, God created physical beings with freedom. He desires that they know Him and choose good. Being physical requires that they be able to navigate in their physical world, which in turn requires some pain to tell them when they are at risk and to serve as a warning to others of risk.

Out of the countless cases where pain protects and warns, there are times when pain mechanisms function for no constructive purpose and nothing can be done to stop them. God sets up the natural order but is not required to micro manage every event so as to assure that each experience is constructive for everyone involved. Just as gravity makes physical life possible but also causes falls, so pain is constructive overall without being helpful to everyone in absolutely every case.

Seemingly pointless suffering is not necessarily completely pointless however. It provides opportunities for compassion and motivates people to develop ways to alleviate suffering, for example. Physical suffering of all types have led to the development of medical discoveries, including anesthetics, vaccinations, prosthetics, pacemakers, and medicines. Progress is even being made to understand the genetic code, the degeneration of which causes birth abnormalities. The cause of seemingly pointless suffering could be irresponsibility on someone's part. Whether or not it was the fault of the person suffering, the outcome can make people determined to be more responsible and prudent.

Christian philosophers have suggested reasons why pointless evil is not evidence against the existence of a good and omnipotent God. Peter van Inwagen suggests that God allows some pointless evil because sin has entered the world and ruptured our relationship with Him. Michael Peterson argues that God allows some pointless evil as part of a world in which moral beings act freely in a physical and moral environment (William Hasker holds a very similar view).[9]

God does not necessarily micro manage the physical world for our comfort, and the onus is on us to understand our environment, work within it, plan, and work to reduce the hazards that cause pain. All this spurs us on to become responsible and caring. Of course God can still intervene providentially on a micro level to make His care and power known. But we know that God is intervening only because (from our vantage point at least) things sometimes do go wrong. If God intervened every time without fail, insuring that nothing unwanted ever happened to anyone, then we fallen creatures would have no reason to think He is there and cares what happens. It would be like the child who said to his Christian parents, I don't think God is blessing and protecting our family because things would always go right anyway; they always do. To this the parents said, maybe we should pray some things go really wrong so you will see things don't just go right by themselves. It is the fact that things sometimes do go wrong that allows us to see the power of God, especially in response to prayer and faith.

God is not unfair if He does not intervene when things "go wrong," nor is He unfair to those who seem to have been given less in the way of physical abilities, health, or longevity. Everything we receive from God is from His grace, and by definition grace is undeserved. God does not owe each of us seventy-five years of life, perfect health, or anything else. Birth abnormalities or health problems (and troubles of many kinds) can help us realize what is important in life and how short life is with the result that we spend our time on what is important. They can help us depend on God. They can provide the irritant that develops the pearl of our character.

If we assume that the goal of this world is the maximal happiness of every creature, it is difficult to reconcile it with a good God. But if there is a higher good and it sometimes conflicts with lower goods like happiness, then a good being like God would choose the higher good. That higher good is the fullest possible revelation of God Himself, who is goodness. For humans, to know God and become like Him is a higher good than momentary pleasure or the absence of pain. Like a responsible parent, God must sometimes forfeit pleasure in creatures for the sake of something more important, such as development of good character – which is linked to an even higher good, which is the knowledge of Himself. Achieving the highest goods sometimes requires that we face challenges, struggles, and setbacks.

As with parenting, there is no guarantee that those difficulties will produce the desired effect. Because as part of God's grand plan we are free beings, we can choose bitterness over gratitude, self-pity over self-determination, laziness over honest effort, selfishness over love, and so on.

This world holds great possibilities for good, but no guarantees of it. It is up to us to make use of the opportunities provided by our fallen world.

Only a fallen world like ours provides the opportunity to see and experience many aspects of God, such as forgiveness, compassion, and providential protection. And only a fallen world allows us as humans to develop similar qualities ourselves. To become forgiving, people have to sin against us; to become compassionate there has to be pain, to trust God's protection there has to be danger, to be determined to do good we have to face and overcome obstacles. So pain and suffering present us with opportunities not only to see these qualities in God but also to mirror the character of God ourselves – thereby revealing Him even more. That is part of our being in the image of God in the fullest sense.

The development of moral and rational beings requires that actions have consequences. If we do not see that evil causes real damage, we will not shun it and instead choose good and God. But that consistency of cause and effect also means that innocent people will be hurt by evil intentions. People will be hurt by gossip, lies, bullets, and terrorist's bombs. God has given us the awesome opportunity to do good, but that also means that failure brings awesome consequences. If the possibility of bad consequences were not very real then the responsibility would not be very real.

Morality and rationality also require a consistent physical environment so that we can plan and carry out actions. If the cold did not consistently make people freeze, and wearing a coat did not consistently protect them from cold, then there would be no reason for us to give someone a coat to keep them warm. But that consistency also means that people who go without coats will freeze. Similarly, people who go without food starve. However, God can intervene sometimes and change events for a special purpose. He may do so, for example, in response to prayer or to provide credentials for His spokespersons (as we see with prophets and apostles in the Bible).

The consistent operation of the natural world means that sometimes there will be natural disasters. Wind will cause damage, rivers will overflow, and so on. God could providentially control these phenomena and limit the range of natural possibilities so that wind does not blow hard enough to damage structures and it never rains hard enough to flood. Even in our fallen world He does limit damage at times, but other times He does not. That is because like other kinds of suffering, natural disasters make us realize our limits, move us to depend on God; motivate us to plan, discover, work together, and the like. They also make us realize that not all is right between ourselves and our creator: we need to be reconciled to Him.

That said, there is no doubt that many times God does prevent evil, not only natural disasters but also the effects of moral evil, which He does through the operations of conscience, law enforcement, defensive use of military deterrence, and more. It is impossible for us to know just how much evil God prevents, but we have each heard of things like a narrow escape from a traffic accident, a visit to a doctor for something minor that uncovers cancer just in time, people escaping a burning building just before it collapses, a bullet ricocheting harmlessly off a belt buckle, a child falling from a building and landing unhurt on a bush, a person just missing an encounter with a vicious criminal, and countless other instances of providence. Yet even God's intervention is bound to be misunderstood and distrusted. If Hitler had died as an unknown teenager, how many people would be shaking their heads saying, how could a loving and all powerful God allow such a terrible thing?

This relates to an interesting insight from chaos theory, which deals with the effect of changes in highly complex systems where the parts within it affect other parts. It turns out that even where the causes and effects are rigidly determined, the outcome cannot be predicted (at least not by humans). That is because when one thing affects another thing, which affects another thing, then even a minute difference at the beginning quickly produces a big difference as events unfold. Weather is one example of such a system. One quip is that the difference in the way a butterfly flaps its wings can eventually determine whether or not there will be a hurricane.

So if minute differences can eventually cause major changes, it is possible that God would allow some tragedy now in order to bring about a greater good much later. If it is impossible to detect the minute differences that eventually produce major weather systems, how much more difficult would it be to know whether some tragedy would result in good within the human realm – a realm much more complex than weather. Therefore, how could a skeptic say that an evil event could produce no good, or that the good it could produce could never outweigh the bad it leaves in its wake?

One area where suffering is widely thought to have no purpose is animal pain. Animals certainly seem to be innocent victims, yet we have to be careful not to project onto them human levels of consciousness and its pains. Even the higher animals have limited awareness, memory, ability to think abstractly, and so on. As with humans, God has not been unkind or unjust if He does not give them a long or trouble free existence. And as with people, no one creature experiences the total amount of pain. The problem of pain for humans or other creatures comes down to justifying the amount of pain each individual feels, not a theoretical sum of all pains, which no one experiences. If any being experiences the sum of all misery, it is God Himself, who is aware of all evil, suffering, and lost opportunity for good. He willingly allows Himself to be touched by it all. Moreover, God suffered supremely in the person of Christ.

Life is, mercifully, of limited duration. So no pain lasts a very long time, nor can anyone inflict pain for very long. And pain ends permanently for those who accept the free gift of forgiveness and are brought into wonderful, intimate fellowship with God in heaven. Only those who refuse His grace are left with suffering that will never be healed or made ultimately meaningful. Yet in the broader picture even their tragic refusal contributes to a higher good in that it reveals God's justice – which is a good in itself and need not be a form of love.

God's justice is also the cause of some sufferings in this life. In some cases God allows people to have trouble because they deserve it. Justice is built into the natural order, so for example, protracted anger or worry bring health problems, recklessness causes accidents, laziness results in want; and so on. Some consequences of wrongdoing are psychological, in the form of a poor self image, guilty conscience, and the like; as an English proverb says, "there is no hell like a troubled conscience."[10] In other cases justice comes through divinely ordained human processes, such as police, courts, and prisons.

So to sum up, there are many reasons why the God of theism, and more specifically, the God of Christianity, fits with this fallen world. We could consider many more, some of which have nothing to do with the issue of evil.

The Problems of Evil and Worldviews

The explanation for pain and evil offered by the Christian worldview competes with explanations offered by other worldviews. And insofar as worldviews include more than answers to pain and evil, we can evaluate them according to how well they interpret a lot of other things.

Worldviews interpret the broadest possible array of subjects, such as why humans are the way they are, what is right and why, what makes for a just society, what forces have directed history, why the universe is as it is, what will happen in the future, and so on.

Does Evil Point to the Existence of God?

Some have argued that (ironically) the existence of evil helps demonstrate the existence of God. It is argued that if God does not exist then there are no objective moral values. But evil exists, so there are objective moral values. So God must exist as well.

It could form an inductive argument, or more specifically, an argument to the best explanation. This argument is sometimes cast as simply an argument for God's existence, without including the existence of evil. It says that objective moral values exist and therefore God exists. Notice that the argument is not claiming that only theists are moral people, or that one can't decide what is moral without believing in God, or that one can have no basis whatsoever for right and wrong without God. Instead it turns on the idea that there are objective moral values. More specifically, it looks at the basis, or foundation, or ultimate grounding of moral values. Without God, the argument claims, there is no ultimate foundation for morals.

When people say evil exists they usually mean (perhaps without realizing it) that evil is something objective – not just a matter of opinion. They mean that some things are evil whether we think so or not, the way that London is north of Paris whether we think so or not.

Not everyone agrees that some morals are objective. Some would claim that moral values are purely subjective, that is, that what is right is whatever we decide is right. That would make right and wrong something akin to matters of taste. If you think adultery is right and I think it is wrong, it is not much different from you thinking chocolate ice cream is best while I prefer vanilla. Some would claim that moral values are relative, that is, they can change from situation to situation; from culture to culture for example. Others would say that right and wrong is simply a matter of pragmatics, that is, what works in a situation.

But if pressed, most people would be uncomfortable with these options. Can we really say that the holocaust was right for those who believed in it? Or that it was wrong for British culture but right for German culture? Or, could slavery ever be right if it works out for us pragmatically?

Subjectivists, relativists, and pragmatists often tout their views as better able to promote tolerance. Yet in so doing they are implying that tolerance is always right for everyone! That sounds a lot like those who claim that some moral values are objective – true whether we think so or not.

Those who argue from the existence of evil to the existence of God say that for there to be a "problem of evil" there has to be objective right and wrong. When people point to evils like abuse of children and war and claim that God could not exist, they mean that abuse of children and war are objectively wrong. They don't just mean that those things don't suit their personal preferences, or that there is something wrong with them only in their culture.

The argument goes on to say that if morals are objective there must be a moral being who is above the human race. That is because, in part, we've already established that right and wrong must transcend humanity. Even if the whole human race thought torturing babies for fun is right, or genocide is right, it would still be wrong. We cannot explain objective morals by means of a thing or impersonal power above the human race, because they are not moral. Rocks and electricity are not moral. Only personal beings are moral.

Of course not everyone agrees with the moral argument. One objection is that it depends on requiring that right and wrong be a matter of what God commands (the divine command theory). But one problem with the divine command theory is that in order to know that what God commands is good, we have to have some idea of good that is independent of God. An answer to that objection is that we may have independent knowledge of what is right (because God gave us a conscience), yet God is ultimately the ground of right and wrong. A further problem with the divine command theory is that if what is right is purely a matter of God's will, it is arbitrary and tomorrow He could command that randomly murdering children is right. In answer to that, most Christians would say that right and wrong is a matter not of God's will purely, but of His nature; so He won't change His will tomorrow, or command something outrageous.[11]

Other objections come from attempts since the Enlightenment to ground morals in something other than God. A lot of modern thought grounds ethics in our common human needs, or our common evolution. But those who uphold the moral argument would answer that these do not make for objectively binding obligations. So what if we would like our race to survive? The defender of the moral argument would say that our wanting the race to survive does not create an objectively binding moral obligation. Besides, what if we decide that the best way for the human race to survive is to have slavery – would it then be right?

There are atheists who believe morals are objective and are not grounded in things like evolution, need, or opinion. Supposedly, they just exist. The theist would answer that morals don't just exist, floating out in space; they exist in persons. Even if they do "just exist," why would we humans be bound to obey them? If we really do have a duty to obey them, we have a duty to someone; and that someone must be God.[12]

Reasons to Accept God's Existence

The Bible says that everyone can know some very basic things about God because of creation, "for since the creation of the world His invisible attributes, His eternal power and divine nature, have been clearly seen, being understood through what has been made...." (Rom. 1:20). Psalm 19:1 says that "the heavens are telling of the glory of God." The revelation is nonverbal (v. 3) and reaches every part of the earth (v. 4). This is known as "general" revelation because it is available to everyone.

The Bible is not specific as to just how everyone can make an inference from the world to God's existence. Traditional thinking has divided the subject into two main approaches, which have each been used for centuries. First, that the universe exists at all shows there is a God (the cosmological argument), and second, the order apparent around us shows that there is a God (the teleological argument). Within these basic approaches there are many different specific arguments, which vary as to their success. Examining them in detail would easily take a book of its own so we will give only the gist of one contemporary variation of each.

The Universe Must Have Been Created

An argument that has attracted a lot of attention in recent years is called the kalam cosmological argument. It argues for one alternative within each of three pairs of alternatives. The first is that the universe either had a beginning or had no beginning (i.e., is eternal), and the kalam argument tries to show that it had a beginning. The second choice is that the beginning of the universe was either caused or uncaused (i.e., came into existence by itself), and the kalam argument tries to show that it was caused. The final step says that the cause of the universe either was or was not a personal being (i.e., a person rather than a force).

The argument for the first alternative gets a little technical, but it is necessary to show that the universe had a beginning because an eternal universe would not need a creator. But if it had a beginning then it is easier to show that it had a creator.

To argue against an eternal universe, the kalam argument shows that such an idea is fraught with problems. If the universe had no beginning, then there had to be an actual infinite number of things stretching backwards eternally (such as an infinite number of physical events). Now an actually infinite number of things is different from a theoretical infinite, such as a mathematical concept. Remember your math teacher told you that a line is an infinite set of points? Well, of course that is a theoretical infinite. If you got a microscope you would see that the pencil line is made of a finite amount of graphite; and we know that the graphite is composed of a finite number of molecules. No one believes that there are an infinite number of molecules, atoms, or subatomic particles making up that line. The "infinite" is a theoretical infinite. You can talk about theoretical infinites, but translating that to the real world and making actual infinites is an entirely different matter. Like trying to get an infinite number of grains of sand, there is no way to do it by adding one grain at a time. You cannot add the final grain and say, at last I have an infinite amount of sand. In the same way you cannot add one event to another event and finally say that you have an infinite number of events.

The idea that there cannot be an infinite number of events does not normally bother us because we are used to thinking of events stretching forward to eternity. But with the beginning of the universe we have to say that there is an eternity behind us, with no beginning; so the present moment is the end of an eternal number of events. It's like saying we started with an infinitely high negative number and we finally counted down to zero. But that would be impossible because you cannot start from an infinitely high number; there is no beginning of infinitely high numbers. It seems that if you could somehow start from an infinitely high negative number you could never reach this moment. It's like saying I started with an infinite pile of sand and I got rid of it grain by grain. If you got rid of it, it was not infinite. If you could count down to zero, you did not start with an infinite number. The point is that, similarly, if the universe had an infinite past you could never reach the present moment. You could never get to today any more than you could count down from an infinitely high negative number or get rid of an infinite amount of sand.

Another problem with the idea that the past is infinite (and thus does not need a God to begin it) is that paradoxes abound when we try to envision an actual infinite number of things. If a hotel had an infinite number of rooms and there were no vacancies because each room had an occupant, the hotel could still add another guest by making each occupant move to the next room over.[13] In fact, though full, the hotel could still accommodate an infinite number of new guests just by moving them over to other rooms; and the hotel would still have the same number of occupants as when it started, namely, an infinite number!

Proponents of the kalam argument say that paradoxes like these show that an actual infinite number of things is impossible. Critics say that the paradoxes arise because we do not know much about the nature of infinity. Christian philosophers J. P. Moreland and William

Craig respond that, on the contrary, infinite set theory is highly developed and well understood – the paradoxes arise precisely because we do understand sets with an infinite number of members.[14]

Besides the issue of infinite sets, modern science gives us reason to believe that the universe had a beginning. It appears to be expanding, which means that if you project back in time, it must have started from some point. It does not appear that it could be expanding and contracting in billions of year cycles because it does not have enough matter to generate the gravity necessary to pull back in on itself. Furthermore, the universe is winding down (the second law of thermodynamics), so if it is infinitely old, why isn't it all wound down? It is like putting an ice cube in a pan of water. Eventually the ice is melted and the pan is one temperature. If the universe is winding down, for example, to a uniform temperature, and that has been going on forever, why isn't the process complete?

So if we conclude that the universe had a beginning, then we have to decide if that beginning was either caused or uncaused. We can infer that the universe had a cause since every physical thing we know about has a cause. The burden of proof is on the person who wants to say that the universe is the only thing we know that just popped into existence by itself.[15]

If the beginning of the universe was caused, that cause was either personal or impersonal (like a force). It must have been personal because before the beginning of the universe there was nothing. The cause had to be in some sense timeless as well as immaterial, and that best fits a mind rather than a thing. If it were a timeless, impersonal force, there would be no way to explain why the universe came into existence at a particular point in time rather than in eternity past (the kalam argument has already argued that the universe does not have an eternal past). The only way to explain it is to say the cause was a person who could make a decision to begin the universe.[16]

So if the kalam argument is successful, then we can show that the universe was caused by a personal being.

The Conditions For Life Are No Accident

As science has learned more about what it takes for life to exist, it has become increasingly clear just how astonishingly unlikely it is that those conditions came together. The obvious conclusion is that the universe has been deliberately fine tuned for life. And as evidence has mounted in this area, theists have argued more convincingly that God's design is the best explanation for the existence of life.

The argument is based on the fact that there are highly specific qualities that allow for life. The amount of gravity has to be just right, which means that the size of the earth has to be just right. If it were too big there would be too much gravity and everything would be crushed into the ground. If it were too small there would not be enough gravity to hold an atmosphere. And that atmosphere has to be composed of the right chemicals to allow for life. Too, the earth has to stay within a very narrow temperature range. Temperatures in the universe range from near absolute zero, where molecules barely move, to millions of degrees, where the heat rips all molecules apart. Life exists in the thinnest sliver of the possible range of temperatures. Even the wind speed on earth cannot be too high for life to exist. On the other hand, if there were little or no wind, the extreme heat near the equator and cold near the poles would not even out as much as they do, and a smaller portion of the earth would be inhabitable.

Besides all of these, there are far less obvious factors. The characteristics of carbon have to be just right, the earth has to have enough metals, and so on.

The forces acting across the entire universe have to be just right as well. For example, physicist Paul Davies says that if the universal forces of gravitation or electromagnetism were off by as little as one part in 10^{40} (remember, that's a one with forty zeros after it!) planets like our would not have existed. It is said that seconds after the big bang, the density of the universe must have been within about one part in 10^{60}.[17] Oxford Physicist Roger Penrose calculates that the odds of the existence of the necessary special low-entropy condition arising by chance is one in $10^{10(123)}$.[18]

These are staggering odds. To get a better grasp of them, consider for example the possibility that your job is to find someone hiding anywhere in the world. The odds that they are the first person you encounter after you are dropped out of an airplane at random anywhere on the globe is 1 in 6×10^9. Yet the odds that some of these factors required for life would happen by chance is more like the chances of finding, on the first attempt, a single electron that has been randomly placed anywhere in the entire universe! The chance of that happening is about 1 in 10^{80}. Just to illustrate how big a number that is, if everyone on earth counted, at the rate of one a second, the number of electrons in a single teaspoon of water, it would take over 10 million years to finish.[19]

The odds of just one or two of these conditions happening by chance is hard to comprehend. But for life to exist, dozens of these factors have to happen together. To calculate that, you have to multiply the odds of them happening separately. The unlikelihood of such a thing staggers our comprehension. Which conclusion is more rational, that it is all coincidence, or that someone designed it? Which conclusion requires that a person turn a blind eye to the evidence?

Reasons to Accept Christianity

If successful, the cosmological argument proves the existence of a creator; the design argument proves a designer; the moral argument a moral being. These have to be put together in order to demonstrate the existence of the God of theism. Theism is the view that there is a God who is omnipotent, omniscient, omnipresent, holy, and creator.

Christianity fills in the details, adding that God is also Triune, author of the Bible, provider of salvation by grace through Christ, and so on. Arguments for the existence of God do not bring us all the way to the Christian God, and that has been a matter of some controversy. However, most people would recognize that we can prove a complex conclusion only by adding up a number of arguments. No one expects, for example, to convict a criminal with one piece of evidence. Rather, a lot of evidence is added up to the conclusion. Neither should we expect that one argument will prove the Christian God. The Christian should be allowed, like anyone else, to add up arguments to demonstrate the conclusion (an approach called a cumulative case).

The Bible seems to recognize a difference between knowing the sort of God described by theism and knowing the God of Christianity, who is theologically more detailed. According to Romans 1:19-21, everyone can know basic things about God because of creation, which reveals His "eternal power and divine nature." But Paul also says later (Rom. 10:14-15) that people cannot know the truth of the gospel (that God saves by grace through Christ, and so on) without special revelation (i.e., the Bible). Someone must tell them the message. They cannot get it from looking at creation.

People can look around them and understand the basics of God's existence, but not the truth of the gospel. This is illustrated by Paul earlier in his life when he persecuted Christians. At the time he earnestly thought he was serving God. When Christ appeared to him on the Damascus road Paul had to ask, "Who are You, Lord?" (Acts 9:5). As a Christian looking back on his pre-conversion opposition to the gospel, he said that he had "acted ignorantly in unbelief" (1 Tim. 1:13). Christ had predicted that people would think they were serving God by killing His followers (John. 16:2).

So, the more detailed beliefs of Christianity (as opposed to mere theism), available in the Bible, cannot be validated by merely looking at trees and sunsets. It has to be validated differently. Many claims tout many books as revelation to one degree or another: the Koran, the Book of Mormon, the Hindu Vedas, to name only a few. The question is, which if any is genuinely supernatural?

In history God has given a number of ways to show fallen people who really speaks for Him. One way is miracles. When God asked Moses to lead His people out of Egypt, he was concerned that they would think he was acting on his own (Exod. 4:1). God gave him a number of miraculous signs to show them, and because of the signs they were convinced (Exod. 4:31). Centuries later when Israel apostatized to the point that they were confused even about which God was the true one, Elijah proposed a decisive test: whichever God could light up the sacrifice by fire was obviously the living God (1 Kings 18:24). The very events that founded Israel were all miracles – the birth of Isaac, the exodus, and the granting of the Law. So were the founding events of the church, including the virgin birth and resurrection.

Not everyone who sees such miracles responds, but some do. Nicodemus did (John 3:2), as did the proconsul who saw Paul blind Elymas (Acts 13:12). So did "many" who saw the raising of Lazarus (John11:45) and Tabitha (Acts 9:36, 40); as well "all" who saw the healing of Aeneas (Acts 9:35). Christ expected that people would respond to miracles (John 10:38), and John said he recorded Christ's "signs" so that people "may believe" (John 20:31).

These days there is much more doubt about miracles. Skeptic philosopher David Hume (1711-76) wrote the first influential attack. Also, there has been a rise in naturalism as a world view, which tries to explain everything non-supernaturally. So using miracles as evidence for Christianity today would require laying quite a bit of groundwork; it is nowhere near as simple as it once was.[20]

God has also used prophecy as a special type of sign to demonstrate the divine origin of the message. The predictions of a true prophet will never fail, a fact which separates true from false prophets (Deut. 18:22; Isa. 46:9-10). There have been remarkable fulfillments of prophecy in history, such as those relating to the cities of Tyre and Sidon.[21] Christ offered detailed prophecy about Himself as evidence that His claims were genuine (Luke 24:44-46).

God also offers His power to affect history as proof. Those who call on a false God will not be helped, whereas He can answer prayer by changing even world events (Isa. 45:20, 46:2, 7).

Miracles and prophecy validated the messenger and his message (though again, groundwork is needed to use them today). The messages fit into a prophetic tradition, which is presented as a cohesive whole. Carefully interpreted, the parts do not contradict. This is remarkable considering the Bible was written in three languages on three continents by over forty authors from every conceivable walk of life. Furthermore, it covers the most controversial of subjects.

We would expect that if the Bible is God's message, it would be the most distributed book in history. And it is. There have been more copies in more languages than any other book. Furthermore, it is the best attested work of ancient times in that it has more manuscripts from which to make an accurate translation than any other ancient document. This is all the more significant in light of the fact that throughout history there have been intense efforts to suppress the Bible, especially during the crucial founding period when the copies were few and not yet widely spread.

Some who defend Christianity would point further to remarkably changed lives of followers, beginning with the early church and continuing today. John Calvin, for example, points out that simple men like Peter and John were transformed into profound thinkers. Paul suddenly espoused the very beliefs he had persecuted.[22]

Some have objected that Christianity is morally inadequate (skeptical British philosopher Bertrand Russell, for example[23]). Sociologist Alvin J. Schmidt answers with an extensive study on the positive effects of Christianity through the centuries. They include elevating the value of: life, of sexual morality, the status of women, compassion and charity, hospitals and health care, economic freedom, abolition of slavery, and more.[24]

Many who would support the faith also point to a God-given, immediate awareness that Christianity is true. John Calvin, for example, said that "the testimony of the Spirit is more excellent than all reason."[25] Classical apologist William Lane Craig rigorously demonstrates Christianity with evidence yet says that evidence only confirms a God-given inner assurance.[26]

There is obviously much more to say about reasons to believe given by those who believe in God and Christianity. The bottom line is, Christ promised that those who are serious about knowing the truth will find it (John 7:17; Matt. 7:7-11; cf. Jer. 29:13).

The Problem of Evil and our Ignorance

The unexamined assumption underlying much of the discussion on the problem of evil is that we human beings are qualified to examine the nature and extent of evil and draw conclusions about God. A person who is skeptical typically has concluded that the kind of evil or the amount of it is too much and there cannot be a loving and all powerful God. Though believers do not deny God's existence, they can secretly doubt that He cares very much about them, or, they can question His wisdom.

But what makes any of us think we are qualified to judge such things? What makes us think that our tiny intellects can sufficiently grasp such things as the mysteries of God's will, the requirements to produce various types of good, or the ultimate effects of pain and evil? I have adapted from Christian philosopher William Alston some reasons why we are not qualified to draw conclusions about such things.[27]

First, we simply do not have enough data. We don't know enough about the secrets of the human heart. People can hide their sins and true motives. Furthermore, in drawing conclusions about the rightness or wrongness of people's actions, we tend to underweight important factors such as motivation, intent, and attitudes (especially attitudes like self-centeredness). So when God punishes someone it may seem unfair. This is especially the case in our day when wrong behavior is often regarded as a disease rather than a choice.

Not only do we not know the human heart, we do not know much about the universe. So the skeptic has no way of knowing whether God could have produced a world with just as much good but without floods, earthquakes, viruses, and so on. Nor do we know much about the past or the future, especially the after-life. As we pointed out in chapter eleven, no one can claim that they know enough about heaven to say it could never compensate for the sufferings of this life.

Not only do we lack data, but secondly, our minds are not even capable of holding enough information at one time to make judgments about such things as different possible worlds. Drawing conclusions requires holding a certain amount of information in one's mind. The kinds of subjects we have to deal with are just too huge to be able to do that.

Then, even if we had enough data and our minds could process it all, we do not know which things in the universe could be different from the way they are and which things have to be just as they are. Is it even possible, for example, for water to be chemically different so that it supports life but can't drown anyone?

And even if we knew which things were possible, we do not necessarily know all the possibilities. There could be possibilities we do not know about. As Alston says, "If we don't know whether or not there are possibilities beyond the ones we have thought of, we are in a very bad position to show that there can be no divine reasons for permitting evil."[28]

Besides not knowing what exists, what does not exist, what is possible and what is necessary, we do not know all values (that is, things that are good or desirable). There may be some desirable things that we are not even aware of. Even if a type of pain or suffering is not worth it based on what we know, there might be values of which we are completely unaware that would make it all worthwhile.

Even if we knew everything that is valuable, we could not make judgements involving all values. That is because, like making decisions about all relevant data, it would require that our minds hold vast amounts of information. There is no reason to think we have the cognitive horsepower to do it.

Clearly, it is no simple matter to say that the pain and suffering in this world could not be worth it. We cannot even point to a particular case of pain and suffering and say that a good and all powerful God would not allow it. A conclusive statement about even one event would require that we know a vast amount.

Something we have not even begun to pursue is the fact that anyone who rejects the notion of a good and all powerful God must have his own explanation for things. Whatever the alternate world view, it has problems. For example, how can atheism explain order, especially beneficial order? How could the human mind become so complex as to think abstractly, through the medium of language, and in terms of things like beauty and values? Could we really have developed all that without a creator, just from a need to find berries and escape from tigers?

A specific form of atheism, Communism, once dominated a large portion of the globe. It held sway over hundreds of millions, promising utopia. But rather than deliver life without limits it died in mere decades, weakened by the failure of its central prophecies and by economic gangrene, and strangled by the tyrants and bureaucracies it spawned. Such was the fate of one alternative to Christianity that for awhile seemed invincible.

Even after a lot has been said about why God would allow pain and evil, there is still some mystery and plenty of room for faith. But the skeptic is left with plenty of challenges of his own. Each of us must decide for ourselves what to believe. As philosopher William James pointed out, we do not have the luxury of avoiding the question of God; it is thrust upon us. We are like a man lost in a blizzard who comes to a fork in the road. We must choose one or the other, and if we refuse the choice we will only freeze to death.

GOING FARTHER

1. Recount an argument that someone made which would have convinced you except for knowledge that you had which was not included in their argument (make up an example if you can't recall one). How does that relate to God and the problem of evil?

2. Make up an example of a deductive proof; an inductive proof. Can you think of an inductive argument whose conclusion is so likely to be true that virtually no one would doubt it? What objections, however unreasonable, might a stubborn skeptic raise? Is the conclusion any less sure even though irrational objections could be raised?

3. What degrees of certainty can we have for the following statements?
Bachelors are unmarried.
2 + 2 equals 4.
The totality of something is at least as great as any of its parts.
Something that is red is red.
Caesar was a Roman leader.
Margaret Thatcher was Prime Minister of Great Britain.

Oxygen is a gas at room temperature.
It is unsafe to walk down a dark alley.
The world's oil supply is diminishing.
The stock market will reach a new high in the next fifteen years.
Though evil exists, a good and all-powerful God exists.

4. How does the atheist's moral outrage imply the existence of God?

5. Can you think of examples of intricate and beneficial order that came about by accident rather than by a being?

6. Think of a tragedy that seems impossible to reconcile with the existence of a good and all-powerful God (e.g., a school bus accident with multiple fatalities, a plague that kills indiscriminately). What would we have to know to be able to say for sure that a good and all-powerful God would never have allowed it?

NOTES

1. David K. Naugle argues that even how we comprise a worldview is itself dependent on our own worldview. David K. Naugle, *Worldview: The History of a Concept* (Grand Rapids, MI: William B. Eerdmans, 2002), 254-56.

2. Moore drew attention to this feature of reasoning. So on a superficial level two people might agree that "if p is true then q is true." One of them might agree with a conclusion on grounds that p is in fact true. So he or she argues,

if p then q
p
therefore, q

But the second person believes that q is false more than he believes that p is true. So although he believes it is the case that "if p is true then q" is true, he argues,

if p then q
not q
therefore, not p

So as Moore would have it, we have to be sensitive to how certain we are of different things. We cannot allow something we are sure of to be overturned by something we are less sure of. Conversely, something we are more sure of (q) should overturn something we are less sure of (p).

3. Harold Netland suggests (personal correspondence, 26 March 2005) that the G. E. Moore shift would apply only where we are comparing a deductive argument for the conclusion that God does not exist (due to evil) with an independent deductive argument for the conclusion that God does exist. But, he maintains that when it comes to a cumulative case argument [where we are considering the total force that various arguments and evidences have on a single conclusion], we are not entitled to reject the evidence against God from evil on grounds that we have other reasons for believing in God. Evil must be assessed along with other factors. I agree that

considering a cumulative case is different from considering independent deductive arguments. I also think that a cumulative case would be stronger if answers to a particular contrary argument could be given (which is why I have offered answers to the problem of evil). However, I think that within a cumulative case, being convinced of one or more propositions (or premises) still has a bearing on what we think of other premises in a way similar to what Moore described. For example, our confidence that a candidate is fit for office may be based on his or her record, testimony of others, and personal experience; and in our minds that may overwhelm one citizen's claim that the candidate has behaved immorally – a claim we conclude is politically motivated. We have no specific knowledge to refute the claim, yet we judge it to be invalid by considering the cumulative factors in favor of the candidate's fitness.

4. R. Douglas Geivett, *Evil and the Evidence for God: The Challenge of John Hick's Theodicy* (Philadelphia, PA: Temple University Press, 1993), Geivett, 17-21.

5. Harold Netland suggested uses of certainty in daily life to get this point across.

6. The essentials of these two examples are used by Alvin Plantinga in various places.

7. That said, our level of belief in something is often rightly limited to our level of evidence. A rational person does not routinely hold beliefs with disregard for evidence. How certain we are that someone is at the door, for instance, is rightly related to how much evidence we have. If we are quite sure that someone knocked, then we are quite sure someone is at the door. On the other hand, if we are uncertain that someone knocked then we are uncertain that someone is at the door. The exact relationship between belief and evidence is, however, highly controversial. Part of the problem has to do with the fact that in some contexts what may count as strong evidence for us may not be so for others. For example, we may rightly regard the feeling of pain in our back as conclusive evidence that it is injured. But the doctor evaluating our insurance claim has only our word for the pain and may suspect that we are lying to get money. Absent evidence on x-rays, we will have trouble proving it to him to the level we believe it ourselves. Our inner certainty about our religious beliefs in some ways parallels the example of back pain more than a knock on the door to the extent that it is dependent on experiences which are not publically verifiable (of course, not everyone's inner certainty about their religious beliefs are highly dependent on their private experiences).

8. Keep in mind that I am including the provability of the premises in calculating how much certainty arguments offer. If we exclude that crucial issue then certainty is easily had; in fact it is normal for valid deductive arguments (which offer certainty if we assume the truth of the premises). But from a practical standpoint we have to include the question of the truth of the premises. Otherwise we would judge to be certain arguments that are deductively valid but perfectly useless. My favorite example is: (1) "Everything Brian Morley thinks is true is in fact true, (2) Brian Morley thinks the Christian God exists; therefore, the Christian God exists. It's deductively sound but no one would accept the premises.

9. Michael L. Peterson, "The Problem of Evil," in *Companion to Philosophy of Religion*, ed. Philip L. Quinn and Charles Taliaferro, Blackwell *Companions to Philosophy* series (Malden, MA: Blackwell, 1997), 398.

10. *The Prentice-Hall Encyclopedia of World Proverbs*, ed. Wolfgang Mieder (New York, NY: MJF Books, 1986), 226.

11. For more on the sorts of issues, see *Does God Exist? The Great Debate*. A debate between J. P. Moreland and Kai Nielsen (Nashville, TN: Thomas Nelson, 1990), chs. 8 and 9.

12. For an overview that favors the moral argument see, J. P. Moreland and William Lane Craig, *Philosophical Foundations for a Christian Worldview* (Downers Grove, IL: InterVarsity, 2003), 490-96. An atheist who believes that ethics in no way requires theism is Kai Nielsen. See, *Why Be Moral* (Buffalo, NY: Prometheus, 1989) and *Ethics Without God*, 2nd ed. (Buffalo, NY: Prometheus, 1989). Supporters of the moral argument include C. S. Lewis, *Mere Christianity* (New York, NY: Macmillan, 1943; rev. 1952), Robert M. Adams, *The Virtue of Faith* (New York, NY: Oxford, 1987), and Linda Zagzebski, "Does Ethics Need God?" *Faith and Philosophy*, Nol. 4, No. 3 (July 1987).

13. This is the so-called "Hilbert's Hotel" example, after mathematician David Hilbert.

14. J. P. Moreland and William Lane Craig, *Philosophical Foundations for a Christian Worldview* (Downers Grove: InterVarsity, IL: 2003), 472.

15. On some interpretations of what takes place at a sub-atomic level, something can come from nothing. But even if it is true that something happens on a sub-atomic level it does not necessarily mean that a similar thing can happen in the visible world (i.e., even if sub-atomic particles could come into existence uncaused that does not mean mountains or houses or universes could). Secondly, we have to be careful what we mean by "nothing." If we mean literally nothing (and not some special state with potential) then there are no powers or potentials to produce anything. See J. P. Moreland, *Scaling the Secular City: A Defense of Christianity* (Grand Rapids: Baker, 1987), 38-41.

16. Moreland and Craig, 479-80.

17. Moreland and Craig, 483. For a general explanation of the teleological argument, see pp. 482-490.

18. Roger Penrose, "Time-Asymmetry and Quantum Gravity," in *Quantum Gravity 2*, ed. C. J. Isham, R. Penrose, and D. W. Sciama (Oxford: Clarendon, 1981), 249; quoted in Moreland and Craig, 483.

19. Assuming there are about 2×10^{23} water molecules in a teaspoon of water. Brian L. Silver, *The Ascent of Science* (New York, NY: Oxford University Press, 1998), 4.

20. David Hume, *An Enquiry concerning [sic] Human Understanding* (1748), section 10. For a critique of Hume on miracles, see Keith E. Yandell, *Hume's 'Inexplicable Mystery': His Views on Religion* (Philadelphia, PA: Temple University Press, 1990), chapter 15, pp. 315-338. On miracles generally, see, *In Defense of Miracles: A Comprehensive Case for God's Action in History*, ed. Douglass Geivett and Gary R. Habermas (Downers Grove, IL: InterVarsity, 1997).

21. See for example, Josh McDowell, *Evidence that Demands a Verdict* (San Bernardino, CA: Here's Life Publishers, 1981), chapter 11.

22. John Calvin, *Institutes of the Christian Religion*, ed. John T. McNeill, trans. Ford Lewis Battles, Library of Christian Classics, vol. 20 (Philadelphia, PA: Westminster, 1960), vol. 1, pp. 90-91; I.viii.11.

23. See for, example, "Can Religion Cure our Troubles?" in *The Basic Writings of Bertrand Russell*, ed. Robert E. Egner and Lester E. Denonn (New York, NY: Simon and Schuster, 1967), pp. 603-604.

24. Alvin J. Schmidt, *How Christianity Changed the World* (Grand Rapids, MI: Zondervan, 2004), 441 pages.

25. Calvin, *Institutes*, I.vii.4; Battles, vol. 1, p. 79.

26. William Lane Craig in Steven B. Cowan, ed., *Five Views on Apologetics*, Counterpoints Series, ed. Stanley N. Gundry (Grand Rapids, MI: Zondervan, 2000), 28.

27. William Alston, "The Inductive Argument from Evil and the Human Condition," in *The Evidential Argument from Evil*, ed. Daniel Howard-Snyder; *The Indiana Series in Philosophy of Religion*, ed. Merold Westphal (Bloomington, IN: Indiana University Press, 1996), 97-125; see especially his summary, 120. What follows has been adapted.

28. Alston, 120.

Chapter fourteen

HOW TO COPE – Lessons from the Ancients (Solomon, Jeremiah, Habakkuk, Paul, and Job)

There is nothing like learning from experts. As someone said, experience may be the best teacher, but it's also the most expensive teacher. If you can learn from another's mistakes you will avoid some very costly lessons.

People of the Bible lived through some horrendous times and experiences. God shares with us their successful coping strategies, which can save us years of failure and grief and can show us the way to a victorious life.

The people in this chapter were not perfect, but they can teach us a lot. We remember Solomon's father King David for his righteousness, though he fell into serious sin with Bathsheba. We remember Solomon himself for his wisdom even though he acted foolishly by marrying foreign women and then falling for their gods. Like the people in this chapter, we need not be perfect to be successful, but like them we do need to overcome our failures and move on.

Solomon – Content with God's Sovereignty

Solomon is just the person to instruct our worldly generation. He had it all. He was perhaps the wealthiest man of his day (and didn't mind flaunting it). He was one of the most powerful persons in that region of the world, and he was a scholar and patron of culture. He even enjoyed international respect. Today it's hard to imagine that much glitz in one person. If anyone could shield himself from pain and suffering it was this worldly-wise, powerful king.

We can benefit from his mistakes by refusing to chase riches and the good life. He tried it all and said that it was all "vanity" (Eccles. 1:2, 5:10). Do not even think about trying to be wealthy, he said. Wealth is elusive, "Like an eagle that flies toward the heavens" (Prov. 23:5). Besides, having it is not fulfilling: "He who loves money will not be satisfied with money" (Eccles. 5:10). And Solomon reminds us that when you die you can't take a thing with you (Eccles. 5:16). Hearses never pull trailers with earthly possessions.

So he can save us from the pain of a misspent life, especially one absorbed in searching for the world's goods – one of the most common mistakes made today. Of course there is nothing wrong with enjoying what you have as long as you have your priorities right and acknowledge who gave you everything. We have to realize too that God has the right to take it away (Eccles. 7:14) for His sovereign purposes.

That points to an important part of the worldview that Solomon eventually developed: he knew that this is God's world, not ours. He made it and runs it according to His wise and sovereign purposes. Because the workings of the world are linked to the mind and heart of its creator, to live righteously is to live well; wise living avoids unnecessary pain.

The idea that we should shape our minds and thus our lives according to the will of God goes against the intellectual flow of the last millennium. The medieval world centered on God, the Renaissance and Enlightenment focused on reality, and our postmodern age focuses on our human perspective (emphasizing society's influence in forming our perspective). But for Solomon, "The fear of the Lord is the beginning of wisdom, and the knowledge of the Holy One is understanding" (Prov. 9:10). Wise living is necessarily God centered.

In a world run by God, the seasons of life go according to His plan, which we cannot necessarily change. As Solomon said, "There is an appointed time for everything. And there is a time for every event under heaven – a time to give birth and a time to die...", and so on for the events of life (Eccles. 3:1, cf. 3:11). There is a certain immutability to what God has decreed (Eccles. 3:2-8, 14). So rather than fret over things we cannot change, we should "rejoice and do good" (Eccles. 3:12), being happy with what God's providence has provided (Eccles.

3:22) without being overly attached to it. We should try to fully enjoy the blessings of each day. It is so easy to focus on the things that are going wrong, what we don't have, what we would like to change, and how we are not getting what others have or what we think we so richly deserve. If we do so we fail to enjoy the many things that are going right, the things we have been blessed with, the people in our lives, the opportunities we have, and so on.

I've benefitted from a number of years of doing photography as a hobby. It has trained me to open my eyes to the many simple blessings that are so easy to pass by – the beauty of the surrounding landscape, plants, the sky; a mother giving a warm hug to a child. One has to make a point of enjoying such things otherwise life's frustrations and all the ugliness in the world can be overwhelming.

A lot of westerners have been attracted to Zen Buddhism because it advocates a peaceful, contented life, enjoying simple blessings. But as it has no concept of God it can offer little more than pleasant experiences. In the center of Solomon's worldview is a God who is both personal and transcendent, who gives life meaning and purpose. When things seem to go wrong we can be assured that behind events there is a plan and infinite wisdom. Knowing that allows us to bear the things we cannot change and enjoy the blessings we have.

Jeremiah – Sure of God's Mercy

It seems that Jeremiah had as much tragedy as Solomon had wealth. When God called him He revealed that his message would be one of judgment, adding the ominous warning that Jeremiah would need divine protection (Jer. 1:14-19). Jeremiah pleaded that he was too young, but God insisted, assuring him (1:8).

A more sorrowful life would be hard to imagine. He saw his people in spiritual and moral decline, facing a crisis over foreign threats. Jeremiah knew what was coming, and it was indeed dismal. For some forty years he warned people who stubbornly refused to listen and who hated him. Through the reign of five Judean kings he faithfully proclaimed God's warnings, only to see his predictions tragically come to pass when Jerusalem starved in a siege that lasted a year and a half, ending in the great city's destruction in 587 BC.

For his faithfulness to God Jeremiah was regarded as a traitor, beaten, and thrown in a dungeon, where he nearly died (37:13-16, 20). Later he was lowered into a muddy cistern where, again, he nearly died

(38:6, 9). It seemed that nearly everyone at one time or other wanted to take the life of this gentle, faithful man (11:19).

Jeremiah felt all this deeply, saying, "I am the man who has seen affliction because of the rod of His wrath" (Lam. 3:1). He felt the Lord had encompassed him "with bitterness and hardship" (Lam. 3:5), making him a "laughingstock to all my people" (Lam 3:14) a "target for the arrow" (Lam. 3:12). He groaned, "He has filled me with bitterness.... I have forgotten happiness" (Lam. 3:15, 17). Few of us will ever observe or experience the depth of Jeremiah's physical and emotional suffering.

Yet in spite of it all, he had a deep and stubbornly held grasp of God's mercy, about which he penned some of the most profound verses in the Bible. He said confidently, "The Lord's lovingkindnesses[1] indeed never cease, for His compassions never fail. They are new every morning; great is Your faithfulness" (Lam. 3:22-23). If anyone could be tempted to doubt God's lovingkindness it was Jeremiah. Yet amidst the rebellion and subsequent carnage Jeremiah had an unwavering confidence that the chastening hand of God was moved by a loving heart. Jeremiah knew it and counted on it every day.

If we could have Jeremiah's confidence in God's sovereign grace we could make it through anything.

He tried to encourage others with assurances of God's eventual mercy. In a letter he told those who had already been taken to Babylon in 597 BC that God would indeed bring them back to the land in seventy years. God said He was still on their side, "'For I know the plans that I have for you,' declares the Lord, 'plans for welfare and not for calamity to give you a future and a hope'" (Jer. 29:11). And though He seemed to have departed, He could always be found: "You will seek Me and find Me when you search for Me with all your heart" (Jer. 29:13).

What seemed to sustain Jeremiah was not only his confidence in God's goodness but his conviction that knowing God was the best thing in life, and all he really needed. "The Lord is my portion," he said (Lam. 3:24). When God is all you want you can never lose. Tragedies and loss only bring you closer to Him, giving you more of what you value. David (Ps. 16:5, 73:26, 119:57, 142:5) and as we shall see, Paul, had the same attitude. No wonder these men were so rugged. Their singular focus on God and resulting peace and joy got them through circumstances that would crush virtually everyone else.

Jeremiah had another often overlooked secret to his spiritual success. Unlike most of us, deep down, he didn't think he deserved better. He asked, "Why should any living mortal, or any man offer complaint in view of his sins?" (Lam. 3:39).[2] Whereas most of us are tempted to think that any bad thing is undeserved and unfair, he felt that he had no right to complain about anything. When any good came his way, he felt it was undeserved. Few of us have that kind of grasp of our place before God. His attitude was the very opposite of self-pity – that crippling flaw that can drive a person to any number of self-destructive behaviors.

Because of Jeremiah's humility, the good things that happened to him meant so much. This led to gratitude, by which he easily saw God's hand where others saw nothing.

Contrast his attitude to the feeling that we deserve a life in which everything goes right all the time. From that presumptuous perspective it is easy to focus on any little thing that isn't perfect, and soon we are struggling with bitterness. When a little thing goes wrong that will take up my valuable time, such as a plumbing problem or car trouble, I sometimes have to stop myself and think, this is a normal part of life, and by God's grace, things are actually going pretty well. I also have to remind myself that this life is mostly about how we respond to challenges and difficulties. I am sure I will never match Jeremiah's hard-won humility and gratitude, but it's something worth striving for.

Habakkuk – Rejoicing In God Alone

An important part of the problem of evil for God's people is the disquieting sense – sometimes suppressed – that what God is allowing isn't quite right. When we feel that way and cannot seem to resolve it, we should think of Habakkuk. He could still function despite wrestling with enigmas that brought him to the brink of despair.

He began his prophetic ministry just before Nebuchadnezzar invaded Judah in 605 BC. The gross immorality engulfing his society vexed him to the core – and as Solomon said, "Oppression drives the wise into madness" (Eccles. 7:7, ESV). Exasperated, he finally cried out to God, "How long, O Lord, will I call for help and you will not hear?" (Hab. 1:2). He asked God how He could tolerate all the violence, wickedness, strife, and injustice (Hab. 1:2-4).

Not only did God not rebuked him for asking, but He gave a very specific answer: He was already working on a grand and decisive solution. The Chaldeans would swoop down violently and destroy the entire place (Hab. 1:5-11). In the end the invaders too would be held guilty (Hab. 1:11).

This certainly resolved Habakkuk's doubt about God's concern over the sins of His people. But that posed what seemed to him to be a worse problem. How could God punish the Jews by means of a people far more wicked? The Chaldeans were infamous for arrogance and cruelty.

God answered by assuring Habakkuk that judgment will fall at the appointed time (Hab. 2:3), and that He indeed scrutinizes people's behavior. He pronounced five woes that cover a wide array of behaviors, including financial abuse of people, getting a person drunk in order to take sexual advantage of them, and idolatry (2:6-19). Thus the answer seemed to be, "Trust me, Habakkuk. I'm very aware of every detail of people's behavior, and when the time is right I will deal with it My way."

Habakkuk then acknowledged God's awesome power and recounted His judgment (Hab. 3:2-15). Knowing what is ahead for his people, he trembled, "waiting quietly for the day of distress" (Hab. 3:16). *But rather than be overwhelmed by the difficulty of the pending situation – or weakened by doubt – he resolutely determined to rejoice and exult in the Lord.* In perhaps the most memorable biblical passage on trusting God, he says,

> Though the fig tree should not blossom and there be no fruit on the vines, though the yield of the olive should fail and the fields produce no food, though the flock should be cut off from the fold and there be no cattle in the stalls, yet I will exult in the Lord, I will rejoice in the God of my salvation. (Hab. 3:17-18).

Have you ever faced or anticipated something really terrible and you could feel yourself starting to panic inside? Perhaps it was medical news, or you were afraid that you or a family member were about to be the victim of a crime; or perhaps you were facing the breakup of a relationship. The situation seems to take your strength away and you wonder how you can face it. At that point you have the same choice Habakkuk had, to succumb to the rising sense of fear, doubt, and despair; or to get hold of yourself and say, no matter what happens I am still going to trust God and rejoice in who He is.

What ultimately made Habakkuk so strong was that, like Jeremiah, he had a deep conviction that even if everything is stripped away God is all that really matters in life – and nothing can take Him away.

Having a sense of joy in the midst of suffering is a mental safeguard. Nehemiah led his people out of a crisis in which they faced a similar serious threat. "Do not be grieved," he said, "for the joy of the Lord is your strength" (Neh. 8:10). Paul said the same thing to the Philippians: "Finally, my brethren, rejoice in the Lord. To write the same things again is no trouble to me, and it is a safeguard for you" (Phil. 3:1).

It's easy to think we would be able to maintain such a spiritual perspective in a crisis – until we suddenly find ourselves in a crisis. When I was about twenty-five and in seminary I was at home one day and heard a knock at the door. I was about to open the door when I heard the voices of two youths outside nervously talking about burglarizing the house. "If we go in now no one will see us," one of them said quietly. Wanting to catch them I backed away from the door. But no one tried to break in. I contacted the police and said I would be happy to wait quietly inside for a few hours (I had a lot of homework anyway) and call back if anyone tried to get in. I invited Bob, a seminary friend of mine over to the house in an effort to end two budding criminal careers. As we are both about six foot four, I thought we would have no trouble overpowering the two twelve year olds if it came to that.

After awhile I checked the peep hole in the door and saw a black Lincoln Continental pull up. Out came two men that looked like organized crime types. Suddenly I thought the boys were merely setting things up for these rough looking men. Now I realized the situation was out of control. I phoned the operator, struggling to keep my voice calm, and got through to the police. But I knew that in a large city like Los Angeles it could take quite a while for help to arrive. The rising sense of panic was very foreign to me since even at that age I had handled lots of emergencies, though they had mostly been medical.

Within a few minutes it became clear that the men were not trying to get into the house I was in. I knew things were back under control again. Still holding the phone, I apologized to the operator for not sounding so calm at one point. I explained that for a moment I really didn't think I would live long enough to complete that phone call. Then she began to feel the emotion of the situation, and with her voice trembling too much to continue, her supervisor finished the call.

We never caught the youthful burglars but I realized that I had some things to work on when it came to maintaining a spiritual perspective when under physical threat. I could have learned some things from Habakkuk.

With that lesson fresh in my mind, it was not long after that I was in another situation in which I sensed I was in danger. A drifter had shown up at the church and needed a place to stay. The church put him in my friend Bob's house. The man was powerfully built and rather quiet. He had moments of friendliness, but mostly he showed a moody, dark side.

Late one Sunday night I was closing up our large church. The place was deserted and very dark. As soon as I got to the most remote part of the grounds, suddenly and silently the drifter emerged from the shadows. He was out for a late walk, he said. He added, in a sinister tone, that he knew he could find me there. After a minute of small talk, and for no apparent reason, he pulled out a very large pocket knife, snapped it open, and started showing me its stained blade.

Although I knew nothing about the man something told me I was in grave danger. He told me again that he knew I would be there. He looked at me, expecting me to be afraid. That made it clear I had something to fear.

Along with my growing sense of danger was the equally strong sense that God was protecting me. This time I had no trouble staying completely calm and conversational, having worked on my attitude following the attempted burglary incident at the house.

As the man who called himself Harry held his knife he kept talking about it with bizarre fascination. His eyes widened, then quickly narrowed to slits, and he said with a little laugh, "You have no idea of the kind of work this knife can do. Yeah, this knife has done a lot of work..." His voice trailed off as he silently revisited dark memories. After a minute or two he ended the conversation and stalked off into the night. I felt that staying calm had made all the difference. I told Bob about the incident, which reinforced his own suspicions.

Not long after, the stranger that some were calling "scary Harry" exchanged a few tense words with another man. In a flash Harry lunged and stabbed him in the upper chest with that knife, and ran. The blow was placed with expert precision, but miraculously, the man lived. The emergency room physician said it had missed his heart by less than a quarter of an inch.

The police detective assigned to the case told a staff member at the church that he was quite familiar with Harry. They strongly suspected him of several murders but since he always terrified witnesses they could never convict him.

As a couple of the church members with whom he had stayed thought back over Harry's time with them they remembered a week during which he had been especially distant, short tempered, and moody. Then he had suddenly disappeared for a few days. When he returned he refused to say anything about where he had been. But he suddenly had a lot of money. Looking back we figured it had something to do with the kind of "work" his knife could do.

I was doubly glad that I had been able to trust God under pressure – at least a little like Habakkuk.

Paul – Seeing the God Behind Our Suffering

Paul is another model of coping with suffering. Because of the false teachers in town Paul felt he should recount his sufferings to the celebrity oriented believers of Corinth (2 Cor. 11:17-18). Unlike your typical celebrity, he had been imprisoned, beaten more times than he could count, five times got thirty-nine lashes, three times was beaten with rods, was stoned, and was shipwrecked three times. Besides the constant danger, he carried the burden of caring for all the churches (2 Cor. 11:23-28). Like the others we have been learning from in this chapter, he suffered much more than most of us ever will.

Paul benefitted from his insight into specific causes of his suffering. Those insights seem to have helped him deal with the difficulties he faced. He knew, for example, that his troubles in Thessalonica were simply a consequence of evil resistance to the gospel. He knew too that God would deal justly with those responsible (1 Thess. 2:14-16). He realized that some of his sufferings were for the ultimate purpose of keeping him dependent on God and helping him relate to others who suffered (2 Cor. 1:4, 9). He also knew that God allowed certain sufferings as a "thorn in the flesh" to keep him from exalting himself (2 Cor. 12:7).

Overarching his understanding of these reasons for suffering was his grand sense that he was participating in the sufferings of Christ. Since for him knowing Christ was of "surpassing value," to gain that knowledge he was willing to "suffer the loss of all things, and count them but rubbish" (Phil. 3:8). Part of that was knowing the "fellowship of his sufferings" (Phil. 3:10). Christ suffered to secure our salvation, and when we accept that salvation we share His sufferings in that we endure the world's hostility toward God and godliness (2 Tim. 3:12).

The Bible says that persecution should come as no surprise (1 John 3:13) because we are no longer part of the world (John 15:19, 17:14). We should take heart that we stand in the long tradition of godly people who got the same treatment, and that our reward in heaven is great (Matt. 5:10-12, Luke 6:22-23). Paul actually rejoiced that he was taking the persecution aimed at Christ, thus "filling up what is lacking in Christ's afflictions" as part of his service to the church (Col. 1:24). It was all part of suffering hardship as a "good soldier of Christ Jesus" (2 Tim. 2:3), and Paul mentally prepared himself by expecting it rather than letting it take him by surprise (1 Thess. 3:4).

Paul could keep on going because he never lost sight of the goal of it all. For him suffering was never pointless, it was for a good purpose. And he kept that purpose in mind, taking solace from it. In the midst of suffering he took pride in the spiritual progress of the Corinthians and was "filled with comfort" and "overflowing with joy" (2 Cor. 7:4, cf. v. 7). When he heard about the stability of the young Thessalonian believers he told them that "in all our distress and affliction we have been comforted about you through your faith" (1 Thess. 3:7).

All of this helped Paul keep suffering in proper perspective. He could say of his considerable suffering that "momentary, light affliction is producing for us an eternal weight of glory far beyond all comparison" (2 Cor. 4:17). If I had endured the likes of Paul's sufferings I doubt I would have consider it "light"!

So rather than viewing suffering in isolation, Paul saw it in light of what it accomplishes and how long eternity lasts. And he did not consider suffering as merely a necessary evil in order to have external spiritual fruit. He kept in mind the fact that the suffering itself produces fruit within our character. It produces endurance, which leads to proven character, which in turn produces a confident hope (Rom. 5:3-4; cf. James 1:3,4).

Paul could rejoice also because he knew that no amount of suffering could separate us from the love of God, not "tribulation, or distress, or persecution, or famine, or nakedness, or peril, or sword" (Rom. 8:35, 38-39).

Understanding the various reasons for suffering can help us the way it helped Paul. Although we might not be certain why a specific thing is happening, we can know in general terms why God lets these sorts of things happen. We can know that suffering keeps us dependent on God, humble, and able to help others who suffer. We can know that some suffering is simply the result of persecution and that we can take heart, knowing that God will someday bring justice. And we can see suffering not in the light of some idyllic life which we could wish for here and now, but for what it is accomplishing eternally.

Job – Developing a Faith that Overcomes

There are a lot of good reasons why God allows pain and evil, and we have explored quite a few in this book. Like Paul, we can draw encouragement from knowing some of those reasons. But from the Book of Job we learn how to handle it when, try as we might, we can think of no reason whatsoever for our troubles.

Job's story is a familiar one. He was "blameless and upright, fearing God and turning away from evil" (1:1, cf. 1:8, 2:3). He cared for people, especially the downtrodden and helpless (29:12-17; 31:13-21). He strove for purity in his inward motivations and attitudes, an emphasis rarely found in Scripture prior to the sermon on the mount (31:1-2, 7, 9, 24-34). Yet his conspicuously blessed life suddenly became a nightmare. And his faith, strong at the beginning (1:21-22), withered under intense suffering. He cursed the day of his birth (3:3-19), began to doubt God's goodness (3:20-23), and eventually called God's goodness into question (e.g., 10:3). He began to imply that God's actions toward him would not stand up to impartial examination (10:3, 31:35).

Job's three friends held to the view that was prevalent in the middle east at the time[3] – and among some in western society today – that blessing and misery are always closely linked to righteousness and sin. In the Hindu and Buddhist concept of karma there is just such a mechanical link. The law of karma works impersonally and infallibly in that you get what you deserve, good or bad, no exceptions. Even some forms of conservative Christianity today link prosperity so closely with God's pleasure that it is a virtual birthright of the righteous: if you are righteous you can expect to be obviously blessed, such as with health and wealth; if you are not so blessed you lack either righteousness or the faith to claim your blessings.

In a sense, Job's three friends were the first health, wealth, and prosperity theologians. They stubbornly insisted that Job's suffering was necessarily the result of some sin. The tragedy of this view is that it adds guilt to suffering. If I believe my troubles are always somehow my fault – because God would never will suffering for the faithful – I will scrutinize my life until I find some deficiency in righteousness or faith, and then blame myself for the troubles. According to this outlook life's troubles are always a scourge and never a motivation to gain a deeper understanding of the complex ways of an all-wise God, nor do they ever goad us to simply trust Him when we cannot understand.

I know of one dear believer who has been influenced by health and wealth views who has endured some of the worst things that this life can bring. Her fine young family broke apart because of the sin of another person, consequently one of her three children wandered far from the Lord. When she had to go back to work to support what was left of her family, she was denied the opportunity to work in a field for which she had advanced training because she was subject to unjust suspicion. As a result she lived in great financial need. Yet because her worldview excluded God working through evil and suffering, she also struggled through countless hours searching for the cause within herself. I suspect to some degree she blamed herself for what was clearly not her fault.

Though Job's three friends (Eliphaz, Bildad, and Zophar) could not think beyond the idea that Job's sufferings were due to his sins, Elihu was not so simplistic. And unlike them he was not rebuked by God for having faulty theology (Job 42:7). Elihu reproved Job for challenging God (34:36-37), pointing out that He is not obligated to repay Job's loyalty with temporal blessings on Job's own human terms (34:33). Besides, he pointed out, we should not obey God merely because it benefits us (34:9). We should remember too that our obedience does not really benefit God because everything is His in the first place (35:7). Whatever the case, God does not owe us an explanation for what He does, "Why do you complain against Him that He does not give an account of all His doings?" (33:13). Far from being inattentive to our situation, we can be assured that God has intimate knowledge of what people do and what they deserve (34:21), and He will "pay man according to his work" (34:11). But God's power and wisdom are far beyond what our small minds can grasp (37:2-24). And from our limited perspective we dare not question His righteousness (35:2).

Unlike Job during his troubles, we know the reason for his sufferings. God was allowing him to be tested in a way that demonstrated something to the angelic realm at the time, and would also benefit readers for thousands of years.

But the point of the Book of Job is not merely to add God's dealings with Satan as one more possible reason why we suffer. God did not even include it in His long speech to Job at the end of the book. The point that God made to Job was simply that He is in full control of things and that He knows so much more than us humans. Not only did He create the earth (38:1-7), but He controls the heavens (38:31-33) and all its natural processes (e.g., 38:26). Even the ocean, which seems so uncontrollable, is under His control (38:8-11). Powerful creatures that are threatening to us are nothing to Him (Behemoth, 40:15-24; Leviathan, 41:1-34). The wicked too are no match for Him (38:13; 40:11-13). Since wisdom itself comes from Him and He is the one who gives it (38:36) or withholds it (39:13-17), it makes no sense for us to question His dealings and integrity (40:8). At the end of the divine statement, Job realized how little he knew compared to God, and he repented (42:1-6).

The Book of Job challenges the age old assumption that there is a close and mechanical link between our behavior and God's recompense. But whether or not we struggle with what appears to us to be undeserved sufferings, the larger point is that we must trust God's wisdom and sovereignty no matter what happens. Try as we might, we will not always be able to understand why we or someone else experience a particular struggle. We will not always be able to figure out why God allowed something to happen. Nevertheless, humble trust in a wise, righteous, and sovereign God is always the right response to life's difficulties.

It is unlikely that in this life we will ever be able to remove all the mysteries of suffering. But we can always deal with them if we maintain a simple, stubborn faith. All our insight on the problem of evil removes neither the need for faith nor the last bit of mystery.

A few years ago a pastor named Tim left a church where he had been for a long time to join our college faculty. He and his wife brought their three teen-aged children across the country. After a successful year on the faculty, he went to the school just as on other days, but he never came home. Without any warning whatsoever, he fell over dead of a heart attack. He was only in his forties.

Two weeks later, with the shock still in the air, I was in the office of another colleague whose family had been close to Tim's for some years. He told me how he had spend many hours thinking, praying, talking to others, and even lying awake at night – all trying to understand why his friend had died. With deep puzzlement lining his face, and rising frustration in his voice, he said to me that it made no sense of any kind. Tim was needed, especially at this time, by his wife, children, friends, and the college. "I just cannot understand it!" he said vehemently. He turned to stare out the window. After a long searching pause he said quietly, "But maybe we're not supposed to understand it.... Maybe that's all part of it."

That brief conversation contained the essence of the Book of Job. It is good to strive to understand the mind and will of God on issues of pain and evil. Yet there will be times when we simply will not understand no matter how hard we try. If we can humbly trust God through the tears, then we have mastered the practical side of the problem of evil.

GOING FARTHER

1. What would you love to change about your life but can't? When you are tempted to become frustrated over those things, what can you instead be thankful for? What objects of beauty and sources of inspiration can you make a point of enjoying on a regular basis?

2. How, specifically, have the worst things in your life (or someone else's) helped you to know God better?

3. In what ways can you, like Habakkuk (Hab. 3:18), rejoice in the God of your salvation no matter how bad life gets?

4. Paul benefitted from insight into various reasons for some of his specific sufferings. He knew that some things kept him humble, other troubles kept him dependent on God, other things were the result of persecution, and so on. Though it is difficult to be definite, can you think of possible reasons for the top five things that have troubled you?

5. What glories of heaven can you look forward to as a way of keeping your earthly troubles in perspective? Might that be perfect physical health, sinless relationships, unbroken intimacy with God?

6. Have you ever suffered over something that, like Job – no matter how hard you try – you simply cannot figure out why God would allow it? What has been your response? If God were to talk to you directly as He did to Job, what do you think He would say?

NOTES

1. The word translated "mercies" in the NKJ and "stead fast love" in the ESV is a broad term that includes "love, grace, mercy, goodness, forgiveness, truth, compassion, and faithfulness," MacArthur Study Bible, 1145.

2. R. K. Harrison says, "When a transgressor is punished for his wrongdoing, he has absolutely no cause for complaint" (cf., 1 Pet. 2:19f.). *Jeremiah and Lamentations: An Introduction and Commentary* (Downers Grove, IL: InterVarsity, 1973), 227. The translators' note in the Net Bible makes a stronger statement, "The point of this verse is that the punishment of sin can sometimes lead to death; therefore, any one who is being punished by God for his sins – and yet is allowed to live – has nothing to complain about!" The Net Bible (Biblical Studies Press, L. L. C., 2003; <www.NetBible.com>), p. 1469.

3. Rene Girard, *Job: The Victim of His People* (Stanford, CA: Stanford University Press, 1987), 122. Robert Gordis observed that this sort of belief was "universally accepted throughout the ancient Near East, from the Nile to the Euphrates." Robert Gordis, *The Book of God and Man* (Chicago, IL: University of Chicago Press, 1965), 137. Both quoted in Larry J. Waters, "Elihu's Theology and His View of Suffering," *Bibliotheca Sacra*, 156 (April-June 1999), p. 149.

CHAPTER FIFTEEN

OUR PART, HERE AND NOW

Actress Theresa Saldana was immediately uneasy about a man who had been phoning her agent and her mother. He had posed as an employee for a producer for whom she had worked. He somehow knew enough about her to trick her mother into giving out her address and phone number. Alarmed, Theresa called the police. But they assumed it was just another fan.

Theresa did not go anywhere alone for a week. When nothing happened, she too began to assume it had been just a fan.

But Arthur Jackson was no ordinary fan. He had seen her in a movie in his native Scotland and became obsessed with her. He began what was described as an imaginary relationship with her. He then flew to the United States to find her. The next eighteen months he spent tracking her, helped by a private detective he hired.

At 10:00 in the morning Theresa walked out of her apartment in Los Angeles to go to her college class. She heard a voice, "Are you Theresa Saldana?" She saw his reflection and instinctively knew it was the man who had been making the mysterious calls.

He suddenly began to attack her, stabbing her over and over. She fought back with all her strength, determined to live.

A crowd immediately gathered. But no one was helping. They stood as if watching a movie or a Shakespearean play. Theresa was screaming as loud as she could, "He's killing me, he's killing me." She concluded that perhaps the bystanders were not helping because they thought it was a family dispute. She wanted them to realize that she was being murdered.

By this time she was starting to fall down from so many wounds. Her lung was punctured and began to collapse. Her aortic artery had been sliced.

A young man delivering bottled water on the second floor heard the screams. He looked out the balcony and saw the crown gathered around, but with so many people he could not see what they were watching. He ran to see if he could help.

On getting through the crowd he saw the attacker on top of his victim. He fought him off, only then realizing that he had a knife. In the struggle he got the knife away and pinned the man on the ground, face down.

Theresa looked up at the only one who had come to her aid. Later she said that she "literally thought he was an angel." She struggled to her feet and walked a ways. But with blood spurting out her lung, she collapsed. She was rushed to the hospital where doctors managed to stay the blood flow and save her life. That began a long period of recovery.

Theresa recalled what the attacker wrote soon after he tried to kill her, "It was very important that I be very careful to concentrate on the vital organs; synonymous with Cupid shooting an arrow into the heart..." It was said that he was in love with her and figured that the only way he could be with her was to kill her and join her in the afterlife. He allegedly believed it was his divine mission to kill her. He said he regretted using a knife because, "a gun would have given me a better chance of reunion with you in heaven."

Arthur Jackson served time in a U.S. prison, and is now in a mental facility in Britain.

The young man who rescued her, Jeffrey Fenn, had always wanted to be in law enforcement. His heroism and national recognition opened the door to a career in the Los Angeles Sheriff's Department, where he is now a sergeant. "I really, really love my job," he said.

In the years since the ordeal, their families have gotten together regularly for their children's birthdays and holidays. "Jeffrey is always part of my life. I would not be here if it wasn't for him," Theresa said.

Like her rescuer, Theresa herself is no bystander. While still recovering from the attack she began to work to get anti-stalking laws in place, and to secure more rights and financial support for victims of crime.[1]

There is an enormous difference between a bystander and a rescuer. One chooses to only think about the situation; the other takes the additional step of becoming involved and making a difference.

We have a similar choice with regard to pain and evil. Most books on the subject help us develop our thoughts on the problem of evil. It is indeed important to understand such things as the origin of pain and suffering, how it relates to our will and God's plan, and how God can be good and all-powerful in spite of it all, and so on. Other treatments exhort us to have faith and not to lose heart in the face of those aspects of evil that seem mysterious and unresolvable. And we indeed need faith because try as we will, there will be aspects of evil that remain opaque to us. But we need to go beyond thinking about pain and evil, and we need to go beyond faith. We need to do something about it.

Pain and evil are opportunities for us to grow in our understanding of the character of God and to manifest it to the world around us. As beings who were made to glorify God by being in His image – by acting as He would act – we are given opportunities to show compassion, forgive, encourage, supply needs, protect people from harm, impart wisdom, bring justice to those who do evil, and a myriad of other things.

Getting involved requires that we do not "merely look out for our own personal interests, but also for the interests of others" (Phil. 2:4). It means going beyond the so called silver rule, which says that we should not do to others what we would not want done to us. That can be fulfilled merely by being passive, by simply not doing harm. But the golden rule says that we should go and do for others what we would want done for us. This requires active involvement, going out of our way to do good.

Finding needs and meeting them requires a new way of looking at the world. There are lots of different ways of seeing the world. We can make a point of seeing how we are not being treated as well as we think we deserve. We can complain about various things that we wish were better. We can be fearful and anxious. We can be angry over what frustrates and annoys us. We can be lost in depression, resigning ourselves to the belief that our lives are in bad shape, and nothing we do will ever make a difference. We can feel self-pity, wondering why such bad things have to happen to us. We can also go beyond seeing the world in a certain way and become active, but active doing the wrong things, such as always trying to get people to meet our needs, or using them to build our personal empire in order to magnify our names, make us comfortable, popular, and secure.

There is no end of ways to see the world around us, and even ways of trying to influence it.

But looking for ways to do good requires that we take our eyes off ourselves and make it our business to serve others and their needs. It has been said that Americans believe you should try to do what is best for yourself, and if you do, perhaps benefits will trickle down to your family, your employer, and your country. It has also been said that Japanese people, on the other hand, believe that you should try to do what is best for your family, your employer, and your country, and if you do perhaps benefits will trickle down to yourself. God's approach is much closer to the latter. As Christ said, "Give, and it will be given to you" (Luke 6:38). As I tell my children, it is not either you help others or you help yourself. God designed the world such that serving others results in the greatest blessing for yourself. I've told them that the greatest blessings in my life have come when I've helped others. Years ago the church I was attending called to ask if I could house a young man from another part of the country while he finished his doctoral exams and looked for a counseling position. I was glad to put him up, and made some contacts for him. When I called an academic dean I knew at a Christian college, he said that they did not need anyone to teach counseling, but they would be interested in having me teach in biblical studies and philosophy. The young man left town without a job, but I've been there sixteen years now.

Nearly thirty years ago I got to know an elder at my church, Sam Ericsson, who was a very successful young attorney. Not long after, he shocked his colleagues by leaving his prestigious firm and generous salary to become the church administrator. He later went on to head the Christian Legal Society, then felt God leading him to start an organization to advance religious liberty around the world. Such an organization could keep doors from closing to the gospel and even open doors that had always been shut. In those first difficult years of starting up Advocates International,[2] he exhausted nearly all his retirement savings, personal savings, and the equity in his house. He and his wife even had to work part-time jobs. When someone asked if he struggled over how God had led him, he said that if God takes away your Mercedes and gives you a Chevy, you just thank Him that He didn't make you ride a bicycle!

Through Sam's organization, God began to work in amazing ways to bring down legal strongholds and protect Christians. In one case, he effectively intervened to save a Christian from being hanged in Pakistan for supposedly dishonoring Muhammad. Advocates intervened when Saudi Arabia threatened to decapitate two Filipino Christians for holding home Bible Studies (the Christians in both Pakistan and Saudi Arabia were released). They got a Mongolian Bible school reopened after it had been shut down by the government. They got the communist Chinese government to clarify that home Bible studies need not register with the government to be under their control.

One day I called his office and was a bit hesitant to ask for him because I knew he was very busy. Over the years he has met with leaders and supreme court justices of foreign countries, and he is responsible for the organization's network of over 30,000 legal professionals in 135 countries. I was told he was unavailable because he was spending the whole day helping a foreign visitor move into his apartment! Later I asked him about it and he said the person needed his help; "besides," he added thoughtfully, "when you help people, things happen."

Sam could have spent his entire career as a highly paid attorney, but where would the thousands of people around the world be who have been helped by his legal and organizational skills? He has made a life verse out of Micah 6:8, "...what does the Lord require of you, but to do justice, to love kindness, and to walk humbly with your God." In so doing he has contributed to the solution to the problem of evil.

There are as many ways to help solve the problem of evil as there are types of evil and suffering – and that is nearly endless. There have been a few occasions where my children, like most children at one time or other, have felt left out of a group. Sitting alone, surrounded by people can be very lonely. My wife Donna has usually said something like, "I'm sorry you had to be by yourself, but the good thing is that this helps you understand what it is like. Now when you see someone sitting alone you can reach out to them and make them feel wanted." I've told them too, that if you forget about yourself and focus on other people – their needs, discouragements, joys, and struggles – and try to add something to their lives, you will have more friends than you can count.

Most of us are drawn to selfless people, those we sense are not using us for their own agenda. Conversely, selfish people are usually lonely people. I told my children about a wedding I went to where the bride and groom were dismayed that hardly anyone had come. They had sent out many invitations and received many promises to attend, but come the day the hall was almost empty and the food they had paid for was unserved. It made me reflect on how little they had been a part of anyone's life. The groom had never bothered to attend anyone else's weddings, funerals, or birthdays. Not only that, but his life had been spent using people. A couple of times over the years I had tried to contact him. When I asked a few people who had known him if they had his phone number, several times I heard, "I don't know where he is and never want to see him again!"

What a contrast to Francisco, a twenty-two year old Bible student in Lima, Peru. As he was walking one day in 1990, a car sped by and launched a mortar attack on the palace nearby. Suddenly police were everywhere. Mistaken for a terrorist, Francisco was arrested and locked in a maximum security prison. He was surrounded by Senderistas, who had been killing so many people that citizens were fleeing into the countryside. Instead of being outraged or depressed by the injustice of his capture, Francisco recognized it as an answer to his prayer to somehow share the love of God with the terrorists who were ravaging his country.

A twenty-four year old university student named Maria asked him if God could ever love and forgive her. It had been one of her tasks to shoot wounded victims in the head to ensure their deaths. She accepted God's love and forgiveness in Christ – and so did sixty other terrorists during the year that Francisco awaited his trial.[3]

Harry Nakos, on the other hand, worked with purely ordinary circumstances. He was an usher at the church I attended. He drove a truck delivering meats, but the highlight of his week was coming to church and making everyone feel welcome. He was always cheerful, always kind, and encouraging. I couldn't imagine anyone not liking Harry. On his delivery route one day he had severe chest pain that turned out to be a heart attack. He was treated, and now others tried to encourage him. He was concerned about his wife and children. A man who had himself suffered a heart attack told him how little it had affected him, and we all said there was no cause for concern. But Harry wasn't persuaded. A few weeks later there was a funeral in the church and quite a few attended. Harry said quietly, almost to himself, that if he were to die hardly anyone would be at his funeral. A friend disagreed. Harry said, "who would come? My family, and perhaps twenty or so others. That's it." He wasn't trying to be gloomy, just realistic.

Sad to say, Harry's unshakable conviction about his health turned out to be right. I got the news that he had suffered a fatal heart attack. His former pastor, radio preacher J. Vernon McGee gave the eulogy. He spoke of Harry's life, and how he had always been there for people, always encouraging and cheering them, doing whatever he could to make them feel welcome and wanted. He ended by saying that he believed God would make him an usher in the next life, welcoming people into heaven. He added rhetorically, that he fully expected Harry to be the first person he would see there, telling each person who arrived how good it was to see them, showing them around, and making them feel at home.

As I looked around the church, I realized just how wrong Harry had been. In attendance were well over a thousand people.

Sam Ericsson's biggest impact has been through his career. Harry's impact came through simply making the most of his contacts with people. Whether through a career, alongside it, or merely within the small circle of our family, the world abounds with opportunities to be a part of the solution to the problem of evil.

In this book we have focused on understanding God and evil. But this is only a part of the solution, the other part consists of what we do. If we need proof that thinking and doing are tightly intertwined, we need look no farther than the legacy of Karl Marx. He is known for his dictum, "Philosophers have only interpreted the world in various ways, the point is, however, to change it." The trouble is that he and his followers tried to change the world according to a faulty understanding of it. The result was the needless deaths of tens of millions, and the enslavement of hundreds of millions.

But if our striving is founded on truth, we can make a powerful difference. The complexities of a right understanding, our efforts and their effects, can be summed up in simple concepts like love, compassion, and justice. They are the sure outcomes of a life that reflects God in thought and deed – a life that glorifies Him through imitation, doing what He would do. Such a life shines brightest in a fallen world.

The struggle is real. Sometimes words and even ideas will fail us. In the foreword to Ellie Wiesel's memoir of the concentration camp, Nobel-Prize winning novelist François Mauriac told of his first meeting with Wiesel, then a young journalist interviewing him. The young man had struggled to hold onto the last shred of faith in God amidst the unspeakable cruelty of the camps, and now he asked how Mauriac could believe in a loving God in such a cruel world. The novelist struggled to answer:

> And I, who believe that God is love, what answer could I give my young questioner.... What did I say to him? Did I speak of that other Israeli, his brother, who may have resembled him – the Crucified, whose Cross had conquered the world? Did I affirm that the stumbling block to his faith was the cornerstone of mine, and that the conformity between the Cross and the suffering of men was in my eyes the key to that impenetrable mystery whereon the faith of his childhood had perished? Zion, however, has risen up again from the crematories and the charnel houses. The Jewish nation has been resurrected from among its thousands of dead. It is through them that it lives again. We do not know the worth of one single drop of blood, one single tear. All is grace. If the Eternal is the Eternal, the last word for each one of us belongs to Him. This is what I should have told this Jewish child. But I could only embrace him, weeping.[4]

GOING FARTHER

1. In what ways have you been a bystander? In what ways a rescuer?

2. When have you struggled and wished you had help? What opportunities do you now have to offer someone the help you never received?

3. What qualities in God would you most like to know deeply? What can you do to get a deep, experiential knowledge of God by imitating that quality yourself?

4. How has God blessed you as you have served others? Would you characterize your outlook as "American," or "Japanese"?

5. Who is the most selfless person you know personally?

6. Have you ever been able to help someone in their struggle with pain or evil without sharing any explanations or ideas about evil?

NOTES

1. From transcript of interview with Saldana and Fenn, Larry King Live, aired July 13, 2004, 21:00 Eastern time. Accessed 2 August 2004. <http://www.cnn.com/TRANSCRIPTS/0407/13/lkl.00.html>.

2. <www.advocatesinternational.org>

3. *Jesus Freaks: Stories of Those Who Stood for Jesus*, by dc Talk and The Voice of the Martyrs (Minneapolis, MN: Bethany House, 1999), 125-6. Johnathan Morley pointed me to this illustration.

4. Weisel, *Night*, 10-11. I was led to this quotation by D. Bruce Lockerbie, *Dismissing God: Modern Writers' Struggle against Religion* (Grand Rapids, MI: Baker, 1998), 243-44.

Conclusion

Pastor and author Mark Buchanan tells of a little girl in his town named Kaitlyn. She and his own four year old daughter would play on the swings and laugh together. But one day when her mother went to pick her up on the school yard she just stood there, seemingly unaware of what was going on around her. She was limp.

They called the ambulance, and later at the hospital the mother was told Kaitlyn had a seizure but would be fine. But she wasn't fine. She began to slur her speech and stumble. Eventually tests revealed she had Batten's disease, a rare degenerative neural disorder that eventually hardens the muscles like a rock. One day she will be unable to swallow or even breathe.

Her family has prayed tearfully, desperately, unceasingly. Their friends and local churches have prayed. She has not gotten any better. Everyone has to watch beautiful little Kaitlyn die slowly.

It is not known if the family next door prays, but their house has been paid up for awhile – and they just won $600,000 in a lottery.[1]

These are the difficult situations that test our faith in God and our understanding of why He allows some things. My wife Donna and I know of another puzzling situation. A man we know is not only exceptionally bright and talented, he is highly motivated to serve the Lord. He has some great ideas and boundless ambition – but even though he is a young man his health is failing.

His back suddenly went out leaving him in excruciating pain, bedridden much of the time. It spasms so badly the muscle action is stressing his heart. And his heart, it was recently discovered, was damaged by an improperly diagnosed infection years ago. Meanwhile, there are drug dealers on the street whose strong bodies enable them to go to extraordinary lengths to keep doing what destroys lives and angers God.

Is life merely senseless, nothing more than "a tale told by an idiot, full of sound and fury, signifying nothing"?[2] Or are we hapless victims of impersonal cosmic forces, as the writing of nineteenth century British novelist Thomas Hardy suggests? Is life, as philosopher Schopenhauer thought, the product of a blind cosmic Will which drives a universal war of all against all, creating a world in which the saint is the one who gives up his will to live? Should we say, along with Ishmael in Moby-Dick, "There are certain queer times and occasions in this strange mixed affair we call life when a man takes this whole universe for a vast practical joke, though the wit thereof he but dimly discerns, and more than suspects that the joke is at nobody's expense but his own."[3] Should we go so far as to join philosopher John Roth in suspecting that God has a dark side, that He is not the pure Being of traditional thought?[4] Or is the very question of cosmic meaning a mere linguistic mirage – an attempt to know Truth when we can know only words and their usage (as some inspired by the philosopher Ludwig Wittgenstein tell us).

Against all of these world views and more, the biblical writers affirm that a loving and just God is in firm control. Consequently, the world does makes sense – but perfect sense only to an omniscient Being. Those of us striving to understand it can find it increasingly comprehensible, yet we should never expect to entirely remove life's mystery and the need for a faith that can hold steady when things do not make sense. And that in itself makes sense, because the point of life is not merely to understand, but to grow in the knowledge of the One who does.

NOTES

1. Adapted from Mark Buchanan, *Your God Is Too Safe* (Sisters, OR: Multnomah, 2001), 80-82.
2. Shakespeare, *MacBeth*, Act v, scene v.
3. Herman Melville, *Moby-Dick* (New York, NY: Barnes and Noble, 1993), 192-3 (ch. 49).
4. John Roth, "A Theodicy of Protest," in *Encountering Evil: Live Options in Theodicy*, ed. Stephen T. Davis (Atlanta, GA: John Knox, 1981), pp. 7-22.

Bibliography

Adams, Marilyn McCord. *Horrendous Evils and the Goodness of God.* Ithaca, NY: Cornell Univ. Press, 1999. 220 p. Focuses especially on evils severe enough to make the sufferer feel life is not worth it. A little technical in places but skillfully written, and by a major scholar. She deals with the subject not just from the standpoint of theism but more specifically, from Christianity.

Adams, Marilyn McCord and Robert Merrihew. *The Problem of Evil,* Oxford Readings in Philosophy. Oxford, UK: Oxford Press, 1990. 230 p. Influential readings on evil.

Basinger, David. "Divine Control and Human Freedom: Is Middle Knowledge the Answer?" *Journal of the Evangelical Theological Society* 36, no. 1 (1993), 55-64.

Carson, D. A. *How Long, O Lord: Reflections on Suffering and Evil.* Grand Rapids, MI: Baker Books; and Leicester, UK: InterVarsity Press, 1990. 275 p. Well rounded and readable introduction to the subject by a top Evangelical scholar.

Ciocci, David M. "Reconciling Divine Sovereignty and Human

Freedom," *Journal of the Evangelical Theological Society* 37, no. 3 (1994), 395-412.

Craig, William Lane. *The Only Wise God: The Compatibility of Divine Foreknowledge and Human Freedom* (1987; reprinted, Eugene, OR: Wipf and Stock, 2000). From an able modern defender of middle knowledge.

Crockett, William, ed. *Four Views on Hell.* Grand Rapids, MI: Zondervan, 1992. 190 p. A lively discussion of this controversial subject.

Davis, Stephen T. ed., *Encountering Evil: Live Options in Theodicy.* Atlanta, GA: John Knox Press, 1981. 182 p. Lively interaction between Stephen T. Davis, John B. Cobb, Jr., David R. Griffin, John H. Hick, and John K. Roth.

——. *God, Reason and Theistic Proofs*, Reason and Religion series (Grand Rapids, MI: Wm. B. Eerdmans, 1997). 204 p. A readable introduction by a prominent philosopher of religion.

Feinberg, John. *The Many Faces of Evil: Theological Systems and the Problem of Evil.* Revised and Expanded. Crossway, 2004.. 544 p.. Well written, thorough, and from a theological as well as philosophical perspective.

Fiddes, Paul S. *The Creative Suffering of God.* Oxford, UK: Clarendon, Oxford Press, 1988. 281 p. Challenges divine impassibility.

Flint, Thomas P. "Two Concepts of Providence," in *Divine and Human Action*, ed. T. V. Morris (Ithaca, NY: Cornell University Press, 1988). A defense of middle knowledge.

Geivett, R. Douglass. *Evil and the Evidence for God: The Challenge of John Hick's Theodicy.* Philadelphia, PN: Temple Univ. Press, 1995. 276 p. Ostensibly a critique of Hick but the book has much broader implications. Written by a professor at Talbot Seminary.

Helm, Paul. *The Providence of God.* Downers Grove, IL: InterVarsity, 1993. 246 p.

Hick, John. *Evil and the God of Love*. Revised. San Francisco, CA: Harper & Row, 1978. 389 p. An excellent historical and philosophical treatment by a major scholar. He contrasts two theodicies: (1) that humanity was created perfect and fell (the Augustinian view), and (2) the view that man was created imperfect and needs pain and suffering to become mature (what he calls the Irenaen view). He argues for the latter.

Howard-Snyder, Daniel, ed. *The Evidential Argument from Evil*. Bloomington, IN: Indian Univ. Press, 1996. 357 p. An excellent collection of readings.

Kelly, Joseph F. *The Problem of Evil in the Western Tradition: From the Book of Job to Modern Genetics*. Collegeville, MN: Liturgical Press, 2002. 245 p. Very readable and thorough introduction to views throughout history.

Larrimore, Mark, ed. *The Problem of Evil: A Reader*. 397p. Oxford, UK: Blackwell, 2001. Classic readings from the Greeks to the present. Includes poets, philosophers, theologians, and scientists.

Leibniz, G. W. *Theodicy*. Reprinted, Chicago, IL: Open Court, 1985. 448 p. A classic.

Lewis, C. S. *The Problem of Pain* (New York, NY: Macmillan, 1962. 160 p. A simple and engaging introduction to the problem of evil.

Molina, Luis de. *On Divine Foreknowledge* (Part IV of the Concordia), trans. Alfred J. Freddoso (Ithaca, NY: Cornell University Press, 1988). Medieval classic on middle knowledge.

Neiman, Susan. *Evil in Modern Thought: An Alternative History of Philosophy*. Princeton, NJ: Princeton University Press, 2002. 358 p. An innovative survey of philosophy from the standpoint of theodicy. Insightful and well-written.

Peterson, Michael L., ed. *The Problem of Evil: Selected Readings*. Notre Dame, IN: Univ. of Notre Dame, 1992. 391 p. Collection of influential readings, some challenging, but all very helpful.

Petrik, James. *Evil Beyond Belief.* M. E. Sharp, 2000. 170 p. Readable introduction; explains clearly some of the technical aspects of the subject.

Plantinga, Alvin. *God, Freedom, and Evil.* 112 p. Reprinted, Grand Rapids, MI: Wm. B. Eerdmans, 1977. Influential work showing, among other things, that evil is logically compatible with a good God.

Reichenbach, Bruce R. *Evil and a Good God.* New York, NY: Fordham Univ. Press, 1982. 198 p. Clear and written from a decidedly philosophical perspective.

Schwarz, Hans. Evil: *A Historical and Theological Perspective.* Minneapolis, MN: Fortress, 1995. 226 p. Overview of major thinkers in history, including contemporary ones.

Stackhouse, John G. Jr. *Can God Be Trusted? Faith and the Challenge of Evil.* New York, NY: Oxford Press, 1998. 196 p. A clearly written introduction.

Swinburne, Richard. *Providence and the Problem of Evil.* Oxford, UK: Clarendon, Oxford Press, 1998. 263 p. A readable and thorough examination of divine providence by one of the foremost philosophers of religion.

Glossary

Note: Underlined words have their own entries within the Glossary, and chapter references indicate where the topic is found within this book.

Analogy. A view advanced through Thomas Aquinas which holds that words used to describe God mean something similar to what they mean when describing other things. Those similar meanings are neither exactly the same (univocal) nor entirely different (equivocal) from their meanings in other contexts. So "knows" means something similar in "God knows John" and "Jones knows John." The meaning of "knows" is different insofar as God's nature is different from Jones's. Yet according to traditional theology, there is similarity between God's way of knowing and Jones's way of knowing because humanity is made in God's image. Besides, if there were no connection between "knows" as applied to God and "knows" as applied to anything else, it is not clear that we could have any idea what it is for God to know something. Analogy can be helpful when it comes to understanding what it means for God to have compassion, be affected by suffering, and so on (ch. 12).

Anthropomorphism. Attributing a human quality to something that is not human, especially God.

Anthropopathism. Attributing a human emotion to something that is not human, especially God.

Aquinas, St. Thomas (1225-74). Theologian and philosopher. Held that we can know God exists apart from the question of evil (ch.13), that greater variety in the universe can result in a fuller revelation of God (the principle of "plenitude"; ch. 5), and that some divine emotions are metaphorical while others are literal (joy and love can be literal because they are not a response from something outside God; ch. 12). He also held that theological statements such as "God is *x*" are analogical, that is, neither exactly like nor entirely unlike statements such as "Jones is *x*." How *x* can be applied to God depends on the nature of God, and how *x* can be applied to Jones depends on the nature of Jones (ch. 12).

Aristotle (384-322 BC). Regarded God as perfect and thus unchangeable, since to change implies imperfection. To change is to change for the better (entailing that God was not perfect to begin with), or for the worse (since change in a perfect being cannot be for the better, so it must be for the worse). As a perfect being God must contemplate only what is perfect, therefore He must contemplate only Himself. He is unaware of the world yet changes it because entities are attracted to Him. God is thus immutable and unaffected by the world and its suffering.

Augustine (354-430). Held that evil is a lack (or privation) of good, and that moral evil arises from a misuse of freewill (chs. 4, 7).

Buddhism. The central doctrines of this religion are that life is suffering, and the way to cease suffering is to cease one's attachment to this world. One can cease such attachment through the ethical teachings of Buddhism. Strictly speaking, Buddhism has no concept of a divine being, though Gautama and Buddhist saints can function like divine beings, and local deities can be infused into Buddhist beliefs.

Chaos. It is thought that systems can be deterministic yet unpredictable because small changes in initial stages can produce huge changes later. The classic illustration is that in weather, supposedly a butterfly flapping its wings can eventually cause a hurricane. This has been used to make the point that some evils which seem to us to have no constructive purpose may have an important role in God's plan (ch. 13).

Christian Science. Founder Mary Baker Eddy taught that things which have no place in God can have no enduring or "real" existence. They are given existence in our minds, thus evils such as sickness can be dealt with on a mental level (ch. 1).

Compatibilism. Compatibilists hold that free will is compatible with determinism. A person's will can be determined by something else, such as their environment or God, yet they are free and responsible for their actions. Typically compatibilists hold that a person is free to do *x* as long as they want to do *x*, even if some other influence caused that desire. It is usually thought that compatibilists cannot argue that evil's existence is due to the fact that God could not both grant free will and guarantee that no one ever does evil (the free will defense). That is because on the compatibilist view He could *guarantee* that free beings act a certain way. The view contrasts with incompatibilism (ch. 4).

Cosmological Argument. Argues that the existence of the universe is evidence for a creator. A recent popular form is the kalam argument (ch. 13).

Determinism. The view that everything that happens has a cause. In some forms of determinism, those causes are natural laws ("scientific determinism"). Simply put, in theological determinism God completely determines what happens such that what we do does not originate from us. We humans are used the way a programmer uses a computer or a carpenter uses a hammer. Determinism entails neither that we can predict events (see chaos), nor that the future will happen regardless of our efforts (see fatalism). Unlike the fatalist, the typical determinist believes that whether we are killed by a missile can depend on whether we took the precaution of going into a bomb shelter.

Deism. A view, popular in the 17th and 18th centuries, which holds that God caused the universe but has since caused nothing else. It was one response to the idea that God is the perfect engineer, and as such does not need to adjust the machine He has made. Like the ultimate watchmaker, He made the perfect watch that never needs adjusting.

The view that God does not need to intervene means that He does not act supernaturally – no miracles or answered prayer; neither does He need to inspire Scripture. Those who emphasized that God made the world perfectly from the start usually also emphasized that what appears to us as an evil is known to God as a good. We are simply ignorant of God's great design (ch. 3).

Double-predestination. The view that God predestines specific people to hell as well as heaven.

Dualism. The view that reality is in two distinct parts such as God and creation, or spirit and matter. In worldviews that are in some sense dualistic, good and evil can be fundamentally opposed and utterly different. In monotheism, which typically holds a form of dualism, God is utterly opposed to evil and judges it. Evil is not an aspect of God. Some forms of dualism such as Zoroastrianism (at least as often construed) hold that the two elements of reality are ultimate, as opposed to monotheism, which typically holds that God alone is ultimate. Such dualism contrasts with monism (ch. 1).

Evidential problem of evil. Argues not that the mere existence of *any* evil counts against God (the logical problem of evil), but rather the amount or type of evil does. Because some evil seems pointless (e.g., there could be as much *good* without some of the evils) the world cannot be the creation of a good God. This is the focus of much of the contemporary discussion of the problem of evil.

Fatalism. The view that nothing we do can change the future. The view is rejected even by most Christians who hold a strong view of predestination. It is not to be confused with determinism (ch. 4).

Fine Tuning argument. A type of teleological argument for the existence of God which holds that crucial elements of the universe and the earth have to exist within a very narrow range for life to exist. It is argued that since this is so unlikely it is evidence of divine design (ch. 13).

Freewill defense. Associated with Augustine, the freewill defense argues that God cannot both grant freewill and guarantee that those who have it will never use it for evil. God is innocent of evil because He did only what is good, that is, create free beings. It is thought to be impossible to have the higher good of freedom without the possibility of evil. It assumes an incompatibilist view of freedom. According to traditional theism (as opposed to Open Theism) God knew ahead of time that free beings would sin, but deemed it worth it to also have beings who freely choose good.

Hard Determinism. Holds that the human will is determined such that freewill is an illusion. Compatibilism holds that the will is determined yet free. Incompatibilism agrees with hard determinism that determinism destroys freewill, but incompatibilism holds that the will is not determined and therefore freedom exists.

Higher goods, argument from (see secondary goods, argument from).

Immutability. God's unchangeableness. It is debated whether God can be affected by things outside Himself (such as suffering) and still be immutable (see passible, impassible).

Impassible. If God is impassible He cannot be affected by anything outside Himself, including suffering. Those who think so usually hold that God is not uncaring but is *above* being affected. Contrasts with the view that God is passible (ch. 12).

Incompatibilism. The view that determinism would undermine freewill. If the will is determined it is not free and responsible. Moderate incompatibilists allow for influences that come short of completely determining that a person will act a certain way. Some forms of incompatibilism require that the person be the orginator of the action. Opposed to incompatibilism and hard determinism.

Kalam argument. A form of the cosmological argument which argues three successive alternatives: either the universe had a beginning or it did not (the kalam argues that it did); that beginning was either cause or uncaused (the kalam argues it was caused); that cause was either personal or an impersonal force (the kalam concludes it was a person).

Kushner, Rabbi Harold. Rabbi Kushner wrote the popular book, *Why Bad Things Happen to Good People*. In it he sees chaos as operating outside God's natural laws, and the source of much suffering. Some suffering occurs within the operation of God's natural laws, because they must operate blindly, without regard to mercy or justice (ch. 1). He also holds that creation is merely creation out of disorder, rather than creation out of nothing (*ex nihilo*). A similar view of creation was held by some ancient Greeks (see Plato), and today by Mormons.

Leibniz, Gottfried (1646-1716). A Christian philosopher who argued in his *Theodicy* that this is the best of all possible worlds in that it has the best balance of good over evil. Thus eradicating evil would also eradicate some types of good. Like Augustine, he held that evil is a lack, or privation, of good. He divided evil into: metaphysical (which is the "mere imperfection" of created things as opposed to the perfection of God), physical evil (suffering), and moral evil (sin; ch. 4).

Libertarian free will. Holds that to be free the will must be undetermined by anything outside it (incompatibilism), and that in fact people *are* free. Hard determinism agrees that the will must be undetermined to be free, but then denies that the will is undetermined and therefore denies the existence of freedom.

Logical problem of evil. The argument that *any* amount of evil counts decisively against the existence of a good and all powerful God. It is generally acknowledged that the argument was successfully answered by A. Plantinga.

Middle Knowledge (*scientia media*). Simply put, the view that God knows what *could* happen, not merely what *will* happen and *cannot* happen. Middle knowledge is midway between what will and what cannot happen. If God has middle knowledge, He knows what free beings would do in every possible situation. So He brings about those circumstances in which beings *freely* choose to do what is in His plan. It is thought that this allows for both sovereignty and free will. The view is associated with the Spanish Jesuit, Luis de Molina (1535-1600; hence molinism, molinist view). He claimed that God used middle knowledge to formulate His decree (roughly, His plan); that is, He used His knowledge of what would happen under all possibilities to decree what would actually take place. It was thought that this affirmed sovereignty while maintaining genuine freewill. The Dominicans, on the other hand, made God's middle knowledge a *consequence* of His decree. So in effect, God *decided* what each person would do in every circumstance. An able proponent of the middle knowledge view in modern times is William Lane Craig.

Modernism. An academic and cultural viewpoint, dominant from the later Renaissance until the late twentieth century, which holds that the world as it exists apart from us can be known with certainty and described objectively in an authoritative way. It was typically thought that such descriptions could be made to correspond to reality, could be built up into entire worldviews, and could be true for all times and perspectives. It accepted reason and science as objective and neutral. It has been challenged by postmodernism.

Molinism. See middle knowledge.

Moltmann, Jurgen (1926-). German theologian who was held as a prisoner by the allies in World War II. He became committed to Christianity and worked out his views in contrast with Marxism and other ideologies. He rejected the traditional doctrine that God is impassible, that is, unaffected by the world, including its sufferings. He also emphasized the future (eschatology) as a way of understanding the present.

Monism. The view that there is fundamentally only one kind of substance, and everything is a different aspect of that one substance. In such worldviews, evil and good are not fundamentally different but are different aspects of the same reality. If a monistic worldview includes God, it is usually a form of pantheism. Monism contrasts with dualism (ch. 1).

Mormons. Following founding Prophet Joseph Smith, Mormons believe that God formed the world out of eternal matter (ch. 1). Generally, the view entails that God cannot be blamed entirely for the world's evils. Mormons also hold that because the fall was necessary, it was something less than sin in the strictest traditional sense (ch. 5).

Omnipotence. The view that God is all powerful. If God can do what is logically contradictory then some answers to the problem of evil are ineffective. Also, if God's power relates to human nature in a way that makes compatibilism true, then the freewill defense is invalid.

Ontological Argument. Attempts to argue for God's existence from the mere idea of God. The basic argument is that, if God is the most perfect possible being He must exist, otherwise He is not the most perfect possible being. It has always been controversial even among theists, but was strengthened in modern times by A. Plantinga and others.

Open Theism. On this view, God does not know the future, thus it is "open" and creation entailed a risk. Nevertheless He is regarded as omniscient because He knows everything that could be an object of knowledge. Supposedly, the future acts of free beings are not objects of knowledge.

Panentheism. Best known in a modern form called Process Theology, panentheism holds that God's relation to the world is like a mind to a body. There is an aspect of God which is above the world, and another aspect which is inextricably linked to it. According to Process theodicy, evil exists because God's power over beings is limited to trying to persuade them to do good. He is not omnipotent in the traditional sense.

Panpsychism. The view that everything, even rocks and plants, have some mental qualities (supposedly evidenced, for example, in the fact that their molecules "cooperate"). Nevertheless only higher beings have minds as such.

Pantheism. The view that everything is God or that God is in everything (ch. 1)

Passible. If God is passible He *can* be affected by something outside Himself, such as suffering. Some believe this is a threat to His immutability (or unchangeableness; ch. 12).

Plantinga, Alvin (1932-). A Christian philosopher who argued effectively against the logical problem of evil, which holds that a good and omnipotent God cannot exist if *any* amount of evil exists. It is generally acknowledged that his defense (see theodicy) assumed an incompatibilist view of freewill. Attention on the problem of evil then shifted to the evidential problem of evil. Plantinga also helped revive the ontological argument for the existence of God.

Plato (c. 428-327 BC). Ancient Greek philosopher who held a view, common at the time, that God formed the world out of eternally existing material. He did not create it out of nothing (*ex nihilo*). This entails that God is not entirely responsible for the world's evils. Variations of this view are held today by Rabbi Kushner, Mormons, and Process theologians (see panentheism).

Plenitude, argument from. A principle which appeared in various forms in much thought from the Greeks to the medievals, according to which God would bring about everything that is possible to bring about. The principle was seen as compatible with a divine source that is infinite. Aquinas held that it is better to have many things rather than fewer things where many things results in greater revelation of God. The idea that greater variety can glorify God better than less variety could be used to argue, for example, that it is better for God to allow situations which manifest the widest variety of good character traits. So while it would be good for Jones to experience circumstances that make him grateful, it would be better for him to also experience circumstances that make him longsuffering, persistent, and forgiving (ch. 5). Interpreted this way, the principle relates to the argument from secondary goods. Plenitude could also be used to find some good in, for example, animal death since death makes life possible for other animals – there being insufficient resources on earth to support such vast numbers of animals if none ever died.

Postmodernism. A complex and multifaceted challenge to modernism (some would say postmodernism predates modernism). As such postmodernists have typically challenged the correspondence view of truth, which holds that what makes a statement true is that it corresponds with (or matches) the world. So "it is raining" is true if it corresponds with droplets falling from the sky. In place of the correspondence view, some postmodernists have held a form of pragmatism, which can hold that "it is raining" is true if believing it works for us. Some postmodernists have held that our knowledge of the world cannot rise above the confines of our language, or our social perspective, or our political interests. They thus typically hold that science is no better at discovering truth about the world than any other field. As a consequence of these and other views, postmodernists have typically held that we can make no statements that are unconditionally true for all peoples, times, and situations. We cannot expect therefore, to come to any full and final understanding of how the world is, to the sort of thing described by a worldview.

Privation. Some, like Augustine, have argued that evil is better understood as the absence of good and has no real positive existence. This allows God to be the cause of everything yet not the cause of evil, because evil is not a thing but merely the lack of something. He did not cause blindness (a lack of sight), rather, He did not grant more grace to be able to see. In granting less grace He did no evil because He alone has all perfections. Sin is the lack of righteousness (e.g., cowardice is a lack of bravery), yet again He did no evil. Augustine argued that God created freewill and we are the cause of the lack of good in our character. We are liable to sin because, unlike God, we are finite (a similar view was held by Leibniz; ch. 4).

Process Theology. See panentheism.

Process Theodicy. See panentheism.

Realism, non-realism. Simply put, to be a realist about something is to believe that it exists apart from our minds (i.e., our thoughts about it). A realist with regard to ethics, for example, holds that some things are right or wrong regardless of whether we think so. A realist with regard to the external world may hold that we can know something about it as it exists apart from us. It is hard to imagine someone holding to the most extreme realism, since no one thinks that things like pain or stories exists apart from our minds. It would also be hard to hold the extreme non-realist position that nothing whatever exists apart from our thoughts about it. There are different types of realism and therefore different non-realisms. A realist may hold that certain types of things exist apart from our minds (e.g., physical objects, moral values) and that our statements about them are true or false because of the way things are in the world. He may further hold that we can know truths about those things as they exist apart from us. A realist with regard to *x* would hold that our statements about *x* are not reducible to statements about something else. For example, a realist with regard to ethical values would hold that our statements about right and wrong are not merely about our preferences. Postmodernism has raised a number of challenges to realism.

Relativism. The view that truth is not objective but relative to a person or viewpoint. The first to propose it was the Greek philosopher Protagoras, who claimed that "man is the measure of all things." Socrates revealed his error by showing that an individual can make a mistake (entailing that there must be a standard by which to judge that a mistake has been made). Radical forms of relativism can be similarly challenged by asking if relativism is true only for the individuals who hold it, or for everyone. Some forms of relativism claim only that a particular area is relative, such as taste (e.g., "beauty is in the eye of the beholder") or ethics. Relativism is often equated with subjectivism, though they can be distinguished. Relativism is somewhat related to the issue of realism versus non-realism.

Secondary goods, argument from. The view that some good things cannot exist without the presence of certain conditions. With regard to the problem of evil, some good things cannot exist without the presence of certain evils. For example, there can be no forgiveness without sin to forgive, no justice without wrongdoing, no mercy without suffering, no longsuffering without persistent undesirable circumstances. Some evils manifest good in God though of course the good qualities would exist in God whether or not they were shown to us. Some evils allow the only opportunity for humans to develop specific character traits. Some of these good traits have no exact corollary in God. For example, danger of physical harm gives us the chance to develop courage, though we would not say that God can be threatened by danger and manifest courage. Many aspects of God's character can be seen without evil, yet even some of these can be seen better in the presence of evil. His wisdom and power, for instance, can be seen better in the outwitting of evildoers, as when He makes their evil deeds serve His good ends (ch. 5).

Spinoza, Baruch (1632-77). Philosopher who is widely considered a type of pantheist because he held that everything is an aspect of God.

Stoics. An ancient philosophy that extolled a type of personal peacefulness which they supposed was in God, an attitude indifferent to the sufferings of others. They regarded God as impassible, unaffected by anything (ch. 12)

Subjectivism. The view that what is true or valuable depends on the individual. Relativism on the other hand holds that what is true or valuable changes from one situation to another (e.g., from one culture to another).

Taoism. An eastern religion that divides reality into two contrasting yet interdependent forces. Yin is dark, decaying, weak, and feminine. Yang is strong, light, forthright, and masculine. The wise person keeps these forces in balance, which requires attentiveness to discern the flow of the Tao (ch. 1).

Teleological Argument. An argument for the existence of God based on the universe showing evidence of design. Sometimes called the design argument. A form of this is the fine tuning argument.

Theodicy. A term invented by G. Leibniz which refers to the endeavor to defend the existence of a good and omnipotent God in the face of evil and suffering. Theodicy is sometimes distinguished from a "defense," which seeks merely to answer an attack on theism (e.g., A. Plantinga). A theodicy has the more ambitious goal of giving a positive case so as to persuade someone of theism.

Voluntarism. The view that the will is primary over the intellect. In theological voluntarism, whatever God wills is good by virtue of His willing it. So He does not choose to will what is good, rather, it is good because He wills it. He could have willed that murder is good.

Zoroastrianism. The ancient Persian religion that holds to the existence of two gods, one good and one evil (ch. 1).

Index

Other books of interest from

Christian Focus

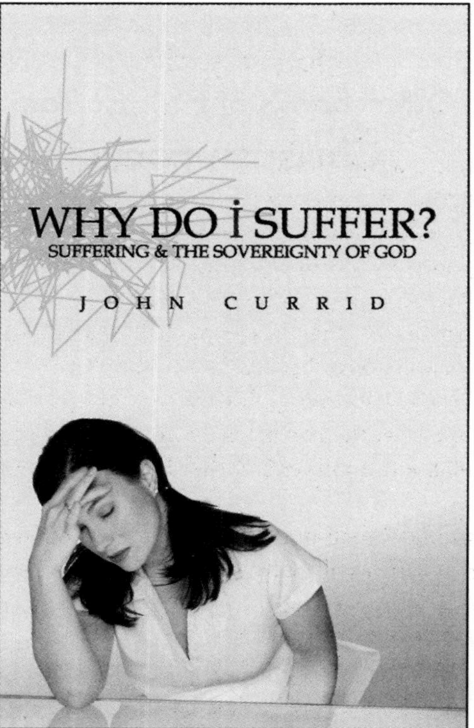
WHY DO I SUFFER?
SUFFERING & THE SOVEREIGNTY OF GOD
JOHN CURRID

Why Do I Suffer?

Suffering and the Sovereignty of God

John Currid

Why *does* God allow suffering?

It's a question that, in one form or another rears its ugly head time and again. Whether it comes from someone who has just lost a loved one, been diagnosed with an incurable illness or even just surveyed the plight of poor in the third world. Every terrorist attack or world disaster raises the question – Where was God in this?

The question is one that has dogged Christians down the ages. A number of answers have been offered – and indeed all worldviews attempt their own response. John Currid brings Biblical teaching to bear. God does work in suffering, he is not a worried observer unwilling or unable to intervene, rather he has a purpose at work and is in control.

As Abraham said "Shall not the Judge of all the Earth do right?"

Grasping that truth will help us as we face the future and ensure that when we are next faced with that most tricky of questions we will know where to begin.

John Currid is Carl McMurray Professor of Old Testament at Reformed Theological Seminary, Jackson, Mississippi. He is a prolific author whose books include well received, multi-volume commentaries on Genesis, Exodus and soon Leviticus.

ISBN 1-85792-954-3

'A wonderful antidote to self-pity' **Jennifer Rees Larcombe**

Why Do Bad Things Happen to Good People?

MELVIN TINKER

Why do Bad Things Happen to Good People?

A Biblical Look at the Problem of Suffering

Melvin Tinker

Why is doing good no guarantee of an easy life? One of the most common objections to the Christian Faith is 'If God created the universe, and is still in control of it, then Why does he allow suffering and injustice?'

Melvin Tinker considers the different opinions people have before investigating the biblical answers about a crucial topic that needs to be faced by an evangelistic church. He looks at the situations biblical characters faced, the opposition to Jesus himself, and the suffering of the early church.

This book provides the key factors behind the benefit and purpose of suffering.

"Right from the first page this book is easy reading, yet it deals with the most difficult subject Christians ever have to face - the question of why a loving God allows suffering. A wonderful antidote to self-pity, I can highly recommend this book to anyone, but particularly to those who struggle to know what to say or how to help when their friends are going through the mill."

Jennifer Rees Larcombe, Christian Herald

"...not only an apologetic and a pastoral help but also puts the reader into immediate contact with Job and the Psalmists as they struggle with the issues for real. The book is a deceptively easy read, written in an everyday style with biblical and contemporary illustrations. It is well worth a read."

Evangelicals Now

Melvin Tinker is Vicar of St John's Newland in Hull. He has written a number of books including *Close Encounters* and *Alien Nation.* Melvin is married to Heather and they have three boys

ISBN 1-85792-322-7

Christian Focus Publications

publishes books for all ages

Our mission statement –

STAYING FAITHFUL

In dependence upon God we seek to help make His infallible Word, the Bible, relevant. Our aim is to ensure that the Lord Jesus Christ is presented as the only hope to obtain forgiveness of sin, live a useful life and look forward to heaven with Him.

REACHING OUT

Christ's last command requires us to reach out to our world with His gospel. We seek to help fulfil that by publishing books that point people towards Jesus and help them develop a Christ-like maturity. We aim to equip all levels of readers for life, work, ministry and mission.

Books in our adult range are published in three imprints.

Christian Focus contains popular works including biographies, commentaries, basic doctrine and Christian living. Our children's books are also published in this imprint.

Mentor focuses on books written at a level suitable for Bible College and seminary students, pastors, and other serious readers. The imprint includes commentaries, doctrinal studies, examination of current issues and church history.

Christian Heritage contains classic writings from the past.

Christian Focus Publications, Ltd
Geanies House, Fearn,
Ross-shire, IV20 1TW, Scotland, United Kingdom
info@christianfocus.com

For details of our titles visit us on our website
www.christianfocus.com